Kaplan Publishing are constantly find[ing] [stu]dents looking for exam success and our on[line resources give] an extra dimension to your studies.

CW01521476

This book comes with free MyKaplan online resources so that you can study anytime, anywhere. **This free online resource is not sold separately and is included in the price of the book.**

Having purchased this book, you have access to the following online study materials:

| CONTENT | | AAT | |
| --- | --- | --- | --- |
| | | Text | Kit |
| Electronic version of the book | | ✓ | ✓ |
| Knowledge Check tests with instant answers | | ✓ | |
| Progress Test | | | ✓ |
| Mock assessments online | | ✓ | ✓ |
| Material updates | | ✓ | ✓ |

## How to access your online resources

**Received this book as part of your Kaplan course?**
If you have a MyKaplan account, your full online resources will be added automatically, in line with the information in your course confirmation email. If you've not used MyKaplan before, you'll be sent an activation email once your resources are ready.

**Bought your book from Kaplan?**
We'll automatically add your online resources to your MyKaplan account. If you've not used MyKaplan before, you'll be sent an activation email.

**Bought your book from elsewhere?**
Go to **www.mykaplan.co.uk/add-online-resources**
Enter the ISBN number found on the title page and back cover of this book.
Add the unique pass key number contained in the scratch panel below.
You may be required to enter additional information during this process to set up or confirm your account details.

This code can only be used once for the registration of this book online. This registration and your online content will expire when the examinations covered by this book have taken place. Please allow one hour from the time you submit your book details for us to process your request.

**Please scratch the film to access your unique code.**

Please be aware that this code is case-sensitive and you will need to include the dashes within the passcode, but not when entering the ISBN.

KAPLAN

PUBLISHING

# MANAGEMENT ACCOUNTING TECHNIQUES

# STUDY TEXT

**Qualifications and Credit Framework**

**Q2022**

This Study Text supports study for the following AAT qualifications:

AAT Level 3 Diploma in Accounting

AAT Level 3 Certificate in Bookkeeping

AAT Diploma in Accounting at SCQF Level 7

**KAPLAN PUBLISHING'S STATEMENT OF PRINCIPLES**

**LINGUISTIC DIVERSITY, EQUALITY AND INCLUSION**

We are committed to diversity, equality and inclusion and strive to deliver content that all users can relate to.

We are here to make a difference to the success of every learner.

Clarity, accessibility and ease of use for our learners are key to our approach.

We will use contemporary examples that are rich, engaging and representative of a diverse workplace.

We will include a representative mix of race and gender at the various levels of seniority within the businesses in our examples to support all our learners in aspiring to achieve their potential within their chosen careers.

Roles played by characters in our examples will demonstrate richness and diversity by the use of different names, backgrounds, ethnicity and gender, with a mix of sexuality, relationships and beliefs where these are relevant to the syllabus.

It must always be obvious who is being referred to in each stage of any example so that we do not detract from clarity and ease of use for each of our learners.

We will actively seek feedback from our learners on our approach and keep our policy under continuous review. If you would like to provide any feedback on our linguistic approach, please use this form (you will need to enter the link below into your browser).

https://forms.gle/U8oR3abiPpGRDY158

We will seek to devise simple measures that can be used by independent assessors to randomly check our success in the implementation of our Linguistic Equality, Diversity and Inclusion Policy

.

**British Library Cataloguing-in-Publication Data**

A catalogue record for this book is available from the British Library.

Published by
Kaplan Publishing UK
Unit 2, The Business Centre
Molly Millars Lane
Wokingham
Berkshire
RG41 2QZ

ISBN: 978-1-83996-966-9

# CONTENTS

**STUDY TEXT**

**Chapter**

**KAPLAN** PUBLISHING

# INTRODUCTION

## HOW TO USE THESE MATERIALS

These Kaplan Publishing learning materials have been carefully designed to make your learning experience as easy as possible and to give you the best chance of success in your AAT assessments.

They contain a number of features to help you in the study process.

The sections on the Unit Guide, the Assessment and Study Skills should be read before you commence your studies.

They are designed to familiarise you with the nature and content of the assessment and to give you tips on how best to approach your studies.

## STUDY TEXT

This Study Text has been specially prepared for the revised AAT qualification introduced in February 2022.

It is written in a practical and interactive style:

- Key terms and concepts are clearly defined.

- All topics are illustrated with practical examples with clearly worked solutions based on sample tasks provided by the AAT in the new examining style.

- Frequent practice activities throughout the chapters ensure that what you have learnt is regularly reinforced.

- 'Pitfalls' and 'examination tips' help you avoid commonly made mistakes and help you focus on what is required to perform well in your examination.

- 'Test your understanding' activities are included within each chapter to apply your learning and develop your understanding.

## ICONS

The chapters include the following icons throughout.

They are designed to assist you in your studies by identifying key definitions and the points at which you can test yourself on the knowledge gained.

 **Definition**

These sections explain important areas of Knowledge which must be understood and reproduced in an assessment.

 **Example**

The illustrative examples can be used to help develop an understanding of topics before attempting the activity exercises.

 **Test your understanding**

These are exercises which give the opportunity to assess your understanding of all the assessment areas.

 **Foundation activities**

These are questions to help ground your knowledge and consolidate your understanding on areas you're finding tricky.

 **Extension activities**

These questions are for if you're feeling confident or wish to develop your higher level skills.

Quality and accuracy are of the utmost importance to us so if you spot an error in any of our products, please send an email to mykaplanreporting@kaplan.com with full details.

Our Quality Co-ordinator will work with our technical team to verify the error and take action to ensure it is corrected in future editions.

## Progression

There are two elements of progression that we can measure: first how quickly students move through individual topics within a subject; and second how quickly they move from one course to the next. We know that there is an optimum for both, but it can vary from subject to subject and from student to student. However, using data and our experience of student performance over many years, we can make some generalisations.

A fixed period of study set out at the start of a course with key milestones is important. This can be within a subject, for example 'I will finish this topic by 30 June', or for overall achievement, such as 'I want to be qualified by the end of next year'.

Your qualification is cumulative, as earlier papers provide a foundation for your subsequent studies, so do not allow there to be too big a gap between one subject and another.

We know that exams encourage techniques that lead to some degree of short term retention, the result being that you will simply forget much of what you have already learned unless it is refreshed (look up Ebbinghaus Forgetting Curve for more details on this). This makes it more difficult as you move from one subject to another: not only will you have to learn the new subject, you will also have to relearn all the underpinning knowledge as well. This is very inefficient and slows down your overall progression which makes it more likely you may not succeed at all.

In addition, delaying your studies slows your path to qualification which can have negative impacts on your career, postponing the opportunity to apply for higher level positions and therefore higher pay.

You can use the following diagram showing the whole structure of your qualification to help you keep track of your progress.

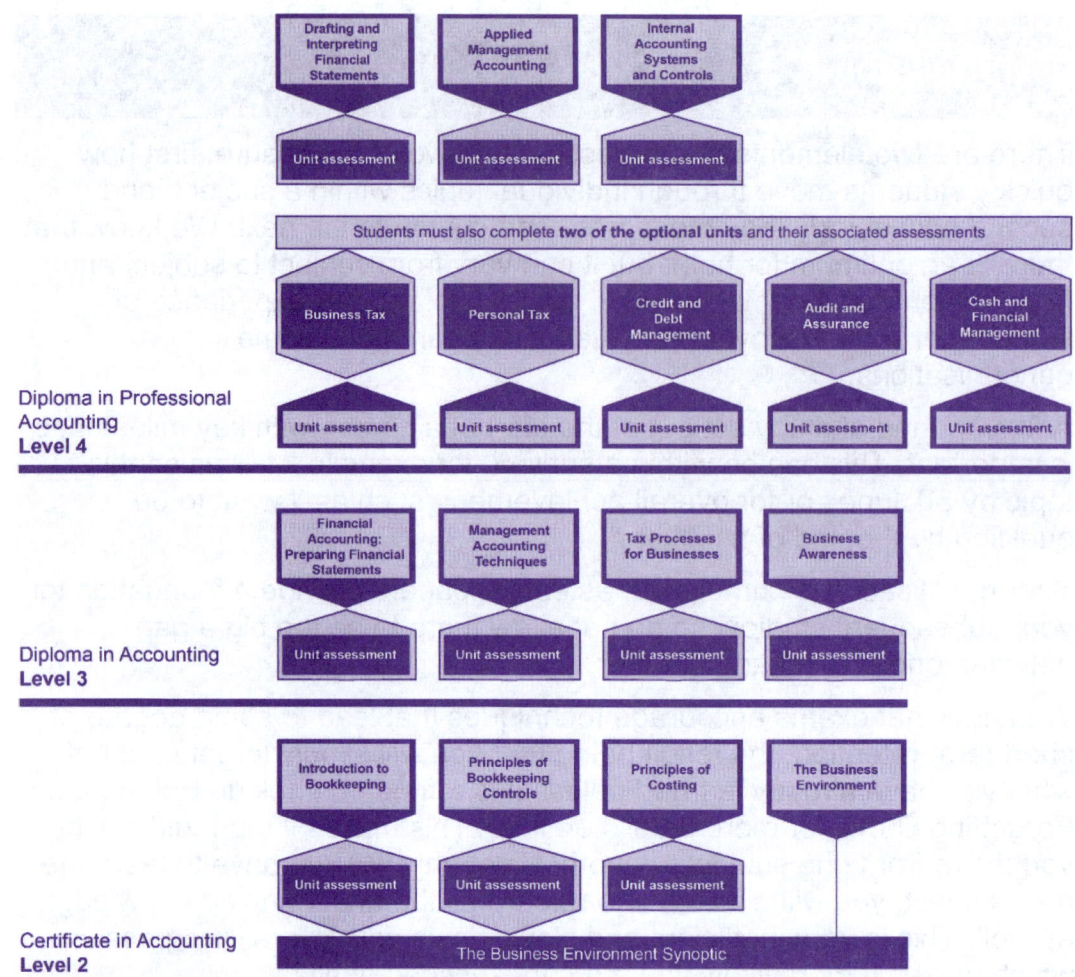

# UNIT GUIDE

## Introduction

Management Accounting Techniques provides students with the knowledge and skills needed to understand the role of management accounting in an organisation, and how organisations use such information to aid decision making.

Students will learn the principles that underpin management accounting methodology and techniques, how costs are handled in organisations, and why organisations treat costs in different ways. Students will be able to recognise different approaches to management accounting and provide informed and reasoned judgements to guide management. They will also learn how to apply these principles and appreciate why effective management accounting is crucial to any organisation.

Students will learn the techniques required for dealing with direct costs and revenues, and with the treatment of short-term overhead costs. They will also learn the techniques required for decision making, using estimates of costs, revenues and cash flow. Students will learn to carry out procedures as they would in a real-world organisation's finance function including: undertake budgetary overhead apportionments and producing recovery rates, carry out basic variance and cost-volume-profit (CVP) analysis, calculate changes in forecast unit costs and profits, calculating working capital measures, producing simple budgets, monitoring cash flow and reporting accounting information.

Students will be required to use spreadsheets when making calculations, manipulating and analysing data, reporting, and forecasting. Skills such as the use of formulas, functions, data analysis tools, sorting and filtering will be vital within accountancy to enable students to perform complex calculations quickly and accurately. After analysis, the data needs to be comprehensively checked and then presented using a range of methods, for example as a structured spreadsheet with pivot tables and charts.

The application of ethical principles is threaded throughout this unit. All work must be carried out with integrity, objectivity and a high degree of professional competence.

This unit builds on the knowledge and skills that students develop at Certificate level in Principles of Costing and prepares them for the Professional level unit Applied Management Accounting. Together, these units give students an underpinning understanding of cost and management accounting principles and the ability to apply relevant techniques.

Management Accounting Techniques is a **mandatory** unit in this qualification.

## Learning outcomes

On completion of this unit the learner will be able to:

- Understand the purpose and use of management accounting within organisations.

- Apply techniques required for dealing with costs.

- Attribute costs according to organisational requirements.

- Investigate deviations from budget.

- Use spreadsheet techniques to provide management accounting information.

- Use management accounting techniques to support short-term decision making.

- Understand principles of cash management.

## Scope of content

To perform this unit effectively you will need to know and understand the following:

**Chapter**

**1 Understand the purpose and use of management accounting within an organisation**

**1.1 Internal reporting calculations**                    1, 2

Learners need to know:

- The purpose of costing, budgeting and internal reporting and

- the importance of providing accurate information to management for the purposes of planning, control and decision-making.

Learners need to be able to:

- calculate revenues, costs, contribution and reported profits for an organisation

- calculate segmented revenues, costs, contribution and reported profits by product.

**1.2 Differences between marginal and absorption costing**                    2, 3

Learners need to understand:

- the difference between product and period costs:

    - some period costs are carried forward in the value of closing inventory under absorption costing

    - in marginal costing only variable costs are included in inventory and period costs are written off in full

- the differences between costing techniques

    - marginal costing

    - absorption costing

- the impact on reported performance of marginal versus full absorption costing in both the short run and the long run

- when each technique is appropriate

**Chapter**

Learners need to be able to:

- calculate:
  - prime cost
  - marginal cost
  - full absorption cost.

## 2 Use techniques required for dealing with costs

| | | |
|---|---|---|
| **2.1** | **Record and calculate materials, labour and overhead costs** | 4, 5, 6 |

Learners need to be able to:

- use appropriate data and information from both manual records and software packages to:
  - prepare and interpret inventory records for materials, work-in-progress and finished goods
  - calculate material and labour costs
  - account for overheads.
  - calculate cost per equivalent unit of finished production.

| | | |
|---|---|---|
| **2.2** | **Prepare cost accounting journals** | 4, 5, 6 |

Learners need to understand:

- principles of cost accounting journal entries for:
  - direct material or indirect materials
  - direct or indirect labour
  - overhead costs.

Learners need to be able to:

- prepare cost accounting journal entries for:
  - materials
  - labour
  - overheads.

**Chapter**

**4**

### 2.3 Apply inventory control methods

Learners need to be able to:

- calculate inventory control and valuation measures:
  - inventory buffers, lead times, minimum/maximum order quantities
    - buffer inventory = re-order level – (average usage × average lead time)
    - re-order level = (average usage × average lead time) + buffer inventory

Note: students will be provided with either buffer inventory or re-order level values when completing calculations.

- maximum inventory level = buffer inventory + maximum re-order quantity
- maximum re-order quantity = maximum inventory level – buffer inventory

Note: students will be provided with either maximum inventory level or maximum re-order quantity values when completing calculations.

- minimum re-order quantity = average usage × average lead time
  - economic order quantity
- = $\sqrt{((2 \times \text{annual usage} \times \text{ordering cost}) \div \text{inventory holding cost})}$
  - compliance with inventory control policies
  - the effect on reported profits of choice of method
- account for inventories using first-in first-out (FIFO) and average cost (AVCO) methods
- analyse closing inventory balances.

**Chapter**

**2**

**2.4    Cost behaviours**

Learners need to understand:

- the implications of different cost behaviours for cost analysis, decision making and reporting:
    - fixed
    - variable
    - semi-variable
    - stepped.

Learners need to be able to:

- use the high-low method to separate fixed and variable cost elements of semi-variable costs.

**2.5    Differences between costing systems**    3, 4, 5

Learners need to understand:

- the appropriate choice of costing system for different business sectors and individual organisations
- the effect of waste on costing inputs and outputs

Learners need to able to:

- record cost information, using different costing systems:
    - job costing
    - batch costing
    - unit costing
    - service costing.

**3    Attribute costs according to organisational requirements**

**3.1    Calculate and attribute overhead costs using traditional methods**    6

Learners need to know:

- different methods of indirect cost recovery:
    - apportionment
    - allocation.

**Chapter**

Learners need to be able to:

- attribute overhead costs to production and service cost centres:
  - apportionment versus allocation
  - direct method
  - step-down method.

**3.2 Calculate overhead recovery rates using traditional methods**   6

Learners need to be able to:

- calculate overhead recovery rates in accordance with suitable bases of absorption:
  - for a manufacturer: machine hours or direct labour hours
  - for a service business: suitable basis for the specific business.

**3.3 Calculate overhead recovery rates using activity-based costing**   6

Learners need to know:

- the concept of activity-based costing:
  - appropriate cost drivers
  - use of cost pools.

Learners need to be able to:

- calculate overhead recovery rates using appropriate cost drivers.

**3.4 Under- or over-recovery of overheads**   6

Learners need to understand:

- how to account for under- or over-recovered overhead costs in accordance with established procedures:
  - making under absorption or over absorption calculations
  - interpreting the significance of under- or over-recoveries of overhead costs on unit costs and total profit.

Chapter

**4 Investigate deviations from budgets**

**4.1 Principles of standard prices/costs and budgeting**      8

Learners need to understand:

- a product's standard price and standard cost

- how standard prices and costs can be used to develop budgets

- different types of budget:
  - fixed
  - flexed
  - rolling

- how operating statements are used to compare budgeted volume and standard revenue/cost versus actual performance

Learners need to be able to:

- prepare budgets for multi-product organisations:
  - revenue
  - materials
  - labour
  - variable overheads
  - fixed overheads
  - non-manufacturing overheads

- flex fixed budgets for actual volume.

**4.2 Calculate variances**      8

Learners need to able to:

- recognise variances as being either favourable or adverse

- calculate variances using flexed budgets

- compare flexed budget versus actual costs and revenues to calculate:
  - sales price variance (total)
  - raw materials variance (total)
  - labour variance (total)
  - variable overhead variance (total)
  - fixed production variance (total).

**Chapter**

**4.3    Analyse and investigate variance**                                      **8**

Learners need to be able to:

- determine the cause and effects of revenue and cost variances

- recognise significant variance for investigation

- report on remedial action to address adverse variances.

**5    Use spreadsheet techniques to provide management accounting information**

**5.1    Organise, record and format data**                                      **10**

Learners need to be able to:

- organise data:

  - design spreadsheets to support:

    - flexing budgets

    - the calculation and analysis of variances

    - production of operating statements

    - overhead absorption and allocation

    - short-term decision making

    - cash budgeting

- ensure data is valid and reliable:

  - select data from different sources

  - enter data manually into appropriate cells and worksheets

  - link data from different sources within the same worksheet/across different worksheets:

    - copying and pasting special values

    - linking

  - remove duplications in data

- format data:

  – formatting cells:

    • advanced formatting i.e. data manipulation, data security, data statistics

    • decimals, whole numbers, thousand separator, %

    • currency, accountancy, general, number

    • show adverse/negative figures with ( ) or –

  – produce/format/adjust charts and graphs:

    • chart production: 3D, exploded, bar, column, pie, line

    • changing chart type

  – chart labelling:

    • axis scale

    • titles

    • legend

- data tables.

**5.2    Use tools to manipulate, analyse and verify data**          10

Learners need to be able to:

- use a range of formulas and functions to perform calculations:

  – mathematical and logical functions using absolute and relative cell referencing:

    • sum

    • average

    • minimum

    • maximum

    • round

    • roundup

**Chapter**

- - rounddown
  - sumif
  - count
  - counta
  - countif
  - IF (simple and nested)
  - VLOOKUP
  - HLOOKUP
  - days
  - statistical techniques:
    - goal seek
    - forecast
- use tools to support analysis of data:
  - data sort/data filter using single and/or multiple criteria
  - conditional formatting (using function)
  - lookup tables:
    - pivot tables
    - pivot charts
  - subtotals:
    - average
    - sum
    - maximum
    - minimum
  - comments box:
    - show
    - hide

- edit and update data:

    – include new data (worksheet/chart)

    – consider if any new data is included in any existing analysis/existing charts

- verify accuracy of data by using formula auditing tools:

    – trace precedents

    – trace dependents

    – show formulas.

**5.3** **Use tools to prepare, protect and present accounting information**       10

Learners need to be able to:

- protect integrity of data:

    – use data validation to restrict data entry and editing

    – protect individual and ranges of cells

- enhance the visual presentation of data:

    – insert/edit headers and footers

    – hide/unhide rows/columns

    – format columns and rows to enhance understanding of data: font type, font colour, size, bold, italics, alignment

    – freezing rows and columns

    – adjust margins, orientation and print area

    – use a range of charts to summarise and present information

    – chart alteration: moving and resizing, changing chart type, in stacked, 3D, exploded formats

    – changing data series: chart colour/format, add/change cell fill colour

    – format charts: altering and formatting scales, axes, labels, data series, data tables.

**Chapter**

**6** **Use management accounting techniques to support short-term decision making**

**6.1** **Estimate and use short-term future revenue and costs**                     7

Learners need to understand:

- the concept of contribution, i.e. revenue minus variable costs.

Learners need to be able to:

- use estimates of relevant future revenue and costs

- use cost-volume-profit (CVP) analysis (both by calculation and by linear break-even chart) to calculate:

    – break-even analysis

    – margin of safety and margin of safety percentage

    – target profit

    – profit-volume ratio.

- interpret and report on CVP analysis.

**6.2** **Examine the effects of changing activity levels**         2, 7, 8

Learners need to understand:

- the effect of changing activity levels on unit revenues, costs and profits.

Leaners need to be able to:

- calculate changes in forecast unit revenues, costs and profits.

Chapter

**7      Understand principles of cash management**

**7.1    Principles of cash budgeting**                    9

Learners need to understand:

- the key differences between cash and profit

- principles of forecasting cash receipts and payments for:

  – sales, purchases and production

  – the acquisition and disposal of non-current assets

  – accounts receivable and payable

  – capital/new loans, repayment of loans and drawings

- the funding methods available for the acquisition of non-current assets:

  – cash

  – part-exchange

  – borrowing – loans, hire purchase

- the suitability of each funding method for the acquisition of non-current assets

- the importance of liquidity and use of resources ratios

- the working capital cycle

Learners need to be able to:

- produce cash budgets

- calculate working capital using resources ratios:

  – inventory holding period (days) = inventories / cost of sales × 365

  – trade receivables collection period (days) = trade receivables / revenue × 365

  – trade payables payment period (days) = trade payables / cost of sales × 365

  – working capital cycle (days) = inventory days + receivable days – payable days.

**7.2    Improving cash flow**

Learners need to understand:

- the importance of liquidity for businesses' survival

- the actions that can be taken if insufficient liquidity:

    - raise additional finance from owners in the form of capital

    - raise additional finance externally in the form of debt

- other methods of improving cash flow:

    - chase receivables

    - delay supplier payments

    - offer prompt payment discounts (PPD)

    - dispose of non-current assets

    - reduce inventory

- how accounting software and the use of automation and visualisation can aid cash flow planning.

## Delivering this unit

This unit links with:

- Level 2 Principles of Costing
- Level 3 Business Awareness
- Level 3 Financial Accounting: Preparing Financial Statements
- Level 4 Applied Management Accounting

# THE ASSESSMENT

## Test specification for this unit assessment

**Assessment type**
Computer based assessment

**Marking type**
Partially computer / partially human marked

**Duration of exam**
2 hours 30 minutes

| Learning outcomes | | Weighting |
|---|---|---|
| 1 | Understand the purpose and use of management accounting within organisations | 10% |
| 2 | Use techniques required for dealing with costs | 15% |
| 3 | Attribute costs according to organisational requirements | 20% |
| 4 | Investigate deviations from budget | 15% |
| 5 | Use spreadsheet techniques to provide management accounting information | 15% |
| 6 | Use management accounting techniques to support short-term decision making | 15% |
| 7 | Understand principles of cash management | 10% |
| Total | | 100% |

# APPRENTICESHIP LEARNERS ONLY

# UNIT LINK TO THE END POINT ASSESSMENT (EPA)

To achieve the Assistant Accountant apprenticeship leaners must pass all of the assessments in the Diploma in Accounting, complete a portfolio and reflective discussion and complete a synoptic/knowledge assessment.

The synoptic/knowledge assessment is attempted following completion of the individual AAT units and it draws upon knowledge and understanding from those units. It will be appropriate for learners to retain their study materials for individual units until they have successfully completed the synoptic assessment for that apprenticeship level.

With specific reference to this unit, the following learning objectives are also relevant to the synoptic assessment:

LO1   Understand the purpose and use of management accounting within organisations.

LO2   Use techniques required for dealing with costs.

LO4   Investigate deviations from budgets.

LO7   Understand principles of cash management

# STUDY SKILLS

## Preparing to study

### Devise a study plan

Determine which times of the week you will study.

Split these times into sessions of at least one hour for study of new material. Any shorter periods could be used for revision or practice.

Put the times you plan to study onto a study plan for the weeks from now until the assessment and set yourself targets for each period of study – in your sessions make sure you cover the whole course, activities and the associated Test your knowledge activities.

If you are studying more than one unit at a time, try to vary your subjects as this can help to keep you interested and see subjects as part of wider knowledge.

When working through your course, compare your progress with your plan and, if necessary, re-plan your work (perhaps including extra sessions) or, if you are ahead, do some extra revision/practice questions.

## Effective studying

### Active reading

You are not expected to learn the text by rote, rather, you must understand what you are reading and be able to use it to pass the assessment and develop good practice.

A good technique is to use SQ3Rs – Survey, Question, Read, Recall, Review:

**1    Survey the chapter**

Look at the headings and read the introduction, knowledge, skills and content, so as to get an overview of what the chapter deals with.

**2    Question**

Whilst undertaking the survey ask yourself the questions you hope the chapter will answer for you.

**3    Read**

Read through the chapter thoroughly working through the activities and, at the end, making sure that you can meet the learning objectives highlighted on the first page.

**4    Recall**

At the end of each section and at the end of the chapter, try to recall the main ideas of the section/chapter without referring to the text. This is best done after short break of a couple of minutes after the reading stage.

**5    Review**

Check that your recall notes are correct.

You may also find it helpful to re-read the chapter to try and see the topic(s) it deals with as a whole.

**Note taking**

Taking notes is a useful way of learning, but do not simply copy out the text.

The notes must:

- be in your own words
- be concise
- cover the key points
- be well organised
- be modified as you study further chapters in this text or in related ones.

Trying to summarise a chapter without referring to the text can be a useful way of determining which areas you know and which you don't.

**Three ways of taking notes**

**1    Summarise the key points of a chapter**

**2    Make linear notes**

A list of headings, subdivided with sub-headings, listing the key points.

If you use linear notes, you can use different colours to highlight key points and keep topic areas together.

Use plenty of space to make your notes easy to use.

**KAPLAN** PUBLISHING

## 3 Try a diagrammatic form

The most common of which is a mind map.

To make a mind map, put the main heading in the centre of the paper and put a circle around it.

Draw lines radiating from this to the main sub-headings which again have circles around them.

Continue the process from the sub-headings to sub-sub-headings.

## Highlighting and underlining

You may find it useful to underline or highlight key points in your study text – but do be selective.

You may also wish to make notes in the margins.

## Revision phase

Kaplan has produced material specifically designed for your final examination preparation for this unit.

These include pocket revision notes and a bank of revision questions specifically in the style of the new syllabus.

Further guidance on how to approach the final stage of your studies is given in these materials.

## Further reading

In addition to this text, you should also read the 'Accounting Technician' magazine every month to keep abreast of any guidance from the examiners.

# 1

# Management accounting

## Introduction

This chapter considers the basic principles of management accounting and management information.

| ASSESSMENT CRITERIA |
| --- |
| Internal reporting calculations (1.1) |

## CONTENTS

1   Management accounting
2   Data and information
3   Cost accounting
4   Terminology
5   Code of Ethics

# 1 Management accounting

## 1.1 Introduction

The primary purpose of **Management accounting** is to provide information for use within an organisation. **Internal users**, such as departmental managers, will require a variety of information to ensure the smooth running of their department.

It is also possible that some **external users**, such as banks, may also review the management accounts of a business.

## 1.2 The purpose of management accounting

The purpose of management accounting is to assist management in the following areas of running a business:

- **Decision making**

  Management accountants use management information to make informed decisions about the future.

- **Planning**

  Management accountants provide the information for the creation of short, medium and long term plans; for example, a short term plan is the preparation of annual budgets.

- **Co-ordinating**

  Planning enables all the different activities/departments in a business to work together towards the same common goal.

- **Controlling**

  The comparison of actual results with the budget helps to identify areas where operations are not running according to plan. Investigating the causes, and acting on the results of that investigation, helps to control the activities of the business.

- **Communicating**

  Preparing plans that are then distributed to departmental managers helps to communicate the aims of the business to those managers.

- **Motivating**

  Plans and budgets should include targets to motivate managers (and staff) and improve their performance. If the target is too difficult, however, it is likely to demotivate and the target is unlikely to be achieved.

# 2 Data and information

## 2.1 Attributes of good information

A management accountant's main objective is to provide information to managers to enable the correct decisions to be made. The information provided may be the same as that required for financial accounting but there are no regulations that need to be applied.

Management information needs to have the attributes of good information. It needs to be ACCURATE:

**A**ccurate

The degree of accuracy depends on the reason why the information is needed. For example:

- a report on the performance of different divisions of a business may show figures to the nearest pound, or nearest thousand pounds.

- when calculating the cost of a unit of output, managers may want the cost to be accurate to the nearest pence.

**C**omplete

Managers should be given all the information they need, but information should not be excessive. For example:

- a complete control report should include all standard and actual costs necessary to aid understanding of the calculations.

- production managers will need the analysis relating to material used or labour efficiency, where-as purchasing managers with need the analysis relating to material prices.

**C**ost-effective

The value of the information should exceed the cost of producing it. Management information is valuable, because it assists decision making. If a decision backed by information is different from what it would have been without the information, the value of information equates to the amount of money saved as a result.

**U**nderstandable

Use of technical language or jargon must be limited. Accountants must always be careful about the way in which they present financial information to non-financial managers.

Relevant

The information contained within a report should be relevant to its purpose. Redundant parts should be removed. For example:

- the sales team may need to know the total cost of producing a unit to calculate the selling price but may not need to know the breakdown into material, labour and overhead costs.

Authoritative

Information should be trusted and provided from reliable sources so that the users can have confidence in their decision making.

Timely

Information should be provided to a manager in time for decisions to be made based on that information.

Easy to use

We must always think about the person using the information we provide and make sure the information meets their needs.

## 2.2    The purpose of internal reporting

Management information can be produced in **any format** that is useful to the business and tends to be produced frequently, for instance **every month**.

To provide information as a basis for informed decision making the types of report that you may come across include:

- Budgeted financial reports – budgeted statement of profit or loss, budgeted statement of financial position

- Segmented reports – reports that are produced for different segments, products or services, of the business

- Variance reports – reports that are produced comparing what the business did (actual results) with what they had planned to do at the start of the period (flexed budget)

- Cash flow forecasts – reports that aim to forecast cash flow into and out of the business

- Cost cards – the detailed breakdown of the cost of a product.

Reports are usually intended to initiate a decision or an action.

If a report describes what happened in the past, a control action may be taken in an attempt to prevent a repeat of this behaviour.

Reports may advise on a certain course of action and recommend what decision should be taken.

# 3 Cost accounting

## 3.1 Cost accounting

**Cost accounting** is usually a large part of management accounting. As its name suggests, it is concerned with **establishing costs**. It developed within manufacturing businesses.

Cost accounting is primarily directed at enabling management to perform the functions of **planning, control** and **decision making**:

(a)  determining costs and profits during a control period

(b)  valuing inventory of raw materials, work in progress and finished goods, and controlling inventory levels

(c)  preparing budgets, forecasts and other control data for a forthcoming control period

(d)  creating a reporting system which enables managers to take corrective action where necessary to control costs

(e)  providing information for decision-making such as pricing.

Items (a) and (b) are traditional **cost accounting roles**; (c) to (e) extend into management accounting.

Cost accounting is not confined to the environment of manufacturing, although it is in this area that it is most fully developed. **Service industries, central and local government, and accountancy and legal practices** make use of cost accounting information. Furthermore, it is not restricted purely to manufacturing and operating costs, but also to administration, selling and distribution and research and development.

# 4 Terminology

## 4.1 Introduction

This section looks at some of the basic terminology you will encounter whilst working through this unit.

## 4.2 Cost object

A **cost object** is anything for which costs can be ascertained. Cost units and cost centres, described below, are types of cost object.

## 4.3    Cost units

A **cost unit** is a unit of product or service in relation to which costs are ascertained.

To help with planning, control and decision making, businesses often need to calculate a cost per unit of output.

A key question, however, is what exactly we mean by a 'unit of output', or '**cost unit**'. This will mean different things to different businesses but we always look at what the business produces.

- A car manufacturer will want to determine the cost of each car and probably different components as well.

- In a printing firm, the cost unit could be the specific customer order.

- For a paint manufacturer, the unit could be a litre of paint.

- An accountancy firm will want to know the costs incurred for each client. To help with this it is common to calculate the cost per hour of chargeable time spent by staff.

Service organisations may use several different cost units to measure the different kinds of service that they are providing.

Examples for a hotel might include:

- Meals served for the restaurant

- Rooms occupied for the cleaning staff

- Hours worked for the reception staff.

A composite cost unit is more appropriate if a service is a function of two variables.  Examples of composite cost units are as follows:

- How much is carried over what distance (tonne-miles) for haulage companies

- How many patients are treated for how many days (patient-days) for hospitals

- How many passengers travel how many miles (passenger-miles) for public transport companies.

## 4.4    Responsibility centres

 **Definition**

A **responsibility centre** is an individual part of a business whose manager has personal responsibility for its performance.

The main responsibility centres are:

- Cost centre
- Revenue centre
- Profit centre
- Investment centre.

A **cost centre** is a production or service location, function, activity or item of equipment whose costs are identified and recorded. A **cost centre** is a part of a business for which costs are determined.

- For a paint manufacturer cost centres might be: mixing department, packaging department, administration, or marketing departments.

- For an accountancy firm, the cost centres might be: audit, taxation, accountancy, word processing, administration, and canteen. Alternatively, they might be the various geographical locations, e.g. the London office, the Cardiff office, the Plymouth office.

- Cost centre managers need to have information about costs that are incurred and charged to their cost centres. The performance of a cost centre manager is judged on the extent to which cost targets have been achieved.

A **revenue centre** is a part of the organisation that earns sales revenue. It is similar to a cost centre, but only accountable for revenues, and not costs.

- Revenue centres are generally associated with selling activities, for example, a regional sales manager may have responsibility for the regional sales revenues generated.

- Each regional manager would probably have sales targets to reach and would be held responsible for reaching these targets.

- Sales revenues earned must be able to be traced back to individual (regional) revenue centres so that the performance of individual revenue centre managers can be assessed.

A **profit centre** is a part of the business for which both the costs incurred and the revenues earned are identified.

- Profit centres are often found in large organisations with a divisionalised structure, and each division is treated as a profit centre.

- Within each profit centre, there could be several costs centres and revenue centres.

- The performance of a profit centre manager is measured in terms of the profit made by the centre.

- The manager must therefore be responsible for both costs and revenues and in a position to plan and control both.

- Data and information relating to both costs and revenues must be collected and allocated to the relevant profit centres.

Managers of **investment centres** are responsible for investment decisions as well as decisions affecting costs and revenues.

- Investment centre managers are therefore accountable for the performance of capital employed as well as profits (costs and revenues).

- The performance of investment centres is measured in terms of the profit earned relative to the capital invested (employed).

 **Test your understanding 1**

**A cost centre is defined as:**

A   A unit of product or service for which costs are accumulated

B   A production or service location, function, activity or item of equipment for which costs are accumulated

C   Costs that relate directly to a unit

D   Costs that contain both a fixed and a variable element

# 5   Code of Ethics

## 5.1   The Code of Ethics for Professional Accountants

The Code of Ethics for Professional Accountants, published by The International Federation of Accountants (IFAC), forms the basis for the ethical codes of many accountancy bodies, including the AAT, ICAEW, ACCA and CIMA.

The Code adopts a principles-based approach. It does not attempt to cover every situation where a member may encounter professional ethical issues, prescribing the way in which he, she or they should respond. Instead, it adopts a value system, focusing on fundamental professional and ethical principles which are at the heart of proper professional behaviour.

A management accountant's responsibility is not just to satisfy the needs of an individual client or employer. It should also be to act in the public interest. In acting in the public interest a management accountant should observe and comply with the fundamental ethical requirements shown in the IFAC Code.

The five key principles are as follows:

**(a)   Integrity**

A person should be straightforward and honest in performing professional work and in all business relationships.

**(b)   Objectivity**

A professional accountant should not allow bias, conflict of interest or undue influence of others to override professional or business judgments.

**(c)   Professional competence and due care**

A professional accountant has a continuing duty to maintain professional knowledge and skill at the level required to ensure that a client or employer receives competent professional service based on current developments in practice, legislation and techniques.

**(d)   Confidentiality**

A professional accountant should respect the confidentiality of information acquired as a result of professional and business relationships and should not disclose any such information to third parties without proper and specific authority unless there is a legal or professional right or duty to disclose.

**(e)  Professional behaviour**

A person should not act in any way that is unprofessional or does not comply with relevant laws and regulations.

Threats to compliance with the fundamental principles can be general in nature or relate to the specific circumstances of an appointment.

General categories of threats to the principles include the following:

- **The self-interest threat** – a threat to a member's integrity or objectivity may stem from a financial or other self-interest conflict.

  This could arise, for example, from a direct or indirect interest in a client, from fear of losing an engagement or having employment terminated.

- **The self-review threat** – there will be a threat to objectivity if any product or judgement made by the member or the firm needs to be challenged or re-evaluated by the same individual subsequently i.e. can you effectively review your own work?

- **The advocacy threat** – there is a threat to a member's objectivity if he, she or they becomes an advocate for or against the position taken by the client or employer in any adversarial proceedings or situation. The degree to which this presents a threat to objectivity will depend on the individual circumstances. The presentation of only one side of the case may be compatible with objectivity provided that it is accurate and truthful.

- **The familiarity or trust threat** – is a threat that the member may become influenced by having:

  - knowledge of the issue

  - a relationship with the client or employer

  - judgement impaired to the extent that the member becomes too trusting.

- **The intimidation threat** – the possibility that the member may become intimidated by threat, by a dominating personality, or by other pressures, actual or feared, applied by the client or employer or by another.

# 6 Summary

In this introductory chapter we looked at some of the basic principles and terminology used in cost and management accounting.

You need to be aware of the difference between **cost units** (individual units of a product or service for which costs can be separately ascertained) and **cost centres** (locations or functions in respect of which costs are accumulated).

## Test your understanding answers

 **Test your understanding 1**

A cost centre is defined as:

B    A production or service location, function, activity or item of equipment for which costs are accumulated.

# Cost classification

2

## Introduction

This chapter considers how costs can be classified and the various uses of classification in management accounting.

| ASSESSMENT CRITERIA |
| --- |
| Internal reporting calculations (1.1) |
| Differences between marginal and absorption costing (1.2) |
| Cost behaviours (2.4) |
| Examine the effects of changing activity levels (6.2) |

## CONTENTS

1 The cost card

2 Cost classification

3 Cost behaviour

4 High low method

# 1    The cost card

## 1.1    Cost cards

A cost card is used to show the breakdown of the costs of producing output based on the classification of each cost.

A cost card can be produced for one unit or a planned level of production. The cost card below is an example of a cost card for a planned level of production i.e. in total.

The following chapters are aimed at being able to build up the total or unit cost.

|  | £ |
|---|---|
| **Direct costs** |  |
| Direct materials | 250,000 |
| Direct labour | 120,000 |
| Direct expenses | 10,000 |
| **Prime cost** (total of direct costs) | 380,000 |
| Variable production overheads | 15,000 |
| **Marginal production cost** (total of direct and variable costs) | 395,000 |
| Fixed production overheads | 35,000 |
| **Absorption cost** (total production cost) | 430,000 |
| Non-production overheads (e.g. administration overhead; selling overhead) | 20,000 |
| **Total cost** | 450,000 |

**Note:** The terminology in this cost card will be explained during your studies.

## 1.2    Product and period costs

A product cost is a cost that relates to the product or service being produced or provided e.g. raw materials.

A period cost is a cost that relates to a time period e.g. monthly rent, annual salaries.

## 2 Cost classification

### 2.1 Purpose of cost classification

Costs can be **classified** (collected into logical groups) in many ways. The particular classification selected will depend upon the purpose for which the resulting analysed data will be used, for example:

| Classification | Purpose |
| --- | --- |
| By element – materials, labour and expenses | Cost control |
| By function – production (cost of sales), and non-production (distribution costs, administrative expenses). | Financial accounts |
| By nature – direct and indirect | Cost accounts |
| By behaviour – fixed, variable, stepped fixed and semi-variable | Budgeting, decision making |

Classification of costs will also be determined by the **type of business** that is being run. For example, fuel for a taxi firm is required for the service they provide whereas fuel for a delivery vehicle for a manufacturing company is not part of the product they produce.

### 2.2 Cost classification by element

Classification by element involves stating costs according to what the cost is as follows:

- **Materials** – includes raw materials for a manufacturer or alternatively the cost of goods that are to be resold in a retail organisation.

- **Labour** – consists of basic pay and also overtime, commissions and bonuses as well.

- **Expenses** – includes electricity, depreciation and rent.

---

### Test your understanding 1

**Classify the following costs for a clothes retailer by element.**

| Cost | Materials | Labour | Expenses |
|---|---|---|---|
| Designer skirts | ☐ | ☐ | ☐ |
| Heating costs | ☐ | ☐ | ☐ |
| Depreciation of fixtures and fittings | ☐ | ☐ | ☐ |
| Cashier staff salaries | ☐ | ☐ | ☐ |

## 2.3 Cost classification by function

For financial accounting purposes costs are split into the following categories:

**Production (Operating costs)**

- **Cost of sales** – also known as **production** costs. This category could include production labour, materials, supervisor salaries and factory rent.

**Non-production (non-operating costs)**

- **Distribution** – this includes selling and distribution costs such as sales team commission and delivery costs.

- **Administrative costs** – this includes head office costs, IT support and HR support.

**Depreciation**

Depreciation is a measure of how much a non-current asset is wearing out or being used up. The classification will depend on which asset is being depreciated. For example:

- Cost of sales – depreciation on a machine in the production line

- Distribution – depreciation of a delivery van

- Administration – depreciation of a computer in the accounts department.

Depreciation can be calculated in two ways:

- The diminishing (reducing) balance method of depreciation allows a higher amount of depreciation to be charged in the early years of an asset's life compared to the later years. This reflects the increased levels of usage of such assets in the earlier periods of their lives.

- The straight line method calculates a consistent amount of depreciation over the life of the asset.

## Test your understanding 2

George plc makes stationery.

**Classify the following costs by function in the table below.**

| Cost | Production | Administration | Distribution |
|---|---|---|---|
| Purchases of plastic to make pens | ☐ | ☐ | ☐ |
| Managing director's bonus | ☐ | ☐ | ☐ |
| Depreciation of factory machinery | ☐ | ☐ | ☐ |
| Salaries of factory workers | ☐ | ☐ | ☐ |
| Insurance of sales team cars | ☐ | ☐ | ☐ |

## 2.4 Cost classification by nature

To be able to account for costs incurred it is necessary to know which costs are associated with the final product/service and which are incurred whilst producing the product/service. Classification by nature is how this is done:

- A **direct cost** is an item of cost that is traceable directly to a cost unit. An example of direct costs for a toy maker producing teddy bears might be:

    Direct material – fur fabric, stuffing

    Direct labour – employee stuffing the bear

    Direct expenses – patent for bear design.

The **total** of all **direct** costs is known as the **prime cost** per unit.

- An **indirect** cost is a cost that cannot be identified with any one finished unit. An example of indirect costs for a toy maker producing a teddy bear might be:

    Indirect material – cleaning products

    Indirect labour – the production line supervisor

    Indirect expenses – rent, rates, electricity.

These costs are incurred as a result of running the business but cannot necessarily be identified to an individual teddy bear.

**Indirect** costs are often referred to as **overheads**.

## Test your understanding 3

Camberwell runs a construction company.

**Classify the following costs by nature (direct or indirect) in the table below.**

| Cost | Direct | Indirect |
|---|---|---|
| Bricks | ☐ | ☐ |
| Plant hire for long term contract | ☐ | ☐ |
| Builders' wages | ☐ | ☐ |
| Accountants' wages | ☐ | ☐ |

## Test your understanding 4

**Direct costs are:**

A    A unit of product or service for which costs are accumulated

B    A production or service location, function, activity or item of equipment for which costs are accumulated

C    Costs that relate directly to a unit

D    Costs that contain both a fixed and a variable element

## Test your understanding 5

P Harrington is a golf ball manufacturer.

**Classify the following costs by nature (direct or indirect) in the table below.**

| Cost | Direct | Indirect |
|---|---|---|
| Machine operators wages | ☐ | ☐ |
| Supervisors wages | ☐ | ☐ |
| Resin for golf balls | ☐ | ☐ |
| Salesmen's salaries | ☐ | ☐ |

# 3 Cost behaviour

## 3.1 Cost classification by behaviour

For **short term** budgeting purposes, management needs to be able to predict **how costs will vary with differing levels of activity** (i.e. the number of units being produced).

For example, if a furniture manufacturer expected to produce 1,000 chairs in a particular month, what should he/she budget for the costs of wood, labour, selling costs, factory heat and light, manager's salaries, etc.? How would these costs differ (if at all) if he expected to produce 2,000 chairs?

To make short term budgeting and forecasting easier, costs are split into the following categories:

- Variable

- Fixed

- Stepped

- Semi-variable.

## 3.2 Variable costs

**Variable costs** are costs that vary with changes in level of activity. Variable costs are **constant per unit** of output and increase in direct proportion to activity.

For example, if you make twice the number of units then the amount (and hence the cost) of raw material used would double.

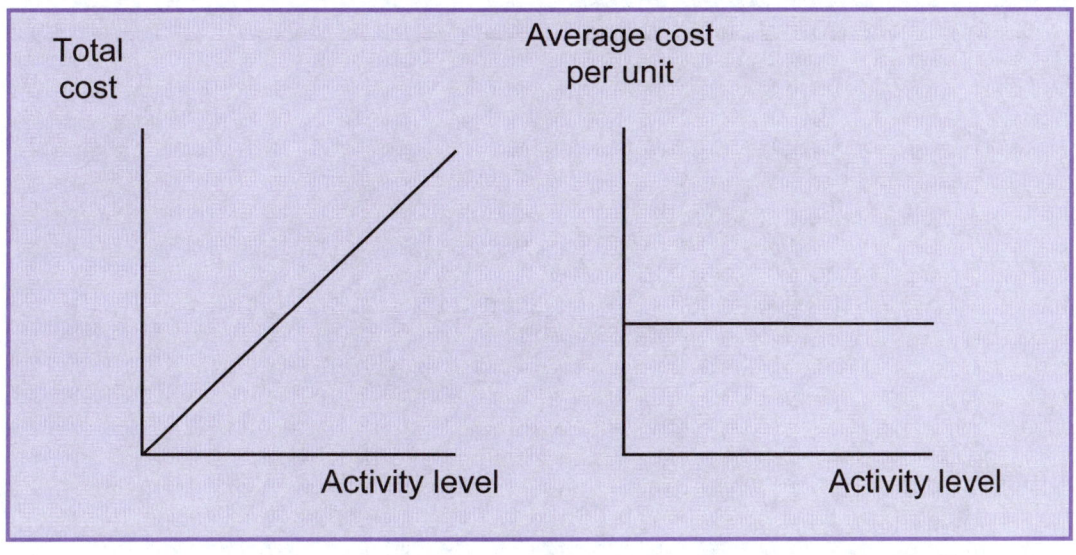

**Example 1**

If a business has total variable costs of £10,000 when it produces 1,000 units what is the variable cost per unit?

£10,000/1,000 = £10

What would be the total variable cost if the activity increased to 2,000 units?

£10 × 2,000 = £20,000

## 3.3 Fixed costs

**Fixed costs** are costs that, in the short term, are not affected by changes in activity level. The total cost stays constant as activity levels change. This leads to a decrease in the cost per unit of output as activity levels increase.

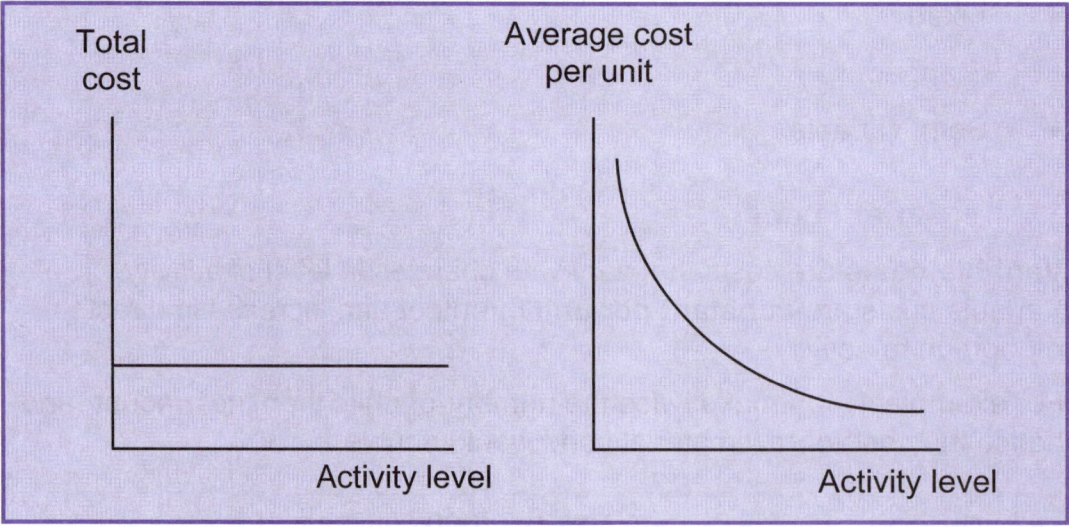

**Example 2**

If a business has total fixed costs of £15,000 when it produces 1,000 units what is the fixed cost per unit?

£15,000/1,000 = £15

If a business has total fixed costs of £15,000 when it produces 3,000 units what is the fixed cost per unit?

£15,000/3,000 = £5

What would be the total fixed cost if the activity increased to 5,000 units?

£15,000

 **Test your understanding 6**

Which of the following best describes a 'pure' fixed cost?

**A cost which:**

A    represents a fixed proportion of total costs

B    remains at the same level up to a particular level of output

C    has a direct relationship with output

D    remains at the same level whenever output changes

## 3.4    Stepped costs

**Stepped fixed costs** are costs that remain fixed up to a particular level of activity, but which rise to a higher (fixed) level if activity goes beyond that range.

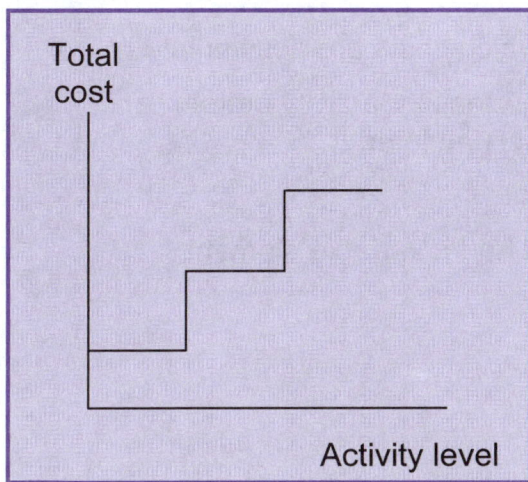

**Example 3**

A business has total fixed costs of £20,000 when it produces 1,000 units but if it goes above this level fixed costs increase by 50%. What would the fixed costs be if the business produced 2,000 units?

£20,000 × 1.5 = £30,000

### 3.5 Semi-variable costs

**Semi-variable costs** are those that have a fixed element and a variable element:

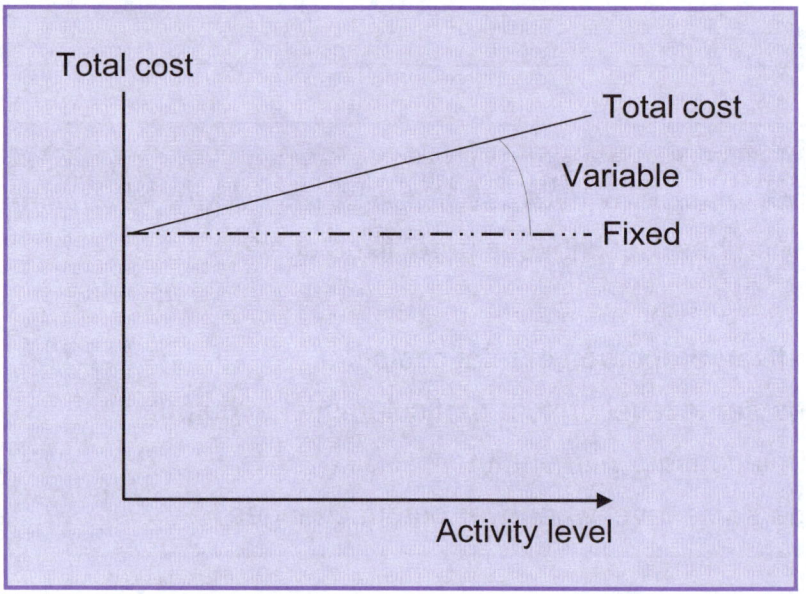

 **Test your understanding 7**

**A semi-variable cost is:**

A     A unit of product or service for which costs are accumulated

B     A production or service location, function, activity or item of equipment for which costs are accumulated

C     A cost that relate directly to a unit

D     A cost that contains both a fixed and a variable element

**KAPLAN** PUBLISHING

## Test your understanding 8

Gilbert plc is a furniture manufacturer.

**Classify the following costs by their behaviour in the table below.**

| Cost | Fixed | Variable | Semi-variable |
|---|---|---|---|
| Director's salary | ☐ | ☐ | ☐ |
| Wood | ☐ | ☐ | ☐ |
| Rent of factory | ☐ | ☐ | ☐ |
| Phone bill – includes a line rental | ☐ | ☐ | ☐ |
| Factory workers wage | ☐ | ☐ | ☐ |

## Test your understanding 9

**Identify the following statements as either true or false.**

| | True | False |
|---|---|---|
| Stepped costs have a fixed and variable element | ☐ | ☐ |
| Fixed costs vary directly with changes in activity | ☐ | ☐ |
| Variable costs have a constant cost per unit | ☐ | ☐ |

## 3.6 Cost behaviour assumptions

To be able to use cost behaviours to produce budgets there are some assumptions that are made:

- Any **change** in cost is only due to change in **activity levels**.

- Costs are assumed to be either **fixed** or **variable**, or at least **separable into these elements**.

- Total fixed costs remain fixed throughout the activity range (unless told otherwise).

- Total variable costs change in direct proportion to volume.

- Economies or diseconomies of scale are ignored; this ensures that **the variable cost per unit is constant**.

- Efficiency and productivity do not change with volume.

- If a cost is **direct** it will have a **variable** cost behaviour.

**Note:** The use of cost behaviour to classify costs only holds in the short term, **in the long term** (by definition) **all costs are variable**.

## 3.7    Identifying cost behaviours

The **behavioural characteristics** of costs are used when planning or forecasting costs at different levels of production or activity.

When producing a forecast, it may be necessary to identify the type of behaviour a cost is exhibiting. It is useful to remember the following:

- Fixed costs are constant in total.

- Variable costs are constant per unit.

- Semi-variable costs are neither constant in total nor constant per unit.

- Stepped fixed costs will be fixed in total to a certain range, increase and then be fixed again.

 **Example 4**

A company has a mix of variable, semi variable, fixed and stepped fixed costs. Identify the behaviour for each of the costs shown below:

**Total cost at different activity levels**

| Cost | 1,000 units £ | 3,000 units £ | 5,000 units £ | 7,000 units £ |
|---|---|---|---|---|
| 1 | 4,500 | 7,500 | 10,500 | 13,500 |
| 2 | 1,830 | 5,490 | 9,150 | 12,810 |
| 3 | 5,000 | 5,000 | 5,000 | 5,000 |
| 4 | 12,250 | 12,250 | 15,000 | 15,000 |

**Cost per unit at different activity levels:**

| Cost | 1,000 units £ | 3,000 units £ | 5,000 units £ | 7,000 units £ |
|---|---|---|---|---|
| 1 | 4.50 | 2.50 | 2.10 | 1.93 |
| 2 | 1.83 | 1.83 | 1.83 | 1.83 |
| 3 | 5.00 | 1.67 | 1.00 | 0.71 |
| 4 | 12.25 | 4.08 | 3.00 | 2.14 |

- **Cost 1** is be a **semi-variable cost** as the total cost changes when activity level change and the cost per unit also changes at the different activity levels.

- **Cost 2** is a **variable cost** as the cost per unit is constant at each activity level.

- **Cost 3** is a **fixed cost** as the total cost does not change as activity level changes.

- **Cost 4** is a **stepped fixed cost** as the total cost is constant then increases to a new constant level and the cost per unit is changing at each activity level.

---

 **Test your understanding 10**

**Identify if the following costs are variable, fixed, stepped fixed or semi-variable.**

|  | 1,500 units | 2,500 units | 3,500 units | 5,500 units |
|---|---|---|---|---|
| Material | £7,500 | £12,500 | £17,500 | £27,500 |
| Labour | £12,000 | £12,000 | £24,000 | £24,000 |
| Rent | £17,000 | £17,000 | £17,000 | £17,000 |
| Electricity | £16,750 | £21,250 | £25,750 | £34,750 |

## 3.8    Stepped fixed costs

If a forecast includes a stepped fixed cost, then information may be provided as to when the step up in cost would occur and by how much.

---

 **Example 5**

A manufacturing business has variable production costs of £3 per unit and fixed costs of £60,000. A further cost is the salary of the factory supervisor of £18,000 per annum. If more than 100,000 units of the product are made, then an additional factory supervisor must be employed at the same salary.

**What is the total cost of production and the cost per unit at the following production levels?**

(i)     60,000 units

(ii)    90,000 units

(iii)   120,000 units

---

| | Production level | | |
|---|---|---|---|
| | 60,000 units £ | 90,000 units £ | 120,000 units £ |
| Variable production costs | | | |
| 60,000 × £3 | 180,000 | | |
| 90,000 × £3 | | 270,000 | |
| 120,000 × £3 | | | 360,000 |
| Fixed costs | 60,000 | 60,000 | 60,000 |
| Supervisor's salary (stepped) | 18,000 | 18,000 | 36,000 |
| Total production cost | 258,000 | 348,000 | 456,000 |
| Cost per unit | £4.30 | £3.87 | £3.80 |

The total costs are made up of both fixed and variable costs but the cost per unit falls as the production quantity increases. This is because the fixed costs are spread over a higher number of units of production.

### 3.9 Semi-variable costs

Changes in activity level may also require the separation of the fixed and variable element of a semi-variable cost. The total fixed cost will remain constant as activity changes but the total variable cost will change in proportion to the activity changes.

The splitting or separating of a semi-variable cost is done by using the high-low method.

## 4 The high low method

### 4.1 High low method

If a semi-variable cost is incurred, it is often necessary to estimate the fixed element and the variable element of the cost for the purposes of budgeting. This can be done using the high low method.

Remember:

**Total cost = Fixed cost + (Variable cost per unit × Activity level)**

**Example 6**

A factory has incurred the following power costs in the last six months with different levels of production in each month:

| | Production units | Power costs £ |
|---|---|---|
| January | 20,000 | 18,000 |
| February | 16,000 | 16,500 |
| March | 18,000 | 17,200 |
| April | 24,000 | 20,500 |
| May | 22,000 | 19,400 |
| June | 19,000 | 17,600 |

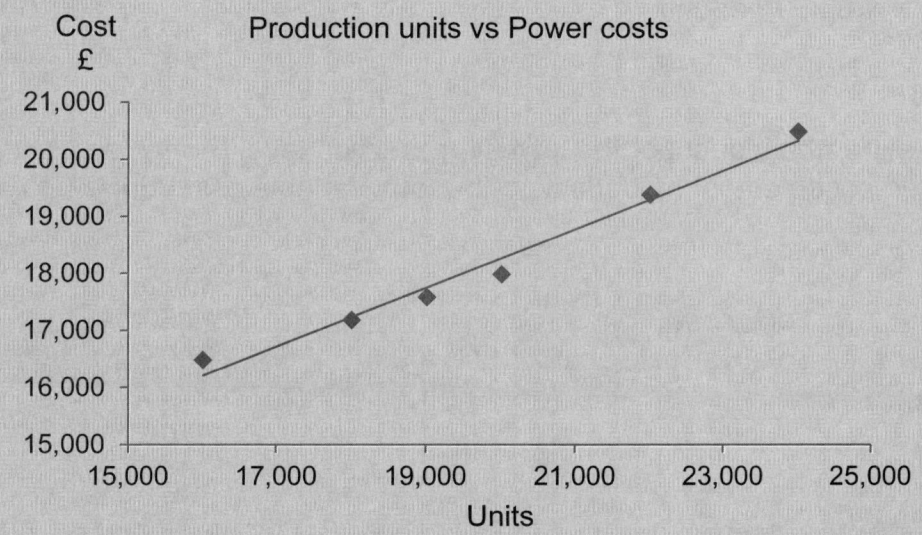

**What are the fixed and variable elements of the power cost?**

**Step 1**

Find the highest and lowest levels of production (activity) and their related costs.

| | | Units | Cost £ |
|---|---|---|---|
| High | April | 24,000 | 20,500 |
| Low | February | 16,000 | 16,500 |

**Step 2**

Find the variable cost element by determining the increased power cost per unit between highest and lowest production levels.

|  |  | Units | Cost £ |
|---|---|---|---|
| High | April | 24,000 | 20,500 |
| Low | February | 16,000 | 16,500 |
|  | Difference | 8,000 | 4,000 |

The power cost has increased by £4,000 for an increase in 8,000 units of production. The variable power cost is therefore:

$$\frac{£4,000}{8,000} = £0.50 \text{ per unit}$$

**Step 3**

Using either the highest or the lowest production level (from step 1) find the fixed cost element by deducting the total variable cost from the total cost.

| | | £ |
|---|---|---|
| April | Total cost | 20,500 |
| | Total variable cost 24,000 × 0.5 | (12,000) |
| | | 8,500 |

| | | £ |
|---|---|---|
| February | Total cost | 16,500 |
| | Total variable cost 16,000 × 0.5 | (8,000) |
| | | 8,500 |

**If production levels of 30,000 units are anticipated next month, what is the expected power cost?**

The semi-variable power cost consists of the fixed cost (£8,500) and a variable cost per unit (£0.50). Therefore, for an activity level of 30,000 units the total cost is predicted to be:

| | £ |
|---|---|
| Variable cost 30,000 × 0.50 | 15,000 |
| Fixed cost | 8,500 |
| Total cost | 23,500 |

**Test your understanding 11**

C Ling has a contract with a customer to produce 4,000, 5,000 or 6,000 units of product.

Revenues and costs for 4,000 units are shown below. Fixed overheads remain constant for the range charted but indirect labour will increase by £2,000 when production reaches 5,500 units.

| Possible production level | 4,000 units |
|---|---|
| | £ |
| Sales revenue | 50,000 |
| Variable costs: | |
|     Material | 2,000 |
|     Labour | 4,000 |
|     Overheads | 6,000 |
| Fixed costs: | |
|     Indirect labour | 12,000 |
|     Overheads | 8,000 |
| Total cost | 32,000 |
| Total profit | 18,000 |
| Profit per unit | 4.50 |

**Calculate:**

- The sales revenue per unit if the contract is for 4,000 units.

- The variable cost per unit if the contract is for 4,000 units.

- The fixed cost per unit if the contract is for 4,000 units.

- The total cost if the contract is for 6,000 units.

- The total profit if the contract is for 6,000 units.

**Test your understanding 12**

**Biscuit Making Company**

The general manager has given you the task of supplying cost data for the manufacture of a specific brand of chocolate biscuit for 20X9 on the basis of projected costs. A cost clerk has given you data on variable and fixed costs, which is relevant over the range of production.

**Complete the budgeted cost schedule for the different levels of production.**

| BUDGETED COST SCHEDULE | | YEAR 20X9 | | | |
|---|---|---|---|---|---|
| | | ACTIVITY (Packets) | | | |
| | | **150,000** | **175,000** | **200,000** | **225,000** |
| Description | | £ | £ | £ | £ |
| Variable costs: | | | | | |
| Direct material | | 12,000 | | | |
| Direct labour | | 9,000 | | | |
| Packing costs | | 1,500 | | | |
| Fixed costs: | | | | | |
| Depreciation costs | | 12,000 | | | |
| Rent and rates | | 26,000 | | | |
| Supervisory costs | | 12,000 | | | |
| Administration costs | | 8,000 | | | |
| Total costs | | 80,500 | | | |
| Cost per packet (2 decimal places) | | 0.54 | | | |

The cost per packet has increased/decreased* because the fixed cost per unit has increased/decreased*

*delete as appropriate

**Test your understanding 13**

The electricity used in a factory has a semi-variable cost behaviour.

**What would be the budgeted electricity cost for the factory if it were to make 75 units?**

| Units | Total cost £ |
|---|---|
| 10 | 120 |
| 50 | 200 |
| 100 | 300 |

A     £150

B     £100

C     £250

D     £137.50

 **Test your understanding 14**

The total production cost for making 10,000 units was £12,000 and the total production cost for making 25,000 was £21,000.

**What is the full production cost for making 40,000 units?**

A     6,000

B     24,000

C     30,000

D     72,667

**Test your understanding 15**

Charlie Ltd is preparing its budget for the next quarter and it needs to consider different production levels.

The semi-variable costs should be calculated using the high low method. If 3,000 units are produced, then the semi-variable cost will be £8,500.

**Complete the table below and calculate the estimated profit per unit at the different activity levels.**

| Units sold and produced | 1,000 | 1,500 | 2,000 |
|---|---|---|---|
| Sales revenue | 25,000 | 37,500 | 50,000 |
| Variable cost | | | |
| Direct materials | 5,000 | 7,500 | 10,000 |
| Direct labour | 2,400 | 3,600 | 4,800 |
| Overheads | 3,600 | 5,400 | 7,200 |
| Semi-variable costs | 4,500 | | |
| Variable element | | 3,000 | 4,000 |
| Fixed element | | 2,500 | 2,500 |
| Fixed cost | 3,500 | 3,800 | 3,500 |
| Total cost | 19,000 | 25,800 | 32,000 |
| Total profit | 6,000 | 12,000 | 18,000 |
| Profit per unit (to 2 decimal places) | 6.00 | 8.00 | 9.00 |

*(handwritten: 25 above 1,500 column; S next to Direct materials; brackets with "3" and "add all", "sales" on right)*

*(handwritten working at bottom:)*

2     − 4,500   3000
      8,500 − 1000
      = 4,000  = 2,000
      4,000 ÷ 2,000 = 2

**Test your understanding 16** 🔵

Wendy Sheds is preparing its budget for the next quarter and it needs to consider different production levels.

The semi-variable costs should be calculated using the high low method. If 300 sheds are produced then the semi-variable cost will be £600.

**Complete the table below and calculate the estimated profit per shed at the different activity levels.**

| Sheds sold and produced | 500 | 750 | 1,000 |
|---|---|---|---|
| Sales revenue | 8,000 | 12,000 | 16,000 |
| Variable cost | | | |
| Direct materials | 800 | 1,200 | 1,600 |
| Direct labour | 760  330 | 1,140 | 1,520 |
| Overheads | 1,440 | 2,160 | 2,880 |
| Semi-variable costs | 900 | | |
| Variable element | | 1,125 | 1,500 |
| Fixed element | | 150 | 150 |
| Fixed cost | 700 | 700 | 700 |
| Total cost | 4,600 | 6,475 | 8,350 |
| Total profit | 3,400 | 5,525 | 7,650 |
| Profit per shed (to 2 decimal places) | 6.80 | 7.37 | 7.65 |

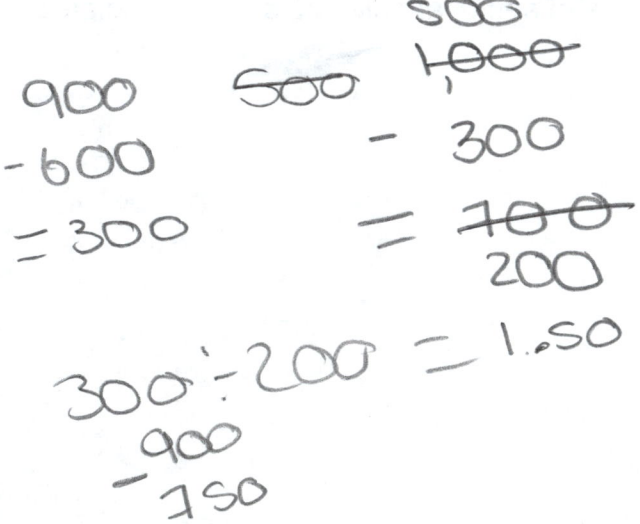

900
−600
=300

500   500
1,000
−   300
=   700
    200

300 ÷ 200 = 1.50

900
−750

**Test your understanding 17**

A manufacturing business has variable production costs of £3 per unit and fixed costs of £50,000. These include rent of £18,000 per annum. If more than 50,000 units of the product are made, then additional floor space must be rented at a cost of £20,000 per annum.

**What is the total cost of production and the cost per unit at the 60,000 units?**

|   | Total | Per unit |
|---|---|---|
| A | £230,000 | £3.83 |
| B | £250,000 | £4.17 |
| C | £268,000 | £4.47 |
| D | £88,000 | £1.47 |

# 5 Summary

Costs can be classified in a variety of different ways for different purposes. The basic classification is into **materials, labour and expenses**, each of which will be dealt with in detail in the following chapters. A further method of classification of costs is between **direct and indirect** costs.

For decision-making and budgeting purposes, it is useful to distinguish costs according to their **behaviour** as production levels change. The basic classifications according to behaviour are **fixed** and **variable** costs although there are also **stepped** costs and **semi-variable** costs. The fixed and variable elements of semi-variable costs can be isolated using the **high low method**.

## Test your understanding answers

### Test your understanding 1

| Cost | Materials | Labour | Expenses |
|---|---|---|---|
| Designer skirts | ☑ | ☐ | ☐ |
| Heating costs | ☐ | ☐ | ☑ |
| Depreciation of fixtures and fittings | ☐ | ☐ | ☑ |
| Cashier staff salaries | ☐ | ☑ | ☐ |

### Test your understanding 2

| Cost | Production | Administration | Distribution |
|---|---|---|---|
| Purchases of plastic to make pens | ☑ | ☐ | ☐ |
| Managing director's bonus | ☐ | ☑ | ☐ |
| Depreciation of factory machinery | ☑ | ☐ | ☐ |
| Salaries of factory workers | ☑ | ☐ | ☐ |
| Insurance of sales team cars | ☐ | ☐ | ☑ |

### Test your understanding 3

| Cost | Direct | Indirect |
|---|:---:|:---:|
| Bricks | ☑ | ☐ |
| Plant hire for long term contract | ☑ | ☐ |
| Builders' wages | ☑ | ☐ |
| Accountants' wages | ☐ | ☑ |

### Test your understanding 4

Direct costs are:

**C**  Costs that relate directly to a unit.

### Test your understanding 5

| Cost | Direct | Indirect |
|---|:---:|:---:|
| Machine operators wages | ☑ | ☐ |
| Supervisors wages | ☐ | ☑ |
| Resin for golf balls | ☑ | ☐ |
| Salesmen's salaries | ☐ | ☑ |

### Test your understanding 6

**D**  Pure fixed costs remain exactly the same in total regardless of the activity level.

### Test your understanding 7

A semi-variable cost is:

**D**  A cost that contains both a fixed and a variable element.

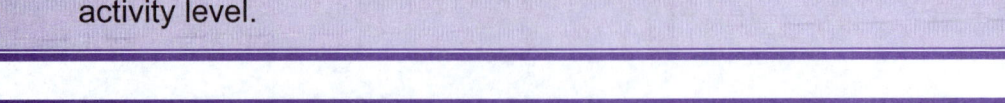

## Test your understanding 8

| Cost | Fixed | Variable | Semi-variable |
|---|:---:|:---:|:---:|
| Director's salary | ☑ | ☐ | ☐ |
| Wood | ☐ | ☑ | ☐ |
| Rent of factory | ☑ | ☐ | ☐ |
| Phone bill – includes a line rental | ☐ | ☐ | ☑ |
| Factory workers wage | ☐ | ☑ | ☐ |

## Test your understanding 9

| | True | False |
|---|:---:|:---:|
| Stepped costs have a fixed and variable element | ☐ | ☑ |
| Fixed costs vary directly with changes in activity | ☐ | ☑ |
| Variable costs have a constant cost per unit | ☑ | ☐ |

## Test your understanding 10

To identify cost behaviours, it is necessary to look at the total costs and the cost per unit.

A **variable cost** will be constant per unit as activity changes – **Material**

A **fixed cost** will be constant in total as activity changes – **Rent**

A **stepped fixed cost** will be constant in total then increase to a new constant level and the cost per unit is changing at each activity level – **Labour**

A **semi-variable cost** will be neither constant in total nor constant per unit as activity changes – **Electricity**

**Test your understanding 11**

- The sales revenue per unit if the contract is for 4,000 units

    50,000/4,000 = £12.50

- The variable cost per unit if the contract is for 4,000 units

    (2,000 + 4,000 + 6,000)/4,000 = £3.00

- The fixed cost per unit if the contract is for 4,000 units

    (12,000 + 8,000)/4,000 = £5.00

- The total cost if the contract is for 6,000 units

    (£3.00 × 6,000) + (12,000 + 2,000) + (8,000) = £40,000

- The total profit if the contract is for 6,000 units

    (£12.50 × 6,000) – £40,000 = £35,000

 **Test your understanding 12**

| BUDGETED COST SCHEDULE | | YEAR 20X9 | | | |
|---|---|---|---|---|---|
| | | ACTIVITY (Packets) | | | |
| | | 150,000 | 175,000 | 200,000 | 225,000 |
| Description | | £ | £ | £ | £ |
| Variable costs: | | | | | |
| Direct material | | 12,000 | 14,000 | 16,000 | 18,000 |
| Direct labour | | 9,000 | 10,500 | 12,000 | 13,500 |
| Packing costs | | 1,500 | 1,750 | 2,000 | 2,250 |
| Fixed costs: | | | | | |
| Depreciation costs | | 12,000 | 12,000 | 12,000 | 12,000 |
| Rent and rates | | 26,000 | 26,000 | 26,000 | 26,000 |
| Supervisory costs | | 12,000 | 12,000 | 12,000 | 12,000 |
| Administration costs | | 8,000 | 8,000 | 8,000 | 8,000 |
| Total costs | | 80,500 | 84,250 | 88,000 | 91,750 |
| Cost per packet (2 decimal places) | | 0.54 | 0.48 | 0.44 | 0.41 |

The cost per packet has **decreased** because the fixed cost per unit has **decreased**.

**Test your understanding 13**

The cost for the electricity for 75 units is:

**C** £250

**Variable cost**

$$\frac{300 - 120}{100 - 10} = £2$$

**Fixed cost**

300 − (100 × 2) = £100

**Cost for 75 units**

100 + (75 × 2) = £250

---

**Test your understanding 14**

**C**

|  | £ |
|---|---|
| Cost of 25,000 units | 21,000 |
| Less cost of 10,000 units | 12,000 |
| Difference = variable cost of 15,000 units | 9,000 |

$$\text{Variable cost per unit} = \frac{£9,000}{15,000} = 60p \text{ each}$$

Fixed costs = total cost − variable costs

Fixed costs = £21,000 − £(25,000 × 0.6) = £6,000

Therefore total cost for 40,000

|  | £ |
|---|---|
| Variable (40,000 × 0.6) | 24,000 |
| Fixed | 6,000 |
|  | 30,000 |

**Test your understanding 15**

| Units sold and produced | 1,000 | 1,500 | 2,000 |
|---|---|---|---|
| Sales revenue | 25,000 | 37,500 | 50,000 |
| Variable cost | | | |
| Direct materials | 5,000 | 7,500 | 10,000 |
| Direct labour | 2,400 | 3,600 | 4,800 |
| Overheads | 3,600 | 5,400 | 7,200 |
| Semi-variable costs | 4,500 | | |
| Variable element | | 3,000 | 4,000 |
| Fixed element | | 2,500 | 2,500 |
| Fixed cost | 3,500 | 3,500 | 3,500 |
| Total cost | 19,000 | 25,500 | 32,000 |
| Total profit | 6,000 | 12,000 | 18,000 |
| Profit per batch (to 2 decimal places) | 6.00 | 8.00 | 9.00 |

Splitting the semi-variable cost:

$$\frac{8,500 - 4,500}{3,000 - 1,000} = \text{£2 per unit}$$

Variable cost (at 3,000 units) = 3,000 × £2 = £6,000

Fixed cost = £8,500 – £6,000 = £2,500

## Test your understanding 16

| Sheds sold and produced | 500 | 750 | 1,000 |
|---|---|---|---|
| Sales revenue | 8,000 | 12,000 | 16,000 |
| Variable cost | | | |
| Direct materials | 800 | 1,200 | 1,600 |
| Direct labour | 760 | 1,140 | 1,520 |
| Overheads | 1,440 | 2,160 | 2,880 |
| Semi-variable costs | 900 | | |
| Variable element | | 1,125 | 1,500 |
| Fixed element | | 150 | 150 |
| Fixed cost | 700 | 700 | 700 |
| Total cost | 4,600 | 6,475 | 8,350 |
| Total profit | 3,400 | 5,525 | 7,650 |
| Profit per shed (to 2 decimal places) | 6.80 | 7.37 | 7.65 |

## Test your understanding 17

B

|  | 60,000 units £ |
|---|---|
| Variable production costs 60,000 × £3 | 180,000 |
| Fixed costs | 50,000 |
| Additional rentals | 20,000 |
| Total production cost | 250,000 |
| Cost per unit | £4.17 |

# Types of costing systems

**3**

## Introduction

We are now going to turn our attention to different types of costing systems. **Marginal costing** is used within management accounting to aid decision making. The marginal cost of a product is the **total variable production costs**. In marginal costing **fixed overheads** are treated as **period costs** and are charged in full against the profit for the period.

**Absorption costing** assigns fixed production overheads to the inventory.

**Job costing** involves individual jobs with different materials and labour requirements (for example, car repairs). **Batch costing**, on the other hand, is suitable for businesses that produce batches of identical items (for example, bars of soap) though batch costs may vary from product to product. **Service costing** is used when an organisation provides a service rather than a product.

| ASSESSMENT CRITERIA | CONTENTS |
|---|---|
| Differences between marginal and absorption costing (1.2) | 1 Marginal costing |
| Difference between costing systems (2.5) | 2 Absorption costing |
| | 3 Absorption versus marginal costing |
| | 4 Types of costing techniques |

# 1 Marginal costing

## 1.1 Marginal costing

Marginal costing values each unit of inventory at the **variable production cost** required to make each unit (the marginal cost). This includes direct materials, direct labour, direct expenses and variable overheads. Variable non-production costs do not form part of the product cost but are subtracted after the cost of sales to calculate **contribution**. No **fixed overheads** (production or non-production) are included in the product costs; they are treated as a **period cost** and deducted in full lower down the statement of profit and loss.

### Definition

The **marginal production cost** is the cost of one unit of product or service which would be avoided if that unit were not produced, or the amount by which costs would increase if one extra unit were produced.

Marginal costing requires knowledge of cost behaviours as costs are split based on whether they are fixed or variable. Semi-variable costs would need to be separated into their fixed and variable elements by using the high-low method. See Chapter 2.

The basic layout for calculating budgeted profit or loss under marginal costing is as follows (with illustrative figures).

|  | £ | £ |
|---|---|---|
| Sales revenue (10,000 × £10) |  | 100,000 |
| Cost of sales (at **marginal/variable** cost, £6) |  | (60,000) |
| Variable non-production costs (£1) |  | (10,000) |
| **Contribution** |  | 30,000 |
| Less:    **Fixed** production costs | 20,000 |  |
|         **Fixed** non- production costs | 2,000 |  |
|  |  | (22,000) |
| Profit for the period |  | 8,000 |

## Test your understanding 1

**XYZ plc**

XYZ plc manufactures toy horses and has produced a budget for the quarter ended 30 June 20X5 (Quarter 1) as follows.

| | |
|---|---|
| Sales | 190 units @ selling price of £12 ✓ |
| Production | 200 units ✓ |
| Opening inventory | 20 units ✓ |
| Variable production cost per unit | −✗ £8 |
| Fixed production overhead | £400 |
| Selling and distribution costs (fixed) | £250 |

**Required:**

**Draft the statement of profit or loss using marginal costing principles**

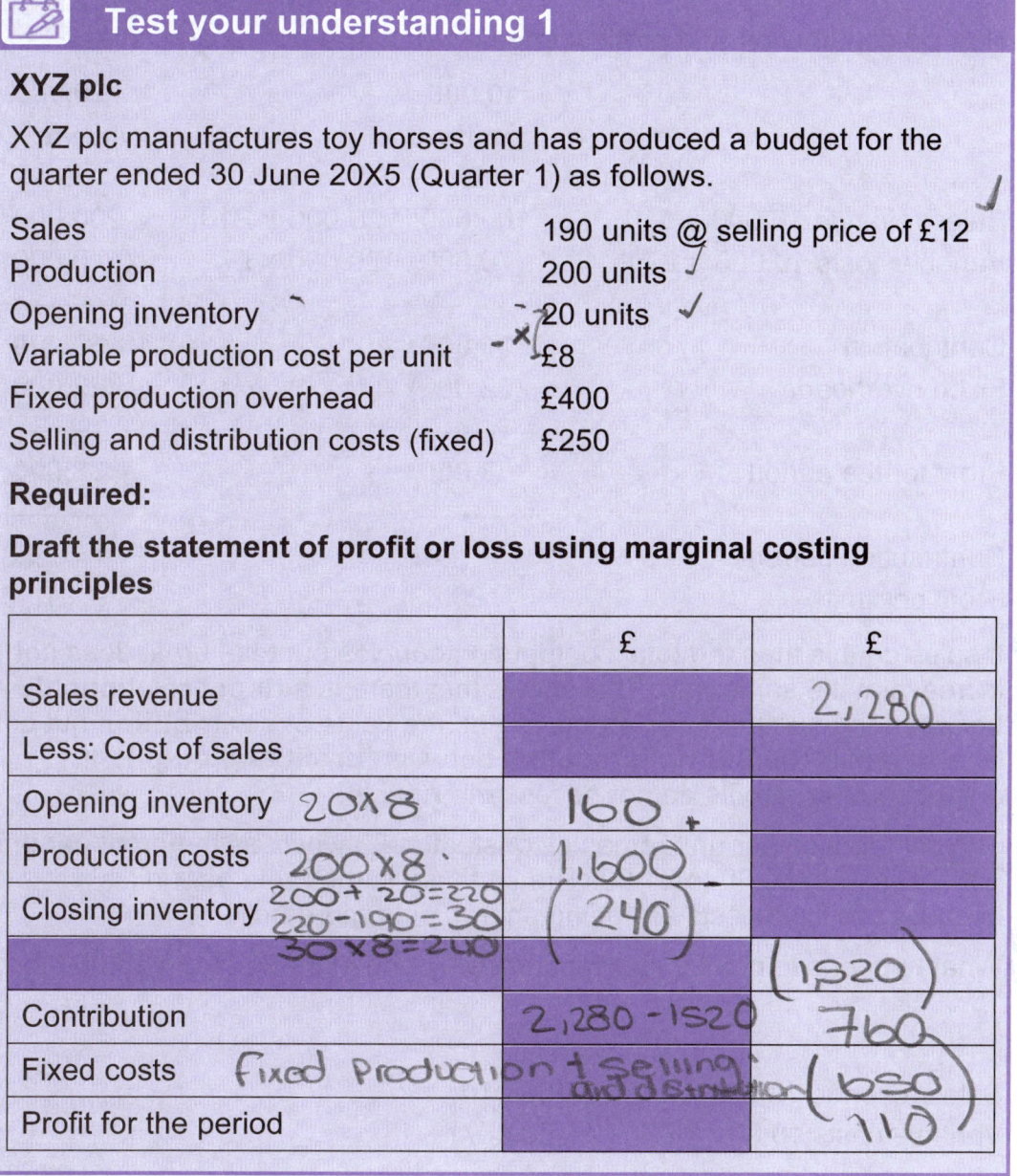

| | £ | £ |
|---|---|---|
| Sales revenue | | 2,280 |
| Less: Cost of sales | | |
| Opening inventory 20×8 | 160 + | |
| Production costs 200×8 | 1,600 − | |
| Closing inventory 200+20=220 220−190=30 30×8=240 | (240) | |
| | | (1520) |
| Contribution | 2,280−1520 | 760 |
| Fixed costs Fixed Production + selling and distribution | | (650) |
| Profit for the period | | 110 |

$\frac{VC}{S}$

## 1.2 Contribution

The concept of contribution is one of the most fundamental in cost and management accounting. Contribution measures the **difference between the sales price of a unit and the variable costs of making and selling that unit**.

Contribution = Sales revenue less all variable costs

## 1.3 Changes in activity level

How do contribution and profit change if we double output and sales?

|  | 10,000 units £ |  | 20,000 units £ |
|---|---|---|---|
| Sales revenue 10,000 × £10 | 100,000 | 20,000 × £10 | 200,000 |
| Variable costs 10,000 × £7 | (70,000) | 20,000 × £7 | (140,000) |
| Contribution | **30,000** |  | **60,000** |
| Fixed overheads | (22,000) |  | (22,000) |
| Profit for the period | **8,000** |  | **38,000** |
| Contribution per unit | £3 |  | £3 |
| Profit per unit | £0.80 |  | £1.90 |

If sales double then the total contribution doubles but total profit does not increase at the same rate. This shows that there is a **direct relationship between** the number of **sales** made and the value of **contribution** but not level of profit. There is **no direct link between profit and output.** If output doubles, profits do not necessarily double.

The contribution per unit remains constant at £3 whereas the profit per unit increases from £0.80 to £1.90. The increase in the profit per unit is because the fixed costs are being shared over more units.

What happens to profit if sales increase by one extra unit from 10,000 to 10,001?

|  | £ |
|---|---|
| Sales revenue 10,001 × £10 | 100,010 |
| Variable costs 10,001 × £7 | (70,007) |
| Contribution | 30,003 |
| Fixed costs | (22,000) |
| Profit for the period | 8,003 |

Total contribution increases £3, but the total fixed overheads do not change so profit also goes up by £3 (i.e. the same as contribution).

The concept of **contribution** is an extremely important one in cost and management accounting. It is important to remember that since contribution measures the **difference between sales price and the variable cost of the unit**, if a product has a positive contribution it is worth making. Any amount of contribution, however small, **goes towards paying the fixed overheads**; if enough units are made and sold such that total contribution exceeds fixed overheads then profit will start to be made. Contribution is more useful for decision making than profit.

# 2 Absorption costing

## 2.1 Absorption costing

Production overheads are recovered by absorbing them into the cost of a product and this process is called absorption costing.

The main aim of absorption costing is to recover overheads in a way that fairly reflects the amount of time and effort that has gone into making a product or service.

Absorption costing involves the following stages:

- allocation and apportionment of overheads to the different cost centres

- reapportionment of service cost centre overheads to the production cost centres

- absorption of overheads into the products.

The stages of absorption costing are covered in more detail in Chapter 6: Overheads. Absorption costing allows businesses to make decisions about pricing policies and value its inventory in accordance with IAS 2 Inventories which defines cost as comprising: 'all costs of purchase, costs of conversion and other costs incurred in bringing the inventories to their present location and condition'.

Absorption costing values each unit of inventory at the total cost incurred to **produce** the unit. This includes direct materials, direct labour, direct expenses, variable production overheads and fixed production overheads. All these costs would be referred to as **product costs**. **Non-production** costs are considered **period costs** and are not included in the cost of a unit but are deducted in full from the gross profit.

**Definition**

**Absorption costing** is a method of building up a full product cost which adds direct costs and a proportion of production overhead cost by means of one or a number of overhead absorption rates.

The basic layout for calculating the budgeted profit or loss under absorption costing is as follows (with illustrative figures).

|  | £ |
|---|---|
| Sales revenue (10,000 × £10) | 100,000 |
| Cost of sales (at full **production** cost, £8) | (80,000) |
|  |  |
| **Gross profit** | 20,000 |
| Less: **Non-production** costs | (12,000) |
|  |  |
| Profit for the period | 8,000 |

 **Example 1**

**XYZ plc**

XYZ plc manufactures toy horses and has produced a budget for the quarter ended 30 June 20X5 (Quarter 1) as follows.

| Sales | 190 units @ selling price of £12 |
|---|---|
| Production | 200 units |
| Opening inventory | 20 units |
| Variable production cost per unit | £8 |
| Fixed production cost per unit | £2 |
| Selling and distribution costs | £250 |

**Required:**

**Draft the statement of profit or loss using absorption costing principles**

**Solution**

Closing inventory = Opening inventory + production – sales

Closing inventory = 20 + 200 – 190 = 30 units

The cost per unit in the cost of sales includes the variable production cost and the fixed production cost.

*190 - 220 = 30*

| | £ | £ |
|---|---|---|
| Sales revenue 190 × £12 | | 2,280 |
| Less: Cost of sales | | |
| Opening inventory 20 × £10 | 200 | |
| Production costs 200 × £10 | 2,000 | |
| Closing inventory 30 × £10 | (300) | |
| | | 1,900 |
| Gross profit | | 380 |
| Non-production costs | | (250) |
| Profit for the period | | 130 |

# 3 Absorption versus marginal costing

## 3.1 Comparison of absorption and marginal costing

Below is a table that compares absorption costing and marginal costing:

| Absorption costing | Marginal costing |
|---|---|
| Costs are split based on **function** – production or non-production | Costs are split based on **behaviour** – variable or fixed |
| Inventory is valued at the **full production cost** (fixed and variable production costs) | Inventory is valued at the **variable production cost only** |
| Sales – cost of sales<br>= **gross profit** | Sales – all variable costs<br>= **contribution** |
| Non-production overheads are deducted after gross profit | Variable non-production overheads are excluded from the valuation of inventory but are deducted before contribution |

| Absorption costing | Marginal costing |
|---|---|
| Fixed costs are split between production and non-production costs | All fixed cost are period costs |
| Adheres to IAS 2 Inventory and can therefore be used for the financial accounts of the business | Does not adhere to IAS 2 Inventory so is mainly used internally for decision making processes |

 **Test your understanding 2**

**Billie Millar**

The following information relates to the manufacture of product Delphinium during the month of April 2005:

| | |
|---|---|
| Direct materials per unit | £10.60 |
| Direct labour per unit | £16.40 |
| Variable overheads per batch | £60,000 |
| Fixed overheads per batch | £80,000 |
| Number of units per batch | 10,000 |

**Task**

**Calculate the prime cost per unit.**

10.60 + 16.40 = 27.00

**Calculate the marginal cost per unit.**

60,000 ÷ 10,000 = 6 + 27.00 = 33.00

**Calculate the absorption cost per unit.**

80,000 ÷ 10,000 = 8 + 33 = 41.00

## Test your understanding 3

The following information has been provided.

|  | Cost per unit £ |
|---|---|
| Direct material | 8.50 |
| Direct labour | 27.20 |
| Variable production overhead | 11.30 |
| Fixed production overhead | 14.00 |
| Selling price | 61.50 |

**Required:**

**Calculate each of the following in £/unit:**

(a)  prime cost   *35.70*

(b)  marginal cost   *47.00*

(c)  absorption cost   *61.00*

(d)  gross profit   *0.50*   *S - AC = GP*

(e)  contribution   *14.50*   *S - VC = C*

*-61.50*

## Test your understanding 4

Crescent Feeds Ltd have produced the following set of cost and management accounting figures for its current accounting period.

|  | £ |  |
|---|---|---|
| Production and sales tonnage | – | 2,500 tonnes |
| Direct labour | 102,000 | *40.80* |
| Admin overheads | 16,500 | *6.60* |
| Direct materials | 210,000 | *84* |
| Direct expenses | 5,250 | *2.10* |
| Fixed production overheads | 20,400 | *8.16* |
| Variable production overheads | 20,000 | *8* |
| Selling and distribution costs (fixed) | 52,300 | *20.92* |

**Calculate for the period:**

- Prime cost   *317,250*

- Marginal cost   *337,250*

- Absorption cost   *357,650*

- Non-production cost    68,800
- Total cost    426,450
- Prime cost per tonne of product    126.90
- Marginal cost per tonne of product    134.90
- Absorption cost per tonne of product    143.06
- Total cost per tonne of product    170.58

## 3.2    Impact of changing inventory levels on profit

The cost of sales calculation in the budgeted statement of profit or loss can be broken down into 3 elements – opening inventory, production and closing inventory. The units within these elements are valued either at marginal cost or absorption cost. The value of the closing inventory is subtracted from the sum of the value of the opening inventory and production to calculate the cost of making sales.

## 3.3    Impact on profit

When inventory levels increase or decrease over the short term i.e. a month, profits will differ under absorption and marginal costing. Over the longer term the differences in inventory will net off and not produce different profits.

Increasing inventory is when closing inventory in the cost of sales is greater than opening inventory. Decreasing inventory is when opening inventory is greater than closing inventory.

- If inventory is increasing then absorption costing will give the higher profit.

- If inventory levels are decreasing then absorption costing will give the lower profit.

- If inventory levels remain constant then the profit values will be the same.

This is because:

- under **marginal costing** all the period's fixed production overheads are charged **in full** against that period's profit, whereas

- under **absorption costing** some of the period's fixed production overheads will be **carried forward** in the closing inventory value and charged to the next period's statement of profit or loss.

This is illustrated in the following example:

**Example 2**

**Worked example of profit differences**

|  | £ per unit |
|---|---|
| Sales price | £15 |
| Prime cost | £4 |
| Variable production costs | £2 |
| Budgeted fixed production overheads | £40,000 per month |
| Budgeted production | 10,000 units per month |
| Budgeted sales | 8,000 units |
| Opening inventory | 500 units |

**Required:**

**Produce a budgeted marginal costing and an absorption costing statement of profit or loss for a month.**

**Solution**

When calculating the profit we will need the number of units in closing inventory. This is given by:

Opening inventory units + production units – sales units

This will be 500 + 10,000 – 8,000 = 2,500 units

**Marginal costing statement of profit or loss**

|  | £ | £ |
|---|---|---|
| Sales revenue (8,000 × £15) | | 120,000 |
| Opening inventory (500 × £6) | 3,000 | |
| Marginal production costs (10,000 × £6) | 60,000 | |
| Closing inventory (2,500 × £6) | (15,000) | |
| Marginal cost of sales | | (48,000) |
| Contribution | | 72,000 |
| Fixed costs | | (40,000) |
| Profit for the period | | 32,000 |

The marginal cost includes the prime cost and the variable production cost. The fixed costs are charged in full against the sales for the period.

**Absorption costing statement of profit or loss**

|  | £ | £ |
|---|---|---|
| Sales revenue (8,000 × £15) | | 120,000 |
| Opening inventory (500 × £10) | 5,000 | |
| Production costs (10,000 × £10) | 100,000 | |
| Closing inventory (2,500 × £10) | (25,000) | |
| | ──── | |
| Absorption cost of sales | | (80,000) |
| | | ──── |
| Profit for the period | | 40,000 |
| | | ──── |

The production cost includes the prime cost of production, the variable production costs plus an amount per unit for the fixed production costs.

The fixed overhead absorbed by each unit is as follows.

$$\frac{\text{Budgeted fixed overheads}}{\text{Budgeted production}} = \frac{£40,000}{10,000} = £4 \text{ per unit}$$

## 3.4 Reconciliation of profits

 **Example 2 (continued)**

In the example above the absorption costing profit is £8,000 higher than the marginal costing profit. Why?

Consider the Cost of sales calculation:

Opening inventory + production – closing inventory

Under absorption costing:

- The opening inventory has been charged with £2,000 of fixed production cost (500 units × £4)

- The £40,000 fixed production costs have been charged to production costs (10,000 units × £4)

- £10,000 of this has then been deducted from the cost of sales as part of the closing inventory value (2,500 units × £4)

- This means that under absorption costing only £32,000 of fixed costs has been charged in this month's statement of profit and loss (£2,000 + £40,000 – £10,000 = £32,000).

MANAGEMENT ACCOUNTING TECHNIQUES

Under marginal costing:

- The full £40,000 of fixed costs as been charged to this month's statement of profit or loss

- The profit under marginal costing is £8,000 lower than under absorption costing as £8,000 more cost has been charged against revenue.

It is possible to calculate the absorption costing profit if the marginal costing profit is known and vice versa, using the information on fixed production costs.

**Absorption costing to marginal costing profit**

The fixed costs are included in the cost of sales as a product cost so they need to be turned into a period charge.

Adjustment:

Deduct the fixed costs in the closing inventory and add back the fixed cost in the opening inventory.

**Marginal costing to absorption costing profit**

There are no fixed costs in the cost of sales so these need to be included as they are charged as a period cost.

Adjustment:

Deduct the fixed costs in the opening inventory and add back the fixed costs in closing inventory.

## Example 2 (continued)

Using the information in the example:

| | |
|---|---|
| Absorption costing profit | £40,000 |
| Less: Fixed costs in closing inventory (2,500 × £4) | –£10,000 |
| Plus: Fixed cost in opening inventory (500 × £4) | £2,000 |
| Marginal costing profit | £32,000 |
| **OR** | |
| Marginal costing profit | £32,000 |
| Less: Fixed costing in opening inventory (500 × £4) | –£2,000 |
| Plus: Fixed costs in closing inventory (2,500 × £4) | £10,000 |
| Absorption costing profit | £40,000 |

There is also a short cut proforma to do this:

| | |
|---|---|
| Absorption costing profit | X |
| Less: Change in inventory × OAR | +/–X |
| | ——— |
| Marginal costing profit | X |

**Note:** The change in inventory is calculated as the opening inventory units less the closing inventory units.

---

### Example 2 (continued)

Using the information in the example:

| | |
|---|---|
| Absorption costing profit | £40,000 |
| Less: Change in inventory × OAR | |
| (500 – 2,500) × 4 | –£8,000 |
| Marginal costing profit | £32,000 |

---

### Test your understanding 5

Voliti Limited has produced the following budgeted figures for a new product it hopes to launch.

| | |
|---|---|
| Direct material | £10 per unit |
| Direct labour | £5 per unit |
| Variable production overheads | £8 per unit |
| Fixed production costs | £19,500 per month |
| Budgeted output | 6,500 units per month |
| Sales price | £30 per unit |

**Month 1**

| | |
|---|---|
| Production | 6,500 |
| Sales | 5,000 |

**Task**

**Complete the statement of profit or loss for month 1 on each of the following bases, and reconcile the resulting profit figures:**

(i)    **Marginal costing principles**

|  | £ | £ |
|---|---|---|
| Sales revenue | | 150,000 |
| Less: Cost of sales | | |
| Opening inventory | 0 | |
| Production costs | 19,500 | |
| Closing inventory | (−39,000) | |
| | | (−130,000) |
| Contribution | | |
| Fixed costs | | ( ) |
| Profit for the period | | |

(ii)   **Absorption costing principles**

|  | £ | £ |
|---|---|---|
| Sales revenue | | |
| Cost of sales | | |
| Opening inventory | | |
| Production costs | | |
| Closing inventory | ( ) | |
| | | ( ) |
| Gross profit | | |
| Non-production costs | | ( ) |
| Profit for the period | | |

The absorption costing profit is *higher/lower** than the marginal costing profit because there are *more/less** fixed costs charged against the sales in the absorption costing statement.

*delete as appropriate*

**Test your understanding 6**

**McTack**

McTack manufactures PCs and has produced a budget for the quarter ended 31 March 20X4 (Quarter 1) using absorption costing as follows.

| | £ | £ |
|---|---|---|
| Sales revenue (100 units @ £500 per unit) | | 50,000 |
| Production cost of 120 units | | |
| Materials | 12,000 | |
| Labour | 24,000 | |
| Variable overhead | 6,000 | |
| Fixed overhead | 6,000 | |
| | 48,000 | |
| Less: Closing inventory (20 × £400) | (8,000) | |
| | | (40,000) |
| | | 10,000 |

**Required:**

**Redraft the statement of profit or loss using marginal costing principles.**

| | £ | £ |
|---|---|---|
| Sales revenue | | |
| Less Cost of sales: | | |
| Opening inventory | | |
| Production costs | | |
| Closing inventory | ( ) | |
| | | ( ) |
| Contribution | | |
| Fixed costs | | ( ) |
| Profit for the period | | |

Reconcile the profits:

## 3.5 Advantages of marginal costing

- Marginal costing avoids needing to allocate, apportion, re-apportion and absorb fixed overheads.

- Fixed costs logically relate to time and so are charged as period costs.

- Profit figures are more consistent with fluctuating sales.

- Used for short term decision-making.

**Note:** It is not ethical to switch between marginal and absorption costing to improve the performance of an area of the business.

## 3.6 Advantages of absorption costing

Absorption costing has a number of advantages:

- The costing technique adheres to the accounting standard for the valuation of inventory (IAS 2) so can be used for **statutory financial reporting**.

- When valuing inventory using absorption costing the total production cost is considered. This means that when deciding on a selling price all production costs should be covered.

- The analysis of under- or over- absorption of overheads is a useful exercise in controlling costs

# 4 Types of costing techniques

## 4.1 Costing systems

There are different types of costing system that are used depending on the type of production a business uses.

- **Specific order costing** is the costing system used when the work done by an organisation consists of **separately identifiable jobs** or **batches**.

- **Continuous operation costing** is the costing method used when goods or services are produced as a direct result of a **sequence of continuous operations or processes**.

## 4.2 Job costing

Job costing is a form of **specific order costing** and it is used in a business where the production is made up of **individual jobs.** Each job is identified to a customer's individual requirements and specifications. The costs are identified for this specific job, coded to it and recorded as job costs. The organisation will add on their required profit margin and quote their price to the customer. Effectively **the job is the cost unit**.

Typical examples of businesses that use job costing would be ship building, civil engineering, construction, aeroplane manufacture, and vehicle repairs.

## 4.3 Job card

Each job is given a separate identifying number and has its own job card. The job card is used to record all of the direct costs of the job and the overheads to be absorbed into the job.

A typical job card might look like this:

### Example 3

| JOB NO | 217 | | |
|---|---|---|---|
| **Materials requisitions** | **Quantity** | **£** | **Total** |
| 0254 G 3578 | 100 kg | 4,200 | |
| 0261 K 3512 | 50 kg | 3,150 | |
| | | ───── | |
| | | | 7,350 |

| **Wages – employees** | **Hours** | **£** | |
|---|---|---|---|
| 13343 | 80 | 656 | |
| 15651 | 30 | 300 | |
| 12965 | 40 | 360 | |
| | ─── | ─── | |
| | 150 | | 1,316 |
| | ─── | | |

| **Overheads** | **Hours** | **£** | |
|---|---|---|---|
| Absorption rate £12 | 150 | 1,800 | 1,800 |
| | | | ───── |
| Total cost | | | 10,466 |
| | | | ───── |

When materials are requisitioned for a job, the issue of materials will be recorded at their issue price on the job cost card.

The labour hours and relevant hourly rate will be transferred onto the card and any expenses that can be directly attributed to a particular job are then coded to the job or jobs they relate to.

When the job is completed an appropriate proportion of administration, selling and distribution overheads will also be included on the job cost card.

---

### ✎ Test your understanding 7

Given below are the direct costs of job number 3,362.

|  |  |  | £ |
| --- | --- | --- | --- |
| Materials requisitions: |  |  |  |
| 15,496 |  |  | 1,044 |
| 15,510 |  |  | 938 |
| 15,525 |  |  | 614 |
| Wages analysis: |  |  |  |
| Employee 13,249 | 40 hours |  | 320 |
| Employee 12,475 | 33 hours |  | 231 |
| Employee 26,895 | 53 hours |  | 312 |

Overheads are apportioned to jobs at the rate of £3.50 per direct labour hour.

**What is the total cost of Job 3,362?**

| JOB NO | 3,362 | | |
| --- | --- | --- | --- |
| **Materials requisitions** | | £ | Total |
| | | | |
| | | ——— | |
| **Wages – employees** | Hours | £ | |
| | | | |
| | ——— | ——— | |
| | | | |
| | ——— | | |
| **Overheads** | Hours | £ | |
| | | | |
| | | ——— | |
| | | | |
| | | ——— | |

The principles behind a job costing system are exactly the same as those in a unit costing system with the **job** being treated as the **cost unit**. A job costing system needs tight controls over the coding of all materials requisitions and hours worked to ensure that each job is charged with the correct direct costs and eventually overheads.

## 4.4 Batch costing

Batch costing is also a form of **specific order costing**. It is suitable for a business that produces **batches of identical units**. For example, a baker may produce loaves of bread in batches.

Each batch of production will have different costs but each unit within the batch should have the same cost. Therefore, the total cost of the batch of production is calculated and divided by the number of units in that batch to find the cost per unit for that batch of production.

As with any costing system the costs to be included in the batch cost are the direct costs of material, labour and any direct expenses plus the overheads that are to be absorbed into the batch. In order to find the cost of each product or cost unit the total cost of the batch must be divided by the number of products in that batch.

---

### Example 4

A paint manufacturer is producing 1,000 litres of matt vinyl paint in 'sea blue'. The direct costs of the production run are:

|  | £ |
|---|---|
| Materials | 1,600 |
| Labour 15 hours @ £10 | 150 |
| Overheads 15 hours @ £16 | 240 |

What is the cost per litre of this batch of paint?

| Batch cost | £ |
|---|---|
| Materials | 1,600 |
| Labour | 150 |
| Overheads 15 hours @ £16 | 240 |
|  | ------ |
| Total batch cost | 1,990 |
|  | ------ |
| Cost per litre | £1.99 |

---

**Test your understanding 8**

A manufacturer of frozen meals produces a batch of 20,000 units of salmon tagliatelli. The direct costs of this batch are:

|  | £ |
|---|---|
| Materials | 15,000 |
| Labour 1,000 hours | 4,200 |

Overheads are to be absorbed at rate of £1.20 per direct labour hour.

**The cost of each portion of salmon tagliatelli is?**

A     £1.20

B     £0.96

C     £2.16

D     £1.02

 **Test your understanding 9**

**Jetprint Limited**

Jetprint Limited specialises in printing advertising leaflets and is in the process of preparing its price list. The most popular requirement is for a folded leaflet made from a single sheet of A4 paper. From past records and budgeted figures, the following data have been estimated for a typical batch of 10,000 leaflets:

| | |
|---|---|
| Artwork (fixed cost) | £65 |
| Machine setting (fixed cost) | 4 hours @ £22 per hour |
| Paper | £12.50 per 1,000 sheets |
| Ink and consumables | £40 per 10,000 leaflets |
| Printers' wages | 4 hours @ £8 per hour per 10,000 leaflets |

General fixed overheads are £15,000 per period during which a total of 600 printers' labour hours are expected to be worked (not all, of course, on the leaflet). The overheads are recovered only on printers' hours.

**Task**

**Calculate the cost (to the nearest pound) for batches of 10,000 and 20,000 leaflets.**

## 4.5    Service costing

Service costing is a form of **continuous operation costing**. The output from a service industry differs from manufacturing for the following four reasons:

- **Intangibility** – the output is in the form of 'performance' rather than tangible or touchable goods or products.

- **Heterogeneity** – the nature and standard of the service will be variable due to the high human input.

- **Simultaneous production and consumption** – the service that you require cannot be inspected in advance of receiving it.

- **Perishability** – the services that you require cannot be stored.

## 4.6    Service cost units

One of the main difficulties in service costing is the establishment of a suitable cost unit. Examples for a hotel might include:

- **Meals served** for the restaurant

- **Rooms occupied** for the cleaning staff

- **Hours worked** for the reception staff.

A **composite cost unit** may be more appropriate. For example, a bus company might use passenger miles or how many passengers travel how many miles.

## 4.7    Cost per service unit

The total cost of providing a service will include the same costs as manufacturing but overheads may make up a larger proportion of the cost than direct costs. It is also possible that labour costs would be the only direct cost incurred by a service provider.

To calculate the cost per service unit the total cost of providing the service is divided by the number of service units used to provide the service.

$$\text{Cost per service unit} = \frac{\text{Total costs for providing the service}}{\text{Number of service units used to provide the service}}$$

**Test your understanding 10**

The canteen of a company records the following income and expenditure for a month.

|  | £ | £ |
|---|---|---|
| Income |  | 59,010 |
| Food | 17,000 |  |
| Drink | 6,000 |  |
| Bottled water | 750 |  |
| Fuel costs | 800 |  |
| Maintenance of machinery | 850 |  |
| Repairs | 250 |  |
| Wages | 15,500 |  |
| Depreciation | 1,000 |  |

During the month the canteen served 56,200 meals. The canteen's cost unit is one meal.

**Calculate the average cost per meal served and the average income per meal served.**

 **Test your understanding 11**

Happy Returns Ltd operates a haulage business with three vehicles. The following estimated cost and performance data is available:

| | |
|---|---|
| Petrol | £0.50 per kilometre on average |
| Repairs | £0.30 per kilometre |
| Depreciation | £1.00 per kilometre, plus £50 per week per vehicle |
| Drivers wages | £300 per week per vehicle |
| Supervision and general expenses | £550 per week |
| Loading costs | £6.00 per tonne |

*[handwritten: 1.80 per km]*

During week number 26 it is expected that all three vehicles will be used, 280 tonnes will be loaded and a total of 3,950 kilometres travelled (including return journeys when empty) as shown in the following table:

*[handwritten calculations:*
*1.80 × 3,950 = 7,110*
*300 × 3 = 900*
*550*
*280 × 6 = 1,680*
*= 3,280*
*+ 7,100*
*= 10,390 ]*

| Journey | Tonnes carried (one way) | Kilometres (one way) |
|---|---|---|
| 1 | 34 | 180 |
| 2 | 28 | 265 |
| 3 | 40 | 390 |
| 4 | 32 | 115 |
| 5 | 26 | 220 |
| 6 | 40 | 480 |
| 7 | 29 | 90 |
| 8 | 26 | 100 |
| 9 | 25 | 135 |
| | 280 | 1,975 |

**Calculate the average cost per tonne-kilometre in week 26 (to 2 decimal places).**

# 5 Summary

**Marginal costing** calculates the **contribution** per unit of a product. In marginal costing units are valued at **variable production cost** and fixed overheads are accounted for as period costs.

In **absorption costing**, units are valued at **variable cost plus fixed production overheads** absorbed using a pre-determined absorption rate.

The differences in these methods give rise to different profit figures which are usually reconciled at the end of an accounting period.

A business that produces **one-off products** for customers, each of which is different, will use a **job costing** system. This treats each individual job as a cost unit and therefore attributes the direct costs to that job, as well as the overheads according to the organisation's overhead absorption basis.

In a business which produces a number of different products in **batches of identical units** then a **batch costing** system is appropriate. Here the costs of each batch of production are gathered together as though the batch was a cost unit and the actual cost per unit is calculated by dividing the batch cost by the number of units produced in that batch.

## Test your understanding answers

 **Test your understanding 1**

There will be closing inventory of 30 units.

Opening inventory + production – sales = closing inventory

Under marginal costing, the closing inventory will be valued at the variable production cost of £8 per unit.

**Marginal costing statement of profit and loss**

|  | £ | £ |
|---|---|---|
| Sales revenue |  | 2,280 |
| Less: Cost of sales |  |  |
| Opening inventory (20 × 8) | 160 |  |
| Production costs (200 × 8) | 1,600 |  |
| Closing inventory (30 × 8) | (240) |  |
|  |  | 1,520 |
| Contribution |  | 760 |
| Fixed costs |  | (650) |
| Profit for the period |  | 110 |

 **Test your understanding 2**

Calculate the prime cost per unit.

10.60 + 16.40 = £27.00

Calculate the marginal cost per unit.

27.00 + (60,000 ÷ 10,000) = £33.00

Calculate the absorption cost per unit.

33.00 + (80,000 ÷ 10,000) = £41.00

## Test your understanding 3

**(a)  Prime cost per unit**

|  | £ |
|---|---|
| Direct material | 8.50 |
| Direct labour | 27.20 |
| | ——— |
| | 35.70 |

**(b)  Marginal cost per unit**

|  | £ |
|---|---|
| Prime cost | 35.70 |
| Variable production overhead | 11.30 |
| | ——— |
| | 47.00 |

**(c)  Absorption cost per unit**

|  | £ |
|---|---|
| Prime cost | 35.70 |
| Variable production overhead | 11.30 |
| Fixed production overhead | 14.00 |
| | ——— |
| | 61.00 |

**(d)  Gross profit per unit**

|  | £ |
|---|---|
| Selling price | 61.50 |
| Less Absorption cost | (61.00) |
| | ——— |
| | 0.50 |

**(e)  Contribution per unit**

|  | £ |
|---|---|
| Selling price | 61.50 |
| Less Marginal cost | (47.00) |
| | ——— |
| | 14.50 |

## Test your understanding 4

- Prime cost (210,000 + 102,000 + 5,250)          £317,250
- Marginal cost (317,250 + 20,000)                £337,250
- Absorption cost (337,250 + 20,400)              £357,650
- Non-production cost (16,500 + 52,300)           £68,800
- Total cost (357,650 + 68,800)                   £426,450
- Prime cost per tonne (317,250 ÷ 2,500)          £126.90
- Marginal cost per tonne (337,250 ÷ 2,500)       £134.90
- Absorption cost per tonne (357,650 ÷ 2,500)     £143.06
- Total cost per tonne (426,450 ÷ 2,500)          £170.58

## Test your understanding 5

(i)    **Marginal costing principles**

|  | £ | £ |
|---|---|---|
| Sales revenue | | 150,000 |
| Less: Cost of sales | | |
| Opening inventory | 0 | |
| Production costs | 149,500 | |
| Closing inventory | (34,500) | |
| | | (115,000) |
| Contribution | | 35,000 |
| Fixed costs | | (19,500) |
| Profit for the period | | 15,500 |

**(ii)   Absorption costing principles**

|  | £ | £ |
|---|---|---|
| Sales revenue |  | 150,000 |
| Cost of sales |  |  |
| Opening inventory | 0 |  |
| Production costs | 169,000 |  |
| Closing inventory | (39,000) |  |
|  |  | (130,000) |
| Gross profit |  | 20,000 |
| Non-production costs |  | (0) |
| Profit for the period |  | 20,000 |

The absorption costing profit is **higher** than the marginal costing profit because there are **less** fixed costs charged against the sales in the absorption costing statement.

The difference of £4,500 is the increase in inventory of 1,500 units × the £3 per unit OAR for fixed overheads.

 **Test your understanding 6**

**McTack – Budgeted profit statement quarter ended 31 March**

Marginal costing format

**Marginal costing statement of profit or loss**

|  | £ | £ |
|---|---|---|
| Sales revenue (100 × £500) |  | 50,000 |
| Less: Cost of sales |  |  |
| Opening inventory | 0 |  |
| Production costs (12,000 + 24,000 + 6,000) | 42,000 |  |
| Closing inventory (20 × £350) | (7,000) |  |
|  |  | (35,000) |
| Contribution |  | 15,000 |
| Fixed costs |  | (6,000) |
| Profit for the period |  | 9,000 |

**Calculation of marginal cost per unit.**

Marginal cost/number of units produced = marginal cost per unit

42,000/120 = £350

**Reconciliation of profits**

|  | £ |
|---|---|
| Absorption costing profit | 10,000 |
| Change in inventory × OAR | |
| (0 – 20) × £50 | –1,000 |
|  | ——— |
| Marginal costing profit | 9,000 |
|  | ——— |

### Test your understanding 7

| JOB NO 3,362 | | | |
|---|---|---|---|
| **Materials requisitions** | | £ | Total |
| 15496 | | 1,044 | |
| 15510 | | 938 | |
| 15525 | | 614 | |
|  | | ——— | |
|  | | | 2,596 |
| **Wages – employees** | Hours | £ | |
| 13249 | 40 | 320 | |
| 12475 | 33 | 231 | |
| 26895 | 53 | 312 | |
|  | ——— | ——— | |
|  | 126 | | 863 |
|  | ——— | | |
| **Overheads** | Hours | £ | |
| Absorption rate £3.50 | 126 | 441 | 441 |
|  | | | ——— |
|  | | | 3,900 |
|  | | | ——— |

## Test your understanding 8

**D**

|  |  | £ |
|---|---|---|
| Materials |  | 15,000 |
| Labour |  | 4,200 |
| Overheads | 1,000 hours @ £1.2 | 1,200 |
|  |  | ——— |
| Total cost |  | 20,400 |
|  |  | ——— |
| Cost per unit | £20,400 ÷ 20,000 = | £1.02 |

## Test your understanding 9

**Jetprint Limited**

|  | 10,000 leaflets | 20,000 leaflets |
|---|---|---|
|  | £ | £ |
| Artwork | 65.00 | 65.00 |
| Machine setting | 88.00 | 88.00 |
| Paper | 125.00 | 250.00 |
| Ink and consumables | 40.00 | 80.00 |
| Printers' wages | 32.00 | 64.00 |
| General fixed overheads (W) | 100.00 | 200.00 |
|  | ——— | ——— |
| Total cost | 450.00 | 747.00 |

**Workings:**

$$OAR = \frac{£15,000}{600} = £25 \text{ per hour}$$

10,000 leaflets £25 × 4 hours = £100

20,000 leaflets £25 × 8 hours = £200

**Test your understanding 10**

Total canteen expenditure = £42,150

Total meals served = 56,200

Average cost per meal served = £42,150 ÷ 56,200 = £0.75 per meal

Average income per meal served = 59,010 ÷ 56,200 = £1.05 per meal

 **Test your understanding 11**

Average cost per tonne-km = £10,390 ÷ 66,325 = £0.16 per tonne-km

Total costs in Week 26

|  | £/km | £ |
|---|---|---|
| Petrol | 0.50 | |
| Repairs | 0.30 | |
| Depreciation | 1.00 | |
| | ——— | |
| | 1.80  × 3,950 = | 7,110 |

|  | £/week |
|---|---|
| Depreciation (£50 × 3) | 150 |
| Wages (£300 × 3) | 900 |
| Supervision and general expenses | 550 |
| Loading costs (£6 × 280) | 1,680 |
| | ——— |
| | 3,280 |
| **Total costs** | **10,390** |

Tonne-kilometres

Costs are averaged over the outward journeys, not the return, as these are necessary, but carry no tonnes.

| Journey | Tonnes carried (one way) × | Kilometres (one way) = | Tonne-kilometres |
|---|---|---|---|
| 1 | 34 | 180 | 6,120 |
| 2 | 28 | 265 | 7,420 |
| 3 | 40 | 390 | 15,600 |
| 4 | 32 | 115 | 3,680 |
| 5 | 26 | 220 | 5,720 |
| 6 | 40 | 480 | 19,200 |
| 7 | 29 | 90 | 2,610 |
| 8 | 26 | 100 | 2,600 |
| 9 | 25 | 135 | 3,375 |
| | 280 | 1,975 | **66,325** |

**KAPLAN** PUBLISHING

# Materials

4

## Introduction

This chapter looks at the procedures that a business should have in place to ensure that records of inventory (materials) are kept accurate and up to date. In particular, it looks at the purchasing of inventory, the valuation of inventory and inventory control.

| ASSESSMENT CRITERIA | CONTENTS |
|---|---|
| Record and calculate material costs (2.1) | 1 Inventory control cycle |
| Prepare costing accounting journals (2.2) | 2 Materials documentation |
| Apply inventory control methods (2.3) | 3 The stores department |
| Differences between costing systems (2.5) | 4 Cost of having inventory |
| | 5 Inventory control systems |
| | 6 Costing issues of raw materials |
| | 7 Work in progress – materials |
| | 8 Material wastage |
| | 9 Integrated bookkeeping – materials |

# 1 Inventory control cycle

## 1.1 Introduction

Inventory often forms the **largest single item of cost** for a business so it is essential that the inventory purchased is the most suitable for the intended purpose.

Inventory includes:

- raw materials or components to be used in the manufacture of products

- items bought to be sold on (retailer or wholesaler)

- items that will be used for general day to day running of the business.

## 1.2 Control of purchasing

When goods are purchased they must be ordered, received by the stores department, recorded, issued to the manufacturing department that requires them and eventually paid for. This process needs a great deal of paperwork and strict internal controls.

Internal control consists of full documentation and appropriate authorisation of all transactions, movements of inventory and of all requisitions, orders, receipts and payments.

If control is to be maintained over purchasing, it is necessary to ensure that:

- only necessary items are purchased

- orders are placed with the most appropriate supplier after considering price and delivery details

- the goods that are actually received are the goods that were ordered and in the correct quantity/quality

- the price paid for the goods is correct (i.e. what was agreed when the order was placed).

To ensure that all of this takes place requires a reliable system of checking and control.

## 1.3 Overview of procedures

It is useful to have an overview of the purchasing process.

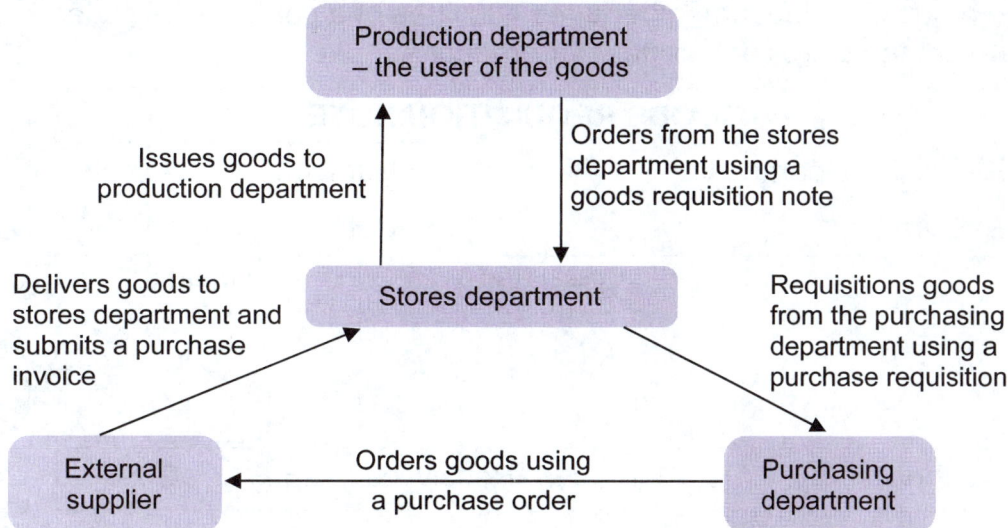

There are many variations of the above system in practice, but it is a fairly typical system and does provide good control over the purchasing and issuing process. Details about the documentation mentioned in the diagram above follows.

# 2 Materials documentation

## 2.1 Goods requisition note (also called 'materials requisition')

The user department (e.g. a production department) will notify the stores department that it requires certain goods using a 'goods requisition note'. This note will be authorised by the departmental manager.

**Example 1**

The production department requires 400 litres of a particular oil coded L04 from the stores department for product A.

| GOODS REQUISITION NOTE | | |
|---|---|---|
| Requiring department: *Production* | Number: *4027* | |
| Required for: *Product A* | Date: *14 April 20X4* | |
| Code | Description | Quantity |
| *L04* | *Oil* | *400 litres* |
| Authorised by: *Factory Manager*    Received by: .............................. | | |

### 2.2 Purchase requisition

It is important that an organisation **controls** the goods that are ordered from suppliers. Only goods that are genuinely necessary should be ordered. Therefore, before any order for goods is placed, a purchase requisition must be completed.

Each purchase requisition must be **authorised** by the appropriate person. This will usually be the storekeeper or store manager.

When the purchase requisition has been completed it is sent to the purchasing department so that the purchase order is prepared.

**Example 2**

The storekeeper completes the requisition to order the 400 litres of oil for production. The code for the type of oil that is to be purchased is L04. Delivery is to be made directly to the stores department by 2 May.

**PURCHASE REQUISITION**

| Date: 15 April 20X4 | | | | Number: 6843 | |
|---|---|---|---|---|---|

Purpose: General machinery maintenance

Goods requisition note (if any): 4027

| Quantity | Material code | Job code | Delivery details | | Purchase order details |
|---|---|---|---|---|---|
| | | | Date | Place | |
| 400 litres | L04 | – | 2 May 20X4 | Stores | |

| Origination department: | Stores |
|---|---|
| Authorisation: | Storekeeper |

Note that the purchase requisition must have the following elements:

- Be dated.

- Be consecutively numbered.

- Include the purpose for which the materials are required, showing any relevant job code where necessary.

- Include a detailed description of the precise materials required.

- Show when and where the goods are required.

- Include space to record the eventual purchase order details.

- Be authorised by the appropriate person in the department placing the purchase requisition.

## 2.3 Purchase order

The person placing the order must first check that the purchase requisition has been authorised by the appropriate person in the organisation.

Once the supplier of the goods has been chosen depending on price, delivery and quality, the price is entered on the purchase order together with details of the goods being ordered. The purchase order is then authorised by the appropriate person in the organisation and dispatched to the supplier.

A copy of the purchase order is sent to the stores department so they know that goods are due and can alert appropriate management if they are not received and to the accounts department to be matched to the supplier's invoice.

An example purchase order is shown below.

---

### Example 3

Rowson Supplies Ltd has been chosen to supply the oil required by production. They agree to deliver the oil at a price of £1.50 per litre.

**PURCHASE ORDER**

To: Rowson Supplies Ltd     Number: 81742

Date: 15 April 20X4

Purchase requisition number: 6843

Please supply in accordance with attached conditions of purchase.

| Quantity | Description/code | Delivery date | Price £ | Per |
|---|---|---|---|---|
| 400 litres | L04 | 2 May 20X4 | 1.50 | Litre |

Your quotation:     £600 (400 litres X £1.50)

Authorisation:     Purchasing Manager

---

## 2.4 Delivery note

A delivery note is sent by the supplier to the stores with the goods being delivered. This will include a description of the goods being delivered along with the quantity. The contents and quality of the items delivered should be checked against the delivery note and this is then signed by the person receiving the goods as evidence that the goods arrived.

Any concerns about the goods (for example, too few, too many, the wrong colour, or the wrong size) should be referred immediately to the appropriate manager before accepting the goods.

### Example 4

400 litres of oil is delivered buy Rowson Supplies.

| ROWSON SUPPLIES LTD – DELIVERY NOTE | | |
|---|---|---|
| Delivery to: French Productions Ltd | | Date: 2 May 20X4 |
| Purchase order no:   81742 | | |
| Delivery note no:     D6582 | | |
| Please supply in accordance with attached conditions of purchase. | | |
| Quantity | Description | Code |
| 400 litres | Oil | L04 |
| Signed: Storeman | | |

## 2.5 Goods received note

When goods are received by the organisation they will be taken to the stores department rather than being delivered directly to the department that will use the goods. This enables the receipt of goods to be controlled. When the goods are received, the stores department will check:

(a)    that the goods that arrive agree in **all** detail to those ordered on the purchase order

(b)    that the details of the delivery note agree with the actual goods delivered.

When the stores department are satisfied with all of the details of the delivery, the details are recorded on a goods received note (GRN).

The GRN is evidence that the goods that were ordered have been received and therefore should be, and can be, paid for. The GRN will, therefore, be sent to the accounts department to be matched with the supplier's invoice.

As evidence of the actual receipt of the goods the GRN is also used for entering receipts of materials in the stores records.

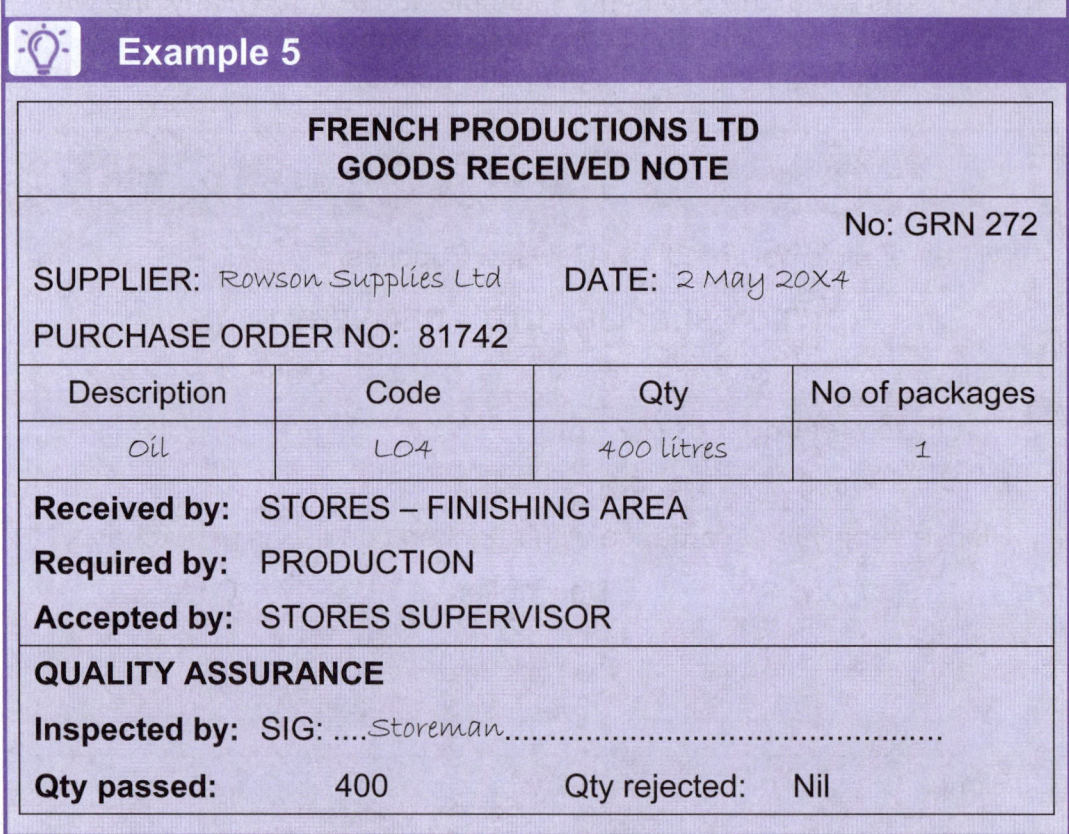

### Example 5

**FRENCH PRODUCTIONS LTD**
**GOODS RECEIVED NOTE**

No: GRN 272

SUPPLIER: Rowson Supplies Ltd    DATE: 2 May 20X4

PURCHASE ORDER NO: 81742

| Description | Code | Qty | No of packages |
|---|---|---|---|
| Oil | LO4 | 400 litres | 1 |

**Received by:** STORES – FINISHING AREA

**Required by:** PRODUCTION

**Accepted by:** STORES SUPERVISOR

**QUALITY ASSURANCE**

**Inspected by:** SIG: ....Storeman......................................................

**Qty passed:** 400        Qty rejected:    Nil

### 2.6    Issues to the user department (production department)

The circle is completed when the stores department issues the goods to the production department. The goods must agree with the original goods requisition note.

### 2.7    Purchase invoice

The purchase invoice for goods details the amount that the receiver of the goods must pay for them and the date that payment is due. The purchase invoice might be included when the goods themselves are delivered, or might be sent after delivery.

The person responsible for payment must check that the details of the purchase invoice agree to the goods received note, the delivery note and the purchase order. This is to ensure that:

- what was ordered was received

- what was received is what is being paid for

- the price charged is that agreed.

Once it is certain that the purchase invoice agrees with the goods that were actually received then the invoice can be authorised for payment by the appropriate person in the organisation.

---

### Example 6

**ROWSON SUPPLIES LTD – PURCHASE INVOICE**

| To: | Ronson Supplies Ltd | Date: | 2 May 20X4 |
|-----|------|------|------|

Purchase order no:   81742

Invoice no:          16582

| | £ |
|---|---|
| For supply and delivery of: | |
| 400 litres of oil L04 @ £1.50 per litre | 600.00 |
| Payment due in 30 days | |

---

## 2.8    Goods returned note

If goods are damaged or are not as ordered, they will be returned to the supplier. A goods returned note will be used, authorised by the stores department's manager.

When unused materials are returned from user departments to the stores, the transaction will be recorded on a document similar to the materials requisition but usually printed in a different colour. It will be completed by the user department that is returning the goods and signed by the storekeeper as evidence that the goods were returned to stores.

When the goods are returned the details on the goods returned note must be checked to the actual goods themselves.

## 2.9    Credit note

If goods have been returned to the supplier, or there is some fault with the invoice (e.g. incorrect price or discount), a credit note will be requested from the supplier.

### Test your understanding 1

Which of the following documents would be completed in each situation?

| | Material requisition | Purchase requisition | Goods received note | Goods returned note |
|---|---|---|---|---|
| Material returned to stores from production | ☐ | ☐ | ☐ | ☐ |
| Form completed by the stores department detailing inventory requirements | ☐ | ☐ | ☐ | ☐ |
| Materials returned to supplier | ☐ | ☐ | ☐ | ☐ |
| Form completed by stores on receipt of goods | ☐ | ☐ | ☐ | ☐ |
| Form completed by production detailing inventory requirements | ☐ | ☐ | ☐ | ☐ |

## Test your understanding 2

**Match the document with the correct situation.**

| | |
|---|---|
| Goods received note | Form completed by the purchasing department to order supplies |
| Purchase order | Form completed by the stores department detailing inventory requirements |
| Purchase requisition | Details the amount due to be paid and the date payment is due by |
| Stores record card | Form received with goods on delivery |
| Delivery note | Document completed to show the movement of inventory |
| Purchase invoice | Document completed by stores on receipt of goods |

# 3 The stores department

## 3.1 Function of the stores department

The stores or inventory department is responsible for the receipt, storage, issue and recording of the raw materials used in the production process.

## 3.2 Receipt of goods

When raw materials are received from suppliers they will normally be delivered to the stores department. The stores personnel must check that the goods delivered are the ones that have been ordered, in the correct quantity, of the correct quality and in good condition using the goods received note and the purchase requisition or purchase order.

## 3.3 Storage of materials

Once the materials have been received they must be stored until required by the production departments.

Storage of materials must be appropriate to their type. For example, foodstuffs must be stored at the correct temperature and wood must be stored in dry conditions. Storage should also be laid out in such a manner that the correct materials can be accessed easily either manually or by machinery.

### 3.4 Issue of materials

When the production departments require raw materials for production, it is essential that the stores department can provide the correct quantity and quality of materials at the time they are required. This will require careful attention to inventory control policies to ensure that the most efficient levels of inventories of raw materials are kept. Inventory control policies are discussed in a later section.

### 3.5 Recording of receipts and issues

In many organisations the stores department is also responsible for the recording of the quantities of raw materials that are received from suppliers and issued to the production departments. This normally takes place on the bin cards or the stores/inventory record card.

## 4 Cost of having inventory

### 4.1 Introduction

Most businesses, whatever their size, will be concerned with the problem of which items to have in inventory and how much of each item should be kept.

There are three forms that inventory can exist in:

- **Raw material** – items that are to be used in the manufacture of products

- **Work in progress** – items that are part way through the manufacturing process

- **Finished goods** – items that have completed the manufacturing process and are ready to be sold.

## 4.2 Functions of inventory

The principal reasons why a business needs to hold inventory are as follows:

(a)     It acts as a buffer in times when there is an unusually high rate of consumption.

(b)     It enables the business to take advantage of quantity discounts by buying in bulk.

(c)     The business can take advantage of seasonal and other price fluctuations (e.g. buying coal in the summer when it is cheaper).

(d)     To prevent any delay in production caused by a lack of raw material so production processes will flow smoothly and efficiently.

(e)     It may be necessary to hold inventory for a technical reason: for example, whisky must be matured.

## 4.3 Costs of having inventory

Holding inventory costs money and the principal 'trade-off' in an inventory holding situation is between the costs of acquiring and storing inventories on the one hand and the level of service that the company wishes to provide on the other.

The **total cost of having inventory** consists of the following:

(a)     **Purchase price**

(b)     **Holding costs**:

    (i)     the opportunity cost of capital tied up

    (ii)     insurance

    (iii)     deterioration

    (iv)     obsolescence

    (v)     damage and pilferage

    (vi)     warehouse upkeep

    (vii)     stores labour and administration costs.

(c)     **Ordering costs**:

    (i)     clerical and administrative expenses

    (ii)     transport costs.

(d)     **Stock-out costs** (items of required inventory are not available):

    (i)     loss of sales, therefore lost contribution

    (ii)     long-term damage to the business through loss of goodwill

    (iii)     production stoppages caused by a shortage of raw materials

    (iv)     extra costs caused by the need for emergency orders.

(e)     **Inventory recording systems costs:**

    (i)     maintaining the stores record card.

## 4.4 Disadvantages of low inventory levels

To keep the holding costs low it may be possible to reduce the volume of inventory that is kept but this can cause some problems:

- Customer demand cannot always be satisfied; this may lead to loss of business if customers become dissatisfied.

- In order to fulfil commitments to important customers, costly emergency procedures (e.g. special production runs) may become necessary in an attempt to maintain customer goodwill.

- It will be necessary to place replenishment orders more frequently than if higher inventories were held, in order to maintain a reasonable service. This will result in higher ordering costs being incurred.

## 4.5 Disadvantages of high inventory levels

To reduce the problems mentioned above management may consider holding high levels of inventory but again this can have issues:

- Storage or holding costs are very high; such costs will usually include rates, rent, labour, heating, deterioration, etc.

- The cost of the capital tied up in inventories, i.e. the cash spent to buy the inventory, is not available to pay other bills.

- If the stored product becomes obsolete, a large inventory holding of that item could, at worst, represent a large capital investment in an unsaleable product whose cash value is only that of scrap.

- If a great deal of capital is invested in inventories, there will be proportionately less money available for other requirements such as improvement of existing production facilities, or the introduction of new products.

- If there is a sudden drop in the price of a raw material after a high level of inventory has already been purchased, then the extra spent over the new lower price represents the opportunity cost of purchasing in advance. It follows that it would seem sensible to hold higher inventories during an inflationary period and lower inventories during a period of deflation.

## 5 Inventory control systems

### 5.1 Introduction

Inventory control is the method of ensuring that the right **quantity** of the right **quality** of the relevant inventory is available at the right **time** and right **place**.

Inventory control is maintained through the use of inventory record cards and by carrying out inventory checks on a regular basis.

There are two main types of inventory control systems:

**(a) fixed quantity system**

In a **fixed order system**, a replenishment order of a fixed size is placed when the inventory level falls to a fixed re-order level. Thus a **fixed quantity** is ordered at **variable intervals of time**. This is the most common system used.

**(b) periodic (cyclical) review system**

In a **periodic review system**, the inventory levels are reviewed at fixed points in time, when the quantity to be ordered is decided. By this method **variable quantities** are ordered at **fixed time intervals**.

Although this may increase the chances of a stock-out (between review times), it has the advantage of being easier to plan the scheduling of inventory counts and orders in advance.

### 5.2 Inventory control methods

Many inventory control systems will incorporate some or all of the following inventory control levels that assist in keeping costs of inventory holding and ordering down, whilst minimising the chances of stock-outs. The control methods are:

- buffer (minimum) inventory and maximum inventory
- re-order level
- re-order quantity – minimum and maximum order quantity
- Economic order quantity (EOQ).

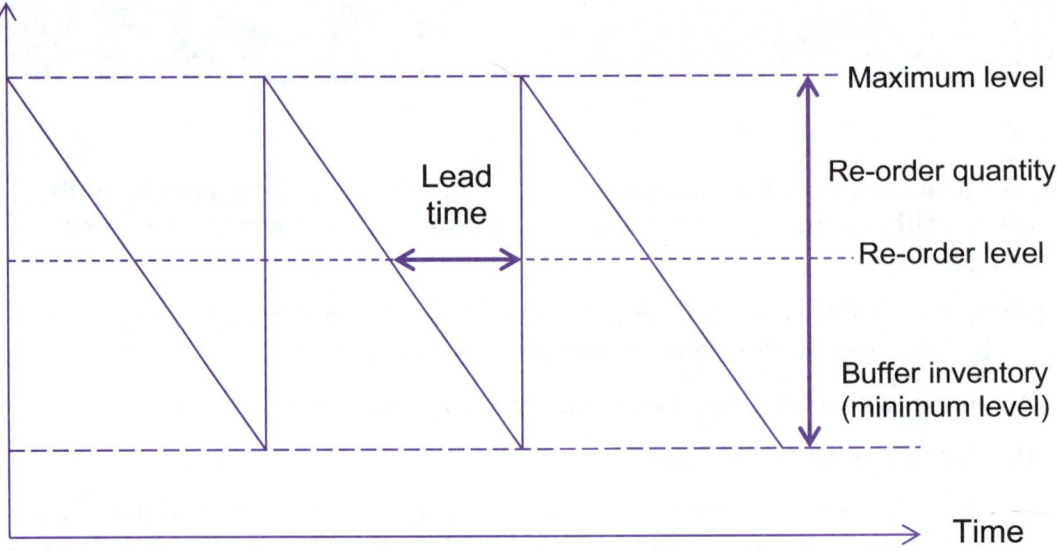

## 5.3    Inventory levels

**Buffer inventory** is also called safety inventory. It is the **minimum level** of inventory to be held.  It is used to reduce the occurrence of running out of inventory.  It is an extra amount that is kept in inventory that is in excess of the forecast demand.  It is used to ensure unexpected demands can be met.

> **Buffer inventory** = re-order level – (average usage × average lead time)

The lead time is the time it takes to receive an order after it has been placed.

The **maximum inventory** level may be determined by available storage space but depending on the information available it can be calculated as:

> **Maximum inventory level** = buffer inventory + maximum re-order quantity

## 5.4    Re-order level

The re-order level is calculated to make sure a company places an order so that it will be delivered before inventory runs out.  It will be determined with reference to the time it takes to receive the order (the lead time) and the inventory requirements during that time (usage).

> **Re-order level** = (average usage × average lead time) + buffer inventory

## 5.5　Re-order quantities

Once the re-order level is reached then an order needs to be placed with the suppliers.

The maximum re-order quantity will put inventory levels back to the maximum inventory level:

> **Maximum re-order quantity** = maximum inventory level – buffer inventory

The minimum re-order quantity will restore inventory to the re-order level, at which point another order will need to be placed

> **Minimum re-order quantity** = average usage × average lead time

 **Example 7**

The demand for a particular product is expected to vary between 10 and 50 units per day. Lead time has been as short as 4 days and as long as 10 days. The company orders 1,500 units at a time and can store a maximum of 1,960 units at any time. The company holds 90 units as buffer inventory. The company operates a 300-day year.

**Calculate the re-order level.**

**Calculate the maximum and minimum re-order quantities.**

**Solution**

| | |
|---|---|
| Re-order level | = average usage × average lead time + buffer inventory |
| | = (10+50)/2 per day × (4+10)/2 days + 90 |
| | = 30 × 7 + 90 |
| | = 300 units |
| Maximum re-order quantity | = maximum inventory level – buffer inventory |
| | = 1,960 – 90 |
| | = 1,870 units |
| Minimum re-order quantity | = average usage × average lead time |
| | = 30 × 7 = 210 units |

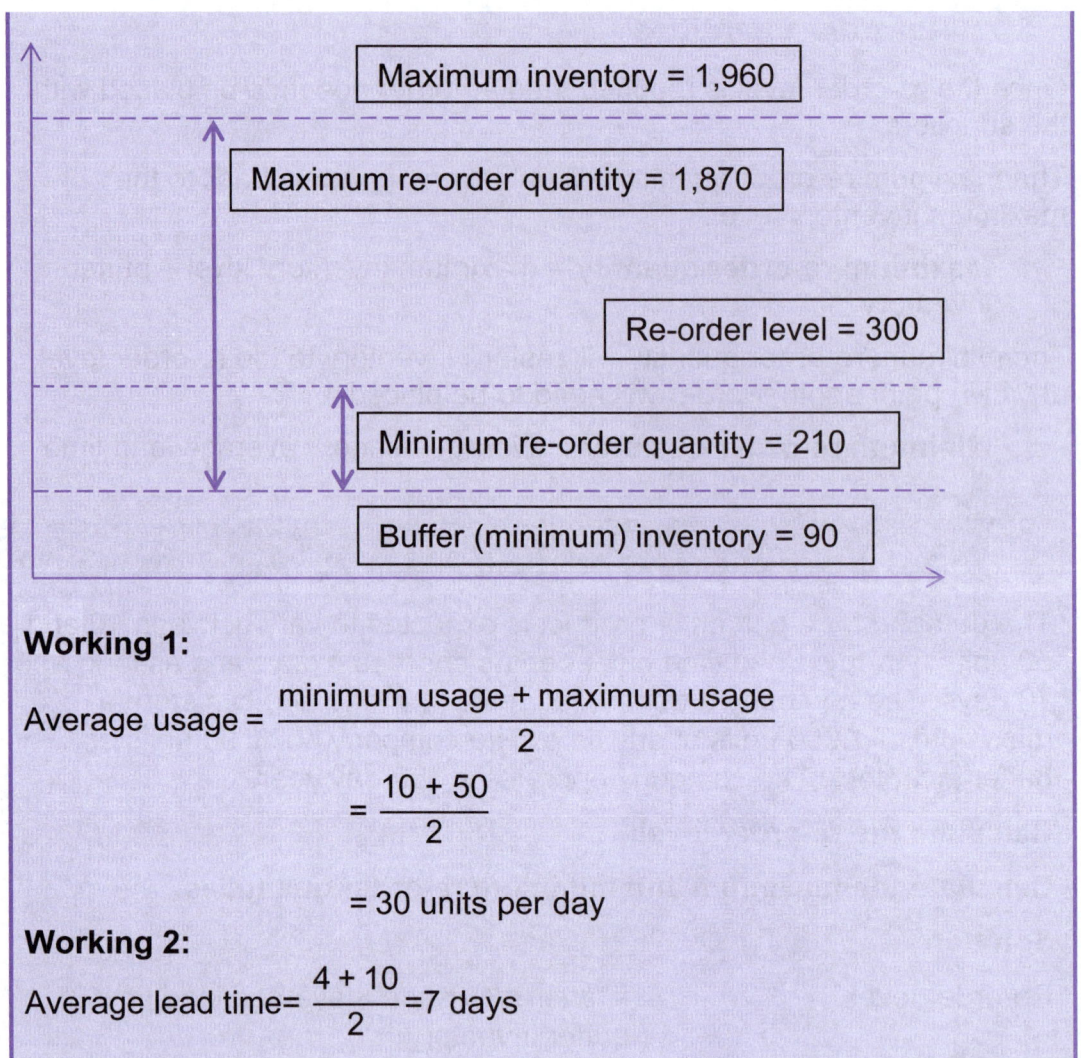

Maximum inventory = 1,960

Maximum re-order quantity = 1,870

Re-order level = 300

Minimum re-order quantity = 210

Buffer (minimum) inventory = 90

**Working 1:**

$$\text{Average usage} = \frac{\text{minimum usage} + \text{maximum usage}}{2}$$

$$= \frac{10 + 50}{2}$$

$$= 30 \text{ units per day}$$

**Working 2:**

$$\text{Average lead time} = \frac{4 + 10}{2} = 7 \text{ days}$$

**Test your understanding 3**

Ravenscar Engineering uses a standard component XZ7.

It estimates the following information regarding this unit:

| | |
|---|---|
| Weekly usage | 30 – 70 units |
| Delivery period | 3 – 7 weeks |

The working year is 50 weeks

Ordering costs are £50.63 per order

It costs £5 per unit per year to store the component.

Ravenscar Engineering orders 225 units in each order when inventory levels reach 490 units. Ravenscar can hold a maximum of 625 units in inventory.

**Calculate the following:**

(i)     Buffer inventory level


(ii)    Minimum re-order quantity


(iii)   Maximum re-order quantity


## 5.6     Economic order quantity (EOQ)

Once the re-order level is reached, an order will be placed. The size of the order will affect:

(a)    average inventory levels (the larger the order, the higher the inventory levels will be throughout the year)

(b)    frequency of orders placed in the year (the larger the order, the longer it will take for inventories to fall to the re-order level, and thus the fewer the orders placed in the year).

Increasing the order size will have two conflicting effects on costs: increased holding costs through higher inventory levels and decreased re-ordering costs due to fewer orders placed in the year.

Under certain 'ideal' conditions (including constant rates of usage and constant lead times) a mathematical model can be used to determine the optimum (economic) order quantity (EOQ) that will minimise the total of these two costs – see graph.

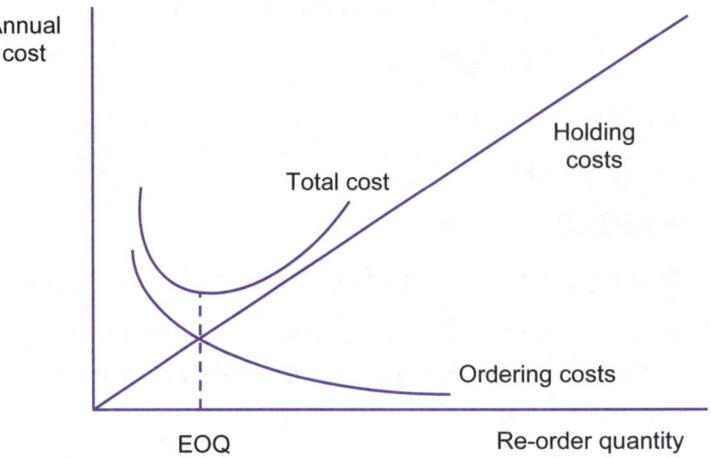

The formula for the economic order quantity is:

$$EOQ = \sqrt{\frac{2 \times C_o \times D}{C_h}}$$

where:  $C_o$ = cost of placing each order (note this is not the cost of the materials purchased but the administrative cost of placing the order).

D = annual demand/usage in units.

$C_h$ = cost of holding **one** unit of inventory for **one** year.

Assumptions of the economic order quantity:

- Demand and lead time are constant and known

- Purchase price is constant

- No buffer inventory is held.

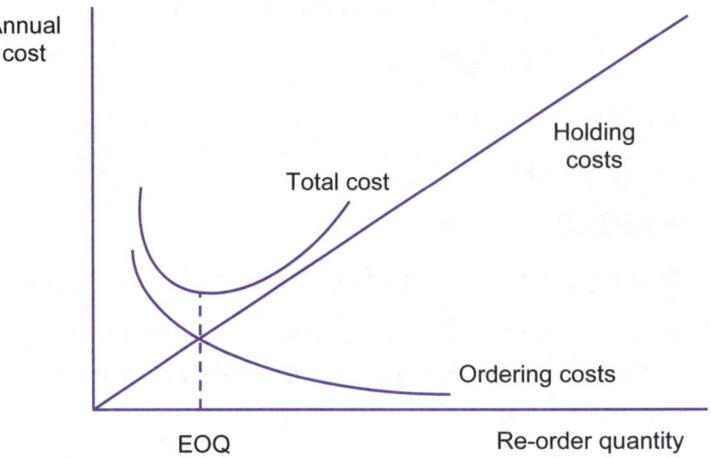

### Example 8

The demand for a particular product is expected be 25 units a day. Each time an order is placed, administrative costs of £15 are incurred and one unit of inventory held for one year incurs £0.10 of holding costs.

The company operates a 300-day year.

**Calculate the economic order quantity.** 225,000

$$\sqrt{2 \times 0.10 \quad \overset{7,500}{} \times 15}$$  2,250,000

$$\overline{\phantom{xxxxxxxxxxxx}}$$
0.10  1,500

**Solution**

$$EOQ = \sqrt{\frac{2 \times Co \times D}{Ch}}$$

$$EOQ = \sqrt{\frac{2 \times £15 \times 7,500}{£0.10}} = 1,500 \text{ units}$$

**Working:**

Annual demand D = days in year × usage per day

D = 300 × 25 = 7,500

---

### Test your understanding 4

Given below is information about one inventory line that a business holds:

Daily usage (units)          20

Lead time (days)              5

The business operates for 250 days a year and keeps 50 units of inventory as buffer inventory.

The cost of placing each order is £20 and it costs £0.20 to hold an item of inventory for one year.

**Calculate the economic order quantity.**

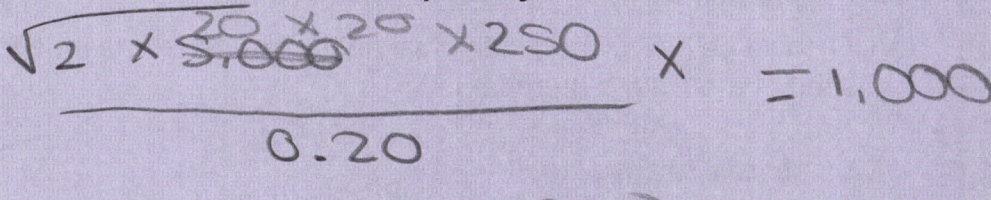

$$\sqrt{2 \times \frac{20 \times 20 \times 250}{5,000}}{0.20} \times = 1,000$$

1,000,000

---

# 6    Costing issues of raw materials

## 6.1    Introduction

The cost of materials purchased will normally be derived from suppliers' invoices but, where many purchases have been made at differing prices, a decision has to be taken as to which cost is used when inventory is issued to the user department (cost centre).

## 6.2 Methods of pricing

Various methods exist including:

(a) FIFO (first in, first out)

(b) Average cost (AVCO).

The choice of method will not only affect the charge to the user department for which the material is required, but also the value of the inventory left in stores.

**NOTE**: the methods do not necessarily mean that inventory is physically issued in a particular order. It is the prices used in the valuation that follow the method.

## 6.3 FIFO and AVCO methods

These systems attempt to reflect the movement of units of material (for example kg or litres) in and out of inventory under different assumptions.

- **FIFO** – assumes that issues will be made based on the oldest prices, leaving the more recent prices in stores. FIFO could be used when products are perishable e.g. milk. FIFO is acceptable by HMRC and adheres to IAS2 Inventories.

- **AVCO** – assumes that the issues into production will be made at an average price. This price is derived from taking the total value of the inventory and dividing it by the total units in inventory thus finding the average price per unit. A new average cost is calculated before each issue to production.

    AVCO could be used when individual units of material are indefinable e.g. sand at a builder's merchants.

## 6.4 The stores record card

It is usual to record quantities of an inventory item (and often inventory values as well) on a **stores record card**. One such card is maintained for each different inventory item, showing receipts of new inventory from suppliers, issues of inventory to production, and balance of inventory remaining on hand.

**Example 9**                                                              97

Sid makes the following purchases of Component X.

| Date | Quantity | Unit price £ | Total cost £ |
|---|---|---|---|
| 10 January | 50 | 1.00 | 50 |
| 20 January | 60 | 1.10 | 66 |
| 30 January | 40 | 1.25 | 50 |

On 25 January Sid issues 70 units for use in production.

On 31 January Sid issues 60 units for use in production.

No inventory was held at the beginning of the month.

**Calculate the value of closing inventory and the cost of inventory issued to production using:**

(a)   a FIFO basis

(b)   an AVCO basis (round the average price per unit to 2 decimal places).

**Solution**

(a)   **FIFO basis**

**Stores Record Card**

Material description:  Component X

Code:                         X100

| | Receipts | | | Issues | | | Balance | |
|---|---|---|---|---|---|---|---|---|
| Date | Quantity | Unit price £ | Total £ | Quantity | Unit price £ | Total £ | Quantity | Total £ |
| 10 Jan | 50 | 1.00 | 50 | | | | 50 | 50 |
| 20 Jan | 60 | 1.10 | 66 | | | | 50 | 50 |
| | | | | | | | 60 | 66 |
| | | | | | | | 110 | 116 |
| 25 Jan | | | | 50 | 1 | 50 | | |
| | | | | 20 | 1.10 | 22 | 40 | 44 |
| | | | | 70 | | 72 | | |

| Date | Quantity | Unit price | Total | Quantity | Unit price | Total | Quantity | Total |
|---|---|---|---|---|---|---|---|---|
| 30 Jan | 40 | 1.25 | 50 | | | | 40 | 44 |
| | | | | | | | 40 | 50 |
| | | | | | | | —— | —— |
| | | | | | | | 80 | 94 |
| 31 Jan | | | | 40 | 1.10 | 44 | | |
| | | | | 20 | 1.25 | 25 | 20 | 25 |
| | | | | —— | | —— | —— | —— |
| | | | | 60 | | 69 | 20 | 25 |
| | | | | —— | | | —— | —— |

## (c)   AVCO basis

**Stores Record Card**

Material description:   Component X

Code:                            X100

| | Receipts | | | Issues | | | Balance | |
|---|---|---|---|---|---|---|---|---|
| Date | Quantity | Unit price £ | Total £ | Quantity | Unit price £ | Total £ | Quantity | Total £ |
| 10 Jan | 50 | 1.00 | 50 | | | | 50 | 50 |
| | | | | | | | —— | —— |
| 20 Jan | 60 | 1.10 | 66 | | | | 50 | 50 |
| | | | | | | | 60 | 66 |
| | | | | | | | —— | —— |
| | | | | | | | 110 | 116 |
| | | | | | | | —— | —— |
| 25 Jan | | | | 70 | 1.05 | 74 | 40 | 42 |
| 30 Jan | 40 | 1.25 | 50 | | | | 40 | 42 |
| | | | | | | | 40 | 50 |
| | | | | | | | —— | —— |
| | | | | | | | 80 | 92 |
| | | | | | | | —— | —— |
| 31 Jan | | | | 60 | 1.15 | 69 | 20 | 23 |
| | | | | | | | —— | —— |
| | | | | | | | 20 | 23 |
| | | | | | | | —— | —— |

**Note:** The average cost per unit is calculated based on what is in stores before the issue occurs. For example:

25 Jan £116 ÷ 110 units = £1.05 therefore the valuation of the issue is 70 units × £1.05 = £74 (rounded to the nearest whole number).

In the exam you will be told how many decimal places the 'per unit' figure and total figure need to be.

---

## Test your understanding 5

Amp plc is a printing company specialising in producing accounting manuals. No formal stores accounting system is in operation at present.

**Complete the following inventory entries using:**

FIFO and AVCO (average cost per unit to two decimal places of a £).

| | |
|---|---|
| Material: | Paper – Code 1564A |
| Opening inventory: | 10,000 sheets – value £3,000 |

| Purchases | | | Issues | |
|---|---|---|---|---|
| 3 May | 4,000 sheets | £1,600 | 6 May | 7,000 sheets |
| 12 May | 10,000 sheets | £3,100 | 15 May | 6,000 sheets |
| | | | 22 May | 7,200 sheets |

**Stores Record Card FIFO**
Material: Paper     Code: 1564A

| Date | Details | Receipts | | Issues | | | Inventory | |
|---|---|---|---|---|---|---|---|---|
| | | Sheets | £ | Sheets | Price | £ | Sheets | £ |
| 1.5 | Opening inventory | 10,000 3,000 | 3,000 | | | | 10,000 | 3,000 |
| 3.5 | Receipt | 4,000 4,000 | 1,600 | | | | 14,000 | 4,600 |
| 6.5 | Issue | | | 7,000 | 0.33 | 2310 | 7,000 | 2290 |
| 12.5 | Receipt | 10,000 | 3100 | | | | 17,000 | 5390 |
| 15.5 | Issue | | | 6,000 | 0.32 | 1920 | 11,000 | |
| 22.5 | Issue | | | | | | | |

| Date | Details | Receipts | | Issues | | | Inventory | |
|------|---------|----------|---|--------|-------|---|-----------|---|
| | | Sheets | £ | Sheets | Price | £ | Sheets | £ |
| 1.5 | Opening inventory | | | | | | | |
| 3.5 | Receipt | | | | | | | |
| 6.5 | Issue | | | | | | | |
| 12.5 | Receipt | | | | | | | |
| 15.5 | Issue | | | | | | | |
| 22.5 | Issue | | | | | | | |

*Stores Record Card AVCO*
*Material:    Paper  Code: 1564A*

**Test your understanding 6**

Cavernelli runs a pizza house. The inventory and usage of pizza bases for December was:

|  |  | Units | Value (£) |
|---|---|---|---|
| Opening inventory | 1 Dec | 200 | 180 |
| Purchases | 3 Dec | 800 | 800 |
| Purchases | 20 Dec | 1,200 | 1,140 |
| Usage | w/e 7 Dec | 400 |  |
|  | w/e 14 Dec | 350 |  |
|  | w/e 21 Dec | 410 |  |
|  | w/e 28 Dec | 475 |  |

**Calculate the value of issues and the closing inventory using the FIFO method of pricing (show figures to the nearest £).**

The issues are priced at the end of each week.

**Stores Record Card FIFO**

Material: Pizza

Code: 1626

| Date | Details | Receipts | | Issues | | | Inventory | |
|---|---|---|---|---|---|---|---|---|
|  |  | Units | £ | Units | Price | £ | Units | £ |
|  |  |  |  |  |  |  |  |  |
|  |  |  |  |  |  |  |  |  |
|  |  |  |  |  |  |  |  |  |
|  |  |  |  |  |  |  |  |  |

**Test your understanding 7**

Kiveton Cleaning Services supplies its employees with protective clothing. One such item is protective gloves.

Records from the stores department for January showed:

1 Jan        Opening inventory
             150 pairs @ £2 each

7 Jan        Purchases
             40 pairs @ £1.90

15 Jan       Issues
             30 pairs

29 Jan       Issues
             35 pairs

**Calculate the value of the issues and the closing inventory if the FIFO method is used to price the usage.**

**Stores Record Card FIFO**

Material:   Protective gloves

Code:       1607

| Date | Details | Receipts | | Issues | | | Inventory | |
|---|---|---|---|---|---|---|---|---|
| | | Pairs | £ | Pairs | Price | £ | Pairs | £ |
| | | | | | | | | |
| | | | | | | | | |
| | | | | | | | | |
| | | | | | | | | |
| | | | | | | | | |
| | | | | | | | | |
| | | | | | | | | |
| | | | | | | | | |

**Test your understanding 8**

Crescent Engineering use a standard component AB3 and the inventory, receipts and issues for the month of September were:

Opening inventory 75 units @ £40 = £3,000.

| Date | Receipts (units) | Unit cost £ | Issues to production (units) |
|---|---|---|---|
| 1 Sept | 100 | 40 | |
| 10 Sept | 75 | 42 | |
| 15 Sept | | | 60 |
| 20 Sept | | | 55 |
| 23 Sept | 45 | 42 | |
| 30 Sept | | | 50 |

The company uses the weighted average cost method for pricing issues and valuing inventory.

**Calculate the total usage for the month and the value of closing inventory (round per unit figures to 2 decimal places and total figures to the nearest £1).**

| **Stores Record Card AVCO** | | | | | | | | |
|---|---|---|---|---|---|---|---|---|
| **Material:** Component AB3 | | | | | | | | |
| **Code:** 010203 | | | | | | | | |
| | Receipts | | | Issues | | | Inventory | |
| Date | Units | Cost | £ | Units | Cost | £ | Units | £ |
| | | | | | | | | |

**Test your understanding 9**

**Navneet Ltd**

Identify the method of inventory valuation and complete the stores record card shown below for steel component Magic, for the month of May 20Y0.

**Note:** Figures in the total columns should be shown to the nearest £. The company's policy is to round prices per unit to two decimal places.

**STORES RECORD CARD FOR STEEL COMPONENT MAGIC**

**Inventory valuation method:**

| Date 20Y0 | Receipts Quantity kg | Cost per kg (£) | Total cost (£) | Issues Quantity kg | Cost per kg (£) | Total cost (£) | Balance Quantity kg | £ |
|---|---|---|---|---|---|---|---|---|
| Balance as at 1 May | | | | | | | 25,000 | 50,000 |
| 9 May | 30,000 | 2.30 | 69,000 | | | | 55,000 | 119,000 |
| 12 May | | | | 40,000 | 2.30 | 84,500 | 15,000 | 34500 |
| 18 May | 20,000 | 2.50 | 50,000 | | | | 35,000 | 84500 |
| 27 May | | | | 10,000 | 2.30 | 23,000 | 25,000 | 61500 |

 **Test your understanding 10**

Dennis plc has the following kg of raw material in inventory:

| Date purchased | Quantity | Cost per kg (£) | Total cost (£) |
|---|---|---|---|
| April 24 | 500 | 1.20 | 600 |
| April 26 | 450 | 1.30 | 585 |
| April 30 | 600 | 1.50 | 900 |

Calculate the cost of issuing 1,000 kg on 1 May and the value of the closing inventory (to the nearest £) using:

- FIFO
- AVCO

## 6.5 Features of the different methods

**FIFO** has the following features:

- In times of rapidly increasing prices, material may be **issued** at an early and unrealistically low price, resulting in the particular job showing an unusually large profit.

- Two jobs started on the same day may show a different cost for the same quantity of the same material.

- In times of rapidly increasing prices FIFO will give a higher profit figure than AVCO.

- FIFO can be used in the production of financial accounts as it is **acceptable to HMRC and adheres to IAS 2 Inventories**.

**AVCO** is a compromise on valuation of inventory and issues and the average price rarely reflects the actual purchase price of the material.

## 6.6 Inventory valuation method and profit

As stated above FIFO will return a higher profit than AVCO if prices are increasing over a time period. If prices are declining AVCO then returns a higher profit. This is due to the valuation of closing inventory and its application in a statement of profit or loss.

**Example 10**

Charlie has the following extract from their inventory card and was wondering which method of inventory valuation would give him the highest profit.

- 1 July Received 100 units at £10 per unit
- 2 July Received 100 units at £11 per unit
- 3 July Issued 150 units to production.

There is no opening inventory.

| Date | Receipts | | | Issues | | | Balance | |
|---|---|---|---|---|---|---|---|---|
| | Qty | Per unit | Total | Qty | Per unit | Total | Qty | Total |
| 1 July | 100 | 10 | 1,000 | | | | 100 | 1,000 |
| 2 July | 100 | 11 | 1,100 | | | | 100 | 1,000 |
| | | | | | | | 100 | 1,100 |
| | | | | | | | 200 | 2,100 |
| 3 July (FIFO) | | | | 100 | 10 | 1,000 | | |
| | | | | 50 | 11 | 550 | 50 | 550 |
| | | | | 150 | | 1,550 | | |

**OR**

| Date | Receipts | | | Issues | | | Balance | |
|---|---|---|---|---|---|---|---|---|
| 3 July (AVCO) | | | | 150 | 10.50 | 1,575 | 50 | 525 |

If we now use the above data to produce a statement of profit or loss for the first few days in July:

### FIFO

The closing inventory is valued at the most recent prices therefore the higher prices.

|  |  | £ |
|---|---|---|
| Sales (illustrative figure) |  | 2,000 |
| Less: Cost of sales |  |  |
| Opening inventory | 0 |  |
| Purchases (from receipts) | 2,100 |  |
| Less: closing inventory | (550) |  |
|  | ⎯⎯⎯ |  |
|  |  | (1,550) |
|  |  | ⎯⎯⎯ |
| Gross profit |  | 450 |

### AVCO

The closing inventory is valued at the oldest prices therefore the lower prices.

|  |  | £ |
|---|---|---|
| Sales (illustrative figure) |  | 2,000 |
| Less: Cost of sales |  |  |
| Opening inventory | 0 |  |
| Purchases (from receipts) | 2,100 |  |
| Less: closing inventory | (525) |  |
|  | ⎯⎯⎯ |  |
|  |  | (1,575) |
|  |  | ⎯⎯⎯ |
| Gross profit |  | 425 |

We can see that FIFO has a higher value of closing inventory (£550) therefore a lower cost of sales (£1,550) which leads to a higher profit.

---

 **Test your understanding 11**

**If raw material prices are rising over time, which method of valuing inventories will give the lowest profit?**

A     FIFO

B     AVCO

# 7 Work in progress – materials

## 7.1 Introduction

During production it is possible that products **are not all completed at the end of a time period** for example the manufacture of cars. This means that the costs are shared between finished (fully completed) units and **work in progress** (partially completed) units.

Work in progress is often referred to as WIP

We need to share the costs incurred in production on a fair basis between units that are completed and those that require more effort to complete them.

## 7.2 Equivalent units

To be able to assign the correct amount of cost to finished and partially completed units of product we use a concept called **Equivalent units (EU)**.

**The calculation of equivalent units:**

If we had 1,000 units that are 50% complete at the end of a period. How many finished units is this equivalent to?

Equivalent units = Number of physical units × percentage completion.

1,000 × 50% = 500 equivalent units (EU).

In other words, we assume we could have made 500 units and finished them instead of half finishing 1,000 units.

**The calculation of the cost per equivalent unit:**

Once we have the number of equivalent units for the completed units and the WIP units we can share the production cost over those equivalent units to calculate the cost per EU.

Cost per EU = Total cost of production ÷ total equivalent units

**Valuation of completed and WIP units:**

Using the cost per equivalent unit and the number of equivalent units we can then fairly value the completed units and the work in progress.

Valuation = cost per EU × number of EU

**Example 11**

DL Ltd is a manufacturer. In Period 1 the following production occurred.

Input = 1,400 units

Completed output = 1,000 units

Work in progress = 400 units

Work in progress = 25% complete

Cost of production = £3,300

**Calculate the cost per equivalent unit and value the completed units and WIP units.**

**Solution**

**The calculation of equivalent units:**

| | | | EUs |
|---|---|---|---|
| Completed | 1,000 × | 100% | 1,000 |
| WIP | 400 × | 25% | 100 |
| Total | | | 1,100 |

**The calculation of the cost per equivalent unit:**

Cost per EU = £3,300/1,100 EU = £3.00 per EU

**Valuation of completed and WIP units:**

Completed units = 1,000 EU × £3.00 = £3,000

WIP units = 100 EU × £3.00 = £300

 **Test your understanding 12**

**WIP**

On 1 March 20X0 production started work on 350 units and at the end of the month there were still 75 units waiting to be finished, these were 60% complete.

The total cost of materials, labour, etc. input during March was £3,696.

*Completed 275 × 100% = 16500 105*
*WIP 75 × 60% = 4500 45*
*= 210*

*210-*

**Required:**

1    What is the cost per equivalent unit:

    A    £8.70

    B    £9.36

    C    £11.55

    D    £12.45

2    Calculate the cost of the completed output and the work in progress (round to the nearest whole £).

    Completed output = £
    Work in progress = £

# 8 Material wastage

## 8.1 Material wastage

In practice wastage of raw material input into production may be due to such things as evaporation, faulty materials supplied or materials damaged in the process.

It could be expressed as a percentage loss of raw materials in the manufacturing or production process.

 **Example 12**

Each unit of a product called 'The Oblong' requires 0.5kg of material that costs £1 per kg. The business expects to produce 11,400 Oblongs in the month of March.

5% of materials are lost during the manufacturing process.

**Calculate the material required for production**

11,400 units × 0.5kg = 5,700kg.

**Calculate the amount of material that is wasted**

5% of material is wasted in the production process, this means that 5,700kg is 95% of the total material required for production.

5,700kg/95 × 5 = 300kg is wasted

> **Calculate the total number of kilograms required**
>
> 5,700kg + 300kg = 6,000kg.
>
> Or 5,700kg/95 × 100 = 6,000kg.

## 8.2 Wastage in production

It is also possible for wastage to occur during the production process, this may be due to such things as items rejected as inferior by quality control, items damaged in the warehouse or theft. The wastage can be expressed as a percentage loss of finished goods.

 **Example 13**

This month, the Production Manager has informed you that 4% of all units produced are being quality tested and will no longer be saleable.

**Complete the budgeted spreadsheet, identifying faulty production and total production required for the months of June and July.**

| Production budget spreadsheet | | |
|---|---|---|
| | June | July |
| Good/fault-free production required | 6,360 | 5,640 |
| Faulty production/wastage | | |
| Total production | | |

**Solution**

| Production budget spreadsheet | | |
|---|---|---|
| | June | July |
| Good/fault-free production required | 6,360 | 5,640 |
| Faulty production/wastage (W1) | 265 | 235 |
| Total production | 6,625 | 5,875 |

**Working 1**

June = 6,360/96 × 4 = 265

July = 5,640/96 × 4 = 235

**Test your understanding 13**

You work for Bracken Ltd as a management accountant. The company makes two products, the Omega and the Vector. Both products use the same type of materials but in different quantities.

One of your jobs is to prepare the production budget. You are given the following information to help you to prepare this budget.

| Forecast sales volumes (units) | Omega | Vector |
|---|---|---|
| Period 7 | 7,200 | 10,340 |

**Production**

*7,800   11,000*

Quality control of the units will mean that <u>4% of Omegas</u> and <u>6% of</u> Vectors will be lost.

**Materials**

*67,500   132,000*

Each Omega requires 9 kg of material and each Vector 12 kg of material

2% of material is lost through wastage during production. *203,572*

**Calculate the production levels and the total material requirement (round the total materials required up to the nearest whole kg)**

---

## 9    Integrated bookkeeping – materials

### 9.1    Introduction

The costs of a business have to be recorded in a bookkeeping system. Many businesses use an **integrated bookkeeping system** where the ledger accounts kept provide the necessary **information for both costing and financial accounting**.

### 9.2    Stores record card (bin card)

Every line of inventory, e.g. component X and material Y, will have a record card showing precisely how much of this item is in inventory. Therefore each time a receipt of a material arrives from a supplier then the stores record card must be updated.

## 9.3 Stores department entries

In many management accounting systems only the quantity of the materials is entered by the stores department as that is the only information that they have.

## 9.4 Accounts department entries

Once the stores record card reaches the accounts department then the correct price of the materials, taken from the purchase invoice will be entered.

The stores record card is an important document that helps to control the movement of materials and assess inventory levels.

## 9.5 Inventory ledger account

The accounting for material is dealt with through a stores ledger account (or the material cost account). This is maintained by the accounting department, the physical inventory shown on these accounts is reconciled with the stores record card. The materials cost account is where the movement of the costs associated with the materials are recorded.

---

### Example 14

**Materials cost account**

| | £ | | £ |
|---|---|---|---|
| Opening balance (1) | | Issues to production (4) | |
| Purchases (2) | | Returns to suppliers (5) | |
| Returns to stores (3) | | Production overheads (6) | |
| | | Statement of profit and loss (7) | |
| | | Closing balance (8) | |

(1) The **opening balance** of materials held in stores at the beginning of a period is shown as a **debit** in the material cost account.

(2) Materials **purchased** on credit are **debited** to the material cost account. Materials purchased for cash would also be a debit.

(3) Materials **returned to stores** cause inventory to increase and so are **debited** to the material cost account.

(4) **Direct materials** used in production are transferred to the **production** account, which is also known as the **Work-In-Progress**. This is recorded by crediting the material cost account.

---

(5)   Materials **returned to suppliers** cause inventory levels to fall and are therefore '**credited** out' of the materials cost account.

(6)   **Indirect materials** are not a direct cost of manufacture and are treated as **overheads**. They are therefore transferred to the production overhead account by way of a **credit** to the materials cost account.

(7)   Any material **write-offs** are '**credited** out' of the material cost account and transferred to the statement of profit or loss where they are written off.

(8)   The **balancing figure** on the materials cost account is the **closing balance** of material at the end of a period. It is also the opening balance at the beginning of the next period.

 **Test your understanding 14**

**What are the correct journal entries the following accounting transactions?**

1   Receipt of material into stores paying on credit:

A   Dr Bank, Cr Materials

B   Dr Trade Payables Control, Cr Materials

C   Dr Materials, Cr Bank

D   Dr Materials, Cr Trade Payables Control

2   Issue of material from inventory to production.

A   Dr Bank, Cr Materials

B   Dr Materials, Cr Bank

C   Dr Materials, Cr Production

D   Dr Production, Cr Materials

3   Receipt of material into stores paying immediately by BACS.

A   Dr Bank, Cr Materials

B   Dr Trade Payables Control, Cr Materials

C   Dr Materials, Cr Bank

D   Dr Materials, Cr Trade Payables Control

4    Return of material from production to stores.

    A    Dr Materials, Cr Bank

    B    Dr Materials, Cr Trade Payables Control

    C    Dr Materials, Cr Production

    D    Dr Production, Cr Materials

 **Test your understanding 15**

**Retail Store Company**

Issues are costed from the warehouse and transport department using the weighted average method.

**Complete the stores ledger card below for an item of inventory in the clothing department for the month of May 20X8 using the weighted average method for costing issues and valuing inventory.**

**Note:** Figures in the total columns should be shown to the nearest £.

The company's policy is to round prices per unit to three decimal places.

| Stores Record Card | | | | | | | | | |
|---|---|---|---|---|---|---|---|---|---|
| **Department:** | | | | | | | **Month:** | | |
| | **Receipts** | | | **Issues** | | | **Balance** | | |
| Date | Quantity | Price £ | Total £ | Quantity | Price £ | Total £ | Quantity | | Total £ |
| 1/5 Balance | | | | | | | 2,420 | | 12,584 |
| 7/5 | 2,950 | 5.500 | 16,226 | | | | | | |
| 11/5 | 3,200 | 5.700 | 18,239 | | | | | | |
| 14/5 | | | | 4,105 | | | | | |
| 21/5 | 1,535 | 5.400 | 8,289 | | | | | | |
| 27/5 | | | | 1,800 | | | | | |
| 30/5 | | | | 2,600 | | | | | |

**What is the double entry for the issue on the 27th May?**

A    Dr Bank, Cr Materials

B    Dr Materials, Cr Bank

C    Dr Materials, Cr Production

D    Dr Production, Cr Materials

# 10 Summary

**Pricing issues** of raw materials and valuing inventories are two of the most important techniques that you need to know about in the topic of materials. We have looked at two main methods of pricing issues and valuing inventories: FIFO and Weighted Average Cost. A common examination task is to ask you to record receipts and issues of materials onto a stores ledger card using one of these methods.

We have also looked at the **documents** involved in the process of purchasing materials and the different inventory control systems (re-order level (two-bin) system and the periodic review system.

Another important part of the topic of materials is that of **inventory control** levels – these assist in keeping the costs of inventory holding and inventory ordering at a minimum, whilst minimising stock-outs at the same time. Make sure that you can calculate the re-order level, the EOQ, the maximum inventory level and the minimum inventory level.

## Test your understanding answers

### Test your understanding 1

|  | Material requisition | Purchase requisition | Goods received note | Goods returned note |
|---|---|---|---|---|
| Material returned to stores from production | ☐ | ☐ | ☐ | ☑ |
| Form completed by the stores department detailing inventory requirements | ☐ | ☑ | ☐ | ☐ |
| Materials returned to supplier | ☐ | ☐ | ☐ | ☑ |
| Form completed by stores on receipt of goods | ☐ | ☐ | ☑ | ☐ |
| Form completed by production detailing inventory requirements | ☑ | ☐ | ☐ | ☐ |

## Test your understanding 2

| | |
|---|---|
| Goods received note | Document completed by stores on receipt of goods |
| Purchase order | Form completed by the purchasing department to order supplies |
| Purchase requisition | Form completed by the stores department detailing inventory requirements |
| Stores record card | Document completed to show the movement of inventory |
| Delivery note | Form received with goods on delivery |
| Purchase invoice | Details the amount due to be paid and the date payment is due by |

## Test your understanding 3

(i)   Buffer (minimum) inventory level:

Re-order level – (average usage × average lead time)

= 490 – (50 × 5) = 240 units

(ii)   Minimum re-order quantity:

Average usage × average lead time

= 50 × 5 = 250 units

(iii)   Maximum re-order quantity:

Maximum inventory – buffer inventory

= 625 – 240 = 385 units

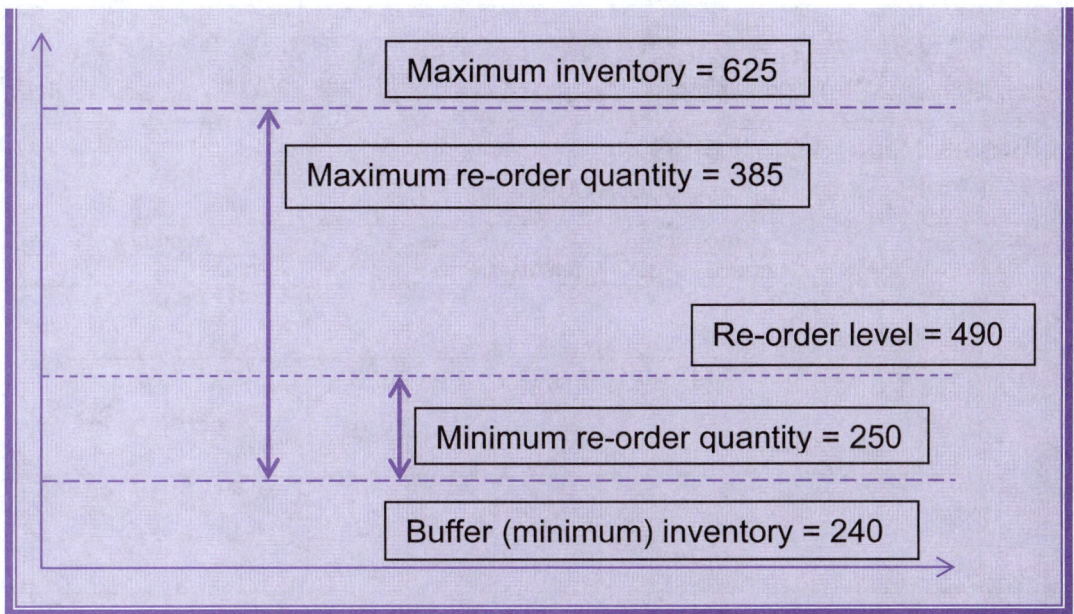

Maximum inventory = 625

Maximum re-order quantity = 385

Re-order level = 490

Minimum re-order quantity = 250

Buffer (minimum) inventory = 240

## Test your understanding 4

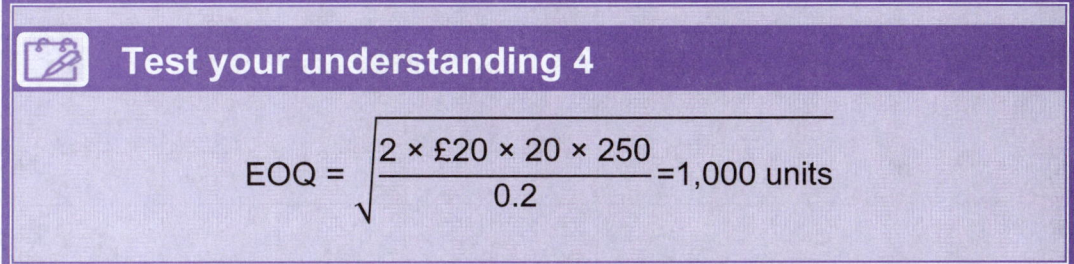

$$EOQ = \sqrt{\frac{2 \times £20 \times 20 \times 250}{0.2}} = 1,000 \text{ units}$$

**Test your understanding 5**

## Stores Record Card FIFO
Material: Paper          Code: 1564A

| Date | Details | Receipts | | Issues | | | Inventory | |
|---|---|---|---|---|---|---|---|---|
| | | Sheets | £ | Sheets | Price | £ | Sheets | £ |
| 1.5 | Opening inventory | | | | | | 10,000 | 3,000 |
| 3.5 | Receipt | 4,000 | 1,600 | | | | 10,000 | 3,000 |
| | | | | | | | 4,000 | 1,600 |
| | | | | | | | 14,000 | 4,600 |
| 6.5 | Issue | | | | | | 3,000 | 900 |
| | | | | 7,000 | 0.30 | 2,100 | 4,000 | 1,600 |
| | | | | 7,000 | | 2,100 | 7,000 | 2,500 |
| 12.5 | Receipt | 10,000 | 3,100 | | | | 3,000 | 900 |
| | | | | | | | 4,000 | 1,600 |
| | | | | | | | 10,000 | 3,100 |
| | | | | | | | 17,000 | 5600 |
| 15.5 | Issue | | | 3,000 | 0.30 | 900 | 1,000 | 400 |
| | | | | 3,000 | 0.40 | 1,200 | 10,000 | 3,100 |
| | | | | 6,000 | | 2,100 | 11,000 | 3,500 |
| 22.5 | Issue | | | 1,000 | 0.40 | 400 | | |
| | | | | 6,200 | 0.31 | 1,922 | 3,800 | 1,178 |
| | | | | 7,200 | | 2,322 | 3,800 | 1,178 |

## Stores Record Card AVCO
Material: Paper          Code: 1564A

| Date | Details | Receipts | | Issues | | | Inventory | |
|---|---|---|---|---|---|---|---|---|
| | | Sheets | £ | Sheets | Price | £ | Sheets | £ |
| 1.5 | Opening inventory | | | | | | 10,000 | 3,000 |
| 3.5 | Receipt | 4,000 | 1,600 | | | | 14,000 | 4,600 |
| 6.5 | Issue | | | 7,000 | 0.33 | 2,310* | 7,000 | 2,290* |
| 12.5 | Receipt | 10,000 | 3,100 | | | | 17,000 | 5,390 |
| 15.5 | Issue | | | 6,000 | 0.32 | 1,920 | 11,000 | 3,470 |
| 22.5 | Issue | | | 7,200 | 0.32 | 2,304 | 3,800 | 1,166 |

*The difference in these two values is the result of rounding the price p/unit to 33p. A more accurate unit price of 32.86p would have valued them both at £2,300.

**Test your understanding 6**

**Stores Record Card FIFO**

Material: Pizza

Code: 1626

| Date | Details | Receipts | | Issues | | | Inventory | |
|------|---------|----------|-----|--------|-------|-----|-----------|-----|
| | | Units | £ | Units | Price | £ | Units | £ |
| 1 Dec | Balance b/f | | | | | | 200 | 180 |
| 3 Dec | Receipt | 800 | 800 | | | | 200 | 180 |
| | | | | | | | 800 | 800 |
| | | | | | | | 1,000 | 980 |
| 7 Dec | Issue | | | 200 | 0.9 | 180 | | |
| | | | | 200 | 1.0 | 200 | 600 | 600 |
| | | | | 400 | | 380 | 600 | 600 |
| 14 Dec | Issue | | | 350 | 1.0 | 350 | 250 | 250 |
| 20 Dec | Receipt | 1,200 | 1,140 | | | | 250 | 250 |
| | | | | | | | 1,200 | 1,140 |
| | | | | | | | 1,450 | 1,390 |
| 21 Dec | Issue | | | 250 | 1.0 | 250 | 1,040 | 988 |
| | | | | 160 | 0.95 | 152 | | |
| | | | | 410 | | 402 | | |
| 28 Dec | Issue | | | 475 | 0.95 | 451 | 565 | 537 |

**Test your understanding 7**

**Stores Record Card FIFO**

Material: Protective gloves

Code: 1607

| Date | Details | Receipts | | Issues | | | Inventory | |
|------|---------|----------|----|--------|-------|----|-----------|-----|
| | | Pairs | £ | Pairs | Price | £ | Pairs | £ |
| 1 Jan | Balance b/f | | | | | | 150 | 300 |
| 7 Jan | Purchases | 40 | 76 | | | | 150 | 300 |
| | | | | | | | 40 | 76 |
| | | | | | | | 190 | 376 |
| 15 Jan | Issues | | | 30 | 2.00 | 60 | 120 | 240 |
| | | | | | | | 40 | 76 |
| | | | | | | | 160 | 316 |
| 29 Jan | Issues | | | 35 | 2.00 | 70 | 85 | 170 |
| | | | | | | | 40 | 76 |
| | | | | 35 | | 70 | 125 | 246 |

**Test your understanding 8**

**Stores Record Card AVCO**

Material: Component AB3

Code: 010203

| Date | Receipts | | | Issues | | | Inventory | |
|---|---|---|---|---|---|---|---|---|
| | Units | Cost | £ | Units | Cost | £ | Units | £ |
| 1 Sept | | | | | | | 75 | 3,000 |
| 1 Sept | 100 | 40.00 | 4,000 | | | | 175 | 7,000 |
| 10 Sept | 75 | 42.00 | 3,150 | | | | 250 | 10,150 |
| 15 Sept | | | | 60 | 40.60 | 2,436 | 190 | 7,714 |
| 20 Sept | | | | 55 | 40.60 | 2,233 | 135 | 5,481 |
| 23 Sept | 45 | 42.00 | 1,890 | | | | 180 | 7,371 |
| 30 Sept | | | | 50 | 40.95 | 2,048 | 130 | 5,323 |

Average cost price 10th September = 10,150 ÷ 250 = £40.60 per unit

Value of issues: £2,436 + £2,233 + 2,048 = £6,717

Closing inventory valuation: £5,323

**Test your understanding 9**

### INVENTORY RECORD CARD FOR STEEL COMPONENT MAGIC
### Inventory valuation method: FIFO

| | Receipts | | | Issues | | | Balance | |
|---|---|---|---|---|---|---|---|---|
| Date 20Y0 | Quantity kg | Cost per kg (£) | Total cost (£) | Quantity kg | Cost per kg (£) | Total cost (£) | Quantity kg | £ |
| Balance as at 1 May | | | | | | | 25,000 | 50,000 |
| 9 May | 30,000 | 2.30 | 69,000 | | | | 55,000 | 119,000 |
| 12 May | | | | 40,000 | 25,000 @ 2  15,000 @ 2.30 | 84,500 | 15,000 | 34,500 |
| 18 May | 20,000 | 2.50 | 50,000 | | | | 15,000  20,000  35,000 | 34,500  50,000  84,500 |
| 27 May | | | | 10,000 | 2.30 | 23,000 | 5,000  20,000  25,000 | 11,500  50,000  61,500 |

 **Test your understanding 10**

- **FIFO**

  Issue = (500 × 1.20) + (450 × 1.30) + (50 × 1.50) = £1,260

  Closing inventory = (600 + 585 + 900) − £1,260 = £825

- **AVCO**

  Issue = (600 + 585 + 900)/(500 + 450 + 600) × 1,000 = £1,345

  Closing inventory = (600 + 585 + 900) − £1,345 = £740

**Test your understanding 11**

**B**   AVCO

 **Test your understanding 12**

1   **C**

Equivalent units of production

| | | |
|---|---|---|
| Completed units | 275 × 100% | 275 |
| WIP | 75 × 60% | 45 |
| | | ———— |
| | | 320 |
| | | ———— |

Cost per equivalent unit = $\dfrac{£3,696}{320}$ = £11.55

2

Completed units = £11.55 × 275 EU = £3,176
Closing WIP = £11.55 × 45 EU = £520

 **Test your understanding 13**

**Production**

Omega = 7,200/96 × 100 = 7,500

Vector = 10,340/94 × 100 = 11,000

**Materials**

Omega = 7,500 × 9kg = 67,500kg

Vector = 11,000 × 12kg = 132,000kg

Total materials = (67,500 + 132,000)/98 × 100 = **203,572kg**

**Test your understanding 14**

1    **D**    Dr Materials, Cr Trade Payables Control

2    **D**    Dr Production, Cr Materials

3    **C**    Dr Materials, Cr Bank

4    **C**    Dr Materials, Cr Production

 **Test your understanding 15**

## Stores Record Card

**Department:** Clothing                                **Month:** May 20X8

| Date | Receipts | | | Issues | | | Balance | |
|---|---|---|---|---|---|---|---|---|
| | Quantity | Price £ | Total £ | Quantity | Price £ | Total £ | Quantity | Total £ |
| 1/5 Balance | | | | | | | 2,420 | 12,584 |
| 7/5 | 2,950 | 5.500 | 16,226 | | | | 5,370 | 28,810 |
| 11/5 | 3,200 | 5.700 | 18,239 | | | | 8,570 | 47,049 |
| 14/5 | | | | 4,105 | 5.490 | 22,536 | 4,465 | 24,513 |
| 21/5 | 1,535 | 5.400 | 8,289 | | | | 6,000 | 32,802 |
| 27/5 | | | | 1,800 | 5.467 | 9,841 | 4,200 | 22,961 |
| 30/5 | | | | 2,600 | 5.467 | 14,214 | 1,600 | 8,747 |

The double entry for the issue on the 27 May is:

**D**    Dr Production, Cr Materials

# Labour

**5**

## Introduction

Labour is a large cost for many organisations. The cost of labour will depend on the remuneration (payment) system used by an organisation for example: annual salary, hourly rates and overtime or piecework payments.

| ASSESSMENT CRITERIA |
| --- |
| Record and calculate labour costs (2.1) |
| Prepare cost accounting journals (2.2) |
| Differences between costing systems (2.5) |

## CONTENTS

1 Employee records

2 Remuneration systems

3 Direct and indirect labour costs

4 Integrated bookkeeping – labour

# 1 Employee records

## 1.1 Personnel record details

When an employee joins an organisation it is necessary to record a number of details about them and the details of their job and pay. The personnel department completes this in the individual employee's personnel record.

The type of details that might be kept about an employee are as follows:

- Full name, address and date of birth.

- Personal details such as marital status and emergency contact name and address.

- National Insurance number.

- Previous employment history.

- Educational details.

- Professional qualifications.

- Date of joining organisation.

- Employee number or code.

- Clock number issued.

- Job title and department.

- Rate of pay agreed.

- Holiday details agreed.

- Bank details if salary is to be paid directly into bank account.

- Amendments to any of the details above (such as increases in agreed rates of pay).

- Date of termination of employment (when this takes place) and reasons for leaving.

**Example 1**

Jonathan Minor started to be employed by your organisation on 1 July 2001 as an engineer in the maintenance department of the organisation. He was born on 22 January 1983. His employee code and clock number are M36084 and his agreed rate of pay is £375.60 per week. He is to be paid in cash.

Complete the employee personnel record for Jonathan.

**Solution**

## PERSONNEL RECORD CARD

### PERSONAL DETAILS

| | | | EMPLOYMENT DETAILS |
|---|---|---|---|
| Surname: MINOR<br>Other names: JONATHAN | Address: 24 Hill St<br>Reading | Emergency contact: Jane MINOR<br>24 Hill St<br>Reading | **Previous Employment History** |
| Date of birth: 22/1/83 | Nationality: British | Sex: M | Employer:    Date: |
| Marital status: Single | | Dependents: None | (1) |
| National Insurance Number: WE 22 41 79 J9 | | | (2) |

### EDUCATIONAL DETAILS

(3)

(4)

| Degree: – | | | | Btec/HND: Engineering | TRAINING DETAILS |
|---|---|---|---|---|---|
| A Levels: 2 | O Levels: 0 | | GCSE: 7 | CSEs: 0 | Course    Date: attended: |
| University attended: | | – | | | |
| College attended: | | Reading | | | |
| Schools attended | | Reading High | | | |
| (with dates): | | (1994 – 1999) | | | |
| | | Reading Junior | | | |
| | | (1987 – 1994) | | | |

### JOB DETAILS

| | | OTHER DETAILS |
|---|---|---|
| Date of joining:  1/7/01 | Clock number:    M36084 | Bank account: |
| Job title:  Engineer | Department:    Maintenance | |
| Rate of pay: | Overtime:    1½ times basic | Date of termination: |
| Date         £ | Holiday:    15 days | |
| 1/7/01        375.60 pw | Pension Scheme: | Reason for leaving: |
| | Joined:    1/7/01 | |

## 1.2 Attendance records

In most businesses, **records** are needed of the time spent by each employee in the workplace (attendance time) and time spent on the operations, processes, products or services whilst there (job time). Such timekeeping provides basic data for statutory records, payroll preparation, ascertainment and control of labour costs of an operation or product, overhead distribution (when based on wages or labour hours) and statistical analysis of labour records for determining productivity.

Attendance may be recorded by using a **register**, in which employees note their times of arrival and departure, or by means of a **time recording clock** which stamps the times on a card inserted by each employee. Alternatively, employees may be required to submit periodic **timesheets** showing the amounts of normal and overtime work; these may also include job times.

## 1.3 Holiday records

An employee will usually have an agreed number of days holiday per year. This will usually be paid holiday for salaried employees but may well be unpaid for employees paid by results or on time rates.

It is important for the employer to keep a record of the number of holiday days taken by the employee to ensure that the agreed number per year is not exceeded.

## 1.4 Sickness records

The organisation will have its own policies regarding payment for sick leave as well as legal requirements for statutory sick pay. Therefore, it will be necessary to keep a record of the number of days of sick leave each year for each employee.

## 1.5 Other periods of absence

A record will need to be kept of any other periods of absence by an employee. These might be perfectly genuine such as jury service or training courses or alternatively unexplained periods of absence that must be investigated.

## 1.6 Source of information

Information about an employee's attendance will come from various sources such as clock cards, time sheets and cost cards.

## 1.7 Clock cards

A **clock card** is a document on which is recorded the starting and finishing time of an employee for ascertaining total actual attendance time.

A clock card is usually some form of electronic or computerised recording system whereby when the employee's clock card is entered into the machine the time is recorded. This will give the starting and finishing time for the day and also in some systems break times taken as well.

Clock cards are used as a source document in the calculation of the employee's earnings.

### Example 2

Example of a clock card:

| Works number: | | | | Name: | |
|---|---|---|---|---|---|
| | | Lunch | | | |
| Week ending | In | Out | In | Out | Hours |
| Monday | | | | | |
| Tuesday | | | | | |
| Wednesday | | | | | |
| Thursday | | | | | |
| Friday | | | | | |
| Saturday | | | | | |
| Sunday | | | | | |
| FOREMAN'S SIGNATURE: ................................................ | | | | | |

## 1.8 Daily timesheets

One of these sheets is filled in by each employee (to indicate the time spent by them on each job) and passed to the cost office each day. The total time on the timesheet should correspond to the time shown on the attendance record. Times are recorded daily meaning there is less risk of times being forgotten or manipulated, but these timesheets create a considerable volume of paperwork. Below is an illustration of a daily timesheet.

## Example 3

| Name: | | Frank Smith | | Date: | | 11/6/X5 |
|---|---|---|---|---|---|---|
| Clock number: | | 3 | | Week number: | | 31 |

| Job order number | Description | Time | | Hours worked | Rate | £ |
|---|---|---|---|---|---|---|
| | | Start | Finish | | | |
| 349 | Servicing Ford Ka Y625 AAB | 9.00 | 11.05 | 2.05 | | |
| 372 | Repair to Range Rover TC03 XYZ | 11.05 | 16.30 | 4.25 | | |
| **Signed:** F Smith | | **Certified:** A Foreman | | | **Office ref:** | |

### 1.9 Weekly timesheets

These are similar to daily timesheets but they are passed to the cost office at the end of the week instead of every day (although entries should be made daily in order to avoid error). Weekly timesheets are particularly suitable where there are few job changes in the course of a week.

# 2 Remuneration systems

### 2.1 Introduction

Employees in a business will be remunerated or paid for the work that they do. There are a variety of different ways in which this payment is calculated. The main systems of remuneration are:

- annual salaries
- hourly rates of pay and overtime payments
- piecework payments
- bonus schemes.

Different types of employees within a business may well be paid according to different systems depending upon which is the most appropriate for the type of work that they perform.

**KAPLAN** PUBLISHING

## 2.2 Annual salaries

Annual salaries tend to be paid to management and non-production staff such as administrators, secretaries, accounts staff, etc. The annual salary is simply divided by the 12 months in the year and that is the amount of gross pay for that employee for the month.

 **Example 4**

The sales manager of a business has an annual salary of £30,000.

**What is the gross amount of his/her pay each month?**

**Solution**

| Monthly gross pay | = | £30,000/12 |
|---|---|---|
| | = | £2,500 |

## 2.3 Hourly rates and overtime payments

Many production and manual workers will be paid for every hour that they work. Normally hourly paid workers will have a standard number of hours that they work each week. If they work for more than this number of hours then they will have worked overtime, which will usually be paid at more than the basic hourly rate.

Overtime has two terms that you need to be aware of – overtime payment and overtime premium.

- The **overtime payment** is the **total** amount paid for hours worked above the normal number of hours.

- The **overtime premium** is the **extra** paid above the normal rate for those overtime hours. For example, if an employee is paid time and a half for any hours above their basic, then the 'half' is the premium.

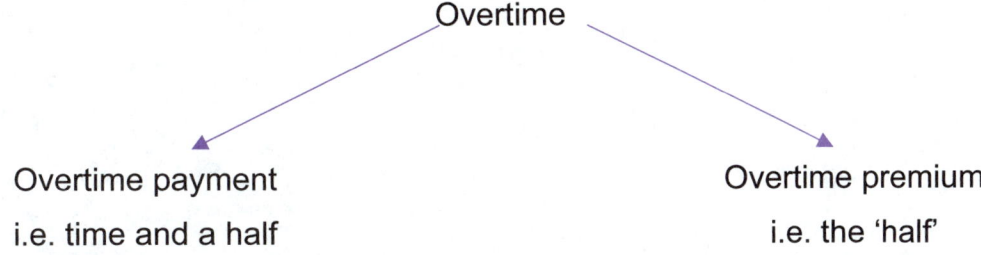

Overtime

Overtime payment

i.e. time and a half

Overtime premium

i.e. the 'half'

This distinction is often necessary for costing purposes, as the premium part of the overtime may be classified separately from the overtime hours at basic rate.

Overtime can be worked for a couple of reasons – **general pressures** in the workplace or to meet the demands of a **specific customer request**. This has an impact on how the overtime is treated in the accounts of a business.

Whether the **overtime premium** is treated as a direct or indirect labour cost will depend upon the reason the overtime was worked:

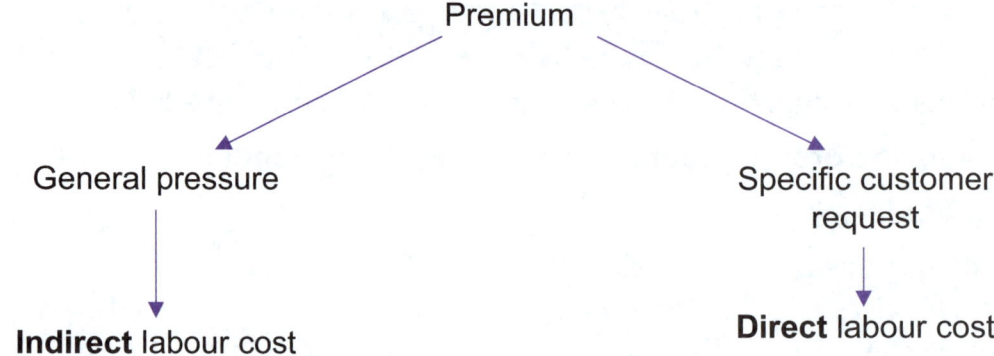

Be careful when answering questions on labour costs – make sure to check what information you are being asked for. Do you need to show the overtime payment or premium? If an exam question asks for the payment then you would split your answer based on normal hours at basic rate and overtime hours at the basic rate plus the premium. If the question asks for premium you would record all the hours worked at a basic rate and then show the premium for the overtime hours separately.

## Example 5

An employee works for a standard week of 40 hours at an hourly rate of pay of £8.20. Any overtime hours are paid at time and a half.

In one week the employee works for 45 hours.

**(i)** **What is the gross pay, showing the overtime payment?**

**(ii)** **What is the gross pay, showing the overtime premium?**

**Solution**

(i)

| | £ |
|---|---|
| Basic hours 40 × £8.20 | 328.00 |
| Overtime payment 5 × (£8.20 × 1.5) | 61.50 |
| | ——— |
| Gross pay | 389.50 |
| | ——— |

(ii)

| | £ |
|---|---|
| Basic hours 45 × £8.20 | 369.00 |
| Overtime premium 5 × (£8.20 × 0.5) | 20.50 |
| | ——— |
| Gross pay | 389.50 |
| | ——— |

## Test your understanding 1

Below is the weekly timesheet for Thomas Yung (employee number Y4791), who is paid as follows:

- For a basic six-hour shift every day from Monday to Friday – basic pay.

- For any overtime in excess of the basic six hours, on any day from Monday to Friday – the extra hours are paid at time-and-a-half.

- For three contracted hours each Saturday morning – basic pay.

- For any hours in excess of three hours on Saturday – the extra hours are paid at double time.

- For any hours worked on Sunday – paid at double time.

**Complete the columns headed Basic pay, Overtime premium and Total pay. Zero figures should be entered in cells where appropriate.**

*Just overtime* (handwritten note)

| Employee's weekly timesheet for week ending 12 December | | | | | | |
|---|---|---|---|---|---|---|
| Name: Thomas Yung | | | | Cost centre: Machining | | |
| Employee number: Y4791 | | | | Basic Pay per hour: £12 | | |
| | Hours spent on: | | Notes | Basic pay £ | Overtime premium £ | Total pay £ |
| | Production | Indirect work | | | | |
| Monday | 6 | 2 | 1 – 3 pm cleaning machinery | 96 | 12 | 108 |
| Tuesday | 2 | 4 | 9 am – 1 pm training course | 72 | 0 | 72 |
| Wednesday | 8 | | | 96 | 12 | 108 |
| Thursday | 6 | | | 72 | 0 | 72 |
| Friday | 6 | 1 | 2 – 3 pm health and safety training | 84 | 6 | 90 |
| Saturday | 6 | | | 72 | 36 | 108 |
| Sunday | 3 | | | 36 | 36 | 72 |
| Total | 37 | 7 | | 528 | 102 | 630 |

## Test your understanding 2

An employee's basic week is 40 hours at a rate of pay of £5 per hour. Overtime is paid at 'time and a half'.

**What is the wage cost of this employee if they work for 45 hours in a week?**

A    £225.00

B    £237.50

C    £300.00

D    £337.50

22S

 **Test your understanding 3**

The following information relates to direct labour costs incurred during July 20Y0:

| | |
|---|---|
| Normal time hours worked | 8,000 hours |
| Overtime at time and a half worked | 1,500 hours |
| Overtime at double time worked | 1,000 hours |
| Total hours worked | 10,500 hours |
| Normal time hourly rate | £7 per hour |

Overtime premiums paid are included as part of direct labour costs.

**What is the total cost of direct labour for the month of July 20Y0.**

A    £91,000

B    £85,750

C    £70,000

D    £73,500

18

## 2.4    Piecework payments

Piecework rates are where the employee is paid per unit of output. The rate will often be based upon the standard (expected) time per unit. This method is an example of 'payment by results'.

 **Example 6**

G MacHue works in the Scottish Highlands producing carved wooden animals for a small company supplying the tourist market. In week 26 G worked 45 hours and production was:

| | **Standard time allowed/unit** |
|---|---|
| 6 Stags | 2.0 hours |
| 5 Otters | 1.5 hours |
| 12 Owls | 1.0 hour |
| 6 Golden Eagles | 2.0 hours |

G is paid £5 per standard hour of production (irrespective of actual time worked).

**What are G's earnings for week 26?**

**Solution**

|  |  | £ |
|---|---|---|
| Stags | 6 × 2 × £5 | 60.00 |
| Otters | 5 × 1.5 × £5 | 37.50 |
| Owls | 12 × 1 × £5 | 60.00 |
| Golden Eagles | 6 × 2 × £5 | 60.00 |
|  |  | 217.50 |

 **Test your understanding 4**

A company operates a piecework system of remuneration. Employees must work for a minimum of 40 hours per week. J produces the following output for a particular week:

| Product | Quantity | Standard time per item (hours) | Total actual time (hours) |
|---|---|---|---|
| Gaskets | 50 | 0.2 | 9 |
| Drive belts | 200 | 0.06 | 14 |
| Sprockets | 100 | 0.1 | 12 |
| Gears | 10 | 0.7 | 6 |
|  |  |  | 41 |

J is paid £6.20 per standard hour worked.

**What are J's earnings for the week?**

A    £129.60

B    £254.20

C    £241.80

D    £498.48

**Advantages of the piecework system**

- It produces a constant labour cost per unit.

- It **encourages efficient work** – an employee taking more than the standard time per unit will only be paid for the standard time. In order for this to motivate, the employee must accept the standard as fair.

To increase motivation, a **differential piecework system** may be implemented, whereby the piece rate is increased for higher output levels.

**Disadvantages of the piecework system**

- Employees **lack security of income**, so may become demotivated.

- The employee can be **penalised** for low levels of production due to factors that are outside his/her control (e.g. machine breakdown).

## 2.5 Guaranteed minimum payment

To overcome these disadvantages, the **straight piecework rate** may be accompanied by a **guaranteed minimum payment** (weekly or daily).

---

### :Ö: Example 7

| | | |
|---|---|---|
| Standard rate per hour | = | £4.50 |
| Guaranteed minimum per week | = | 35 hours |
| Actual production: 10 units @ 3 hours per unit. | | |
| **Calculate the weekly pay.** | | |
| **Solution** | | |
| Standard hours | = | 10 × 3 = 30 hours |
| Pay | = | 30 × £4.50 = £135 |
| Subject to guaranteed minimum pay | = | 35 × £4.50 = £157.50 |
| Therefore weekly pay | = | £157.50 |
| The employee is paid whichever is the highest value. | | |

---

140

 **Test your understanding 5**

Q is paid £3.00 for every unit that is produced but there is a guaranteed wage of £28.00 per eight-hour day. In a particular week Q produces the following number of units:

Monday          12 units
Tuesday         14 units
Wednesday        9 units
Thursday        14 units
Friday           8 units

**Q's wages for the week are:**

A    £176

B    £175

C    £172

D    £171

 **Test your understanding 6**

Continuing with the example of Q above.

**What would be Q's weekly wage if the guarantee were for £140 per week rather than £28 per day?**

A    £176

B    £175

C    £172

D    £171

### 2.6    Bonus schemes

Bonus schemes are a compromise between a day rate and a piecework system. Earnings will comprise:

(a)    a day rate amount, based on hours worked, and

(b)    a bonus based on quantity produced (usually above a certain standard) or on time saved in relation to standard time allowance for the output achieved.

**KAPLAN** PUBLISHING

**Example 8**

On a particular day, F worked for 8.5 hours, producing 15 units. The standard time allowance for each unit is 40 minutes. F's basic hourly rate is £4.50 and is paid a bonus for time saved from standard at 60% of basic hourly rate.

**Calculate F's pay for the day.**

**Solution**

|  |  | £ |
|---|---|---|
| Day rate = 8.5 × £4.50 |  | 38.25 |
| Bonus |  |  |
| Standard time 15 × 40/60 | 10 hours |  |
| Actual time | 8.5 hours |  |
|  | ———— |  |
| Time saved | 1.5 hours |  |
|  | ———— |  |
| Bonus = 1.5 × £4.50 × 60% |  | 4.05 |
|  |  | ———— |
| Total |  | 42.30 |
|  |  | ———— |

## 2.7 Group bonus schemes

In the case of, for example, an assembly line, where it is impossible for an individual worker on the line to increase productivity without the others also doing so, a group bonus scheme may be used. The bonus is calculated by reference to the output of the group and split between the members of the group (often equally).

 **Example 9**

Ten employees work as a group. The standard output for the group is 200 units per hour and when this is exceeded each employee in the group is paid a bonus in addition to the hourly wage.

The bonus percentage is calculated as follows:

$$50\% \times \frac{\text{Excess units}}{\text{Standard units}}$$

The percentage is then applied to the standard hourly wage rate of £7.20 to calculate the bonus per hour for each employee:

The following is one week's record of production by the group:

| | Hours worked | Production units |
|---|---|---|
| Monday | 90 | 24,500 |
| Tuesday | 88 | 20,600 |
| Wednesday | 90 | 24,200 |
| Thursday | 84 | 20,100 |
| Friday | 88 | 20,400 |
| Saturday | 40 | 10,200 |
| | 480 | 120,000 |

**Solution**

The standard number of units for the time worked:

$480 \times 200 = 96,000$ units

The number of excess units produced:

$120,000 - 96,000 = 24,000$ units

The bonus calculation:

$24,000/96,000 \times 50\% = 0.125 = 12.5\%$

Individual hourly bonus:

$£7.20 \times 0.125 = £0.90$

Group bonus:

$480 \times £0.90 = £432$

If K worked for 42 hours and was paid £6.00 per hour as a basic rate what would be the total pay be for this week?

| Basic | = | $42 \times £6.00$ | = | £252 |
|---|---|---|---|---|
| Bonus | = | $42 \times £0.90$ | = | £37.80 |
| Total | | | = | £289.80 |

**Test your understanding 7**

Brown and Jones is a firm of joiners. They have a workshop and employ six craftsmen. One of the employees is engaged on the production of standard doors for a local firm of builders.

This employee is paid a bonus based on time saved. The time saved is paid at a rate of 50% of the basic hourly rate.

In addition to the bonus, hours worked over the basic 40 per week are paid at time and a half.

In the week ended 13 February 20X1 the following details were available.

| | |
|---|---|
| Basic hourly rate | £6.00 |
| Time allowed per standard door | 2 hours |
| Doors produced | 25 |
| Time worked | 45 hours |

**The employee's gross pay for the week ended 13 February 20X1 is:**

A    £270

B    £285

C    £300

D    £315

## 2.8    Holiday pay

As well as the normal payments of wages and salaries, there are other labour costs which include holiday pay and training time.

**Holiday pay** is non-productive, but it is nevertheless charged to the cost of production by allocating the full year's holiday pay to overhead and charging it to production for the whole year.

Alternatively, wages may be allocated at **labour rates inflated to include holiday pay** and other non-productive time costs.

## 2.9    Training time and supervisors' wages

Wages paid during a period of **training** may be charged partly to the job and partly to production overhead. The fact that learners work more slowly than trained employees is offset by the learners' lower rate of pay. Apprentices' remuneration will be charged to a separate account.

Normally, **supervisors' wages** are treated as part of department overhead unless only a particular job is concerned. Where instruction is being given, the remuneration of instructors and supervisors may be included in training time.

## 2.10 Direct labour cost per unit of production or service

Once the direct labour cost has been identified and calculated it can be related to a unit of product or service:

Direct labour cost per unit = total labour cost ÷ total number of units produced.

## 2.11 Direct labour cost per equivalent unit of finished production

In some time periods the units of product or service may not be fully completed with respect to the labour input when the wages are paid. To ensure that each unit is assigned a fair share of the labour cost incurred in the period the cost per equivalent unit (EU) is calculated.

 **Example 10**

A direct worker has been working on 70 units. He/she has fully completed 40 units but 30 units are only 50% complete with regards labour. The direct worker has been paid £165 for the work carried out so far.

**Calculate the cost per equivalent unit**

40 units that are fully complete = 40 × 100% = 40 EU
30 units that are 50% complete = 30 × 50% = 15 EU
Total equivalent units = 40 + 15 = 55 EU
Therefore the direct labour cost per equivalent unit = £165 ÷ 55 = £3 per EU

 **Test your understanding 8**

In July a bonus payment was based on equivalent units. Employees will receive 35% of their basic hourly rate for every equivalent unit in excess of target. Rates of pay are £8. The target production is 400 units.

At the end of July 300 units were completed and there were 200 units of work in progress that was 100% complete for material and 75% complete for labour.

**Calculate the number of equivalent units with regards to labour and the bonus payable.**

# 3 Direct and indirect labour costs

## 3.1 Recap on direct and indirect costs

- A **direct** cost is an item of cost that is traceable directly to a cost unit.

- An **indirect** cost is a cost that either cannot be identified with any one finished unit. Such costs are often referred to as 'overheads'.

We have seen that there are a variety of different methods of remunerating employees and a number of different elements to this remuneration. For costing purposes, the total labour costs must be split between the **direct labour costs**, which can be charged to the units of **production** and any **indirect labour costs**, which are charged as **overheads** to the relevant cost centre.

## 3.2 Production workers

The wages that are paid to the production workers will **on the whole be direct labour costs** so long as they **relate directly** to the production of output, known as basic rate. The direct labour cost will also include the basic rate for any overtime hours but the **overtime premium** may be treated as an indirect cost.

## 3.3 Overtime premium

Whether the overtime premium is treated as a direct or indirect labour cost will depend upon the reasons for the overtime:

- If the overtime is worked due to a customer's specific instruction, then the overtime premium will be treated as a direct labour cost.

- If the overtime is due to general pressure of work, then the premium is treated as an indirect labour cost.

## 3.4 Holiday pay

Holiday pay is normally treated as an **indirect** labour cost as **no production** is occurring.

## 3.5 Training time

The hours paid for the labour force to train are treated as an **indirect** labour cost as **no production** is occurring.

## 3.6    Idle time

Controllable idle time is treated as an indirect labour cost. Uncontrollable idle time is treated as an expense in the costing income statement.

It should obviously be prevented as far as possible. It is important to analyse the causes of idle time so that necessary corrective action can be taken.

There are three groups of causes of idle time:

(a)    Productive causes (e.g. machine breakdown, power failure or time spent waiting for work, tools, materials or instructions).

(b)    Administrative causes (e.g. surplus capacity, policy changes, unforeseen drop in demand).

(c)    Economic causes (e.g. seasonal fluctuations in demand, cyclical fluctuations in demand, changes in demand because of tax changes).

## 3.7    Management and supervisors' salaries

Management salaries and supervisors' salaries are all labour costs that are **not related to actual production** of the cost units, therefore they are all treated as **indirect labour costs**.

---

### Test your understanding 9

G Dickson is a football manufacturer.

**Classify the following costs by nature (direct or indirect) in the table below.**

| Cost | Direct | Indirect |
|---|---|---|
| Basic pay for production workers | ☑ | ☐ |
| Supervisors wages | ☐ | ☑ |
| Bonus for salesman | ☐ | ☑ |
| Production workers overtime premium due to general pressures | ☐ | ☑ |
| Holiday pay for production workers | ☐ | ☐ |
| Sick pay for supervisors | ☐ | ☑ |
| Time spent by production workers cleaning the machinery | ☑ | ☑ |

---

# 4 Integrated bookkeeping – labour

## 4.1 Introduction

The costs of a business have to be recorded in a bookkeeping system. Many businesses use an **integrated bookkeeping system** where the ledger accounts kept provide the necessary **information for both costing and financial accounting**.

## 4.2 Wages control account

Accounting for wages and salaries is based upon two fundamental principles:

- The accounts must reflect the full cost to the employer of employing someone.

- The accounts must show the payable for PAYE and NIC that must be paid over to the HMRC.

There are three accounts to record transactions:

- The wages expense account, which shows the total expense to business i.e. Gross Pay and Employer's NIC.

- The PAYE/NIC account/Trade Union account/Pension account which is used to record the liability owed to HMRC/due to Trade Union/ Pension Company.

- The wages and salaries control account is used as a control. One side of each double entry is put through the control account. This account is cleared out each payroll run and there is never a balance brought down.

The **wages and salaries control account** can also be called the **labour cost account** in a management accounting system.

---

### Example 11

**Wages and salaries control account**

| | £ | | £ |
|---|---|---|---|
| Bank (1) | | Production (4) | |
| HMRC liability (2) | | Production overheads (5) | |
| Pension (3) | | | |
| | ——— | | ——— |
| | ——— | | ——— |

(1) The labour cost **incurred** or **net pay** is paid out of the **bank** to the employees.

(2) The amount of PAYE, Employees and Employers NIC that is owed to the HMRC is recorded in the control account as a debit and in the PAYE/NIC account as a credit or liability.

(3) Pensions, or other payments that are made out of the employees gross wage, will also need to be recorded.

(4) **Direct labour costs** are transferred out of the wages control account via a credit entry to the production account. The production account can also be referred to as Work in Progress (WIP).

(5) **Indirect labour costs** are collected in the production overheads account. They are transferred there via a credit entry out of the wages control account and then debited in the production overheads account.

---

### Test your understanding 10

**What are the correct journal entries the following accounting transactions?**

1 Payment for labour:

    A    Dr Bank, Cr Wages Control

    B    Dr Trade Payables Control, Cr Wages Control

    C    Dr Wages Control, Cr Bank

    D    Dr Wages Control, Cr Trade Payables Control

2    Analysis of direct labour:

A    Dr Bank, Cr Wages Control

B    Dr Wages Control, Cr Bank

C    Dr Wages Control, Cr Production

(D)   Dr Production, Cr Wages Control

3    Analysis of payment for labour relating to overtime premium that was due to a specific customer request:

(A)   Dr Production, Cr Wages Control

B    Dr Production Overheads, Cr Wages Control

C    Dr Wages Control, Cr Production

D    Dr Wages Control, Cr Production Overheads

4    Analysis of payment for labour relating to overtime premium that was due to general work pressures.

A    Dr Wages Control, Cr Production

B    Dr Wages Control, Cr Production Overheads

C    Dr Production, Cr Wages Control

(D)   Dr Production Overheads, Cr Wages Control

## Test your understanding 11

Below is the weekly timesheet for Ekta Plasm (employee number EP0516), who is paid as follows:

- For a basic six-hour shift every day from Monday to Friday – basic pay.

- For any overtime in excess of the basic six hours, on any day from Monday to Friday – the extra hours are paid at time-and-a-third.

- For three contracted hours each Saturday morning – basic pay.

- For any hours in excess of three hours on Saturday – the extra hours are paid at double time.

- For any hours worked on Sunday – paid at double time.

- Any overtime worked is due to general work pressures.

**Complete the columns headed Basic pay, Overtime premium and Total pay. Zero figures should be entered in cells where appropriate.**

| Employee's weekly timesheet for week ending 24 April | | | | | | |
|---|---|---|---|---|---|---|
| **Name:** Ekta Plasm | | | | **Cost centre:** Sewing | | |
| **Employee number:** EP0516 | | | | **Basic Pay per hour:** £9 | | |
| | Hours spent on: | | Notes | Basic pay £ | Overtime premium £ | Total pay £ |
| | Production | Indirect work | | | | |
| Monday | 6 | | | | | |
| Tuesday | 3 | 3 | 10 am – 1 pm training course | | | |
| Wednesday | 8 | | | | | |
| Thursday | 7 | | | | | |
| Friday | 6 | 1 | 2 – 3 pm health and safety training | | | |
| Saturday | 5 | | | | | |
| Sunday | 3 | | | | | |
| Total | 38 | 4 | | | | |

**Complete the Wages Control account below from the timesheet above.**

### Wages control account

| | £ | | £ |
|---|---|---|---|
| Bank | | Production | |
| | | Production overheads | |
| | _____ | | _____ |
| | _____ | | _____ |

# 5 Summary

This chapter has considered the **methods of payment** of labour that may be used by organisations. These may be annual salaries, hourly rates of pay, performance related pay (piecework) and profit related pay (bonus schemes). In order to pay the correct amount to employees there must be detailed recording of the time spent at work by each employee on time sheets or by a time clock and clock cards.

The distribution between **direct and indirect labour** costs is an important one.

Direct labour costs including the following:

- production workers' wages (excluding overtime premiums)

- bonus payments for production workers

- overtime premiums where overtime was worked at the specific request of the customer.

Indirect labour costs include the following:

- holiday pay

- training time

- idle time

- supervisors' salaries

- management salaries

- overtime premiums where overtime was due to the general pressure of work

- production supervisors' wages that cannot be allocated to specific cost units.

## Test your understanding answers

 ### Test your understanding 1

| Employee's weekly timesheet for week ending 12 December | | | | | | |
|---|---|---|---|---|---|---|
| Name: Thomas Yung | | | | Cost centre: Machining | | |
| Employee number: Y4791 | | | | Basic Pay per hour: £12 | | |
| | Hours spent on: | | Notes | Basic pay £ | Overtime premium £ | Total pay £ |
| | Production | Indirect work | | | | |
| Monday | 6 | 2 | 1 – 3 pm cleaning machinery | 96 | 12 | 108 |
| Tuesday | 2 | 4 | 9 am – 1 pm training course | 72 | 0 | 72 |
| Wednesday | 8 | | | 96 | 12 | 108 |
| Thursday | 6 | | | 72 | 0 | 72 |
| Friday | 6 | 1 | 2 – 3 pm health and safety training | 84 | 6 | 90 |
| Saturday | 6 | | | 72 | 36 | 108 |
| Sunday | 3 | | | 36 | 36 | 72 |
| Total | 37 | 7 | | 528 | 102 | 630 |

 ### Test your understanding 2

**B**

| | | |
|---|---|---|
| Basic | = 40 × 5 | = £200 |
| Overtime | = 5 × 5 × 1.5 | = £37.50 |
| Total pay | | = £237.50 |

**Test your understanding 3**

**B**

| | |
|---|---|
| Basic pay 10,500 hrs @ £7 | £73,500 |
| Overtime 1,500 hrs @ 3.5 | £5,250 |
| Overtime 1,000 hrs @ £7 | £7,000 |
| | ———— |
| | £85,750 |
| | ———— |

 **Test your understanding 4**

**C**   £241.80

Multiply the quantity by the standard time per item for each item to give a standard time of 39 hours. This is multiplied by the rate per standard hour. 39 × £6.20 = £241.80.

 **Test your understanding 5**

**A**

Total weekly wage:

| | £ |
|---|---|
| Monday (12 × £3) | 36 |
| Tuesday (14 × £3) | 42 |
| Wednesday (guaranteed) | 28 |
| Thursday (14 × £3) | 42 |
| Friday (guaranteed) | 28 |
| | ——— |
| | 176 |
| | ——— |

## Test your understanding 6

**D**

|  | £ |
|---|---|
| Monday (12 × £3) | 36 |
| Tuesday (14 × £3) | 42 |
| Wednesday (9 × £3) | 27 |
| Thursday (14 × £3) | 42 |
| Friday (8 × £3) | 24 |
|  | ___ |
|  | 171 |
|  | ___ |

As the weekly earnings are above £140, the guaranteed amount is not relevant to the calculations in this instance.

## Test your understanding 7

**C**

Gross wage:

| | |
|---|---|
| Basic pay – 45 hrs @ £6 | £270.00 |
| Overtime – 5 hrs @ £3 | £15.00 |
| Bonus: | |
| 25 doors × 2 hours = 50 hours allowed | |
| Time taken – 45 hours | |
| Time saved – 5 hours × £3 | £15.00 |
| | _____ |
| | £300.00 |
| | _____ |

## Test your understanding 8

Completed units = 300 × 100% = 300 EU

Work in progress units = 200 × 75% = 150 EU

Total EU = 450 EU

Bonus = (450 – 400) × (£8 × 35%) = £140

### Test your understanding 9

| Cost | Direct | Indirect |
|---|---|---|
| Basic pay for production workers | ☑ | ☐ |
| Supervisors wages | ☐ | ☑ |
| Bonus for salesman | ☐ | ☑ |
| Production workers overtime premium due to general pressures | ☐ | ☑ |
| Holiday pay for production workers | ☐ | ☑ |
| Sick pay for supervisors | ☐ | ☑ |
| Time spent by production workers cleaning the machinery | ☐ | ☑ |

### Test your understanding 10

1    Payment for labour:

    **C**    Dr Wages control, Cr Bank

2    Analysis of direct labour:

    **D**    Dr Production, Cr Wages control

3    Analysis of payment for labour relating to overtime premium that was due to a specific customer request:

    **A**    Dr Production, Cr Wages control

4    Analysis of payment for labour relating to overtime premium that was due to general work pressures.

    **D**    Dr Production Overheads, Cr Wages control

**Test your understanding 11**

### Employee's weekly timesheet for week ending 24 April

| Name: | Ekta Plasm | Cost centre: | Sewing |
|---|---|---|---|
| Employee number: | EP0516 | Basic Pay per hour: | £9 |

| | Hours spent on: | | Notes | Basic pay £ | Overtime premium £ | Total pay £ |
|---|---|---|---|---|---|---|
| | Production | Indirect work | | | | |
| Monday | 6 | | | 54 | 0 | 54 |
| Tuesday | 3 | 3 | 10 am – 1 pm training course | 54 | 0 | 54 |
| Wednesday | 8 | | | 72 | 6 | 78 |
| Thursday | 7 | | | 63 | 3 | 66 |
| Friday | 6 | 1 | 2 – 3 pm health and safety training | 63 | 3 | 66 |
| Saturday | 5 | | | 45 | 18 | 63 |
| Sunday | 3 | | | 27 | 27 | 54 |
| Total | 38 | 4 | | 378 | 57 | 435 |

### Wages control account

| | £ | | £ |
|---|---|---|---|
| Bank | 435 | Production | 342 |
| | | Production overheads | 93 |
| | ─── | | ─── |
| | 435 | | 435 |
| | ─── | | ─── |

Production is **direct** labour cost **only** therefore the cost is:

Basic hours less the time spent on non-production activities

£378 – (4 × 9) = £342

Production overheads are the **indirect costs** (the overtime is worked due to general work pressure so is classed as indirect) therefore the cost is:

57 + (4 × 9) = £93

# Overheads

6

## Introduction

This chapter looks at how **overheads** (indirect expenses) are **allocated** or **apportioned** to cost centres and how overheads are then **absorbed** into the cost of a product via an **overhead absorption rate**. This chapter applies **absorption costing principles**.

| ASSESSMENT CRITERIA | CONTENTS |
|---|---|
| Record and calculate overhead costs (2.1) | 1 Expenses |
| Prepare cost accounting journals (2.2) | 2 Overheads |
| Calculate and attribute overhead costs using traditional methods (3.1) | 3 Allocation and apportionment |
| Calculate overhead recovery rates using traditional methods (3.2) | 4 Reapportionment |
| Calculate overhead recovery rates using activity based costing (3.3) | 5 Absorption |
| Under- or over-recovery of overheads (3.4) | 6 Under/over absorption of overheads |
| | 7 Integrated bookkeeping – overheads |
| | 8 Activity based costing |

# 1 Expenses

## 1.1 Introduction

Costs incurred by a business, other than material and labour costs, are known as expenses.

Expenses of a business can cover a wide variety of areas. They might include:

| Production Expenses | Selling and Distribution Expenses | Administration Expenses |
|---|---|---|
| Cost of power | Advertising costs | Rent of office buildings |
| Factory rental | Packaging costs | Telephone bills |
| Light and heat cost | Costs of delivering goods to the customer | Postage costs |
| Depreciation of machinery | Warehouse rental for storage of goods | Auditors fees |

This chapter will mainly focus on the production expenses and how to relate them to the products of a business.

Remember that direct costs are those that can be related directly to a cost unit, whilst indirect costs (overheads) cannot be specifically traced to individual units.

## 1.2 Direct expenses

Expenses are far more likely to be indirect; however, some examples of direct expenses are given below. Direct expenses can be identified with a specific cost unit and are production costs.

- **Royalty or patent costs** payable for use of a particular component, technique, trade name, etc. in the production or service.

- **Sub-contracted charges**: if the business hires another company or a self-employed person to perform a particular function directly related to the product or service provided, this will be treated as a direct expense.

  For example, a building contractor will very often use sub-contractors to carry out electrical and plumbing work on a particular contract. The charge invoiced to the builder for this work (which will include both labour and materials) will be analysed as a direct expense of the contract.

- Expenses associated with **machinery or equipment** used for a particular job: hire charges, maintenance, power, etc.

## 1.3 Indirect expenses

**Indirect expenses** cannot be identified with a specific cost unit. They are far more common and can be categorised in various ways, depending upon the organisational structure of the business and the level of detail required in the cost accounts.

Depending upon their nature, indirect expenses may be:

* production costs (production overheads); or

* non-production costs (non-production overheads).

**NOTE: In the real world the term 'expenses' could include both direct and indirect components. In the exam, however, expenses are always treated simply as 'overheads' with no separation into direct and indirect elements.**

# 2 Overheads

## 2.1 Introduction

There are three categories of indirect costs (making up total overheads):

* indirect materials

* indirect labour

* indirect expenses.

## 2.2 Production and non-production overheads

**Production overheads** are included in the total production cost of a product. They could include factory rent, rates, insurance, light, heat, power and other factory running cost.

Production overheads of a factory can include the following costs:

* heating the factory

* lighting the factory

* renting the factory.

Production may take place over a number of different cost centres and each centre should be assigned with its fair share of overhead cost. There may also be a number of service cost centres that provide support to the production cost centres.

Examples of production cost centres include:

- Assembly

- Machining

- Finishing.

Examples of production service cost centres include:

- Maintenance

- Canteen

- Stores.

For a **service industry**, it is more difficult to make a clear distinction between production and non-production overheads. For example, there is rarely a building that is devoted entirely to the provision of the service itself (i.e. equivalent to a factory) that does not also house the administrative, financial, selling and other functions of the business. Thus it is common to include most, if not all, of a service industry's expenses under the other functional headings described below.

**Non-production overheads** can be split into different categories determined by why or how the cost is incurred:

(a) **Administrative costs**

These include the running costs of non-production buildings; staff and other expenses for non-production departments; management salaries and training costs.

(b) **Selling and distribution costs**

These include sales persons' salaries, commissions; running costs of sales showrooms and offices; delivery vehicle expenses; packaging costs; advertising and promotional costs.

(c) **Finance costs**

These include loan and overdraft interest payable; bank charges; lease interest element; cost of irrecoverable debts.

(d) **Legal and professional charges**

These include auditors', accountants', solicitors', financial advisors' fees; professional subscriptions; professional indemnity insurance; licence costs.

The main reason for wanting to calculate full costs are to value inventories of manufactured goods and also to calculate a selling price based on full costs.

# 3    Allocation and apportionment

## 3.1   Allocation, apportionment and absorption

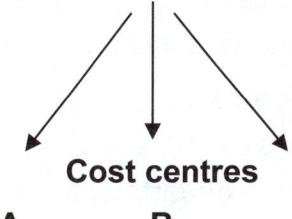

**Step 1:** Allocation or Apportionment

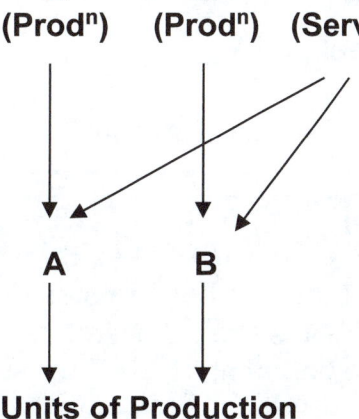

**Step 2:** Reapportion

**Step 3:** Absorb

The purpose of **allocation** and **apportionment** is to attribute production overhead costs to production cost centres.

Where a business has a mix of production and service cost centres any production overheads in the service cost centres are **reapportioned** to the production centres.

The purpose of **absorption** is to assign the production overheads to the units produced by the cost centre.

There are 3 steps to achieving the process:

**Step 1:** Overheads are allocated or apportioned to cost centres using suitable bases.

**Step 2:** Any service centre costs are reapportioned to production centres using suitable bases.

**Step 3:** Overheads are absorbed into units of production using suitable bases.

## 3.2 Allocation

 **Definition**

When an overhead relates entirely to one production or service centre it can be **wholly attributed** to that single production or service centre. This is allocation.

Examples of costs that relate to one specific cost centre are given below:

| Cost centre | Allocated cost |
|---|---|
| Accounts | Accounting overhead |
| Machining department | Insurance of machines |
| Stores | Stores wages |
| Canteen | Maintenance of kitchen equipment |

## 3.3 Apportionment

 **Definition**

When an overhead relates to **more than one** production and/or service centre it is shared over these centres on a fair or suitable basis. This is apportionment.

Examples of bases of apportioning overheads are as follows:

| Nature of cost | Possible bases of apportionment |
|---|---|
| Rent and rates | Floor space (m$^2$) |
| Lighting and heating | Usage of electricity (KwH) |
| Insurance of inventory | Value of inventory |
| Depreciation | Carrying amount of asset |
| Supervisors' salaries | Time spent supervising |

**KAPLAN** PUBLISHING

**Example 1**

**Example of cost allocation and apportionment**

A Ltd has three cost centres: assembly, machining and maintenance. It has the following budgeted overheads costs for the year to December 20X4:

|  | £ |
|---|---|
| Oil for machining department | 2,000 |
| Salary of assembly department supervisor | 20,000 |
| Insurance of machines in machining department | 4,000 |
| Rent of factory | 16,000 |
| Maintenance salaries | 40,000 |
| Canteen costs for factory | 15,000 |
|  | 97,000 |

**Required:**

(a)  Allocate any costs to the relevant cost centres.

(b)  Apportion the costs that cannot be allocated using the information below:

|  | Assembly | Machining | Maintenance | Total |
|---|---|---|---|---|
| Area (m²) | 3,000 | 3,000 | 2,000 | 8,000 |
| No of employees | 15 | 10 | 5 | 30 |

**Solution**

Looking at the overhead costs it is possible to identify 4 costs that are wholly attributable to one centre – Oil for **machining**, supervisors' salary for **assembly**, insurance for the machines in the **machining** department and salaries for the **maintenance** department. These costs are allocated to specific departments.

The remaining costs relate to more than one centre so need to be shared or apportioned across the centres they relate to.

To do this, the calculation is:

$$\frac{\text{Total overhead}}{\text{Total of basis}} \times \text{centre basis}$$

**Rent – area**

Assembly

$$\frac{16,000}{8,000} \times 3,000 = 6,000$$

Machining

$$\frac{16,000}{8,000} \times 3,000 = 6,000$$

Maintenance

$$\frac{16,000}{8,000} \times 2,000 = 4,000$$

**Canteen costs – staff**

Assembly

$$\frac{15,000}{30} \times 15 = 7,500$$

Machining

$$\frac{15,000}{30} \times 10 = 5,000$$

Maintenance

$$\frac{15,000}{30} \times 5 = 2,500$$

It is also possible to use percentages or fractions to share the costs over the cost centres. With some information percentages or fractions will be a quicker and easier to use to perform the apportionment and may save you time in the exam.

| | Assembly | Machining | Maintenance | Total |
|---|---|---|---|---|
| Area (m²) | 3,000 | 3,000 | 2,000 | 8,000 |
| Area as a % | $\frac{3,000}{8,000}$ × 100 = 37.5% | $\frac{3,000}{8,000}$ × 100 = 37.5% | $\frac{2,000}{8,000}$ ×100 = 25% | $\frac{8,000}{8,000}$ ×100 = 100% |
| No of employees | 15 | 10 | 5 | 30 |
| Employees as fractions | $\frac{15}{30} = \frac{1}{2}$ | $\frac{10}{30} = \frac{1}{3}$ | $\frac{5}{30} = \frac{1}{6}$ | $\frac{30}{30} = 1$ |

**Rent – area**

Assembly

16,000 × 37.5% = 6,000

Machining

16,000 × 37.5% = 6,000

Maintenance

16,000 × 25% = 4,000

**Canteen costs – staff**

Assembly

$\frac{1}{2}$ × 15,000 = 7,500

Machining

$\frac{1}{3}$ × 15,000 = 5,000

Maintenance

$\frac{1}{6}$ × 15,000 = 2,500

| Overhead cost | Basis of allocation/ apportionment | Assembly £ | Machining £ | Maintenance £ | Total £ |
|---|---|---|---|---|---|
| Oil | Allocate | | 2,000 | | 2,000 |
| Salary (supervisor) | Allocate | 20,000 | | | 20,000 |
| Insurance | Allocate | | 4,000 | | 4,000 |
| Rent | Floor area | 6,000 | 6,000 | 4,000 | 16,000 |
| Salaries (maintenance) | Allocate | | | 40,000 | 40,000 |
| Canteen | No of employees | 7,500 | 5,000 | 2,500 | 15,000 |
| | | 33,500 | 17,000 | 46,500 | 97,000 |

 **Test your understanding 1**

An organisation has four departments Fixing, Mending, Stores and Canteen.

The budgeted overhead costs for the organisation are as follows:

| | £ |
|---|---|
| Rent | 45,000 |
| Building maintenance costs | 6,000 |
| Machinery insurance | 2,400 |
| Machinery depreciation | 11,000 |
| Machinery running expenses | 6,000 |
| Power | 7,000 |

There are specific costs that are to be allocated to each cost centre as follows:

| | £ |
|---|---|
| Fixing | 5,000 |
| Mending | 4,000 |
| Stores | 1,000 |
| Canteen | 2,000 |

The following information about the various cost centres is also available:

|  | Fixing | Mending | Stores | Canteen | Total |
|---|---|---|---|---|---|
| Floor space (m²) | 15,000 | 8,000 | 5,000 | 2,000 | 30,000 |
| Power usage % | 45 | 40 | 5 | 10 | 100 |
| Value of machinery (£000) | 140 | 110 | – | – | 250 |
| Machinery hours (000) | 50 | 30 |  |  | 80 |
| Value of equipment (£000) | – | – | 5 | 15 | 20 |
| Number of employees | 20 | 15 | 3 | 2 | 40 |
| Value of stores requisitions (£000) | 100 | 50 | – | – | 150 |

**Task**

**Allocate and apportion the costs to the four departments.**

| Overhead cost | Basis | Fixing £ | Mending £ | Stores £ | Canteen £ | Total £ |
|---|---|---|---|---|---|---|
| Specific overheads |  |  |  |  |  | 12,000 |
| Rent |  |  |  |  |  | 45,000 |
| Building maintenance |  |  |  |  |  | 6,000 |
| Machinery insurance |  |  |  |  |  | 2,400 |
| Machinery depreciation |  |  |  |  |  | 11,000 |
| Machinery running cost |  |  |  |  |  | 6,000 |
| Power |  |  |  |  |  | 7,000 |
|  |  |  |  |  |  | 89,400 |

## Test your understanding 2

Ray Ltd has the following four production departments:

- Machining 1
- Machining 2
- Assembly
- Packaging

The budgeted overheads relating to the four production departments for Quarter 3 20X5 are:

|  | £ | £ |
|---|---|---|
| Depreciation |  | 80,000 |
| Rent and rates |  | 120,000 |
| Indirect labour costs: |  |  |
| Machining 1 | 40,500 |  |
| Machining 2 | 18,300 |  |
| Assembly | 12,400 |  |
| Packaging | 26,700 |  |
| Total |  | 97,900 |
| Assembly costs |  | 15,600 |
| Total overheads |  | 313,500 |

Overheads are allocated or apportioned to the production departments on the most appropriate basis. The following information is also available:

| Department | Carrying amount of non-current assets (£000) | Square metres occupied | Number of employees |
|---|---|---|---|
| Machining 1 | 1,280 | 625 | 8 |
| Machining 2 | 320 | 250 | 4 |
| Assembly | 960 | 500 | 3 |
| Packaging | 640 | 1,125 | 7 |
| Total | 3,200 | 2,500 | 22 |

Complete the overhead analysis sheet below (round to the nearest £)

Overhead analysis sheet

|  | Basis | Machining 1 | Machining 2 | Assembly | Packaging | Total |
|---|---|---|---|---|---|---|
| Depreciation |  |  |  |  |  |  |
| Rent and rates |  |  |  |  |  |  |
| Indirect Labour cost |  |  |  |  |  |  |
| Assembly costs |  |  |  |  |  |  |
| TOTAL |  |  |  |  |  |  |

# 4 Reapportionment

## 4.1 Introduction

The next stage is to apportion the service cost centre total costs to the production cost centres that make use of the service cost centre. This process is known as **reapportionment** or secondary apportionment.

This is done because the aim is to have all the production costs identified with a **production** cost centre so that we can then work out the cost of the units that the production cost centre produces.

## 4.2 A single service centre

 **Example 2**

A business has one service centre, the canteen, which serves two production centres. The overhead costs for a period have been allocated and apportioned between the three departments as given below.

|  | Production A | Production B | Canteen |
|---|---|---|---|
| Overhead | £10,000 | £15,000 | £12,000 |
| Number of employees | 100 | 200 |  |

Reapportion the canteen's overheads to the production departments on the basis of the number of employees.

## Solution

Exactly the same technique is used to reapportion as is used to apportion.

| | Department A £ | Department B £ | Canteen £ |
|---|---|---|---|
| Overhead | 10,000 | 15,000 | 12,000 |
| Number of employees | 12,000 ÷ 300 × 100 = 4,000 | 12,000 ÷ 300 × 200 = 8,000 | (12,000) |
| Total overhead for production department | 14,000 | 23,000 | |

 **Test your understanding 3**

The cost of the stores department and the personnel department of RFB plc are to be reapportioned across the other cost centres.

**What bases would you recommend for each cost?**

**Stores department**

A    Number of employees

B    Floor space

C    Number of issues to production

D    Kilowatt hours

**Personnel department**

A    Number of employees

B    Floor space

C    Number of issues to production

D    Kilowatt hours

## 4.3    Two service centres

When there are two or more service centres that need to re-apportion costs to production cost centres there are a couple of options:

(a)    The service centres only supply services to the production cost centres i.e. they do not provide services to each other.

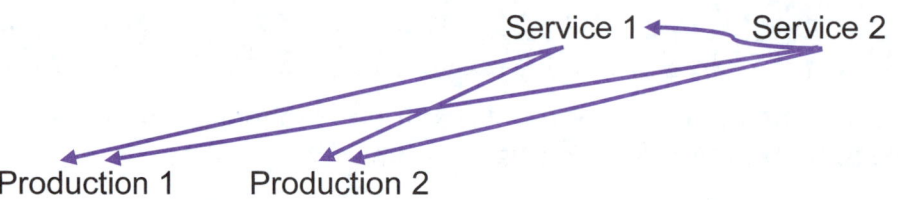

Service 1          Service 2

Production 1    Production 2

(b)    One of the service centres (number 2 in diagram) provides services to the production cost centres and to the other service centre. The remaining service centre (number 1 in the diagram) only provides services to the production cost centres.

Service 1          Service 2

Production 1    Production 2

## 4.4    The direct method

This is used in situation (a) above i.e., where the service centres do not supply services to each other.

 **Example 3**

A business has two production centres, departments A and B, and two service centres, a canteen and a maintenance department.

The costs allocated and apportioned to the four departments are:

|  | £ |
|---|---|
| Production A | 50,000 |
| Production B | 60,000 |
| Canteen | 8,000 |
| Maintenance | 10,000 |

The following information related to the service centres:

|  | Production A | Production B |
|---|---|---|
| Usage of maintenance dept | 40% | 60% |
| Usage of canteen | 45% | 55% |

The maintenance department supplies 40% of its services to department A, 60% to department B and nothing to the canteen.

The canteen supplies 45% to department A, 55% to B and nothing to the maintenance department.

|  | Dept A £ | Dept B £ | Canteen £ | Maintenance £ |
|---|---|---|---|---|
|  | 50,000 | 60,000 | 8,000 | 10,000 |
| Reapportionment of maintenance | (40%) 4,000 | (60%) 6,000 | – | (10,000) |
| Reapportionment of canteen | (45%) 3,600 | (55%) 4,400 | (8,000) | – |
| Total | 57,600 | 70,400 | 0 | 0 |

It does not matter which service cost centre you re-apportion first when using this method.

## 4.5 The step down method

This is used in situation (b) above i.e., where one of the service centres supplies services to the other.

 **Example 4**

A business has two production centres, departments A and B, and two service centres, a canteen and a maintenance department. The costs allocated and apportioned to the four departments are:

|  | £ |
|---|---|
| Production A | 50,000 |
| Production B | 60,000 |
| Canteen | 8,000 |
| Maintenance | 10,000 |

The following information related to the service centres:

| | Production A | Production B | Canteen |
|---|---|---|---|
| Usage of maintenance dept | 40% | 45% | 15% |
| Usage of canteen | 45% | 55% | – |

The maintenance department supplies 40% of its services to department A, 45% to department B and 15% to the canteen. The canteen supplies 45% to department A, 55% to B and nothing to the maintenance department.

**Step 1:** Identify the service centre whose services are used by the other service department and apportion its costs to all the departments. In this case the maintenance department services the canteen so the maintenance costs are apportioned first.

**Step 2:** Now apportion the new total costs of the canteen i.e. its original costs (£8,000) plus its share of the maintenance costs (£1,500) to the production departments.

| | Dept A £ | Dept B £ | Canteen £ | Maintenance £ |
|---|---|---|---|---|
| | 50,000 | 60,000 | 8,000 | 10,000 |
| Reapportionment maintenance | (40%) 4,000 | (45%) 4,500 | (15%) 1,500 | (10,000) |
| Reapportionment canteen | (45%) 4,275 | (55%) 5,225 | (9,500) | – |
| Total | 58,275 | 69,725 | 0 | 0 |

**Test your understanding 4**

Adam has a factory with two production departments, machining and painting, which are serviced by the maintenance and quality control departments.

Relevant information for a particular period is as follows:

|  | Machining | Painting | Maintenance | Quality Control |
|---|---|---|---|---|
| Apportioned overheads | £20,000 | £40,000 | £10,000 | £15,000 |
| Maintenance | 30% | 60% |  | 10% |
| Quality Control | 50% | 50% |  |  |

**Required:**

**Using the step down method reapportion the apportioned overheads and calculate the total overheads for each production department.**

|  | Machining £ | Painting £ | Maintenance £ | Quality control £ |
|---|---|---|---|---|
| Apportioned overheads | 20,000 | 40,000 | 10,000 | 15,000 |
| Reapportionment of maintenance |  |  |  |  |
| Reapportionment of quality control |  |  |  |  |
| Total |  |  |  |  |

# 5 Absorption

## 5.1 Introduction

Having collected all indirect production costs in the production cost centres via overhead allocation and apportionment/reapportionment, the total overhead of each production cost centre must be charged to the **output of the production cost centres**.

### Definition

**Overhead absorption** is the charging of a production cost centre's overhead costs to the cost units produced by the cost centre.

The **absorption rate** is calculated at the start of the period and is therefore **based on budgeted activity** and on **budgeted overheads**. Various bases for absorption exist and the most suitable one should be chosen depending on the situation.

## 5.2 One product business

If only one type of product is being produced it is possible to calculate the overhead absorption rate (OAR) using the planned production in units.

$$\frac{\text{Budgeted overhead}}{\text{Budgeted units produced}}$$

Once we know how much overhead each unit is absorbing we can calculate the full production cost per unit.

### Example 5

Henry produces one product. Each unit of the product uses £20 worth of material and £10 of labour. Henry has two production centres, assembly and finishing. The following overheads are expected to be incurred:

| | |
|---|---|
| Rent and rates | £12,000 |
| Light and heat | £15,000 |

The assembly department occupies twice the floor area of the finishing department. Production is budgeted for 1,000 units.

Calculate the assembly overhead cost per unit, the finishing overhead cost per unit and hence the total cost per unit.

**Solution**

**Step 1**

Apportion the overheads to the cost centres, on the basis of size, therefore in the ratio of 2 to 1.

| Overhead | Basis | Total £ | Assembly £ | Finishing £ |
|---|---|---|---|---|
| Rent and rates | Area 2:1 | 12,000 | 8,000 | 4,000 |
| Light and heat | Area 2:1 | 15,000 | 10,000 | 5,000 |
| | | 27,000 | 18,000 | 9,000 |

**Step 2**

Calculate an overhead absorption rate per unit for each department.

Overhead per unit

Assembly

$$\frac{\text{Budgeted overhead}}{\text{Budgeted units produced}} = \frac{£18,000}{1,000} = £18 \text{ per unit}$$

Finishing

$$\frac{\text{Budgeted overhead}}{\text{Budgeted units produced}} = \frac{£9,000}{1,000} = £9 \text{ per unit}$$

**Step 3**

| Total production cost per unit: | £ |
|---|---|
| Direct costs | |
|     Materials | 20 |
|     Labour | 10 |
| Overheads | |
|     Assembly | 18 |
|     Finishing | 9 |
| | 57 |

### 5.3 Multi-product business

The use of an absorption rate per unit is fine for one-product businesses/cost centres, but **may be inappropriate for multi-product businesses**.

---

 **Example 6**

Sam produces pocket calculators and has one production department, incurring £15,000 overheads. Sam has planned production of 5,000 units.

$$\text{Overhead absorption rate per unit} = \frac{£15,000}{5,000} = £3/\text{unit}$$

Suppose Sam instead makes 3,000 pocket calculators and 2,000 scientific calculators. The scientific calculators take up twice as much time to produce as the pocket calculators. The total overhead is the same as before. The overhead absorption rate per unit produced will be the same as before:

$$\text{Overhead absorption rate per unit} = \frac{£15,000}{3,000 + 2,000} = £3/\text{unit}$$

Decide whether this is a reasonable basis to absorb overheads.

**Solution**

This is probably not a reasonable basis. The scientific calculator takes longer to make and would involve the use of more of the indirect costs (e.g. supervisor's time). It is therefore necessary to choose an absorption basis that best reflects the demand of that product on the production department through which it passes. It may be more appropriate to calculate an overhead absorption rate per hour.

---

Bases commonly used as an **alternative to the rate per unit**, when more than one product is involved, are as follows.

(a) rate per direct labour hour

(b) rate per machine hour.

The calculation is as before but rather than dividing by budgeted units, budgeted activity it used:

$$\frac{\text{Budgeted overhead}}{\text{Budgeted activity}}$$

Whichever method is used, the result will still only be a **rough estimate** of what each product costs as it is based on budgeted figures.

**Example 7**

Sam makes 3,000 pocket calculators and 2,000 scientific calculators. The scientific calculators take up 2 hours to produce and the pocket calculators take only 1 hour to produce. The total overhead is the same as before. The overhead absorption rate per hour produced will be:

$$\text{Overhead absorption rate per unit} = \frac{£15,000}{3,000 \times 1 + 2,000 \times 2} = £2.14/\text{unit}$$

This then needs to be assigned on a per unit basis.

The pocket calculators take one hour to produce so will be charged with one hour's worth of overhead = £2.14

The scientific calculators take two hours to produce so will be charged with two hours' worth of overhead = £2.14 × 2 = £4.18

The difference in unit overhead charges should reflect the effort that has been made in producing the units.

 **Test your understanding 5**

Bertram manufactures three products, the cost of each being:

|  | A | B | C |
|---|---|---|---|
| Direct materials | £14.40 | £25.60 | £36.00 |
| Direct labour |  |  |  |
|    Machining | 2 hours | 1.5 hours | 2 hours |
|    Assembling | 2 hours | 2.5 hours | 1 hour |

Planned production is:

Product A     10,000 units
Product B     20,000 units
Product C     40,000 units

Production overheads for the forthcoming year are estimated at £120,000.

**Calculate the budgeted overhead absorption rate per product based on direct labour hours?**

|   | A<br>£/unit | B<br>£/unit | C<br>£/unit |
|---|---|---|---|
| A | 1 | 0.75 | 1 |
| B | 2 | 2 | 1.5 |
| C | 1 | 1.25 | 0.5 |
| D | 4 | 4 | 3 |

## 5.4    Service industry

One of the main difficulties in service costing is the establishment of a suitable cost unit. Service organisations may use several different cost units to measure the different kinds of service that they are providing. Examples for a hotel might include:

- Meals served for the restaurant

- Rooms occupied for the cleaning staff

- Hours worked for the reception staff.

A composite cost unit is more appropriate if a service is a function of two variables. Examples of composite cost units are as follows:

- How much is carried over what distance (tonne/miles) for haulage companies.

- How many patients are treated for how many days (patient/days) for hospitals.

- How many passengers travel how many miles (passenger/miles) for public transport companies.

 **Example 8**

There are 60 rooms in a hotel, 60% of which were occupied last night and require cleaning and maintenance. The hotel incurs the following costs:

|   | £ |
|---|---|
| Cleaning products | 50 |
| Repairs | 250 |
| Wages | 1,500 |

The hotels cost unit is rooms occupied.

**Required:**

Calculate the average cost per room occupied.

**Solution** Total hotel expenditure = £1,800

Total rooms occupied = 60 × 60% = 36 rooms

Average cost per room occupied = £1,800 ÷ 36 = £50 per room

## 5.5 Choosing an absorption rate

The choice of which rate to be used depends largely on the nature of the operations concerned.

There is no correct method but in order to produce useful information it will always be preferable to choose an absorption rate which is in some way related to the costs being incurred.

- if the overhead consisted mainly of depreciation of machinery then it would be sensible to use the machine hour rate.

- if the overhead consisted mainly of the salaries of supervisors who supervise the workforce then it would make sense to use the labour hour rate.

### Example 9

A factory has two production departments, cutting and finishing. The budgeted overheads and production details are:

|  | Cutting | Finishing |
|---|---|---|
| Budgeted overhead | £100,000 | £80,000 |
| Budgeted direct labour hours | 10,000 | 40,000 |
| Budgeted machine hours | 60,000 | 5,000 |

The cutting department is a machine intensive department whilst finishing is labour intensive.

The factory makes two products, the Pig and the Cow. The production details for these are:

|  | Pig | Cow |
|---|---|---|
| Direct labour hours |  |  |
| Cutting | 1 | 2 |
| Finishing | 4 | 6 |
| Machine hours |  |  |
| Cutting | 8 | 6 |
| Finishing | 2 | 2 |

Calculate the overhead cost to be absorbed into each product using an appropriate absorption rate for each cost centre.

**Solution**

**Step 1: Choose and calculate the absorption rates**

It makes sense to use the machine hour rate for the machine intensive cutting department and the labour hour rate for the labour intensive finishing department.

$$\text{Cutting – machine hour rate} = \frac{£100,000}{60,000} = £1.67/\text{machine hr}$$

$$\text{Finishing – labour hour rate} = \frac{£80,000}{40,000} = £2/\text{labour hr}$$

**Step 2: Absorption into unit costs**

|  | £ |
|---|---|
| Product Pig |  |
| Cutting 8 hours × £1.67 | 13.36 |
| Finishing 4 hours × £2 | 8.00 |
|  | 21.36 |
| Product Cow |  |
| Cutting 6 hours × £1.67 | 10.02 |
| Finishing 6 hours × £2 | 12.00 |
|  | 22.02 |

As the cutting cost centre is machine intensive then a machine hour absorption rate will best reflect how the overhead is incurred and, as the finishing cost centre is labour intensive, a direct labour hour rate is most appropriate in this cost centre.

Which rate should be used? Possibly both – **it depends upon the nature of the overheads**.

 **Test your understanding 6**

Pears plc manufactures children's clothing. The General Manager is concerned about how the costs of the various garments it produces are calculated.

|  | Overhead cost £000 | Numbers employed | Labour hours | Material issued £000 | Machine hours |
|---|---|---|---|---|---|
| **Production departments** |  |  |  |  |  |
| Cutting | 187 | 10 | 400 | 180 | 12,000 |
| Sewing | 232 | 15 | 300 | 240 | 28,000 |
| Finishing | 106 | 8 | 12,000 | 90 |  |
| **Service departments** |  |  |  |  |  |
| Stores | 27 | 2 |  | – |  |
| Maintenance | 50 | 3 |  | 90 |  |
| Totals | 602 | 38 | 12,700 | 600 | 40,000 |

**Using the overhead analysis sheet below, apportion:**

(a) (i) stores department's costs to the production and maintenance departments

(ii) maintenance department's costs to the cutting and sewing departments only.

Select the most suitable basis for each apportionment and state the bases used on the overhead analysis sheet. (Calculations to the nearest £000.)

**Overhead analysis sheet**

| | PRODUCTION | | | SERVICE | | TOTAL |
|---|---|---|---|---|---|---|
| | Cutting | Sewing | Finishing | Stores | Maintenance | |
| | £000 | £000 | £000 | £000 | £000 | £000 |
| Overheads | 187 | 232 | 106 | 27 | 50 | 602 |
| Apportion store Basis: | | | | | | |
| Apportion maintenance Basis: | | | | | | |
| Total | | | | | | |

(b) What would be the overhead rate for the three production departments if cutting and sewing were highly mechanised and finishing required high human input:

| | Cutting | Sewing | Finishing |
|---|---|---|---|
| A | 17.58 | 10.04 | 9.17 |
| B | 5.55 | 7.39 | 2.89 |
| C | 5.28 | 7.03 | 2.75 |
| D | 21.10 | 18.73 | 9.17 |

# 6   Under/over absorption of overheads

## 6.1   Introduction

**Overhead absorption rates** are calculated at the start of the accounting period. They are based on **budgeted** overhead costs and the budgeted volume of activity; they are **pre-determined**.

The reason for this is that management will need to know the **budgeted cost of each unit of production** in order to be able to make decisions about the products and the sales and production. This requires not only budgeted figures for direct materials, direct labour and direct expenses, but also for overheads.

## 6.2   Absorption of overheads

During the accounting period the cost of each unit produced will include overheads based upon the pre-determined budgeted overhead absorption rate.

But what happens if:

(a)    the **actual production levels** are different from the budgeted levels and/or

(b)    the **actual overheads** for the period are different from the budgeted overheads?

If either or both of these occur, the use of the predetermined absorption rate will result in an **over- or under-absorption of overheads** (sometimes referred to as over or under recovery of overheads.)

There is a 3 step procedure for calculating an under or over absorption:

**Step 1**

Calculate the OAR = Budgeted overhead ÷ Budgeted activity

**Step 2**

Calculate how much overhead has been absorbed by actual activity

Absorbed = OAR × Actual activity

**Step 3**

Compare the actual overhead cost with the absorbed overhead

Absorbed > Actual = over absorbed

Absorbed < Actual = under absorbed

 **Example 10**

A factory budgets to produce 10,000 units, its budgeted overhead is £30,000 and the budgeted direct labour hours are 4,000.

The factory actually produced only a total of 8,000 units in the coming year, due to a machine breakdown, in 3,200 labour hours. In addition, the cost of machine repairs resulted in actual factory overheads amounting to £34,000.

The factory absorbs the overhead based on labour hours.

What is the under- or over-absorbed overhead?

**Solution**

**Step 1** – calculate the budgeted overhead absorption rate

$$\text{OAR} = \frac{\text{Budgeted overhead cost}}{\text{Budgeted activity}} = \frac{£30,000}{4,000}$$

$$= £7.50 \text{ per direct labour hour}$$

**Step 2** – calculate the overhead absorbed by actual production

Absorbed = OAR × Actual activity

= £7.50 × 3,200 hours

= £24,000

**Step 3** – calculate the under- or over-absorption

Under- or
over-absorption = Actual overhead cost – Absorbed overhead cost

= £34,000 – £24,000

= £10,000

The absorbed overhead is less than the actual overhead so there has been an under-absorption of the overhead.

## 6.3 Under and over absorption of overheads

Over-absorbed overhead during a period is treated as an addition to profit, because it is an adjustment to allow for the fact that too much overhead cost has been charged. Under absorption is a reduction in profit as it is an adjustment to allow for the fact that the overhead charged in the period is less than the overhead costs incurred.

## 6.4 The significance of under or over absorption of overheads

The amount of under or over absorbed overhead should not usually be large, provided the budgeting is realistic and provided the actual results meet budgeted expectations.

If a large amount of under or over absorption occurs the reasons are usually:

- Actual overhead expenditure was higher than budgeted, possibly due to poor control over actual spending or vice versa.

- Actual overhead expenditure was much higher or lower than budgeted due to poor budgeting of overhead expenditure.

- The actual volume of activity was higher or lower than expected for operational reasons that the production manager should be able to explain.

**Test your understanding 7**

The actual overheads for a department were £6,500 last period and the actual output was 540 machine hours. The budgeted overheads were £5,995 and the budgeted output was 550 machine hours.

(a) **What is the OAR?**

     A     £11.82

     B     £10.90

     C     £12.04

     D     £11.10

(b) **How much overhead will be absorbed into production?**

     A     £6,622

     B     £5,994

     C     £5,886

     D     £6,383

(c) **What is the under- or over-absorption of the overheads?**

     A     £122 over

     B     £506 under

     C     £614 under

     D     £117 under

 **Test your understanding 8**

A company budgeted to spend fixed overheads of £5 per hour in a given month. The actual activity level for the month was 10,000 hours and the actual overhead expenditure was £48,000.

Calculate the over or under absorption of overheads for the month.

 **Test your understanding 9**

You have been asked to calculate the under- or over- absorption in a production division, this division is highly automated and operates with expensive machinery, which is run wherever possible on a 24-hour a day, seven days a week basis.

The following information relates to this division for July 20Y0:

| | |
|---|---|
| Total budgeted departmental overheads | £400,000 |
| Total actual departmental overheads | £450,000 |
| Total budgeted direct labour hours | 3,000 |
| Total budgeted machine hours | 10,000 |
| Total actual direct labour hours | 2,500 |
| Total actual machine hours | 9,000 |

(a)  **What is the budgeted fixed overhead absorption rate for the division for July 20Y0, using the most appropriate basis of absorption?**

    A    £50.00

    B    £40.00

    C    £45.00

    D    £44.44

(b)  **What is the value of the overhead absorbed into production?**

    A    £500,000

    B    £405,000

    C    £360,000

    D    £444,400

(c)  **What is the under- or over absorption for the division?**

    A    £50,000 under

    B    £50,000 over

    C    £90,000 over

    D    £90,000 under

 **Test your understanding 10**

R Noble and Sons are a firm of agricultural engineers based in North Yorkshire.

They have a large workshop from which they operate. The business is divided into cost centres which include:

- Machining

- Fabrication

- Canteen

- Stores

A summary of their budgeted overhead for the three months ended 31 March 20X1 showed:

| | £ |
|---|---|
| Depreciation of machinery | 5,000 |
| Insurance of machinery | 2,100 |
| Heat and light | 800 |
| Power | 1,750 |
| Rent and rates | 2,250 |
| | 11,900 |

Other relevant costs and data for the period showed:

| | Machining | Fabrication | Stores | Canteen |
|---|---|---|---|---|
| No of employees | 2 | 2 | 1 | 0 |
| Value of plant | £40,000 | £19,000 | £2,500 | £1,000 |
| Floor area (sq m) | 300 | 350 | 100 | 50 |
| Kilowatt hours | 600 | 500 | 400 | 250 |
| Material requisitions | 195 | 99 | – | – |
| Direct labour hours | 1,600 | 1,067 | – | – |

**(a)   Complete the overhead analysis sheet below (round to the nearest £).**

**Overhead analysis sheet**

| | BASIS | PRODUCTION | | SERVICE | | TOTAL |
|---|---|---|---|---|---|---|
| | | Machining | Fabrication | Stores | Canteen | |
| Dep'n of machinery | | | | | | |
| Insurance of machinery | | | | | | |
| Heat and light | | | | | | |
| Power | | | | | | |
| Rent and rates | | | | | | |
| Sub-total | | | | | | |
| Reapportion canteen | | | | | ( ) | |
| Reapportion stores | | | | ( ) | | |
| TOTAL | | | | | | |

**(b)** **What would be the overhead rate per kilowatt hour for the production departments?**

|   | Machining | Fabrication |
|---|---|---|
| A | £12.15 | £9.22 |
| B | £4.56 | £4.32 |
| C | £37.38 | £46.57 |
| D | £24.30 | £13.17 |

The actual Kilowatt hours for the period were, machining 614 hours and fabrication 495 hours.

The actual overhead for the period was, machining £7,960 and fabrication £3,800.

**(c)** **Based on the OAR calculated in (b) what would be the under or over absorption in each department?**

|   | Machining | Fabrication |
|---|---|---|
| A | £500 over | £764 under |
| B | £764 over | £500 under |
| C | £500 under | £764 over |
| D | £764 under | £500 over |

# 7 Integrated bookkeeping – overheads

## 7.1 Introduction

The costs of a business have to be recorded in a bookkeeping system. Many businesses use an **integrated bookkeeping system** where the ledger accounts kept provide the necessary **information for both costing and financial accounting**.

## 7.2 Production overheads account

The production overhead account is where the movement of the costs associated with the overheads (indirect costs) are recorded.

---

### Example 11

**Production overheads**

| | £ | | £ |
|---|---|---|---|
| Actual overhead cost (1) | | Absorbed overheads (2) | |
| Over-absorbed (3) | | Under-absorbed (4) | |

1 The **actual cost** of all the indirect costs is recorded as a **debit** in the production overheads account. The credit is either in the bank or payables account. The actual cost will be made up off all the indirect production costs – material, labour and expenses.

2 The overheads that are **absorbed into production** (WIP) are recorded as a **credit** in the production overhead account. This is calculated as the **budgeted OAR × actual activity**.

3 When the account is balanced at the end of the period and the **balancing amount** is required to make the **debit** side of the account match the credit side we have an **over-absorption** of overheads.

4 When the account is balanced at the end of the period and the **balancing amount** is required to make the **credit** side of the account match the debit side we have an **under-absorption** of overheads.

---

## 7.3 The adjustment for under-/over-absorption

The adjustment for an **under-absorbed overhead** is made as a **debit** to the costing **statement of profit or loss**. If the overheads have been under-absorbed, we need to **decrease profit** and increase the expense in the costing statement of profit or loss.

|  | £ |
|---|---|
| Revenue | X |
| Cost of sales (using budgeted overhead absorption rates) | X |
|  | ——— |
| Gross profit | X |
| Less: Under-absorption of fixed overheads | (10,000) |
|  | ——— |
| Adjusted gross profit | X |
|  | ——— |

The accounting entry for this adjustment would be as follows.

|  |  | £ | £ |
|---|---|---|---|
| Debit: | Statement of profit or loss | 10,000 |  |
| Credit: | Production overheads |  | 10,000 |

The adjustment for an **over-absorbed overhead** is made as a **credit** to the costing **statement of profit or loss**. If the overheads have been over-absorbed, we need to **increase profit** and decrease the expense in the costing statement of profit or loss.

|  | £ |
|---|---|
| Revenue | X |
| Cost of sales (using budgeted overhead absorption rates) | X |
|  | ——— |
| Gross profit | X |
| Add: Over-absorption of fixed overheads | 10,000 |
|  | ——— |
| Adjusted gross profit | X |
|  | ——— |

The accounting entry for this adjustment would be as follows.

|  |  | £ | £ |
|---|---|---|---|
| Debit: | Production overheads | 10,000 |  |
| Credit: | Statement of profit or loss |  | 10,000 |

 **KAPLAN** PUBLISHING

**Test your understanding 11**

**What are the correct journal entries the following accounting transactions?**

1    Indirect material issued from stores:

A    Dr Bank, Cr Material

B    Dr Production overheads, Cr Material    ✓

C    Dr Material, Cr Bank ✗

D    Dr Material, Cr Production overheads

2    Indirect wages analysed in the wages control account:

A    Dr Production, Cr Wages control

B    Dr Wages control, Cr Production          *Indirect wages go to Paid*

C    Dr Wages control, Cr Production overheads

D    Dr Production overheads, Cr Wages control    ✓

3    Production overheads absorbed into the cost of production:

A    Dr Production, Cr Production overheads    ✓

B    Dr Production overheads, Cr Statement of profit or loss

C    Dr Production overheads, Cr Production

D    Dr Statement of profit or loss, Cr Production overheads

4    Over-absorption of overheads

A    Dr Production, Cr Production overheads

B    Dr Production overheads, Cr Statement of profit or loss    ✓

C    Dr Production overheads, Cr Production

D    Dr Statement of profit or loss, Cr Production overheads

**Test your understanding 12**

During period 5, the month of May 20X1, Lester Bird's under- and over-recovery of overhead per cost centre was:

| Cost centre | Overhead absorbed | Actual overhead | (under)/over-absorbed |
|---|---|---|---|
| | £ | £ | £ |
| Painting | 3,950 | 4,250 | (300) |
| Finishing | 2,950 | 3,150 | (200) |
| Trimming | 1,640 | 1,600 | 40 |
| Firing | 2,750 | 2,600 | 150 |
| | £11,290 | £11,600 | (310) |

**Post the total figures to the overhead account, showing the transfer of the under-absorption to the costing statement of profit or loss.**

**Production overhead control account**

| | £ | | £ |
|---|---|---|---|
| | | | |
| £ | | £ | |

 **Test your understanding 13**

**Biscuit Making Company**

The general manager has asked you to monitor the absorption of overheads for the production departments for November 20X8.

Company policy is to absorb overheads on the following basis.

| Department | Basis |
|---|---|
| Mixing | Per £ of labour cost |
| Baking | Machine hours |
| Packing | Labour hours |

Budgeted and actual data for November 20X8 is:

|  | Mixing | Baking | Packing |
|---|---|---|---|
| Budgeted overheads | £164,000 | £228,900 | £215,000 |
| Actual labour hours worked |  |  | 16,000 |
| Budgeted labour hours |  |  | 17,200 |
| Actual machine hours |  | 16,100 |  |
| Budgeted machine hours |  | 16,350 |  |
| Actual labour costs | £63,700 |  |  |
| Budgeted labour costs | £65,600 |  |  |

**Calculate the budgeted overhead absorption rate for each department.**

|  | Mixing £ | Baking £ | Packing £ |
|---|---|---|---|
| Budgeted overhead absorption rate |  |  |  |

**Complete the tables and production overhead account.**

| PRODUCTION OVERHEAD SCHEDULE Month: | | | |
|---|---|---|---|
|  | Mixing £ | Baking £ | Packing £ |
| Budgeted overheads |  |  |  |
| Actual overheads | 171,500 | 224,000 | 229,000 |
| Overhead absorbed |  |  |  |

|  | Mixing £ | Baking £ | Packing £ |
|---|---|---|---|
| Over-absorbed overheads |  |  |  |
| Under-absorbed overheads |  |  |  |

**Production overhead control account**

| | £ | | £ |
|---|---|---|---|
| | _____ | | _____ |
| £ | | £ | |
| | _____ | | _____ |

# 8 Activity based costing

## 8.1 Introduction

**Activity based costing** (ABC) is an alternative approach to product costing. It is a form of absorption costing, but, rather than absorbing overheads on a production volume basis it firstly allocates them to cost pools before absorbing them into units using cost drivers.

- A **cost pool** is an activity that consumes resources and for which overhead costs are identified and allocated. For each cost pool there should be a cost driver.

- A **cost driver** is a unit of activity that consumes resources. An alternative definition of a cost driver is the factor influencing the level of cost.

## 8.2 ABC versus absorption costing

Imagine the machining department of a business that makes clothing. In a traditional absorption costing system, the overhead absorption rate would be based on machine hours because many of the overheads in the machining department would relate to the machines, for example power, maintenance and machine depreciation.

Using only machine hours as the basis would seem fair, however not only does the machining department have machine related costs, but also in an absorption costing system it would have had a share of rent and rates, heating and lighting apportioned to it. These costs would also be absorbed based on machine hours and this is inappropriate as the machine hours are not directly responsible for the rent or rates.

ABC overcomes this problem by not using departments as gathering points for costs, but instead it uses activities to group the costs (cost pools) which are caused (driven) by an activity.

There would be an activity that related to each of the following: power usage, machine depreciation and machine maintenance. Machining would not pick up a share of personnel costs or rent and rates as these would be charged to another activity. For example:

- the cost of setting up machinery for a production run might be driven by the number of setups (jobs or batches produced)

- the cost of running machines might be driven by the number of machine hours for which the machines are running

- the cost of order processing might be related to the number of orders dispatched or to the weight of items dispatched

- the cost of purchasing might be related to the number of purchase orders made.

ABCs flexibility reduces the need for arbitrary apportionments.

Using ABC should lead to more accurate product and/or service costs being calculated.

### 8.3    Calculating the overhead recovery rate using ABC

There are five steps to calculating an activity based cost:

**Step 1: Group production overheads into activities, according to how they are driven.**

A cost pool is the grouping of costs relating to a particular activity which consumes resources and for which overhead costs are identified and allocated. For each cost pool, there should be a cost driver.

**Step 2: Identify cost drivers for each activity, i.e. what causes these activity costs to be incurred.**

A cost driver is a factor that influences (or drives) the level of cost.

**Step 3: Calculate a cost driver rate for each activity.**

The cost driver rate is calculated in the same way as the absorption costing OAR. However, a separate cost driver rate will be calculated for each activity, by taking the activity cost and dividing by the cost driver information.

**Step 4: Absorb the activity costs into the product.**

The activity costs should be absorbed by applying the cost driver rate into the individual products.

**Step 5: Calculate the overhead cost per unit of product.**

Once all the overhead has been absorbed into the product it is possible to calculate an overhead cost per unit:

Overhead cost per unit = total overhead absorbed ÷ total number of units

**Example 12**

A manufacturing business makes a product in two models, model M1 and model M2. Details of the two products are as follows:

|  | Model M1 | Model M2 |
|---|---|---|
| Annual sales | 8,000 units | 8,000 units |
| Number of sales orders | 60 | 250 |
| Sales price per unit | £54 | £73 |
| Direct material cost per unit | £11 | £21 |
| Direct labour hours per unit | 2.0 hours | 2.5 hours |
| Direct labour rate per hour | £8 | £8 |
| Special parts per unit | 2 | 8 |
| Production batch size | 2,000 units | 100 units |
| Setups per batch | 1 | 3 |

**Step 1: Group production overheads into activities, according to how they are driven**

**Step 2: Identify cost drivers for each activity.**

|  | £ | Cost driver |
|---|---|---|
| Setup costs | 97,600 | Number of setups |
| Material handling costs | 42,000 | Number of batches |
| Special part handling costs | 50,000 | Number of special parts |
| Invoicing | 31,000 | Number of sales orders |
| Other overheads | 108,000 | Direct labour hours |
| | ———— | |
| Total overheads | 328,600 | |
| | ———— | |

**Step 3: Calculate a cost driver rate for each activity.**

**Calculate the total of each of the drivers for the production levels.**

|  | M1 | M2 | Total |
|---|---|---|---|
| Number of batches | 8,000/2,000 = 4 | 8,000/100 = 80 | 84 |
| Number of setups | 4 × 1 = 4 | 80 × 3 = 240 | 244 |
| Special parts | 8,000 × 2 = 16,000 | 8,000 × 8 = 64,000 | 80,000 |
| Number of sales orders | 60 | 250 | 310 |
| Direct labour hours | 8,000 × 2 = 16,000 | 8,000 × 2.5 = 20,000 | 36,000 |

**Calculate the overhead cost per driver for each activity.**

| Activity | Cost | ÷ | | Total driver | = Cost per driver |
|----------|------|---|---|--------------|-------------------|
| | £ | | | | £ |
| Setups | 97,600 | 244 | setups | | 400 |
| Materials handling | 42,000 | 84 | batches | | 500 |
| Special parts handling | 50,000 | 80,000 | special parts | | 0.625 |
| Invoicing | 31,000 | 310 | sales orders | | 100 |
| Other overheads | 108,000 | 36,000 | labour hours | | 3 |

**Step 4: Absorb the activity costs into the product.**

| Activity | | M1 | M2 | Total |
|----------|---|-----|-----|-------|
| | | £ | £ | £ |
| Setups | £400 × 4 | 1,600 | | |
| | £400 × 240 | | 96,000 | 97,600 |
| Materials handling | £500 × 4 | 2,000 | | |
| | £500 × 80 | | 40,000 | 42,000 |
| Special parts handling | £0.625 × 16,000 | 10,000 | | |
| | £0.625 × 64,000 | | 40,000 | 50,000 |
| Invoicing | £100 × 60 | 6,000 | | |
| | £100 × 250 | | 25,000 | 31,000 |
| Other overheads | £3 × 16,000 | 48,000 | | |
| | £3 × 20,000 | | 60,000 | 108,000 |
| | | ───── | ───── | ───── |
| | | 67,600 | 261,000 | 328,600 |

**Step 5: Calculate the overhead cost per unit of product**

M1 = £67,600 ÷ 8,000 units = £8.45

M2 = £261,000 ÷ 8,000 units = £32.63 (rounded to 2 decimal places)

**Test your understanding 14**

DRP has recently introduced an Activity Based Costing system. It manufactures three products:

|  | Product D | Product R | Product P |
|---|---|---|---|
| Budgeted annual production (units) | 100,000 | 100,000 | 50,000 |
| Batch size (units) | 100 | 50 | 25 |
| Machine set-ups per batch | 3 | 4 | 6 |
| Purchase orders per batch | 2 | 1 | 1 |
| Processing time per unit (minutes) | 2 | 3 | 3 |
| Budgeted number of batches | 1,000 | 2,000 | 2,000 |

Three cost pools have been identified. Their budgeted costs for 20X4 are as follows:

Machine set-up costs £150,000

Purchasing of materials £70,000

Processing £80,000

**The cost per unit attributed to Product R for machine set ups is**

£ _0.52_

**The cost per unit attributed to Product D for processing time is**

£ _0.24_

**Test your understanding 15**

P operates an activity based costing (ABC) system to attribute its overhead costs to cost objects.

In its budget for the year ending 31 August 20X6, the company expected to place a total of 2,895 purchase orders at a total cost of £110,010. This activity and its related costs were budgeted to occur at a constant rate throughout the budget year, which is divided into 13 four-week periods.

During the four-week period ended 30 June 20X6, a total of 210 purchase orders were placed at a cost of £7,650.

**The over-recovery of these costs for the four-week period was:**

A    £330

B    £350

C    £370

D    £390

*(handwritten)*
110,000 ÷ 2,895 = 38
210 × 38 = 7980
7980 − 7650 = 330

## 8.4    Advantages and disadvantages of activity based costing

**ABC has a number of advantages:**

- It provides a more accurate cost per unit. As a result, pricing, sales strategy, performance management and decision making should be improved.

- It provides much better insight into what causes (drives) overhead costs.

- ABC recognises that overhead costs are not all related to production and sales volume.

- In many businesses, overhead costs are a significant proportion of total costs, and management needs to understand the drivers of overhead costs in order to manage the business properly. Overhead costs can be controlled by managing cost drivers.

- It can be applied to calculate realistic costs in a complex business environment.

- ABC can be applied to all overhead costs, not just production overheads.

- ABC can be used just as easily in service costing as in product costing.

**Disadvantages of ABC:**

- ABC will be of limited benefit if the overhead costs are primarily volume related or if the overhead is a small proportion of the overall cost.

- It is impossible to allocate all overhead costs to specific activities.

- The choice of both activities and cost drivers might be inappropriate.

- ABC can be more complex to explain to the stakeholders of the costing exercise.

- The benefits obtained from ABC might not justify the costs.

---

### Test your understanding 16

**Which of the following statements are correct (tick all that apply)?**

|  |  | Correct? |
|---|---|---|
| (i) | A cost driver is any factor that causes a change in the cost of an activity. | ☐ |
| (ii) | For long-term variable overhead costs, the cost driver will be the volume of activity. | ☐ |
| (iii) | Traditional absorption costing tends to under-allocate overhead costs to low-volume products. | ☐ |

# 9 Summary

This chapter has considered how the overheads of a business are gathered together and traced through to the cost units to which they relate. Under the **absorption costing** approach, the budgeted overheads of the business are collected together in each of the cost centres, either by **allocation**, if the overhead relates to only one cost centre or by **apportionment** on a fair basis if the overhead relates to a number of cost centres.

Once the overheads have been allocated and apportioned, the next stage is to **reapportion** any **service** cost centre overheads into the production cost centres. Care must be taken here where the service cost centres provide their service to other service cost centres. In these cases, the step down method is required to reapportion the service cost centre overheads.

When all of the budgeted overheads are included in the production cost centres, an **absorption rate** must be calculated. In many cases this will be either on a direct labour hour basis or on a machine hour basis. This will depend on the nature of the business and the nature of the cost centre.

The overhead absorption rate is based upon the budgeted overheads and the budgeted production level. This rate is then used to include the overheads in the production throughout the accounting period. If the activity levels and/or the amount of the overhead are different to the budgeted figures, then the overhead will be either **over- or under-absorbed**. An adjustment is made for this when the costing statement of profit or loss is prepared.

**Activity based costing** (ABC) is a form of absorption costing, but, rather than absorbing overheads on a production volume basis it firstly allocates them to **cost pools** before absorbing them into units using **cost drivers**.

## Test your understanding answers

### Test your understanding 1

|  | Production | | Service | | Total |
|---|---|---|---|---|---|
|  | Fixing £ | Mending £ | Stores £ | Canteen £ | £ |
| Overheads allocated directly to cost centres | 5,000 | 4,000 | 1,000 | 2,000 | 12,000 |
| Overheads to be apportioned Rent Basis: floor space | | | | | |
| 45/30 × 15,000 | 22,500 | | | | 45,000 |
| 45/30 × 8,000 | | 12,000 | | | |
| 45/30 × 5,000 | | | 7,500 | | |
| 45/30 × 2,000 | | | | 3,000 | |
| Building maintenance Basis: floor space | | | | | 6,000 |
| 6/30 × 15,000 | 3,000 | | | | |
| 6/30 × 8,000 | | 1,600 | | | |
| 6/30 × 5,000 | | | 1,000 | | |
| 6/30 × 2,000 | | | | 400 | |
| Machinery insurance Basis: machine value | | | | | 2,400 |
| 2400/250 × 140 | 1,344 | | | | |
| 2400/250 × 110 | | 1,056 | – | – | |
| Machinery depreciation Basis: machine value | | | | | 11,000 |
| 11,000/250 × 140 | 6,160 | | | | |
| 11,000/250 × 110 | | 4,840 | – | – | |
| Machinery running expenses Basis: machine hours | | | | | 6,000 |
| 6,000/80 × 50 | 3,750 | | | | |
| 6,000/80 × 30 | | 2,250 | – | – | |
| Power Basis: power usage percentages | | | | | 7,000 |
| £7,000 × 45% | 3,150 | | | | |
| £7,000 × 40% | | 2,800 | | | |
| £7,000 × 5% | | | 350 | | |
| £7,000 × 10% | | | | 700 | |
| Allocated and apportioned costs | 44,904 | 28,546 | 9,850 | 6,100 | 89,400 |

**Test your understanding 2**

**Overhead analysis sheet**

|  | Basis | Machining 1 | Machining 2 | Assembly | Packaging | Total |
|---|---|---|---|---|---|---|
| Dep'n | Carrying amount | 32,000 | 8,000 | 24,000 | 16,000 | 80,000 |
| Rent and rates | Square meters | 30,000 | 12,000 | 24,000 | 54,000 | 120,000 |
| Indirect labour cost | Allocated | 40,500 | 18,300 | 12,400 | 26,700 | 97,900 |
| Assembly costs | Allocated | – | – | 15,600 | – | 15,600 |
| TOTAL |  | 102,500 | 38,300 | 76,000 | 96,700 | 313,500 |

 **Test your understanding 3**

Stores – **C**

Personnel – **A**

 **Test your understanding 4**

|  | Machining £ | Painting £ | Maintenance £ | Quality control £ |
|---|---|---|---|---|
| Apportioned overheads | 20,000 | 40,000 | 10,000 | 15,000 |
| Reapportionment of maintenance | 3,000 | 6,000 | (10,000) | 1,000 |
|  |  |  |  | ——— |
|  |  |  |  | 16,000 |
| Reapportionment of quality control | 8,000 | 8,000 |  | (16,000) |
|  | ——— | ——— |  |  |
| Total | 31,000 | 54,000 |  |  |
|  | ——— | ——— |  |  |

## Test your understanding 5

**B**

|  | A | B | C | Total |
|---|---|---|---|---|
| Production (units) | 10,000 | 20,000 | 40,000 | 70,000 |
| **Production hours** | | | | |
| Machining | 20,000 | 30,000 | 80,000 | 130,000 |
| Assembly | 20,000 | 50,000 | 40,000 | 110,000 |
| Total hours | 40,000 | 80,000 | 120,000 | **240,000** |

$$\text{Overhead per direct labour hour} = \frac{£120,000}{240,000} = £0.50$$

|  | A | B | C |
|---|---|---|---|
|  | £ | £ | £ |
| Overheads | (4 hr × £0.50) | (4 hr × £0.50) | (3 hr × £0.50) |
|  | = 2.00/unit | = 2.00/unit | = 1.50/unit |

## Test your understanding 6

**(a)**

| Overhead analysis sheet | PRODUCTION | | | SERVICE | | TOTAL |
|---|---|---|---|---|---|---|
|  | Cutting | Sewing | Finishing | Stores | Maintenance |  |
|  | £000 | £000 | £000 | £000 | £000 | £000 |
| Overheads | 187 | 232 | 106 | 27 | 50 | 602 |
| Apportion store Basis: Mat issued | 8 | 11 | 4 | (27) | 4 | |
| Apportion maint'nce Basis: Mach hours | 16 | 38 | | | (54) | |
| Total | 211 | 281 | 110 | | | 602 |

(b) **A**

| | Cutting | Sewing | Finishing |
|---|---|---|---|
| Apportioned o/heads | £211,000 | £281,000 | £110,000 |
| Machine hours | 12,000 | 28,000 | |
| Labour hours | | | 12,000 |
| Absorption rates | £17.58 | £10.04 | £9.17 |

 **Test your understanding 7**

(a) **B**

£5,995/550 hours = £10.90

(b) **C**

£10.90 × 540 = £5,886

(c) **C**

£6,500 – £5,886 = £614 under-absorbed

 **Test your understanding 8**

Step 1: Calculate budgeted overhead absorption rate (OAR):

OAR = £5 per hour

Step 2: Calculate absorbed overhead

Absorbed overhead = £5 × 10,000 hours

= £50,000

Step 3: Compare overhead absorbed with actual overhead incurred

Absorbed overhead = £50,000 > actual overhead £48,000

therefore £2,000 over-absorption

**Test your understanding 9**

(a) **B** £40.00

£400,000 ÷ 10,000

(b) **C** £360,000

£40 × 9,000

(c) **D** £90,000 under

£450,000 – £360,000

 **Test your understanding 10**

(a) **Overhead analysis sheet**

|  | BASIS | PRODUCTION | | SERVICE | | TOTAL |
|---|---|---|---|---|---|---|
|  |  | Machining | Fabrication | Stores | Canteen |  |
| Dep'n of machinery | Value of plant | 3,200 | 1,520 | 200 | 80 | 5,000 |
| Insurance of machinery | Value of plant | 1,344 | 638 | 84 | 34 | 2,100 |
| Heat and light | Floor area | 300 | 350 | 100 | 50 | 800 |
| Power | Kw hours | 600 | 500 | 400 | 250 | 1,750 |
| Rent and rates | Floor area | 844 | 984 | 281 | 141 | 2,250 |
| Sub-total |  | 6,288 | 3,992 | 1,065 | 555 | 11,900 |
| Reapportion canteen | No of employees | 222 | 222 | 111 | (555) |  |
| Reapportion stores | Material requisitions | 780 | 396 | (1,176) |  |  |
| TOTAL | Value | 7,290 | 4,610 |  |  | 11,900 |

| | Machining | Fabrication |
|---|---|---|
| (b)   **A** | £12.15 | £9.22 |

|  |  | Machining | Fabrication |
|---|---|---|---|
| (c) | C | £500 under | £764 over |

| Machining actual | = | £7,960 |
|---|---|---|
| Machining absorbed | = | £12.15 × 614 = £7,460 |
| Under absorption |  | £500 |
| Fabrication actual | = | £3,800 |
| Fabrication absorbed | = | £9.22 × 495 = £4,564 |
| Over absorption |  | £764 |

## Test your understanding 11

1    B
2    D
3    A
4    B

## Test your understanding 12

**Production overhead control account**

|  | £ |  | £ |
|---|---|---|---|
| Actual overhead | 11,600 | Absorbed overhead | 11,290 |
|  |  | Under-absorbed costing SOPL | 310 |
|  | 11,600 |  | 11,600 |

## Test your understanding 13

|  | Mixing £ | Baking £ | Packing £ |
|---|---|---|---|
| Budgeted overhead absorption rate | £2.50 per £1 direct labour | £14 per machine hour | £12.50 per labour hour |

### PRODUCTION OVERHEAD SCHEDULE

### Month: November 1998

|  | Mixing £ | Baking £ | Packing £ |
|---|---|---|---|
| Budgeted overheads | 164,000 | 228,900 | 215,000 |
| Actual overheads | 171,500 | 224,000 | 229,000 |
| Overhead absorbed | 159,250 | 225,400 | 200,000 |

|  | Mixing £ | Baking £ | Packing £ |
|---|---|---|---|
| Over-absorbed overheads |  | 1,400 |  |
| Under-absorbed overheads | 12,250 |  | 29,000 |

### Production overhead control account

|  | £ |  | £ |
|---|---|---|---|
| Actual overhead | 624,500 | Absorbed overhead | 584,650 |
|  |  | Under absorbed | 39,850 |
|  | ——— |  | ——— |
|  | 624,500 |  | 624,500 |
|  | ——— |  | ——— |

**Test your understanding 14**

**Machine set up costs for Product R**

Budgeted machine set-ups:

| Product | Number of units | Number of batches | Number of set ups |
|---------|-----------------|-------------------|-------------------|
| D | 100,000 | 100,000/100 = 1,000 | 1000 × 3 = 3,000 |
| R | 100,000 | 100,000/50 = 2,000 | 2,000 × 4 = 8,000 |
| P | 50,000 | 50,000/25 = 2,000 | 2,000 × 6 = 12,000 |
| | | | **23,000** |

OAR per set up= £150,000 ÷ 23,000 = £6.52

Unit cost of R: = £6.52 × 8,000 set ups ÷ 100,000 units = **£0.52**

**Processing costs for Product D**

Budgeted processing minutes:

| Product | Number of units | Number of minutes | Total processing minutes |
|---------|-----------------|-------------------|--------------------------|
| D | 100,000 | 2 | 200,000 |
| R | 100,000 | 3 | 300,000 |
| P | 50,000 | 3 | 150,000 |
| | | | **650,000** |

OAR per minute = £80,000 ÷ 650,000 = £0.12

Unit cost of D = £0.12 × 2 minutes = **£0.24**

 **Test your understanding 15**

**A**

Cost driver rate = £110,010 ÷ 2,895 = £38 for each order

|  | £ |
|---|---|
| Cost recovered: 210 orders × £38 | 7,980 |
| Actual costs incurred | 7,650 |
| | ———— |
| Over-recovery of costs for four-week period | 330 |

## Test your understanding 16

| | | Correct? |
|---|---|:---:|
| (i) | A cost driver is any factor that causes a change in the cost of an activity. | ☑ |
| (ii) | For long-term variable overhead costs, the cost driver will be the volume of activity. | ☑ |
| (iii) | Traditional absorption costing tends to under-allocate overhead costs to low-volume products. | ☑ |

Statement (i) provides a definition of a cost driver. Cost drivers for long-term variable overhead costs will be the volume of a particular activity to which the cost driver relates, so Statement (ii) is correct. Statement (iii) is also correct. In traditional absorption costing, standard high-volume products receive a higher amount of overhead costs than with ABC. ABC allows for the unusually high costs of support activities for low-volume products (such as relatively higher set-up costs, order processing costs and so on).

# Short-term decision making

# 7

## Introduction

There are a number of calculations that can be completed to aid decision making in the short term. Within this chapter we will consider the cost profit volume (CVP) calculations.

| ASSESSMENT CRITERIA |
| --- |
| Estimate and use short-term future revenue and costs (6.1) |
| Examine the effects of changing activity levels (6.2) |

## CONTENTS

1  Relevant costing
2  Cost-volume-profit (CVP) analysis

# 1 Relevant costing

## 1.1 Introduction

When assisting management in making **short term** decisions only costs or revenues that are **relevant** to the decision should be considered. Any form of decision-making process involves making a choice between two or more alternatives.

For decision making, it is necessary to identify the costs and revenues that will be affected as a result of taking one course of action rather than another. The costs that would be affected by a decision are known as relevant costs.

Since relevant costs and revenues are those which are different, the term effectively means costs and revenues which change as a result of a decision.

Even though the costs and revenues are only being estimated it is important to ensure that the calculations are made knowing as much detail as possible or that any assumptions are stated. This will maintain the integrity of the information and should demonstrate professional competence.

## 1.2 Relevant costs and revenues

 **Definition**

Relevant costs and revenues are those costs and revenues that **change as a direct result of a decision that is taken**.

A relevant cost is a **future, incremental cash flow** arising as direct result of a decision being taken:

- **Future costs and revenues** – costs and revenues that are going to be incurred sometime in the future due to the decision being taken.

- **Incremental costs and revenues** – any extra cost or revenue generated by the decision that would not arise otherwise e.g. an extra amount of fixed costs due only to the decision.

- **Cash flows rather than profits** – actual cash being spent or received should be used when making the decision. Profits can be manipulated by accounting concepts like depreciation. Cash flows are more reliable.

A relevant cost or revenue could also be referred to as an avoidable cost.

 **Definition**

An **avoidable cost** is any cost that would only occur as a result of taking the decision. If the decision did not go ahead then the cost would not be incurred so it is avoidable.

## 1.3 Non-relevant costs and revenues

Costs or revenues that can be ruled out when making a decision come under the following categories:

- **Sunk costs** – past or historic costs that cannot be changed e.g. any cost incurred due to research and development that has already been carried out will not apply after the decision has been made.

- **Committed costs** – costs that are **unavoidable** and will be incurred whether or not the project is done.

- **Non-cash flow costs** – depreciation and carrying amounts are accounting concepts, not actual cash flows and are not relevant costs.

 **Test your understanding 1**

**Which of the following is not a relevant cost/revenue?**

A    Variable cost

B    Research and development costs that have already been incurred

C    Incremental fixed costs

D    Increase in sales revenue

## 1.4 Fixed and variable costs

It is usually assumed that a **variable cost** will be **relevant** to a decision as when activity increases the total variable cost incurred increases. There is a direct relationship between production activity and variable costs. However there are some situations where this may not be true.

**Example 1**

A company is considering a short-term pricing decision for a contract that would use 1,000 kg of material A. There are 800 kg of material A in inventory, which was bought some time ago for £3 per kg. The material in inventory could be sold for £3.50 per kg. The current purchase price of material A is £4.50.

**What is the relevant cost of material A for this contract?**

**Solution**

The cost per kg of material is considered to be a variable cost but you also need to consider whether the cost is a future cost for it to be relevant.

The company has already got 800 kg in inventory so this does not need to be purchased. The £3 per kg is an old purchase price i.e. a past or historic cost so it is not relevant. The material would therefore be valued at the current re-sale value of £3.50 per kg.

The company will need to buy a further 200 kg to complete the contract. This would be valued at the current purchase price of £4.50.

The total relevant cost of material A is:

| | |
|---|---|
| 800 kg × £3.50 = | £2,800 |
| 200 kg × £4.50 = | £900 |
| Total relevant cost = | £3,700 |

Unless told otherwise variable costs and the variable element of the semi-variable costs are relevant to a decision.

**Fixed costs** tend to come under the umbrella of committed costs so are not relevant. Be careful though because if the fixed cost were to step up as a direct result of a decision taken then the extra cost would be relevant as it is an incremental cost.

**Example 2**

MCL Plc absorbs overheads on a machine hour rate, currently £20 per hour, of which £7 is for variable overheads and £13 is for fixed **overheads. The company is deciding whether to undertake a contract in** the coming year. If the contract is accepted it is estimated that the fixed costs will increase by £3,200 for the duration.

**What are the relevant overhead costs for this decision?**

**Solution**

The variable cost per hour is relevant as this cost would be avoidable of the contract were not undertaken. The relevant cost is therefore £7 per machine hour.

The fixed cost per hour is an absorption rate. This is not an indication of how much actual overheads would increase by. The £3,200 extra fixed cost is relevant as it is an incremental or extra cost.

With regards short-term decision making we assume that on the whole **fixed costs** are **non-relevant** costs so we can approach decisions using the **marginal costing technique**.

# 2 Cost-volume-profit (CVP) analysis

## 2.1 Introduction

Cost volume profit analysis looks at the link between costs, levels of activity and profits generated. It is used to make short term decisions and answer questions such as:

- how many units do we need to sell to make a certain profit?

- how many units do we need to sell to cover our costs?

- by how much will profit fall if the price is lowered by £1?

- what will happen to our profits if we rent an extra factory but find that we can operate at only half capacity?

## 2.2 The approach to CVP analysis

**CVP analysis** makes a number of assumptions as follows.

- Costs are assumed to be either **fixed** or **variable**, or at least **separable into these elements**.

- Fixed costs remain fixed throughout the activity range charted.

- Variable costs change in direct proportion to volume.

- Economies or diseconomies of scale are ignored; this ensures that **the variable cost per unit is constant**.

- Selling prices do not change with volume.

- Efficiency and productivity do not change with volume.

- It is applied to a single product or static mix of products.

- We look at the effect a change in volume has on **contribution** (not profit). Therefore we use **marginal costing**.

- Volume is the only factor affecting cost.

- **Contribution per unit** = selling price per unit – total variable cost per unit.

While some of the assumptions may seem unrealistic, over the short-term considered, they are often a **reasonable approximation** of the true position.

There are a number of calculations and formulas that make up CVP analysis:

- Breakeven point

- Margin of safety

- Target profit

- Profit/volume ratio.

You will need to learn these formulae for the exam.

## 2.3    Breakeven point

 **Definition**

The **breakeven point** is the volume of sales at which neither a profit nor a loss is made.

When there is no profit or loss we can assume that total fixed costs equal total contribution:

Sales revenue – variable costs = total contribution – fixed costs = profit

- If profit is zero then total contribution must equal the fixed costs.

- Contribution per unit is constant therefore we can calculate the number of units required to break even as follows:

$$\text{Breakeven point (units)} = \frac{\text{Fixed cost}}{\text{Contribution/unit}}$$

When a company breaks even its total costs will equal total revenue. Calculating the breakeven point can be useful for management because it shows the minimum volume of sales which must be achieved to avoid making a loss in the period.

At break-even point, total contribution is just large enough to cover fixed costs.

 **Example 3**

Rachel's product, the 'Steadyarm', sells for £50. It has a variable cost of £30 per unit. Rachel's total fixed costs are £40,000 per annum.

**What is her breakeven point?**

**Solution**

To break even we want just enough contribution to cover the total fixed costs of £40,000.

We therefore want total contribution of £40,000.

Each unit of sales gives contribution of £50 – £30 = £20.

Therefore the breakeven point in units:

$$= \frac{\text{Total fixed costs}}{\text{Contribution per unit}} = \frac{£40,000}{£20} = 2,000 \text{ units}$$

We can show that this calculation is correct as below.

| | £ |
|---|---|
| Total contribution (2,000 units × £20) | 40,000 |
| Total fixed costs | (40,000) |
| | ——— |
| Profit/loss | 0 |
| | ——— |

Breakeven point can also be expressed in sales revenue **terms**. We know we have to sell 2,000 units to breakeven and we know the selling price is £50. The breakeven point in sales revenue is **therefore** £100,000.

| | £ |
|---|---|
| Sales revenue (2,000 units × £50) | 100,000 |
| Variable costs (2,000 units × £30) | (60,000) |
| | ——— |
| Total contribution | 40,000 |
| Total fixed costs | (40,000) |
| | ——— |
| Profit/loss | 0 |
| | ——— |

**NOTE**: If the break-even point is 'part' of a unit it is prudent to round the figure up to the nearest whole unit. For example, if the break-even point is 3.2 units we would need to fully make the 4th unit as we cannot sell 0.2 of a unit. If we only made and sold 3 units we would not break even as we need a further 0.2 of a unit to cover the costs.

## 2.4 Margin of safety

 **Definition**

The **margin of safety** is the amount by which the anticipated (budgeted) sales can fall before the business makes a loss.

The margin of safety is the difference between budgeted sales volume and **break-even point**. It can be expressed in absolute units or relative percentage terms.

Margin of safety (units) = Budgeted sales units − Breakeven sales units

$$\text{Margin of safety (\%)} = \frac{\text{Budgeted sales units} - \text{Breakeven sales units}}{\text{Budgeted sales unit}} \times 100$$

Margin of safety is a useful analysis of business risk as it looks at what might happen to profit if the actual sales volume is less than budgeted.

**Example 4**

Rachel's product, the 'Steadyarm', sells for £50. It has a variable cost of £30 per unit. Rachel's total fixed costs are £40,000 per annum. Rachel is expecting to achieve sales of 2,500 units.

**What is her margin of safety?**

**Solution**

To calculate the margin of safety we first need to know the breakeven point in units. From the previous example we know that for Rachel to breakeven she needs to sell 2,000 units.

$$= \frac{\text{Total fixed costs}}{\text{Contribution per unit}} = \frac{£40,000}{£20} = 2,000 \text{ units}$$

We can then work out the margin of safety in units:

= Budgeted sales units – Breakeven sales units

= 2,500 – 2,000 = 500 units

And then the margin of safety as a percentage of budgeted sales units

$$= \frac{\text{Budgeted sales units} - \text{Breakeven sales units}}{\text{Budgeted sales unit}} \times 100$$

$$= \frac{2,500 - 2,000}{2,500} \times 100 = 20\%$$

Margin of safety can also be expressed in sales revenue terms. In the example above we know we have a margin of safety of 500 units and the selling price for each of these units is £50. The sales revenue margin of safety is therefore £25,000.

## 2.5    Achieving a target profit

A similar approach to the breakeven point calculation can be used to find the **sales volume at which a particular profit is made**.

When calculating the breakeven point we wanted to find the number of units that would mean that contribution equalled fixed costs, i.e. zero profit. Now if we know the required profit we can add this to the fixed costs to find the amount of contribution we need to cover both the fixed costs and to generate the required profit.

Sales volume to achieve a particular profit:

$$= \frac{\text{Total fixed costs} + \text{required profit}}{\text{Contribution/unit}}$$

### Example 5

Information as in Rachel example above but we now want to know how many units must be sold to make a profit of £12,000.

To achieve a profit of £12,000, we require sufficient contribution firstly to cover the fixed costs (£40,000) and secondly, to give a profit of £12,000. Therefore our required contribution is £52,000.

$$= \frac{\text{Total fixed costs} + \text{required profit}}{\text{Contribution/unit}}$$

$$= \frac{£40,000 + £12,000}{£20}$$

$$= \quad 2,600 \text{ units}$$

We can show that this is the case with a summarised statement of profit or loss account.

|  | £ |
|---|---|
| Sales revenue (2,600 × £50) | 130,000 |
| Variable cost (2,600 × £30) | (78,000) |
| Total fixed costs | (40,000) |
| | |
| Profit | 12,000 |

A required profit could also be achieved by changing the **selling price** rather than the sales volume.

**Example 6**

Information as in Rachel example above but we now want to know how much the sales price needs to change to be able to make a profit of £12,000.

To achieve a profit of £12,000, we require sufficient contribution firstly to cover the fixed costs (£40,000) and secondly, to give a profit of £12,000. Therefore our required contribution is £52,000.

This means that the contribution per unit needs to be:

$$= \frac{\text{Total fixed costs} + \text{required profit}}{\text{Budgeted sales volume}}$$

$$= \frac{£40,000 + £12,000}{2,500}$$

$$= \quad £20.80$$

This means that contribution needs to increase from £20 to £20.80 – an increase of £0.80. To do this the sales price can be increased by £0.80 to £50.80.

We can show that this is the case with a summarised statement of profit or loss account.

|  | £ |
|---|---|
| Sales revenue (2,500 × £50.80) | 127,000 |
| Variable cost (2,500 × £30) | (75,000) |
| Total fixed costs | (40,000) |
|  |  |
| Profit | 12,000 |

**Test your understanding 2**

| Product | Batman | Robin |
|---|---|---|
| Budgeted sales and production | 500,000 | 750,000 |
| Machine hours required | 1,000,000 | 3,750,000 |
| Sales revenue (£) | 5,000,000 | 9,000,000 |
| Direct materials (£) | 1,000,000 | 2,250,000 |
| Direct labour (£) | 1,250,000 | 2,625,000 |
| Variable overheads (£) | 1,500,000 | 1,500,000 |
| Fixed costs £ | 1,000,000 | 2,450,000 |

The latest sales forecast is that 480,000 units of Product Batman and 910,000 units of Product Robin will be sold during the year.

**Complete the table below to calculate the following:**

(i)    budgeted breakeven sales, in units, for each of the two products

(ii)   the margin of safety (in units) for each of the two products

(iii)  the margin of safety as a percentage (to two decimal places)

(iv)  If only Robins were made how many would be needed to make a profit of £280,000? (assume fixed costs are product specific).

| Product | Batman | Robin |
|---|---|---|
| Fixed costs (£) | 1,000,000 | 2,450,000 |
| Unit contribution (£) | 2.50 | 3.50 |
| Breakeven sales (units) | 400,000 | 700,000 |
| | | |
| Forecast sales (units) | 480,000 | 910,000 |
| | | |
| Margin of safety (units) | 80,000 | 210,000 |
| Margin of safety (%) | 16.67% | 23.08% |
| Target profit (units) | | 780,000 |

2625000          6,375,000

**Test your understanding 3**

A business has a contract with a customer to produce 4,000 units of product.

Revenues and costs for 4,000 units are shown below.

| Possible production level | 4,000 units |
| --- | --- |
| | £ |
| Sales revenue | 50,000 |
| Variable and semi-variable costs: | |
| Material | 2,000 |
| Labour | 4,000 |
| Overheads | 6,000 |
| Fixed costs: | |
| Indirect labour | 12,000 + |
| Overheads | 8,000 + |
| Target profit for contract | 20,000 |

The labour cost is a semi-variable cost. The fixed cost is £2,000 and the variable cost is £0.50 per unit.

**Use the table below to calculate the required number of units for this contract to achieve its target profit. Enter the contribution per unit to two decimal places.**

| Calculation of required number of units | £ |
| --- | --- |
| Fixed costs | 22,000 |
| Target profit | 20,000 |
| Fixed cost and target profit | 42,000 |
| | |
| Sales revenue | 50,000 |
| Variable costs 2000 + (4,000 × 0.5) | 10,000 |
| Contribution | 40,000 |
| Contribution per unit 40,000 / 4000 | 10 |
| | |
| Required number of units to achieve target profit | 4,200 |

## 2.6    Breakeven charts

We can show our analysis diagrammatically in a breakeven chart.

**Breakeven chart showing fixed and variable cost lines**

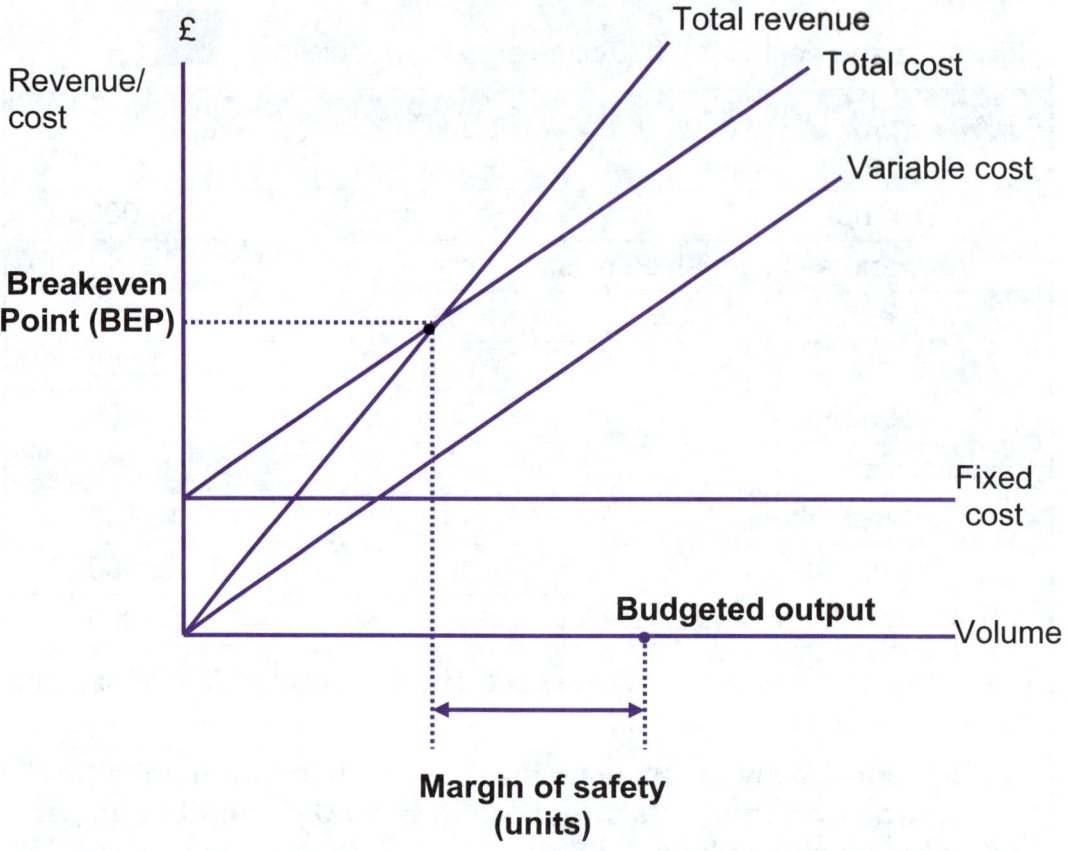

Break-even point is where total revenues and costs are the same. At sales volumes below this point there will be a loss and above this point a profit. The amount of profit or loss can be read off the chart as the difference between the total revenue and cost lines.

The margin of safety is the difference between budgeted sales volume and breakeven sales volume.

To make the diagram clearer we can show it with only the total cost line on the graph.

**Breakeven chart showing total cost line**

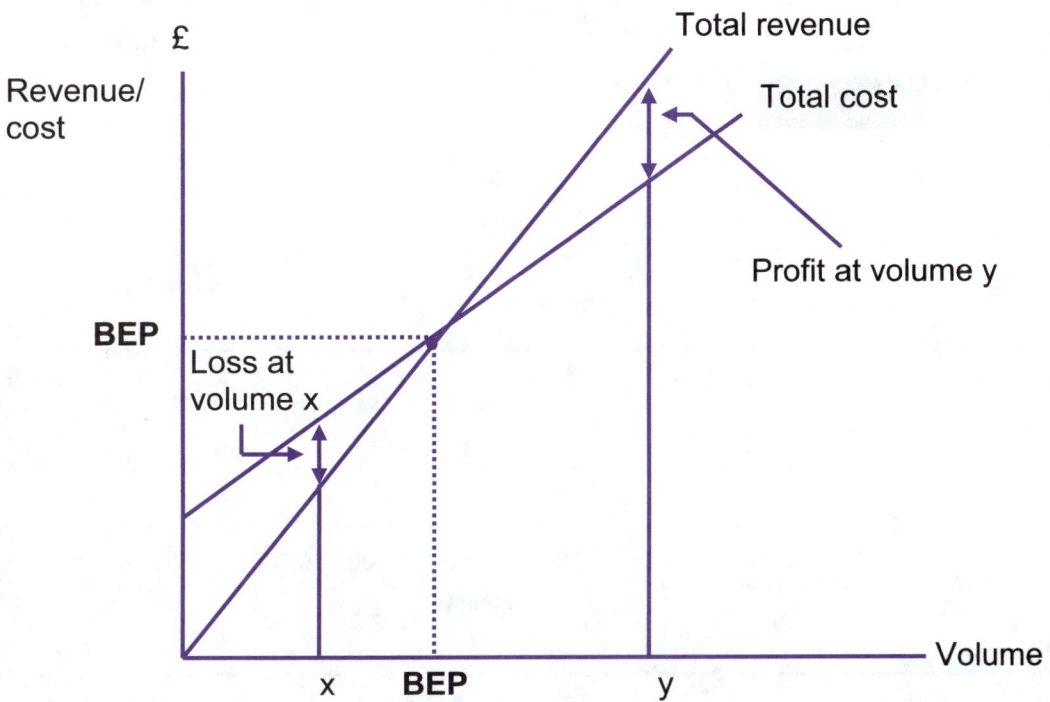

 **Test your understanding 4**

**APSTEL Limited**

The following information relates to a month's production of APSTEL Limited, a small manufacturing company mass producing a single product.

| | |
|---|---|
| Materials per unit | £4 |
| Labour per unit | £6 |
| Selling price per unit | £17 |
| Planned level of sales per month | 7,000 units |

**Required:**

(a)  Read off an approximate breakeven point in sales value and units.

(b)  Calculate the breakeven point in units using the formula.

(c)  Calculate the margin of safety as a percentage of budgeted sales.

(d)  Calculate how many units APSTEL would have to sell if they required a profit of £100,000?

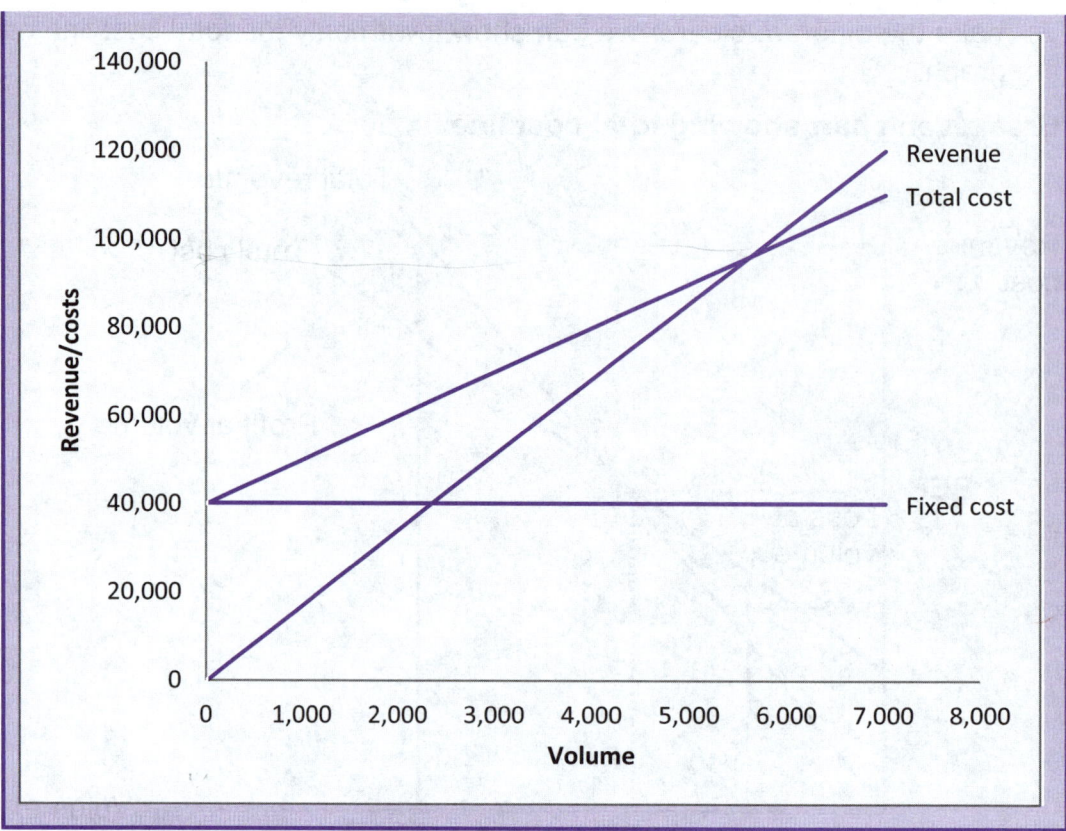

## 2.7     Profit/Volume ratio

   **Definition**

The **P/V ratio** is a measure of the rate at which profit (or, strictly, contribution) is generated with sales volume, as measured by revenue.

An alternative name which provides a more accurate description is the **contribution/sales (C/S)** ratio.

$$\text{P/V ratio} = \frac{\text{Contribution per unit}}{\text{Selling price per unit}} \text{ or } \frac{\text{Total contribution}}{\text{Total revenue}}$$

It tells us what **proportion or percentage of the selling price is contributing to our fixed overhead and profits**.

If, for example, the P/V ratio was 40% this would mean that 40% of the selling price was contribution which means therefore that the remaining 60% is variable cost.

It can be **used in the breakeven point and the target profit** calculations to be able to calculate the answer **in terms of sales value** (rather than volume).

Breakeven point in sales value = $\dfrac{\text{Total fixed costs}}{\text{P/V ratio}}$

Sales value giving a profit £X = $\dfrac{\text{Total fixed costs + required profit}}{\text{P/V ratio}}$

When using the P/V ratio in calculations the **decimal format** is used rather than the percentage i.e. 0.4 rather than 40%.

---

 **Example 7**

We return to the 'Steadyarm' example, where the product sells for £50, has a variable cost of £30 per unit and fixed costs and £40,000 per annum.

**What value of sales revenue will give a profit of £12,000?**

Sales value giving profit £12,000 means that the required contribution is £52,000.

$= \dfrac{\text{Total fixed costs + required profit}}{\text{P/V ratio}}$

$= \dfrac{£40,000 + £12,000}{0.4 \text{ (W)}}$

$=$ £130,000

This corresponds with 2,600 units (as before) at £50 sales value per unit.

**Working:**

P/V ratio = $\dfrac{\text{Contribution}}{\text{Selling price}} = \dfrac{£20}{£50} = 0.4$

---

 **Test your understanding 5**

Camilla makes a single product, the Wocket. During 20Y1 she plans to make and sell 3,500 Wockets and has estimated the following:

|  | Per unit |
| --- | --- |
|  | £ |
| Selling price | 16 |
| Material | 4 |
| Labour | 6 |
| Variable overhead | 2 |

Total fixed costs are budgeted to be £12,000

Target profit £150,000

**Required:**

(a)  Calculate the contribution per unit earned by each Wocket. *£4*

(b)  Calculate the P/V ratio. *0.25*

(c)  Calculate Camilla's breakeven point in units. *3,000*

(d)  Calculate Camilla's breakeven point in revenue. *48,000*

(e)  Calculate Camilla's margin of safety in units. *500*

(f)  Calculate Camilla's margin of safety in revenue. *8,000*

(g)  Calculate Camilla's margin of safety as a percentage of budgeted sales (2 decimal places). *14.29%*

(h)  Calculate the sales revenue that Camilla would require to meet her target profit. *648,000*

---

### 📝 Test your understanding 6

DH is considering the purchase of a bar/restaurant which is available for £130,000. It has been estimated that the weekly fixed costs will be as follows:

|                          | £   |
|--------------------------|-----|
| Business rates           | 125 |
| Electricity              | 75  |
| Insurances               | 60  |
| Gas                      | 45  |
| Depreciation             | 125 |
| Telephone                | 50  |
| Advertising              | 40  |
| Postage and stationery   | 20  |
| Motor expenses           | 20  |
| Cleaning                 | 10  |

*570*

*0.6*

*= 950*

The contribution to sales ratio is 60%.

**The weekly breakeven sales value of the business is:**

A    £800

B    £970

C    £850

D    £950

## 2.8    Profit-volume (P/V) chart

Break-even charts show both costs and revenues over a given range of activity but it is not easy to identify exactly what the loss or profit is at each volume of sales. A graph that shows the profit or loss at any given activity is called a profit/volume chart. Given the assumptions of constant selling price and variable unit costs at all volumes of output, the profit volume chart shows profit or loss as a straight line.

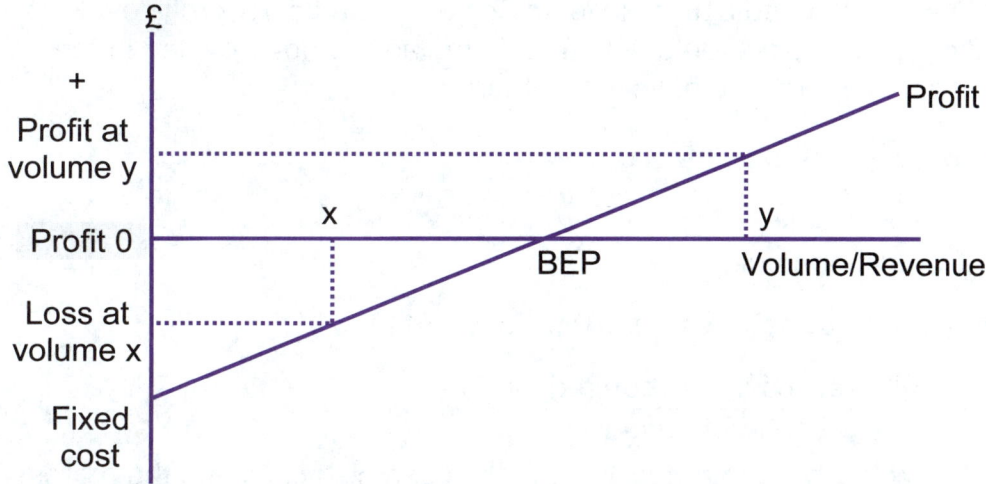

Note that at a **sales volume of nil**, the **total loss** will be the same as the business's **fixed costs**.

# 3 Summary

In this chapter we have considered the approaches required to make short-term decisions about operating levels. CVP analysis recognises that changes in profit arise from changes in contribution which, in turn, is directly related to activity levels. Thus, we can use contribution per unit to calculate the required activity level to achieve a particular profit level, including zero (breakeven point). The formulae are not provided in the exam so make sure you have learnt them.

**Breakeven point in units**

$$\frac{\text{Fixed cost}}{\text{Contribution/unit}}$$

**Sales volume to achieve a particular profit**

$$\frac{\text{Total fixed costs + required profit}}{\text{Contribution/unit}}$$

If we **know the breakeven point**, then we can also calculate the margin of safety.

**Margin of safety (units)**

Budgeted sales units – Breakeven sales units

**Margin of safety (%)**

$$\frac{\text{Budgeted sales units – breakeven sales units}}{\text{Budgeted sales units}} \times 100\%$$

**Profit/Volume ratio or C/S ratio**

$$\frac{\text{Contribution per unit}}{\text{Selling price}}$$

**Breakeven point in sales revenue terms (£)**

$$\frac{\text{Fixed cost}}{\text{C/S ratio}}$$

**Sales revenue (£) to achieve a particular profit**

$$\frac{\text{Total fixed costs + required profit}}{\text{C/S ratio}}$$

## Test your understanding answers

### Test your understanding 1

**B** Research and development costs that have **already been incurred**.

This is a sunk cost and not relevant to a future decision.

### Test your understanding 2

| Product | Batman | Robin |
|---|---|---|
| Fixed costs (£) | 1,000,000 | 2,450,000 |
| Unit contribution (£) | 2.50 | 3.50 |
| Breakeven sales (units) | 400,000 | 700,000 |
| | | |
| Forecast sales (units) | 480,000 | 910,000 |
| | | |
| Margin of safety (units) | 80,000 | 210,000 |
| Margin of safety (%) | 16.67% | 23.08% |
| Target profit (units) | | 780,000 |

**Unit contribution**

Calculate the revenue and each variable cost per unit based on budget. Sales revenue less variable costs = contribution

Batman £10 – (2 + 2.50 + 3) = £2.50

Robin £12 – (3 + 3.5 + 2) = £3.50

**Target profit**

$$\frac{2,450,000 + 280,000}{£3.50} = 780,000 \text{ units of Robin}$$

## Test your understanding 3

| Calculation of required number of units | £ |
|---|---|
| Fixed costs (12,000 + 8,000 + 2,000) | 22,000 |
| Target profit | 20,000 |
| Fixed cost and target profit | 42,000 |
| | |
| Sales revenue | 50,000 |
| Variable costs (2,000 + (4,000 × 0.5) + 6,000) | 10,000 |
| Contribution | 40,000 |
| Contribution per unit | 10.00 |
| | |
| Required number of units to achieve target profit | 4,200 |

## Test your understanding 4

(a) **Breakeven point from graph**

Approx £97,000 sales and 5,700 units.

(b) **Breakeven point in units**

$$\frac{\text{Fixed cost}}{\text{Contribution/unit}}$$

$$= \frac{£40,000}{£7}$$

= **5,715 units (rounding up)**

(c) **Margin of safety (%)**

$$\frac{\text{Budgeted sales units} - \text{breakeven sales units}}{\text{Budgeted sales units}} \times 100$$

$$= \frac{7,000 - 5715}{7,000} \times 100$$

= **18.36%**

**KAPLAN** PUBLISHING

(d) **Target profit**

$$\frac{\text{Total fixed costs} + \text{required profit}}{\text{C/S ratio}}$$

$$= \frac{140,000}{7}$$

= **20,000 units**

---

### 📝 Test your understanding 5

(a) **Contribution per unit**

= Selling price per unit – Variable cost per unit

= £16 – £12 = **£4**

(b) **P/V ratio**

PV ratio = 4/16 = **0.25**

(c) **Breakeven point (units)**

= Total fixed costs/Contribution per unit

= £12,000/£4 = **3,000 units**

(d) **Breakeven point (revenue)**

= Breakeven point (units) × sales revenue per unit

= 3,000 units × £16 = **£48,000**

(e) **Margin of safety (units)**

= budgeted sales – breakeven point

= 3,500 – 3,000 = **500 units**

(f) **Margin of safety (revenue)**

= margin of safety (units) × sales revenue per unit

= 500 × £16 = **£8,000**

(g) **Margin of safety (%)**

= (budgeted sales – breakeven point)/budgeted sales × 100%

= (3,500 – 3,000)/3,500 × 100% = **14.29%**

(h) **Sales revenue to meet the target profit**

(£12,000 + £150,000)/0.25 = **£648,000**

**Test your understanding 6**

**D** £950

Weekly fixed costs are £570; C/S ratio is 0.6 therefore weekly breakeven sales £570/0.6 = £950.

# Budgets and variance analysis

## Introduction

In this chapter we are going to look at how to produce basic budgets, why budgets differ from actual results and the variances that arise.

| ASSESSMENT CRITERIA | CONTENTS |
|---|---|
| Principles of standard prices/costs and budgeting (4.1) | 1 Standard costing |
| Calculate variances (4.2) | 2 Types of budgets |
| Analyse and investigate variances (4.3) | 3 Variance analysis |
| | 4 Causes of variances |
| Examine the effects of changing activity levels (6.2) | 5 Sub-division of variances |
| | 6 Solutions for variances |

# 1 Standard costing

## 1.1 Standard costing

Standard costing provides detailed information to management as to why actual performance differs from expected performance.

Standard costing systems are widely used because they provide cost data which can be used for many different purposes, including the following:

(a) To assist in budget setting and evaluating performance.

(b) To act as a control device by highlighting those activities that do not conform to plan and thus alerting managers to those situations which may be 'out of control' and hence in need of corrective action.

(c) To provide a prediction of future costs to be used in decision-making.

(d) To simplify the task of tracing costs to products for inventory valuation.

(e) To provide a challenging target that individuals are motivated to achieve.

An effective standard costing system relies on standard cost reports, with variances clearly identified, presented in an intelligible form to management as part of the overall cost reporting cycle.

A **standard cost** is the planned unit cost of a product or service. It is an indication of what a unit of product or service **should** cost. Standard costs represent 'target' costs and they are therefore useful for planning, control and motivation. They are also commonly used to simplify inventory valuation.

There are four main types of cost standards.

- **Basic standards** – these are **long-term standards** which remain unchanged over a period of years. Their sole use is to show trends over time for items such as material prices, labour rates, and labour efficiency. They are also used to show the effect of using different methods over time. Basic standards are the least used and the **least useful** type of standard.

- **Ideal standards** – these standards are based upon **perfect operating conditions**. Perfect operating conditions include: no wastage; no scrap; no breakdowns; no stoppages; no idle time. In search for perfect quality, companies can use ideal standards for pinpointing areas where close examination may result in large cost savings. Ideal standards may have an **adverse motivational impact** because they are unlikely to be achieved.

- **Attainable standards** – these standards are the **most frequently encountered** type of standard. They are based **on efficient (but not perfect) operating conditions.** These standards include allowances for the following: normal or expected material losses; fatigue; machine breakdowns. Attainable standards must be based on a high performance level so that with a certain amount of hard work they are achievable (unlike ideal standards).

- **Current standards** – these standards are based on **current levels of efficiency** in terms of allowances for breakdowns, wastage, losses and so on. The main disadvantage of using current standards is that they **do not provide any incentive to improve** on the current level of performance.

In order to prepare budgets we need to know what an individual unit of a product or service is expected to cost.

- A standard cost may be based on either marginal costing or absorption costing.

- Standard costs also provide an easier method of accounting since it enables simplified records to be kept.

- Once estimated, standard costs are usually collected on a standard cost card.

## Example 1

K Ltd manufactures Product K. Information relating to this product is given below.

Budgeted production for the year: 900 units

Standard details for one unit:

Direct materials:      50 square metres at £5.00 per square metre

Direct wages:         Bonding department 20 hours at £4.50 per hour

                              Finishing department 10 hours at £4.80 per hour

Budgeted costs and hours per annum are as follows:

|  | £ | Hours |
|---|---|---|
| Variable overhead | | |
| Bonding department | 45,000 | 30,000 |
| Finishing department | 25,000 | 25,000 |
| Fixed overhead apportioned to this product: | | |
| Production | 36,000 | |
| Selling, distribution and administration | 27,000 | |

**Note:** Variable overheads are recovered (absorbed) using hours; fixed overheads are recovered on a per unit basis.

**Required:**

Prepare a standard cost card in order to establish the standard cost of one unit of Product 20K and enter the following subtotals on the card:

1     prime cost

2     marginal cost

3     total absorption cost

4     total standard cost.

**Solution:**

| Standard cost card – Product K | £ per unit |
|---|---|
| Direct materials (50 × £5.00) | 250 |
| Direct labour: | |
| Bonding (20 hours at £4.50) | 90 |
| Finishing (10 hours at £4.80) | 48 |
| | —— |
| 1    **Prime cost** | **388** |
|       Variable overhead: | |
|       Bonding (£45,000/30,000 × 20 hours) | 30 |
|       Finishing (£25,000/25,000 × 10 hours) | 10 |
| | —— |
| 2    **Marginal cost** | **428** |
|       Production overheads (£36,000/900) | 40 |
| | —— |
| 3    **Total absorption cost** | **468** |
|       Non-production overheads (£27,000/900) | 30 |
| | —— |
| 4    **Total standard cost** | **498** |
| | —— |

## 2 Types of budgets

### 2.1 Budgets

Budgets are prepared for number of reasons:

- To forecast future activity levels

- To communicate goals and objectives

- To plan for the use of resources – materials, labour, money

- To control the different departments

- To motivate by setting achievable targets

These are mostly the same as the aims of management accounting.

### 2.2 Rolling budgets

A rolling budget is a budget (usually annual) kept continuously up to date by adding another accounting period (e.g. month or quarter) when the earliest accounting period has expired. The remaining budget is re-forecast, as well as the new period being added.

Rolling budgets are suitable if accurate forecasts cannot be made for example, in a fast moving environment, or for any area of business that needs tight control.

 **Example 2**

A typical rolling budget might be prepared as follows:

(1) A budget is prepared for the coming year (say January – December) broken down into suitable, say quarterly, control periods.

(2) At the end of the first control period (31 March) a comparison is made of that period's results against the budget. The conclusions drawn from this analysis are used to update the budgets for the remaining control periods and to add a budget for a further three months, so that the company once again has budgets available for the coming year (this time April – March).

(3) The planning process is repeated at the end of each three-month control period.

**Advantages of rolling budgets**

- planning and control will be based on a more accurate budget

- rolling budgets reduce the element of uncertainty in budgeting since they concentrate on the short-term when the degree of uncertainty is much smaller

- there is always a budget that extends into the future (normally 12 months)

- it forces management to reassess the budget regularly and to produce budgets which are more up to date

**Disadvantages of rolling budgets**

- rolling budgets are costlier and time consuming than some other budgets as they are constantly being updated

- may demotivate employees if they feel that they spend a large proportion of their time budgeting or if they feel that the budgetary targets are constantly changing

- there is a danger that the budget may become the last budget 'plus or minus a bit'

- an increase in budgeting work may lead to less control of the actual results

- issues with version control, as each month the full year numbers will change

- confusion in meetings as to each numbers the business is working towards; this can distract from the key issues, as managers discuss which numbers to achieve

## 2.3 Fixed budgets

 **Definition**

A **fixed budget** is a budget produced for a **single** activity level.

A fixed budget is produced at the beginning of the period and is used to provide information as to the aims and objectives that the organisation is working towards in that particular period.

The simplest form of a budget report compares the original budget against actual results.

**Example 3**

241

|  | Fixed budget |
|---|---|
| Units produced and sold | 1,000 |
|  | £ |
| Sales revenue | 10,000 |
| Material costs | 1,300 |
| Labour costs | 2,600 |
| Fixed overheads | 1,950 |
| Operating profit | 4,150 |

## 2.4 Flexed budgets

### Definition

A **flexed or flexible budget** is one which, by recognising cost behaviour patterns, is designed to change as volume of activity changes.

Flexed budgets are produced using cost behaviour and nature principles:

- **Variable costs** increase in direct proportion to activity, i.e. as activity increases so do the costs. Variable costs are constant per unit.

- **Direct costs** are assumed to be variable costs.

- **Fixed costs** are constant as activity increases. Fixed costs per unit decrease as activity increases.

- **Stepped costs** are fixed to a certain level of activity and then the cost steps up to a new fixed level.

- **Semi-variable costs** are costs that have a fixed and a variable element. The cost therefore increases as activity increases (the variable element) but will not have a zero cost at zero activity (the fixed element). The elements of the cost can be separated by using the high-low method.

- **Sales revenue** is assumed to have a variable behaviour unless stated otherwise i.e. the more units that are sold the more revenue there is and there is a constant selling price per unit.

**Example 4**

If we flex the fixed budget in example 3 assuming 1,200 units are produced and sold.

|  | Fixed budget | Working: | Flexed budget |
|---|---|---|---|
| Units produced and sold | 1,000 |  | 1,200 |
|  | £ |  | £ |
| Sales revenue | 10,000 | 10,000/1,000 ×1,200 | 12,000 |
| Material cost | 1,300 | 1,300/1,000 × 1,200 | 1,560 |
| Labour cost | 2,600 | 2,600/1,000 × 1,200 | 3,120 |
| Fixed overheads | 1,950 | N/A | 1,950 |
| Operating profit | 4,150 |  | 5,370 |

 **Test your understanding 1**

Victor Ltd is preparing its budget for the next quarter and it needs to consider different production levels.

**Complete the table below to calculate the flexed budgets for 1,500 units and 2,000 units.**

| Units sold and produced | 1,000 | 1,500 | 2,000 |
|---|---|---|---|
| Sales revenue | 40,000 |  |  |
| Variable costs: |  |  |  |
| Direct materials | 4,000 |  |  |
| Direct labour | 3,800 |  |  |
| Fixed overhead | 10,700 |  |  |
| Total cost | 18,500 |  |  |
| Total profit | 21,500 |  |  |
| Profit per unit (to 2 decimal places) | 21.50 |  |  |

## 2.5    Functional budgets

A functional budget is a budget of revenue and/or expenditure which applies to a particular function of the business. The main functional budgets are:

- sales

- production

- raw material usage

- raw material purchases

- labour

- variable and fixed overheads

- non-manufacturing overheads.

### Example 5

Newton Ltd manufactures two products. The expected sales for each product are shown below.

|  | Product 1 | Product 2 |
|---|---|---|
| Sales in units | 3,000 | 4,500 |
| Sales price per unit | £50 | £75 |

Opening inventory of finished goods is expected to be:

|  |  |  |
|---|---|---|
|  | 500 units | 700 units |

Closing inventory of finished goods is budgeted as:

|  |  |  |
|---|---|---|
|  | 200 units | 300 units |
| Material requirements are: | 2 kg per unit | 3 kg per unit |

The opening inventory of material is expected to be: 4,300 kg

Closing inventory expected levels are: 2,200 kg

Material prices are expected to be 10% higher than this year and current prices are £1.10/kg

Labour

| | | |
|---|---|---|
| Hours per unit | 3 | 1 |

Labour is to be paid at the rate of £9/hour

Production overheads per labour hour are:

Variable £3.00 per labour hour

Fixed £5.00 per labour hour

Newton has estimated that delivery costs will be £7,000 and other administration will incur £8,500

**Calculate the following:**

**(a)   The total budgeted revenue**

| | Product 1 | Product 2 |
|---|---|---|
| Sales in units | 3,000 | 4,500 |
| Sales price per unit | £50 | £75 |
| Total revenue | £150,000 | £337,500 |

Total revenue = £150,000 + £337,500 = **£487,500**

**(b)   The number of units that need to be produced to meet the sales target.**

Opening inventory of finished goods is ready to be sold so does not need to be produced, this is deducted from the sales forecast.  The closing inventory of finished goods needs to be produced on top of those that Newton wishes to sell so they are added onto the sales forecast.

| | Product 1 | Product 2 |
|---|---|---|
| Sales forecast | 3,000 | 4,500 |
| – opening inventory | (500) | (700) |
| + closing inventory | 200 | 300 |
| Production budget | **2,700** | **4,100** |

**(c)   The total quantity of material to be used.**

| | Material |
|---|---|
| Product 1 usage 2,700 × 2 kg | 5,400 |
| Product 2 usage 4,100 × 3 kg | 12,300 |
| Materials usage budget | **17,700 kg** |

**(d)** **The quantity of material to be purchased and the value of the purchases.**

There is already 4,300 kg of material in stores ready to be used (opening inventory) in production so these do not need to be bought. Newton wants to have 2,200 kg left once this production has been completed so these need to be bought in.

| | |
|---|---:|
| Material usage (from (c)) | 17,700 |
| – opening inventory | (4,300) |
| + closing inventory | 2,200 |
| | |
| **Material purchases budget** | **15,600 kg** |
| Material price per kg £1.10 × 1.1 | £1.21 |
| Material purchases budget (value) | **£18,876** |

**(e)** **The number of hours of labour and the cost of this labour.**

| | Skilled |
|---|---:|
| Product 1 hours 2,700 × 3 | 8,100 |
| Product 2 hours 4,100 × 1 | 4,100 |
| **Labour budget (hours)** | **12,200** |
| Labour rate per hour | £9.00 |
| Labour budget | **£109,800** |

**(f)** **The total overhead budget.**

| | | |
|---|---|---:|
| Variable costs | 12,200 hours × £3.00 | 36,600 |
| Fixed costs | 12,200 hours × £5.00 | 61,000 |
| | | **£97,600** |

**(g)** **The non-manufacturing budget**

| | |
|---|---:|
| Delivery | 7,000 |
| Administration | 8,500 |
| | **£15,500** |

# 3 Variance analysis

## 3.1 Analysis of a fixed budget and the actual results

The essential feature of any budgetary control system is the process of comparing budget with actual results. The difference between these figures is usually referred to as a variance.

### Definition

An **adverse variance** occurs when the actual costs exceed the budgeted costs or when the actual revenue is less than the budgeted revenue.

A **favourable variance** occurs when the actual cost is less than the budgeted cost or when the actual revenue exceeds the budgeted revenue.

### Example 6

Using the information in example 3 assuming the actual production and sales were 1,200 units

|  | Fixed budget | Actual | Variance |
|---|---|---|---|
| Units produced and sold | 1,000 | 1,200 | 200 F |
|  | £ | £ | £ |
| Sales revenue | 10,000 | 11,500 | 1,500 F |
| Material costs | 1,300 | 1,040 | 260 F |
| Labour costs | 2,600 | 2,125 | 475 F |
| Fixed overheads | 1,950 | 2,200 | 250 A |
| Operating profit | 4,150 | 6,135 | 1,985 F |

Using a fixed budget as a control method can create problems if actual production and/or sales levels differ from the budgeted production levels. If we consider the variances above:

- Actual revenue is greater than budgeted but is this purely because we sold more units or is it because we sold them at a higher price?

- Actual material and labour costs are lower than budget but more units were produced so is this because we were more efficient with the usage of the material or use of the employee's time?

- Actual overheads are more than expected. Is this related to production levels or the actual cost itself?

If this control process is to be valid and effective, it is important that the variances are calculated in a meaningful way. One of the major concerns here is to ensure that the budgeted and actual figures reflect the same activity level. To overcome this issue budgets are flexed to match the actual production level.

## 3.2 Variance analysis using flexed budgets

When completing a budgetary control report using flexed budgets the flexed budget is prepared based on the actual activity level. This ensures that any variance discovered is not due to a change in activity level i.e. the number of units produced. Any variances identified will be due to the price charged or the amount used per unit of product. For example:

- If a material variance was discovered it would be due to the number of kg used per unit or the price paid per kg.

- If a labour variance was discovered it would be due to the number of hours worked per unit or the rate paid per hour.

The sub-division of variances into price/rate and usage/efficiency are covered on the Professional Diploma in Accounting level but you need to be aware that the sub-division exists. They are used to provide a guideline for control action by individual managers. This will be covered in more detail in a later section of this chapter.

 **Example 7**

Continuing with the figures from example 4 were the fixed budget was flexed to the production and sales of 1,200 units – the **like for like** variances are:

|  | Flexed budget | Actual | Variance | Percentage change |
|---|---|---|---|---|
| Units produced and sold | 1,200 | 1,200 | 0 | 0 |
|  | £ | £ | £ | % |
| Sales revenue | 12,000 | 11,500 | 500 A | 4.17 |
| Material cost | 1,560 | 1,040 | 520 F | 33.33 |
| Labour cost | 3,120 | 2,125 | 995 F | 31.89 |
| Fixed overheads | 1,950 | 2,200 | 250 A | 12.82 |
| Operating profit | 5,370 | 6,135 | 765 F | 14.25 |

It is now possible to see:

- Actual revenue is adverse so we must have been selling at a lower price as we are now comparing using the same volume of sales.

- Actual material costs are still favourable so the usage of material or the price paid per kg of material was better than budgeted.

- Actual labour costs are still favourable so the efficiency of the staff or the rate paid per hour was better than budgeted.

- Actual fixed overheads were more than budget. Since they should not change when activity levels change this must be due an inaccurate budget or an unexpected expense occurring.

- Overall profit is more than budget – this we can be reasonably sure is because we have kept better control of the material and labour costs than planned.

- The most significant variances, calculated as a percentage of budget, are the material and labour favourable variances. The least significant is the adverse sales revenue variance.

---

 **Test your understanding 2**

Victor Ltd is comparing its budget for the quarter with the actual revenue and costs incurred.

| | Budget | Actual |
|---|---|---|
| Volume sold and produced | 1,000 | 1,400 |
| | £ | £ |
| Sales revenue | 40,000 | 60,000 |
| Less costs: | | |
| Direct materials | 4,000 | 6,000 |
| Direct labour | 3,800 | 5,300 |
| Fixed overheads | 10,700 | 13,600 |
| Operating profit | 21,500 | 35,100 |

Complete the table below to show a flexed budget and the resulting variances.

| | Flexed | Actual | Variance | F or A |
|---|---|---|---|---|
| Volume sold | | 1,400 | | |
| | £ | £ | £ | |
| Sales revenue | | 60,000 | | |
| Less costs: | | | | |
| Direct materials | | 6,000 | | |
| Direct labour | | 5,300 | | |
| Fixed overhead | | 13,600 | | |
| Operating profit | | 35,100 | | |

## Test your understanding 3

Youssef Ltd is preparing its budget for the next quarter and it needs to consider different production levels.

Complete the table below and calculate the estimated profit per unit at the different activity levels.

| Units sold and produced | 1,000 | 1,500 | 2,000 |
|---|---|---|---|
| Sales revenue | 80,000 | | |
| Variable cost | | | |
| Direct materials | 8,000 | | |
| Direct labour | 7,600 | | |
| Overheads | 14,400 | | |
| Fixed cost | 7,000 | | |
| Total cost | 37,000 | | |
| Total profit | 43,000 | | |
| Profit per unit (to 2 decimal places) | 43.00 | | |

Youssef Ltd is now comparing its budget for the quarter with the actual revenue and costs incurred.

| | Budget | Actual |
|---|---|---|
| Volume sold | 1,000 | 1,200 |
| | £ | £ |
| Sales revenue | 80,000 | 100,000 |
| Less costs: | | |
| Direct materials | 8,000 | 9,000 |
| Direct labour | 7,600 | 9,300 |
| Overheads | 14,400 | 17,500 |
| Fixed cost | 7,000 | 7,100 |
| Operating profit | 43,000 | 57,100 |

**Complete the table below to show a flexed budget and the resulting variances, indicating if it is a favourable (F) or adverse (A) in the final column.**

| | Flexed budget | Actual | Variance value | Favourable or Adverse |
|---|---|---|---|---|
| Volume sold | | 1,200 | | |
| | £ | £ | £ | |
| Sales revenue | | 100,000 | | |
| Less costs: | | | | |
| Direct materials | | 9,000 | | |
| Direct labour | | 9,300 | | |
| Overheads | | 17,500 | | |
| Fixed cost | | 7,100 | | |
| Operating profit | | 57,100 | | |

## 3.3 Reconciliation of actual with budget

Once the variances have been calculated it should be possible to reconcile the actual profit with the budgeted profit.

- An adverse variance will decrease the budgeted profit so this is subtracted from budgeted profit.

- A favourable variance will increase the budgeted profit so this is added to the budgeted profit.

## Example 8

| Flexed budget profit | | | 5,370 |
|---|---|---|---|
| | | Variance | |
| | | £ | |
| Sales revenue | Subtract | 500 A | |
| Material costs | Add | 520 F | |
| Labour costs | Add | 995 F | |
| Fixed overheads | Subtract | 250 A | |
| Actual profit | | | 6,135 |

# 4 Causes of variances

## 4.1 Investigation of variances

To be able to control aspects of the business, management will need to investigate why the variances have happened. To decide which variances to investigate management will consider:

- The **size** of the variance – is it significant compared to the cost incurred?

- The **cost** of investigating the variance – will it cost less to investigate and put it right than the variance itself?

- Whether it is **adverse or favourable** – some companies will only investigate the adverse variances?

- **Ability to correct** the variance – is the variance controllable in house (hours worked by staff) or uncontrollable (price charged by suppliers)?

## 4.2 Causes of variances

Differences between actual values and budgeted values can occur for a number of reasons. The original explanation for how each variance arose must come from the line manager responsible for that particular cost. The explanations for each variance will then be brought together by the management accountant when producing a variance or exception report for senior management.

One of the main reasons is that when producing a budget we are trying to predict the future. Prediction of the future is not an exact science and it is therefore extremely difficult to get it 100% correct.

This leads to the budgeted figures not being as accurate as they could be and therefore actual values are different from these.

## 4.3 Sales variances

A sales variance could occur for a number of reasons:

- **Price changes** – selling the product at a higher or lower price. This could happen if **discounts** are offered to the customer or discounts are removed or reduced, a price drop is required to remain **competitive** and/or an enforced price change due to **legislation**.

- **Volume changes** – higher or lower volumes are sold than expected. This could be due to a successful or unsuccessful **advertising** campaign; changes in buyers' **habits**; a problem with production may reduce availability and/or changes in **market** conditions.

When comparing a flexed budget with actual results the volume changes are already accounted for by changing the volume in the budget to match actual sales volume.

## 4.4 Material variances

When comparing a flexed budget with actual results we are looking at the material cost per unit of product. This can be broken down into the quantity of raw material that is used per unit and the price paid for the raw material.

Flexed versus actual comparisons remove the effect on cost that is due to the number of units manufactured.

A material variance can have a number of causes when we consider the raw material used to produce the product:

- **Price changes** – an increase or decrease in the price per unit of **material** purchased. This could be due to suppliers changing prices, loss or introduction of a **bulk discount**, higher delivery charges and/or a change in the **quality** of the material.

- **Usage changes** – an increase or decrease in the amount of material used. This could be due to more **efficient** or less efficient working conditions and/or a change in the **quality** of the materials purchased.

- **Quality** – if production uses a **higher quality** material then it will **cost more** to purchase. If a **lower quality** material is used it will be **cheaper** to purchase.

- **Combination of quality and quantity**. Higher quality costs more but may well lead to less wastage so use less. Lower quality costs less but may lead to more wastage so use more.

## 4.5    Labour variances

When comparing a flexed budget with actual results we are looking at the labour cost per unit of product. This can be broken down into the hours of labour worked and the rate paid per hour.

Flexed versus actual comparisons remove the effect on cost that is due to the number of units manufactured.

Variances in labour costs can be caused by:

- **Rate changes** – a higher or lower hourly rate is paid to the employees than expected. If a **higher grade** of labour is used then they will require **higher remuneration**. If a **lower grade** of labour is used then they will require **lower remuneration**. There could be an increase in the basic rate of pay (minimum wage) or a bonus may have been paid.

- **Efficiency** of staff or the **hours worked** to produce output. If the actual time taken is **longer** than budgeted then this will **cost more** but if actual time taken is **shorter** than budgeted then it will **cost less**. This could be due to change in the grade of labour as the more experience the staff the more efficient they are assumed to be.

- **Overtime**. If there is extra time needed to complete the production then this may have to lead to having to pay some staff overtime. This is often paid at a **higher rate** than normal hours. This will **increase** the labour costs due to both increased hours and increased rates of pay.

## 4.6    Fixed overheads variances

Fixed overheads should not change when activity levels change so the cause of any variance when comparing the flexed and actual figures is due to the budgeted **expenditure** being different from actual expenditure.

## 4.7    Interdependence between variances

In many cases the explanation for one variance might also explain why other variances occur. For example:

- Using cheaper materials would result in a drop in the price paid for materials (a favourable variance in the purchasing department) but using cheaper materials in production might increase the wastage rate (an adverse variance in the production department).

- An increase in wastage due to using cheaper material may reduce the productivity of the labour force leading to increased working hours to meet production demands (an adverse labour variance).

- Employees trying to improve productivity (work fewer hours) in order to win a bonus (increase in cost) might use materials wastefully in order to save time (an adverse material variance).

**Test your understanding 4**

Victor Ltd has calculated the following variances.

**Discuss the possible causes for the variances.**

| | Flexed budget | Actual | Variance value | Favourable or Adverse |
|---|---|---|---|---|
| Volume sold | 1,400 | 1,400 | | |
| | £ | £ | £ | |
| Sales revenue | 56,000 | 60,000 | 4,000 | F |
| Less costs: | | | | |
| Direct materials | 5,600 | 6,000 | 400 | A |
| Direct labour | 5,320 | 5,300 | 20 | F |
| Fixed overhead | 10,700 | 13,600 | 2,900 | A |
| Operating profit | 34,380 | 35,100 | 720 | F |

# 5 Sub-division of variances

## 5.1 Sub-division of variances

Variances can be sub-divided to provide more detail:

- Sales variances can be sub-divided into the variance due to the quantity sold (volume variance) and the variance due to the sales prices charged (price variance).

- Material variances can be sub-divided into the variance due to quantity of the materials used (usage variance) and the variance due to the price paid for the materials (price variance).

- Labour variance can be sub-divided into the variance due to the hours worked (efficiency variance) and the variance due to the rate paid per hour (rate variance).

**Test your understanding 5**

A company has a higher than expected staff turnover and as a result staff are less experienced than expected.

**As an indirect result of this, are the labour rate variances and material variances likely to be adverse or favourable?**

| | Labour rate | Material usage |
|---|---|---|
| A | Favourable | Favourable |
| B | Adverse | Favourable |
| C | Favourable | Adverse |
| D | Adverse | Adverse |

 **Test your understanding 6**

A company is obliged to buy sub-standard materials at lower than standard price because nothing else is available.

**As an indirect result of this purchase, are the materials usage variance and labour efficiency variance likely to be adverse or favourable.**

| | Material usage | Labour efficiency |
|---|---|---|
| A | Favourable | Favourable |
| B | Adverse | Favourable |
| C | Favourable | Adverse |
| D | Adverse | Adverse |

**Note:** You will not be asked to calculate the subdivisions, but you will be expected to answer discursive tasks that require knowledge of their subdivision.

**Test your understanding 7**

**Which of the following could be the cause of an adverse sales volume variance for garden furniture?**

(i)      The company offers discounts on sales prices in order to maintain business.

(ii)     Poor weather leads to a reduction in sales.

(iii)    A strike in the factory causes a shortage of finished goods.

A      (i) and (ii) only

B      (i) and (iii) only

C      (ii) and (iii) only

D      All of them

# 6 Solutions for variances

## 6.1    Possible courses of action for correction of variances

Each variance should be considered in turn and any interdependence should be considered before solutions can be arrived at. Following are a number of possible solutions for variances that arise:

- Lower the price of the finished goods to increase volume of sales.

- Increase advertising to improve volume of sales without impacting on price.

- A change of supplier may be an option for improving prices for materials.

- Negotiation of bulk or trade discounts for materials purchased.

- Updating machinery may make the usage of materials better and may also improve the efficiency of the labour force.

- Better quality control over the materials that are used in production may reduce wastage.

- Better supervision of staff may reduce idle time and errors in production.

- Increased training may reduce errors and make the staff more efficient.

- Closer monitoring of budgets may make the budgets more accurate.

This list is not exhaustive and it would be necessary to take each variance in turn and investigate the best way to improve the situation.

# 7 Summary

This chapter has demonstrated how **cost behaviours** are used to predict costs at activity levels different to budget and to produce **flexed** budgets. It will be necessary to be able to identify cost behaviours and use them to produce a flexed budget to then compare with actual results or **calculate variances**.

Another important aspect of this chapter is **analysis of variances** including possible causes and solutions to these variances.

# Test your understanding answers

## Test your understanding 1

| Units sold and produced | 1,000 | 1,500 | 2,000 |
|---|---|---|---|
| Sales revenue | 40,000 | 60,000 | 80,000 |
| Variable costs: | | | |
| Direct materials | 4,000 | 6,000 | 8,000 |
| Direct labour | 3,800 | 5,700 | 7,600 |
| Fixed overhead | 10,700 | 10,700 | 10,700 |
| Total cost | 18,500 | 22,400 | 26,300 |
| Total profit | 21,500 | 37,600 | 53,700 |
| Profit per unit (to 2 decimal places) | 21.50 | 25.07 | 26.85 |

## Test your understanding 2

| | Flexed budget | Actual | Variance value | Favourable or Adverse |
|---|---|---|---|---|
| Volume sold | 1,400 | 1,400 | | |
| | £ | £ | £ | |
| Sales revenue | 56,000 | 60,000 | 4,000 | F |
| Less costs: | | | | |
| Direct materials | 5,600 | 6,000 | 400 | A |
| Direct labour | 5,320 | 5,300 | 20 | F |
| Fixed overhead | 10,700 | 13,600 | 2,900 | A |
| Operating profit | 34,380 | 35,100 | 720 | F |

## Test your understanding 3

| Units sold and produced | 1,000 | 1,500 | 2,000 |
|---|---|---|---|
| Sales revenue | 80,000 | 120,000 | 160,000 |
| Variable cost | | | |
|     Direct materials | 8,000 | 12,000 | 16,000 |
|     Direct labour | 7,600 | 11,400 | 15,200 |
|     Overheads | 14,400 | 21,600 | 28,800 |
| Fixed cost | 7,000 | 7,000 | 7,000 |
| Total cost | 37,000 | 52,000 | 67,000 |
| Total profit | 43,000 | 68,000 | 93,000 |
| Profit per unit (to 2 decimal places) | 43.00 | 45.33 | 46.50 |

| | Flexed budget | Actual | Variance value | Favourable or Adverse |
|---|---|---|---|---|
| Volume sold | 1,200 | 1,200 | | |
| | £ | £ | £ | |
| Sales revenue | 96,000 | 100,000 | 4,000 | F |
| Less costs: | | | | |
| Direct materials | 9,600 | 9,000 | 600 | F |
| Direct labour | 9,120 | 9,300 | 180 | A |
| Overheads | 17,280 | 17,500 | 220 | A |
| Fixed cost | 7,000 | 7,100 | 100 | A |
| Operating profit | 53,000 | 57,100 | 4,100 | F |

**Test your understanding 4**

| | Flexed budget | Actual | Variance value | Favourable or Adverse |
|---|---|---|---|---|
| Volume sold | 1,400 | 1,400 | | |
| | £ | £ | £ | |
| Sales revenue | 56,000 | 60,000 | 4,000 | F |
| Less costs: | | | | |
| Direct materials | 5,600 | 6,000 | 400 | A |
| Direct labour | 5,320 | 5,300 | 20 | F |
| Fixed overhead | 10,700 | 13,600 | 2,900 | A |
| Operating profit | 34,380 | 35,100 | 720 | F |

**Sales revenue**

As the budget has been flexed to match actual sales volume the variance can only be due to price. Victor must have been able to sell at a higher price than budgeted.

**Direct materials**

An adverse variance could be due to an increase in the price paid per unit of raw material or an increase in the volume used in production.

**Direct labour**

A favourable variance could be due to a decrease in the hours worked to produce the output or a decrease in the hourly rate of pay.

**Fixed overhead**

An adverse variance could be due to understating the budget or an unknown expense occurring.

### Test your understanding 5

**C**

Less experienced staff are likely to be paid at a lower rate and therefore the labour rate variance will be favourable.

Usage of materials is likely to be adverse as the staff are less experienced, thus there will be more wastage and a higher level of rejects.

### Test your understanding 6

**D**

Usage of materials is likely to be adverse as the materials are sub-standard, thus there will be more wastage and a higher level of rejects.

Time spent by the labour force on rejected items that will not become output leads to higher than standard time being spent per unit of output, therefore efficiency will decline.

### Test your understanding 7

**C**

Option (i) will cause an adverse sales price variance but would hopefully lead to a favourable volume variance.

Options (ii) and (iii) will both impact on the volume of garden furniture to be sold.

# Principles of cash budgeting

## Introduction

The term cash in this chapter is used to describe bank account balances as well as coins and notes; and cash payments include cheque payments, BACS, direct debits and standing orders.

The majority of businesses will wish to make a profit. This means that, over a period of time, revenue needs to exceed costs. However, even if the business is making a profit, it must also have cash funds available to pay suppliers, employees and other expenses.

Cash is a business's most important asset as without cash it is not possible to pay for the running of the business. Managers must forecast and monitor cash flows to ensure the business does not become bankrupt.

| ASSESSMENT CRITERIA |
| --- |
| Principles of cash budgeting (7.1) |
| Improving cash flow (7.2) |

## CONTENTS

1  Cash flow versus profit

2  Calculating cash flows

3  Cash budgets

4  Liquidity

5  Working capital

6  Raising finance

7  Accounting software for cash flows

# 1 Cash flow versus profit

## 1.1 Cash flow and profit

Cash and profit are not the same thing. It is possible for a business to make a profit but to also run short of cash.

- Profit is a figure on the Statement of profit or loss.

- Cash is a current asset on the Statement of financial position.

A typical Statement of profit or loss is shown below:

|  | £000 |
|---|---|
| **Revenue** | X |
| Cost of sales | (X) |
| **Gross profit** | X |
| Distribution costs | (X) |
| Administrative expenses | (X) |
| **Operating profit** | X |
| Finance costs | (X) |
| **Profit before tax** | X |
| Tax | (X) |
| **Profit for the period** | X |

A typical Statement of financial position is shown below:

|  | £000 |
|---|---|
| **Non-current assets** | |
| Property, plant and equipment | X |
| Other tangible assets | X |
| Goodwill | X |
|  | X |
| | |
| **Current assets** | |
| Inventories | X |
| Trade and other receivables | X |
| Cash and cash equivalents | X |
|  | X |
| | |
| **Total assets** | **X** |
| | |
| **Equity and liabilities** | |
| **Equity** | |
| Share capital | X |
| Share premium account | X |
| Revaluation reserve | X |
| Retained earnings | X |
| | |
| **Total equity** | X |
| | |
| **Non-current liabilities** | |
| Bank loans | X |
| Long-term provisions | X |
|  | X |
| | |
| **Current liabilities** | |
| Trade and other payables | X |
| Tax liabilities | X |
| Bank overdrafts and loans | X |
|  | X |
| | |
| **Total liabilities** | **X** |
| | |
| **Total equity and liabilities** | **X** |

## 1.2    The difference between cash and profit

There are a number of reasons why the profit of a business is not the same as cash in the bank:

- **Revenue** is recorded in the Statement of profit or loss when it is earned i.e. when the sale happens, but this is not necessarily when the cash is received.  A business may make sales on credit sales creating receivables (customers who owe money to the business).

- **Costs** are recorded in the Statement of profit or loss when incurred i.e. when the purchase happens, but this is not necessarily when the cash is paid.  A business may have credit terms with its suppliers creating payables.

- **Accruals** (accrued expenses) are an expense that has been incurred in the current accounting period but has not been paid by the period end.  As it has been incurred the expense needs to be recognised in the Statement of profit or loss, the liability to pay for the expense is set up in the Statement of financial position.

  For example: A business has a year end of 31 December 20X1.  In January 20X2 a telephone bill for £600 covering November X1 to January X2 was received.  Assuming the £600 relates to 3 months of telephone expense then £400 (2/3 × £600) relates to the year ending 31 December 20X1.  The £400 reduces the profit for the year ending December 20X1 but the cash will not be affected until the bill is paid.

  This will decrease profit but will not fully impact the cash flow.

- **Prepayments** (prepaid expenses) are an expense that has been paid for in advance as it relates to a period following the current accounting period.  Although payment has been made, the expense does not relate to the current period so it is not yet recognised against the profit.

  For example: A business has a year end of 31 December 20X1.  The bank statement shows £1,500 being paid for insurance.  The insurance period was 1 January 20X1 to 31 March 20X2, which means that three months of the next period have been prepaid.  £1,500 has left the bank but only £1,200 (12/15 × £1,500) will be charged against the profit.

  This will impact the cash flow as cash is being spent but the expense has not been fully accounted for in this year's Statement of profit or loss.

- **Depreciation** is charged to the Statement of profit or loss, reducing profit, but it does not have any effect on cash.  It is a non-cash expense.

- **Provisions for doubtful debts** are charged as expenses but they are not cash flows and will not reduce the cash balance of the business.

- **Purchases of non-current assets** are often large cash outflows of a business but the only amount that is charged to the Statement of profit or loss is the annual depreciation charge and not the entire cost of the non-current asset.

- **Sale of non-current assets** will result in an inflow of cash to the business but the figure appearing in the Statement of profit or loss is not the sales proceeds but any profit or loss made on the sale.

- **Financing transactions,** such as issuing additional share capital and taking out or repaying a loan, will result in large cash flows in or out of the business with no effect on the profit figure.

---

### Example 1

A business has £50,000 profit, calculate the cash based on the following:

|  | Add/deduct |
|---|---|
| Profit | £50,000 |
| Depreciation charge of £4,500 | |
| Purchase of non-current assets for £8,000 | |
| Capital of £15,000 was introduced | |
| Cash | |

**Solution**

|  | Add/deduct |
|---|---|
| Profit | £50,000 |
| Depreciation charge of £4,500 | + £4,500 |
| Purchase of non-current assets for £8,000 | - £8,000 |
| Capital of £15,000 was introduced | +£15,000 |
| Cash | £61,500 |

Depreciation is not an actual cash flow; it is an accounting concept. In the Statement of profit or loss it has been deducted to calculate profit. To make the profit reconcile with the cash it needs to be added back on.

The purchase of the non-current asset will have decreased the cash in the bank but will not have been recorded in the Statement of profit or loss. The profit will need to be reduced to reconcile with the cash balance.

---

The capital introduced would have increased the cash into the business but will not have been recorded in the Statement of profit or loss. To reconcile the profit to cash, the capital will be added to the profit.

---

 **Test your understanding 1**

**Which of the following items would adversely affect a company's profit but not affect its cash flow?**

A    A tax charge

B    Interest paid on a bank loan

C    Depreciation of a non-current asset

D    Repayment of a loan

**Which of the following items would adversely affect a company's cash flow but not affect its profit?**

A    A tax charge

B    Interest paid on a bank loan

C    Depreciation of a non-current asset

D    Repayment of a loan

---

# 2    Calculating cash flows

## 2.1    Introduction

To be able to produce a cash budget the actual cash a business spends and receives during a time period needs to be calculated. Figures from the Statement of profit or loss and Statement of financial position will be used for these calculations.

## 2.2 Forecasting cash flows

A lot of information is needed in order to produce a cash budget.

### Sales information

The usual starting point for information for a cash budget will be sales quantities and prices. This information will normally be provided by the sales or marketing director or manager. Both the quantity of sales and the price that will be charged are vital information for a cash budget.

### Production information

Details such as the amount of production, the levels of closing inventories and the labour hours to be worked should all be available from the production manager or director. The production manager may also have information about variable and fixed expenses of the factory but equally that information may come from the accountant.

The production manager or director may also be able to provide information about any planned capital expenditure or any planned sales of non-current assets.

### Accounting information

Further information will come from the **accounts department** in the form of materials prices, labour hour rates, variable and fixed costs, details of sales of non-current assets. The accounts department or the credit control department will also have the information required to determine the payment pattern of receivables and payables.

### Forecast information

The information provided by the different departments will be current or past information. This information will need to be amended to allow for any adjustments or alterations foreseen for future periods.

There are a number of different techniques that can be used to produce forecasted figures.

## 2.3 Calculating cash flows

The preparation of a cash budget relies on identifying the expected payment patterns for receipts and payments by accounting for differences in timings arising from selling or purchasing goods and services on credit terms and on cash terms and deposits made in advance.

## Cash receipts from receivables

 **Example 2**

Opening receivables are £20,000 and closing receivables are £28,000. Revenue for the period has been £24,000.  Assuming that all the sales were on credit.

**How much cash has been received from receivables in the period?**

**Solution**

**Trade receivables**

| | | | |
|---|---|---|---|
| Opening balance | 20,000 | Cash **received** | 16,000 |
| Sales | 24,000 | Closing balance | 28,000 |
| | ——— | | ——— |
| | 44,000 | | 44,000 |
| | ——— | | ——— |

Instead of using a T account:

cash received = sales plus opening balance less closing balance

$\qquad$ = 24,000 + 20,000 – 28,000

$\qquad$ = 16,000

## Cash payments to payables

 **Example 3**

Opening payables are £5,000 and closing payables are £6,500. Purchases for the period have been £4,500.  Assuming that all the purchases were on credit.

**How much cash has been paid to payables in the period?**

**Solution**

**Trade payables**

| | | | |
|---|---|---|---|
| Cash **paid** | 3,000 | Opening balance | 5,000 |
| Closing balance | 6,500 | Purchases | 4,500 |
| | ——— | | ——— |
| | 9,500 | | 9,500 |
| | ——— | | ——— |

Instead of using a T account:

cash paid = purchases plus opening balance less closing balance

    = 4,500 + 5,000 – 6,500

    = 3,000

### Non-current assets

A business may buy (acquisition of) or sell (disposal of) a non-current asset and the cash paid or received for this will be classed as a cash outflow or inflow.

It may be necessary to calculate this cash flow with reference to the Statement of profit or loss and the Statement of Financial Position.

 **Example 4**

New fixtures and fittings were purchased in a part exchange deal. The trade in price for the old fittings was £2,400 and the new fitting had a list price of £6,000.

**What was the cash outflow for this purchase?**

**Solution**

£6,000 – £2,400 = £3,600 cash outflow.

In some cases, you may need to work out the cash paid for additions or received from a sale by looking at figures for total assets not individual ones. In such cases make sure you include the depreciation charge for the period.

**Example 5**

The carrying value of non-current assets at the start of the period is forecast to be £60,000 and the carrying value at the end of the period is forecast to be £74,000. Depreciation for the period will be £20,000. The company will pay for any additions immediately by cash.

**Calculate the cash to be paid for any additions.**

**Solution**

### Carrying value of NCA

| | | | |
|---|---|---|---|
| Opening balance | 60,000 | Depreciation charge | 20,000 |
| Cash **paid** for additions | 34,000 | Closing balance | 74,000 |
| | ――――― | | ――――― |
| | 94,000 | | 94,000 |
| | ――――― | | ――――― |

Instead of using a T account:

Cash paid for additions = Closing CV + depreciation – Opening CV

   = 74,000 + 20,000 – 60,000

   = 34,000

The accounting concept of depreciating non-current assets over their useful economic life may mean that when the asset is disposed or sold the cash received does not match the value of the asset in the accounting records. This can lead to a profit or loss on disposal. This figure is not an actual cash flow.

 **Example 6**

During the year a machine was sold that had originally cost £70,000. When the machine was sold it had a carrying value of £46,000. The loss on disposal was £10,000.

**What was the cash inflow from this sale?**

**KAPLAN** PUBLISHING

**Solution**

Disposal

| Machine cost | 70,000 | Accumulated depreciation* | 24,000 |
|---|---|---|---|
| | | Loss on disposal | 10,000 |
| | | Cash received | 36,000 |
| | ——— | | ——— |
| | 70,000 | | 70,000 |
| | ——— | | ——— |

* calculated by subtracting the carrying value (£46,000) from the cost (£70,000).

**Alternative working:**

If the carrying value of the assets is £46,000 and a loss on disposal of £10,000 was made, then the cash received must have been £10,000 less than the carrying value. Therefore cash received = £36,000.

 **Example 7**

The business decided to sell off one of its spare warehouse. The building had been depreciated at 5% on cost for the 5 years of ownership. The original purchase price was £100,000. There was a gain on disposal of £24,000.

**What was the cash received from this sale?**

**Solution**

Disposal

| Building cost | 100,000 | Accumulated depreciation* | 25,000 |
|---|---|---|---|
| Gain on disposal | 24,000 | Cash received | 99,000 |
| | ——— | | ——— |
| | 124,000 | | 124,000 |
| | ——— | | ——— |

* calculated by taking 5% of the original cost and multiplying it by the 5 years the building was owed for (100,000 × 5%) × 5.

Instead of using a T account:

Cash received = Carrying value of the sold asset plus gain on disposal

= (100,000 – (100,000 × 5% × 5 years)) + 24,000

= 75,000 + 24,000

**= 99,000**

### Non-cash items

Depreciation may be included in some of the other expenses within the Statement of profit or loss. Depreciation is a non-cash item so it will need to be adjusted for.

 **Example 8**

Expenses include a depreciation charge for £10,000. Total expenses are £30,000. All expenses are being settled on cash terms.

**Calculate the cash flow for expenses in the period.**

**Solution**

The cash flow for expenses is: £30,000 – £10,000 = £20,000.

### Period expenses

There are some expenses that are paid as they are incurred. For example, wages tend to be paid in the month that they are earned by the employees so no adjustments are usually required to turn the Statement of profit or loss figure into a cash flow figure.

 **Test your understanding 2**

An extract from the accounts for R U Bear for the quarter ended 31 March is as follows:

|  | £ |
|---|---|
| Revenue | 210,325 |
| Purchases | 32,657 |
| Wages | 50,100 |
| Rent | 15,000 |
| Insurance | 7,851 |
| Electricity | 21,039 |

The insurance includes depreciation of £3,500

Receivables at 1/1 were £18,695 and at 31/3 were £15,985

Payables at 1/1 were £965 and at 31/3 were £1,054

**Calculate the actual cash receipts and cash payments for the quarter to 31 March.**

|  | £ |
|---|---|
| Sales receipts |  |
| Purchases |  |
| Wages |  |
| Rent of office |  |
| Insurance of machinery |  |
| Electricity |  |

## Test your understanding 3

Marvin and Pea is a small cookery school.

An extract from the accounts for the month of June is as follows:

|  | £ |
|---|---|
| Revenue | 3,000 |
| Purchases | 1,400 |
| Wages | 500 |
| Insurance | 200 |
| Electricity | 75 |

Wages are paid in the following month. The wages for April were £475 and May were £450.

Receivables at 1/6 were £1,520 and at 30/6 were £1,400

Payables at 1/6 were £400 and at 30/6 were £520

**Calculate the actual business cash receipts and cash payments for the month of June.**

|  | £ |
|---|---|
| Sales receipts |  |
| Purchase payments |  |
| Wages paid |  |
| Insurance |  |
| Electricity |  |

## Other cash inflows and outflows

A business will also have the following inflows and outflows that will need to be calculated/forecast:

- Receipts and payments of relating to the raising of capital or a new loan.

- Payments made to the owners of a business (drawings or dividends)

- Other costs such as the payment of taxes to the government.

# 3    Cash budgets

## 3.1    Cash budget

A cash budget or cash flow forecast is an **estimate of all of the cash inflows and outflows for the period**.

Cash budgets are prepared:

- to show when cash surpluses are likely to occur

- to show when large and unusual items can be paid for

- to show where there is inadequate cash to finance any plans

- to act as an indicator of when surplus cash can be invested

- to provide a basis of control for the forthcoming year

- centrally, as this eliminates duplication of 'buffer inventory' of cash and allows cross subsidisation of divisions.

**Example of a receipts and payments cash budget**

|  | July £ | Aug £ | Sept £ |
|---|---|---|---|
| **RECEIPTS** e.g. cash sales, receipts from receivables, capital introduced |  |  |  |
| **Total receipts** |  |  |  |
| **PAYMENTS** e.g. cash purchases, credit payments, rent, other expenses |  |  |  |
| **Total payments** |  |  |  |
| Net cash flow |  |  |  |
| Opening cash balance |  |  |  |
| **Closing cash balance** |  |  |  |

Once cash in and out flows are applied to the opening cash figure, the closing cash balance at the end of each period can be estimated and management can plan to take any necessary action. For example:

- if there is a cash deficit then agreement with the bank can be sought for an overdraft facility

- if there is a cash surplus then the treasury department may look into short-term investment.

 **Example 9**

At 1 December 20X2 Carrot expects to have a cash balance of £4,000. It is estimated that cash from sales in December, January and February will be £48,000 each month. Cash payments for expenses each month are estimated to be £42,000 but some new equipment must be purchased at a cost of £24,000 paid for in February.

**Prepare the cash budget for the next three months and determine the net cash position at the end of each of the three months.**

**Solution**

| Cash budget | December | January | February |
|---|---|---|---|
| | £ | £ | £ |
| Cash inflows | 48,000 | 48,000 | 48,000 |
| Cash outflows: | | | |
| Expenses | (42,000) | (42,000) | (42,000) |
| Capital expenditure | | | (24,000) |
| Net cash inflow/(outflow) | 6,000 | 6,000 | (18,000) |
| Opening cash balance | 4,000 | 10,000 | 16,000 |
| Closing cash balance | 10,000 | 16,000 | (2,000) |

The closing cash balance at the end of each month is calculated by adding or subtracting the net cash flow for the month to or from the cash balance at the start of the month. The closing cash balance of one month becomes the opening cash balance the following month.

This indicates to management that although there will be cash in the bank at the end of December and January, there is expected to be a shortage at the end of February. Management can then use this information to plan for this eventuality by, for example, arranging for a bank overdraft or bank loan or selling some surplus assets.

Remember that a cash budget monitors cash – do not include any non-cash items i.e. depreciation.

### 3.2 Credit sales and purchases

Sales and purchases are often made on credit meaning that cash receipts or cash payments are not received or made until subsequent periods.

The cash budget needs to show when the actual cash is expected to be received/paid rather than the actual sales/purchases in the period.

**Lagging of receipts**

Lagging is the time it takes between buying goods and paying for them, i.e. the time it takes for receivables to pay their debts. Lagging of receipts affects a business's cash inflow as it will not match the sales revenue shown in the financial accounts.

From past experience it should be possible for a business to estimate how long the receivables take to pay and this can be used to estimate cash inflows to a business.

 **Example 10**

A business makes sales on credit. From past experience the credit controller expects cash to be received as follows:

- 10% in the month of sale
- 40% in the month after sale
- 50% two months after sale.

**Calculate the cash receipts for December to March.**

|  | Dec £ | Jan £ | Feb £ | Mar £ |
|---|---|---|---|---|
| Sales revenue | 10,000 | 12,000 | 14,000 | 16,000 |
|  |  |  |  |  |
| In the month of sale (10%) | 1,000 | 1,200 | 1,400 | 1,600 |
| One month after sale (40%) | – | 4,000 | 4,800 | 5,600 |
| Two months after sale (50%) | – | – | 5,000 | 6,000 |
|  |  |  |  |  |
| Total receipts | 1,000 | 5,200 | 11,200 | 13,200 |

**Example 11**

The information in the previous example could also be laid out as follows:

| Sales | Dec £ | Jan £ | Feb £ | Mar £ |
|---|---|---|---|---|
| Total sales | 10,000 | 12,000 | 14,000 | 16,000 |
| Income from sales: | | | | |
| Dec | 1,000 | 4,000 | 5,000 | – |
| Jan | | 1,200 | 4,800 | 6,000 |
| Feb | | | 1,400 | 5,600 |
| Mar | | | | 1,600 |
| Total cash received | 1,000 | 5,200 | 11,200 | 13,200 |

 **Test your understanding 4**

The details for the credit sales that need to be included in the cash budget are as follows.

|  | £ |
|---|---|
| April | 40,000 |
| May | 30,000 |
| June | 20,000 |
| July | 25,000 |

Recent debt collection experience has been as follows:

In the month of sale       40%

One month after sale    60%

**Required:**

**Forecast the cash receipts from receivables for May to July.**

| Sales | April | May | June | July |
|---|---|---|---|---|
| Total sales | 40,000 | 30,000 | 20,000 | 25,000 |
| Amounts received | 16,000 | | | |
| Income from sales: | | | | |
| April | | 24,000 | | |
| May | | 12,000 | 18,000 | |
| June | | | 8,000 | 12,000 |
| July | | | | 10,000 |
| Total cash received | | 36,000 | 26,000 | 22,000 |

---

### 📝 Test your understanding 5

The following data and estimates are available for ABC Ltd:

| | April £ | May £ | June £ | July £ | August £ |
|---|---|---|---|---|---|
| Sales | 60,000 | 74,000 | 90,000 | 100,000 | 120,000 |

**Notes:**

(1)   20% of sales are for cash.   *Deduct units first to work out*

(2)   The remainder is received 30% in the month following the sale and 70% two months after the sale.

**Required:**

**Prepare the cash receipts budgets for June, July and August.**

| | June £ | July £ | August £ |
|---|---|---|---|
| Cash received: | 72,000 | 80,000 | 96,000 |
| April | 33600 | | |
| May *(70%)* | 17760 | 41440 | |
| June *(30%)* | 18000 | 21600 | 50400 |
| July *(20%)* | | 20,000 | 24,000 |
| August | | | 24000 |
| Total cash received | 69,360 | 83,040 | 98,400 |

## Lagging of payments

Businesses will buy goods on credit and take time to make the payment to the supplier (payable). To be able to complete the cash budget for payments the timing and value of the payments needs to be calculated.

The calculation for the payments to payables is similar to that for receipts from receivables – calculate the total cost to be paid and then lag the payments in line with forecast timings.

 **Example 12**

A business estimates that its credit purchases for February and March will be £14,000 but will increase by 10% each month thereafter. Its payment pattern to payables is that 60% are paid in the month after the purchases and the remaining 40% two months after the purchase.

**What are the payments to payables for the three months of March, April and May?**

|  | February £ | March £ | April £ | May £ |
|---|---|---|---|---|
| Purchases | 14,000 | 14,000 | 15,400 | 16,940 |
| | | | | |
| Payments to payables | | | | |
| One month after purchase | | 8,400 | 8,400 | 9,240 |
| Two months after purchase | | | 5,600 | 5,600 |
| | | | | |
| Cash payments | | 8,400 | 14,000 | 14,840 |

**Test your understanding 6**

DG purchases in May were £100,000 and these are expected to increase by £10,000 per month for the next three months. All purchases are on credit terms. Payables are paid as follows:

* 50% in the month of purchase

* 30% in the month after purchase

* 20% two months after purchase.

**Complete the table below to identify the total purchase payments forecast for July and August.**

|  | May £ | June £ | July £ | August £ |
|---|---|---|---|---|
| Purchases |  |  |  |  |
|  | ——— | ——— | ——— | ——— |
| Payments to payables |  |  |  |  |
| May |  |  |  |  |
| June |  |  |  |  |
| July |  |  |  |  |
| August |  |  |  |  |
|  |  |  | ——— | ——— |
| Cash payments |  |  |  |  |
|  |  |  | ——— | ——— |

## Loans

A business may take out a bank loan to be able to pay for new purchases. The receipt of the loan would be included in the receipts section of the cash budget. A loan will need to be paid back to the bank. There are 2 parts to a loan repayment – the **capital (principal) repayment** and the **interest charged** on the loan – these will both feature in the payments section of the cash budget.

## Labour costs

Labour costs are normally paid in the month in which they are incurred. Labour cost can be calculated based on units produced (piecework), standard or actual hours worked and/or an annual salary.

Overtime payments/premiums may also be incurred in labour costs.

## Other costs and receipts

Care should be taken with other costs, for example administration or distribution costs, as they may include a certain amount which relates to depreciation. Depreciation is not a cash flow and therefore this amount should be excluded from the cash budget.

Examples of other costs and receipts include:

- **Interest received** – in practice the amount of the interest will be calculated on a daily basis. For cash budgeting purposes the amount of interest will normally be calculated on the positive cash balance at the end of the month.

- **Overdraft interest** – as with interest received, the amount of overdraft interest will be calculated on a daily basis. For cash budgeting purposes the amount of overdraft interest will normally be calculated on the basis of the amount of the overdraft outstanding at the end of the previous month.

 **Test your understanding 7**

Flattyre is preparing cash payment figures to include in a cash budget. The following information was provided by the production manager.

- Purchases are paid two months after the date of purchase.

| | February | March | April | May | June | July |
|---|---|---|---|---|---|---|
| Purchases (£) | 70,000 | 72,000 | 77,000 | 80,000 | 83,000 | 85,000 |
| Wages (£) | 15,000 | 17,000 | 17,000 | 18,000 | 18,000 | 18,500 |
| Expenses (£) | 6,000 | 6,500 | 6,750 | 7,000 | 7,000 | 7,750 |

- Wages are paid in the month that they are incurred and expenses are paid in the month after they are incurred. The figures are:

- Expenses include £3,000 each month for depreciation.

- A new machine is to be purchased in May at a total cost of £40,000. Payment for the machine is to be made in 8 equal instalments starting in June. This machine is to be depreciated monthly on a straight line basis at 25% per annum.

**Complete the table below for the payments section of the cash budget for Flattyre for the three months ended July.**

|  | May £ | June £ | July £ |
|---|---|---|---|
| Purchases |  |  |  |
| Wages |  |  |  |
| Expenses |  |  |  |
| New machine |  |  |  |
| Total payments |  |  |  |

# 4 Liquidity

## 4.1 Liquidity

Liquidity is the measure of surplus cash and near cash, over and above the level required to meet obligations. The main sources of liquidity are usually:

- cash in the bank

- short term investments that can be cashed in easily and quickly

- cash inflows from normal trading operations (cash sales and payments by receivables for credit sales)

- an overdraft facility or other ready source of extra borrowing.

Liquid assets consist of both cash and items that could or will be converted into cash within a short time, with little or no loss. They include some investments, for example:

- deposits with banks or building societies where a minimum notice period for withdrawal is required

- investments in government securities, which in the UK are called gilt-edged inventories (or 'gilts')

- other liquid assets are trade receivables and, possibly, inventory.

Trade receivables should be expected to pay what they owe within a fairly short time, so receivables are often considered a liquid asset for a business.

Inventory is less liquid than receivables as it needs to be sold to then become a receivable balance then cash. In some businesses, such as retailing, inventory will be used or re-sold within a short time, to create sales for the business and cash income.

Liquidity can be boosted if a business has an unused overdraft facility, so that it could go into the overdraft with its bank if it needed to.

### 4.2    Improving liquidity

One of the objectives of cash budgeting is to provide a basis or reference point against which actual cash flows can be monitored. Comparing actual cash flows with the budget can help with:

*   identifying whether cash flows are much better or worse than expected (variance analysis)

*   predicting what cash flows are now likely to be in the future, and in particular whether the business will have enough cash (or liquidity) to survive.

Possible decisions that could be taken to deal with forecast short-term cash deficits include:

*   additional short-term borrowing

*   negotiating a higher overdraft limit with the bank

*   the sale of short-term investments, if the company has any

*   using different forms of financing to reduce cash flows in the short term

*   changing the amount of discretionary cash flows, deferring expenditures or bringing forward revenues. For example:

    –    reducing the dividend paid to shareholders

    –    postponing nonessential capital expenditure

    –    bringing forward the planned disposal of non-current assets

    –    reducing inventory levels reducing the cash tied up in the assets

    –    shortening the time taken to collect receivables, perhaps by offering a prompt payment discount (PPD)

    –    delaying payment to payables.

For longer term liquidity issues it may be necessary to raise additional finance:

*   internally, from the owners of the business in the form of equity

*   externally, in the form of debt such as a loan

# 5 Working capital

## 5.1 Working capital

 **Definition**

Working capital is the short-term net assets of the business made up of inventory, receivables, payables and cash.

Working capital is the capital available for conducting the day to day operations of an organisation. It is normally expressed as the excess of current assets (trade receivables, inventory and cash) over current liabilities (trade payables, other payables and overdraft).

Working capital management is the management of all aspects of both current assets and current liabilities, to minimise the risk of insolvency whilst maximising the return on assets.

The liquidity of a business, particularly its operational activities, is therefore related to its working capital and in particular its inventory, receivables and short-term payables. A business that has good liquidity is unlikely to have serious cash flow problems. When a liquid business has to make a cash payment, it should be able to obtain the money from somewhere to do it. Normally, the cash to pay suppliers and employees comes from the cash received from trade receivables.

## 5.2 Working capital cycle

The working capital cycle (cash cycle) is the length of time between the company's outlay on raw materials, wages and other expenditure and the inflow of cash from the sale of goods.

The faster a firm can 'push' items around the cycle the lower its investment in working capital will be:

The working capital cycle:

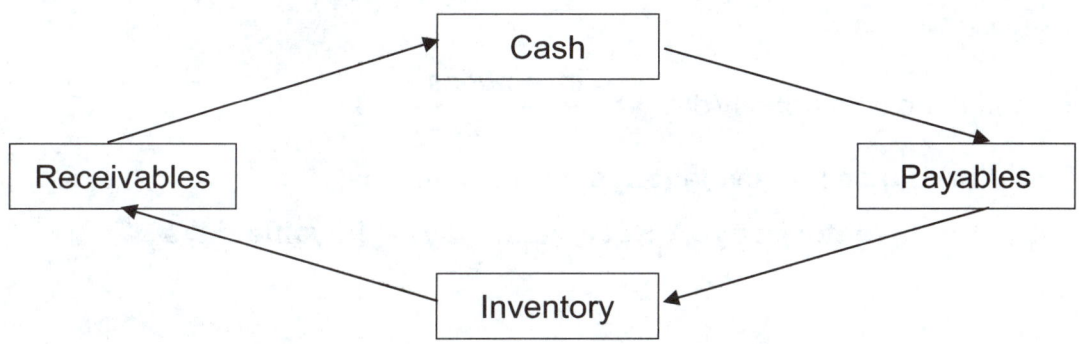

Time line:

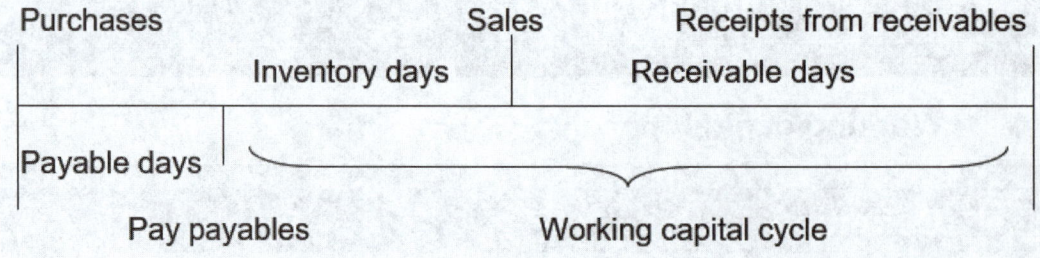

Trying to shorten the working capital cycle may have detrimental effects elsewhere, with the organisation lacking the cash to meet its commitments and losing sales since customers will generally prefer to buy from suppliers who are prepared to extend trade credit, and who have items available when required.

Any assessment of the length of the cycle must take into account the nature of the business involved. A supermarket chain will tend to have a very low or negative cycle – they have very few, if any, credit customers but they have a high inventory turnover and they can negotiate quite long credit periods with their suppliers.

## 5.3 Calculating the working capital cycle

The working capital cycle (cash cycle) can be calculated in days using the following formulae:

$$\text{Trade receivable collection period (days)} = \frac{\text{trade receivables}}{\text{revenue}} \times 365$$

Ideally we would want to use credit sales in this calculation as some of the revenue may be from cash sales. If the credit sales figure is not available, then the next best alternative is revenue.

$$\text{Trade payable payment period (days)} = \frac{\text{trade payables}}{\text{cost of sales}} \times 365$$

Ideally we would want to use credit purchases in this calculation. If the credit purchases figure is not available, then the next best alternative is to use cost of sales.

$$\text{Inventory holding period (days)} = \frac{\text{inventories}}{\text{cost of sales}} \times 365$$

The **Working capital cycle (days)** is calculated as:

**Inventory days + Receivable days – Payable days**

**Example 13**

Below are the relevant details from the Statement of financial position and Statement of profit or loss from Parcel.

Extract from the Statement of financial position

|                            | £000  |
|----------------------------|-------|
| **Current assets**         |       |
| Inventories                | 500   |
| Trade receivables          | 1,000 |
| Cash and cash equivalents  | 200   |
| **Trade payables**         | (900) |

Extract from the Statement of profit or loss

|                     | £000    |
|---------------------|---------|
| Revenue             | 5,000   |
| Cost of sales       | (3,000) |
|                     | ——————  |
| Gross profit        | 2,000   |
| Operating expenses  | (500)   |
|                     | ——————  |
| Profit for the year | 1,500   |

**Calculate the working capital cycle.**

Trade receivable collection period (days) $= \dfrac{\text{trade receivables}}{\text{revenue}} \times 365$

$$= \dfrac{1,000}{5,000} \times 365 = 73.0 \text{ days}$$

Trade payable payment period (days) $= \dfrac{\text{trade payables}}{\text{cost of sales}} \times 365$

$$= \dfrac{900}{3,000} \times 365 = 109.5 \text{ days}$$

Inventory holding period (days) $= \dfrac{\text{inventories}}{\text{cost of sales}} \times 365$

$$= \dfrac{500}{3,000} \times 365 = 60.8 \text{ days}$$

Working capital cycle = 60.8 + 73.0 − 109.5 = 24.3 days

**Test your understanding 8**

**Which is the correct formula for the working capital cycle?**

A      Receivable days – inventory days – payable days

B      Receivable days – inventory days + payable days

C      Receivable days + inventory days – payable days

D      Receivable days + inventory days + payable days

 **Test your understanding 9**

A business has an inventory holding period of 20 days, receives payment from its customers in 60 days and pays its payables in 45 days.

**What is the working capital cycle in days for the business?**

A      5 days

B      53 days

C      35 days

D      125 days

 **Test your understanding 10**

A business has working capital cycle of 50 days, receives payment from its customers in 30 days and pays its payables in 40 days.

**What is the inventory holding period in days for the business?**

A      40 days

B      60 days

C      20 days

D      120 days

**Test your understanding 11**

A business provides the following information:

| | |
|---|---|
| Trade receivables | £8m |
| Trade payables | £4m |
| Inventory | £8.6m |
| Sales (80% on credit) | £60m |
| Material purchases (all on credit) | £36m |
| Cost of sales | £50m |

**Calculate the business's working capital cycle (to the nearest day)?**

 **6** **Raising finance**

## 6.1 Introduction

At various stages in a business's life cycle the management may find that there is a need to raise additional finance. There are many reasons why a business may need to raise additional finance but the most common are:

- to fund working capital
- to increase working capital
- to reduce payables
- to purchase non-current assets
- to acquire another business.

The need to raise the finance may be highlighted by a deficit in the cash budget, by management decisions regarding investment in non-current assets, or by the business strategy of growth by acquisition.

## 6.2 The form of finance required

When deciding which type of finance to use, it is important to consider the specific circumstances of the business and the purpose for which the finance is required.

In the rest of this chapter we will consider different types of finance available for funding the acquisition of non-current assets. As a rule of thumb the time scale of the finance should match the time scale of the reason for the finance.

## 6.3 Acquisition of non-current assets

Not only will a business require enough cash to pay its payables and expenses, such as wages, when they fall due, but most businesses will also need to **invest in additional or replacement non-current assets** on a fairly regular basis.

Non-current assets are distinguished from current assets by the following characteristics, they:

- are long-term in nature

- are not normally acquired for resale

- are could be tangible or intangible

- are used to generate income directly or indirectly for a business

- are not normally liquid assets (i.e. not easily and quickly converted into cash without a significant loss in value).

In many cases a business will not have enough cash to purchase the non-current assets required to maintain or expand operations and will therefore need to raise finance in order to fund the purchase.

### Cash

If a business does have 'spare' cash, or a cash surplus, then this could be used to fund the purchase of non-current assets. The amount and length of time the cash is available for would need to be considered. Non-current assets do not tend to be easily of quickly converted in to cash so if there is any uncertainty of value or duration of the surplus then this would not be a feasible option.

If cash is used, then the business will take full ownership of the non-current asset and the all the risks and rewards are passed to them.

Non-current assets generally cost a lot of money and are purchased with the intention that they be used over a period of years. For most businesses the full purchase cost cannot be funded from cash available in the business, and so other financing methods must be found.

### Overdraft

It may be possible to negotiate a bank overdraft for a fixed period in terms of a maximum available facility. The bank would undertake to advance anything up to, say £50,000, and the business can take advantage of the facility as and when it needs to.

Bank overdrafts have the following features:

- interest will generally be at a variable rate, calculated on a day-to-day basis with reference to the bank's base rate. Although the interest rate on an overdraft may be typically higher than on a loan, the important point about overdraft interest is that it is calculated daily on the amount of the actual overdraft rather than on a fixed amount as would be the interest on a loan.

- flexibility. The business only pays interest on the amount actually drawn, although there may be an additional flat charge of perhaps 0.25% on the maximum facility.

- overdrafts are (technically) repayable on demand and should never be regarded as substitutes for adequate medium term finance.

### Part-exchange

Part of the purchase price of the asset is satisfied by transferring ownership of another asset to the seller. This is frequently seen in the case of motor vehicles, and represents a disposal of the old asset and a purchase of the new asset at the same time.

The valuation of the old asset may be lower than if it was sold privately. It is highly unlikely that the part exchange value will cover the cost of the new asset so extra cash will still need to be sourced.

### Loan

A bank or other lender could lend the business cash to pay for the asset, at a negotiated interest rate. Often the loan will be secured on the asset, so that it can be sold directly for the benefit of the bank or lender in the event of non-payment or liquidation.

A term loan with a bank is a loan for a fixed amount, for an agreed period on pre-arranged terms. The loan can be tailored to meet the requirements of the borrower. It can be taken out for a period which matches the assets which it is financing and the repayment terms can be negotiated to match with the cash flows from the asset or the other business cash flows. Term loans can be for virtually any period and the repayment terms can be negotiated with the bank:

- Interest rates may be fixed or variable and they tend to be lower than that on an overdraft.

- There are a variety of methods of repaying interest and capital.

- The loan can be drawn upon in stages, e.g. 50% now and 50% in three months' time.

In most cases a bank loan is most appropriate for the purchase of major assets which will hopefully provide income over the loan period out of which the loan interest and repayments can be made.

**Hire purchase**

If a non-current asset is to be purchased by the business, but there is not enough cash available for an outright purchase, one simple method is to purchase the asset on a hire purchase scheme.

The business makes regular payments to the finance company (comprising capital amounts plus interest) but the asset remains the finance company's property until the last regular payment is made, when the business can elect to take over the asset's full ownership. This method can be used for machinery, vehicles and computer equipment.

Hire purchase and instalment credit arrangements can be set up quickly and can generally offer fairly flexible repayment terms. The security for the 'advance' is clearly provided by the asset being purchased. If payment is not completed, then the asset is re-possessed by the finance company.

The main disadvantage of a hire purchase agreement is that the total payment for asset can far outweigh the cash purchase price.

 **Example 14**

Enterprise Limited is considering entering into a hire purchase agreement to purchase non-current assets of a value of £2 million.

The amount of interest payable on the £2 million is £584,979. There are 47 regular monthly payments with an option to purchase the asset in the last month for an additional £53,888. Enterprise Limited wishes to own the asset at the end of the hire purchase agreement. The term is 48 months at an APR of 13.2%.

**Required**

**Calculate the monthly and total cost of the hire purchase for Enterprise Limited.**

**Solution**

**Monthly cost**

Enterprise Limited will be paying the £53,888 in the final month to own the asset so the cost that needs to be spread over 47 months = £2,000,000 + £584,979 – £53,888 = £2,531,091

Monthly repayments = £2,531,091 ÷ 47 = £53,853

**Total cost**

Total cost of hire purchase = (£53,853 × 47) + 53,888 = £2,584,979

Which can also be calculated as £2,000,000 + £584,979 = £2,584,979

As we have seen, there is a variety of forms of finance available to a business. Each of these forms of finance has different characteristics and different costs and it is vital that the most appropriate and cheapest form of finance is chosen to meet the funding requirements of each situation.

# 7 Accounting software for cash flows

## 7.1 Management information

As we saw in Chapter 1, a management accountant's main objective is to provide information to managers to enable the correct decisions to be made. Management information can take any format that is useful.

## 7.2 Automation and visualisation

When producing cash flow forecasts and budgets spreadsheets can be very useful. One of the most useful functions of a spreadsheet is being able to input formulae to enable calculation to happen automatically when data is input in specific cells. Most spreadsheet software also allows for graphs and charts to be produced, allowing users of the reports to visually see how the cash levels change over time.

### Example 15

Preparing budgets and forecasts are classic applications of spreadsheets, as they allow estimates to be changed without having to recalculate everything manually. Here is an extract from a cash flow forecast:

|  | A | B | C | D | E |
|---|---|---|---|---|---|
| 1 | Cashflow forecast for 20X2 | | | | |
| 2 | Month | Jan | Feb | Mar | Apr |
| 3 | Sales receipts | £1,867 | £1,828 | £1,893 | £1,939 |
| 4 | | | | | |
| 5 | Payments | | | | |
| 6 | Puchases | £1,691 | £1,644 | £1,701 | £1,798 |
| 7 | Overheads | £57 | £57 | £57 | £57 |
| 8 | Bank Loan | £12 | £12 | £12 | £12 |
| 9 | VAT | £160 | | | |
| 10 | Overdraft interest | £2 | | | |
| 11 | Total payments | £1,922 | £1,713 | £1,770 | £1,867 |
| 12 | | | | | |
| 13 | Net cash flow | -£55 | £115 | £123 | £72 |
| 14 | Opening balance | -£134 | -£189 | -£74 | £49 |
| 15 | Closing balance | -£189 | -£74 | £49 | £121 |
| 16 | | | | | |

The key formulae in this statement are:

Total payments e.g. = sum(B6:B10)

Net cash flow = B3-B11

Closing balance = B13+B14

Displaying this data graphically can help to see trends

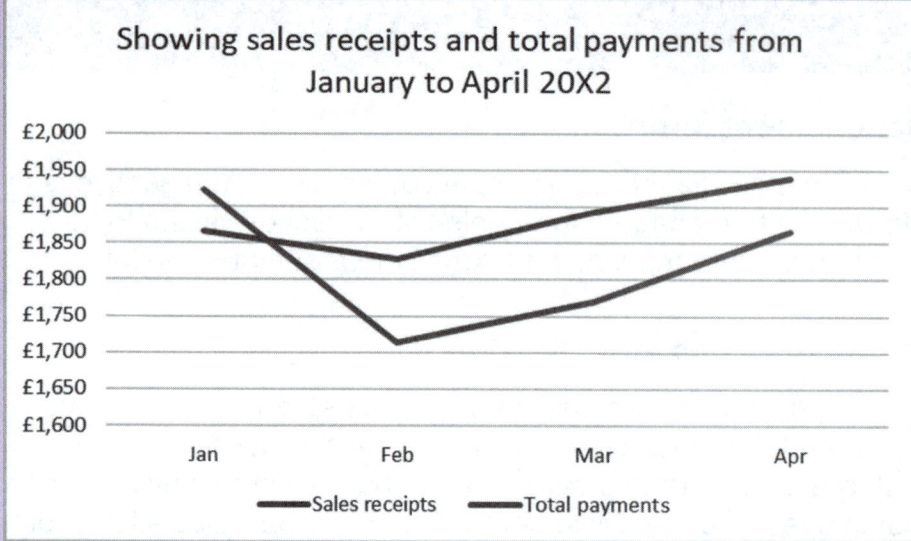

Receipts and payments are both increasing but payments are increasing more rapidly as the payments line is steeper.

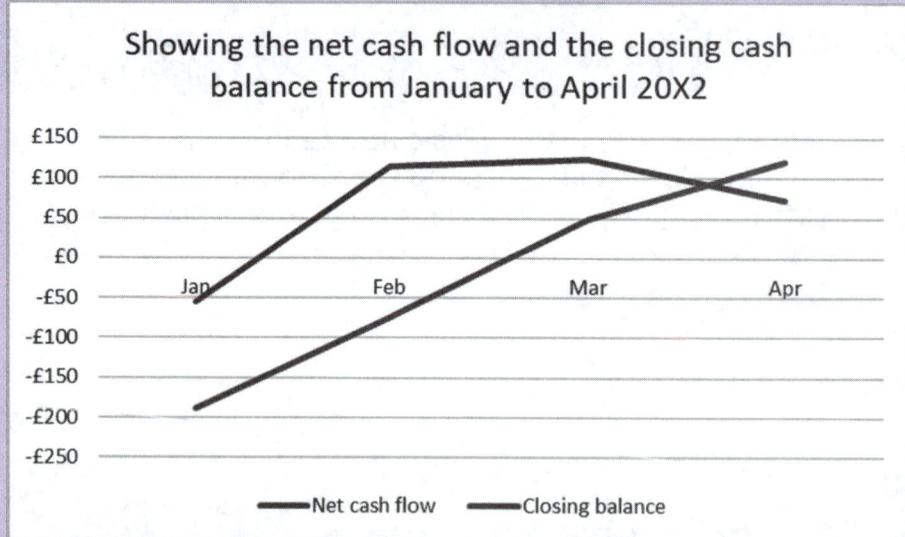

The closing cash balance has been steadily improving but the net cash flow is falling again.

Using other spreadsheet tools manager would be able to forecast what could happen to the cash flows if the general trends continued.

Spreadsheets are covered in much more detail in Chapter 10.

# 8 Summary

This chapter demonstrates the principles of cash budgeting. It has highlighted the differences between cash and profit and the importance of managing cash and liquid funds to maintain and run a business

It has demonstrated how the forecast sales revenue and purchases values do not necessarily reflect the cash in and out flows required for a cash budget. This is because of a delay in receiving receipts from receivables and delays in paying payables.

There are many choices facing a business that needs to raise finance but it is important that the right choice of the form of finance is made. This will start with an initial consideration of the reason for the additional finance and to match the option with the life of the asset.

## Test your understanding answers

 **Test your understanding 1**

Which of the following items would adversely affect a business's profit but not affect its cash flow?

**C**    Depreciation of a non-current asset

Which of the following items would adversely affect a business's cash flow but not affect its profit?

**D**    Repayment of a loan

Options A and B would affect both cash and profits. Option C would affect profits only.  Option D would affect cash only.

The tax charge would be recorded in the SOPL as an expense, this will reduce the profit.  The cash outflow to pay the tax charge would reduce the cash on the SOFP of the business.

The interest paid on a bank loan is recorded as an expense (finance cost) on the SOPL therefore reducing profit.  The interest would be paid with cash reducing the cash flow in the business.

Depreciation of a non-current asset is an accounting principle.  It is recorded as an expense in the SOPL, reducing profit but no cash is actually spent.  The depreciation reduced the value of the non-current assets on the SOPF.

Repaying a loan is an outflow of cash which would affect the cash on the SOFP.  The record of the loan is a liability on the SOFP so there is no impact on profit.

 **Test your understanding 2**

|  | £ |
|---|---|
| Sales receipts | 18,695 + 210,325 – 15,985 = 213,035 |
| Purchases | 965 + 32,657 – 1,054 = 32,568 |
| Wages | 50,100 |
| Rent of office | 15,000 |
| Insurance | 7,851 – 3,500 = 4,351 |
| Electricity | 21,039 |

## Test your understanding 3

| | £ |
|---|---|
| Sales receipts | 1,520 + 3,000 – 1,400 = 3,120 |
| Purchase payments | 400 + 1,400 – 520 = 1,280 |
| Wages paid | (from May) 450 |
| Insurance | 200 |
| Electricity | 75 |

## Test your understanding 4

| Sales | April | May | June | July |
|---|---|---|---|---|
| Total sales | 40,000 | 30,000 | 20,000 | 25,000 |
| Amounts received | 16,000 | | | |
| Income from sales: | | | | |
| April | | 24,000 | | |
| May | | 12,000 | 18,000 | |
| June | | | 8,000 | 12,000 |
| July | | | | 10,000 |
| Total cash received | | 36,000 | 26,000 | 22,000 |

## Test your understanding 5

| | June £ | July £ | August £ |
|---|---|---|---|
| Receipts of cash | | | |
| Cash sales 20% | 18,000 | 20,000 | 24,000 |
| Credit sales 80% | 72,000 | 80,000 | 96,000 |
| Cash received: | | | |
| April | 33,600 | | |
| May | 17,760 | 41,440 | |
| June | 18,000 | 21,600 | 50,400 |
| July | | 20,000 | 24,000 |
| August | | | 24,000 |
| Total cash received | 69,360 | 83,040 | 98,400 |

## Test your understanding 6

| | May £ | June £ | July £ | August £ |
|---|---|---|---|---|
| Purchases | 100,000 | 110,000 | 120,000 | 130,000 |
| Payments to payables | | | | |
| May | 50,000 | 30,000 | 20,000 | |
| June | | 55,000 | 33,000 | 22,000 |
| July | | | 60,000 | 36,000 |
| August | | | | 65,000 |
| Cash payments | | | 113,000 | 123,000 |

## Test your understanding 7

| | May £ | June £ | July £ |
|---|---|---|---|
| Purchases | 72,000 | 77,000 | 80,000 |
| Wages | 18,000 | 18,000 | 18,500 |
| Expenses | 3,750 | 4,000 | 4,000 |
| New machine | 0 | 5,000 | 5,000 |
| Total cash payments | 93,750 | 104,000 | 107,500 |

**Test your understanding 8**

**Answer C**

Receivable days + inventory days – payable days

 **Test your understanding 9**

**Answer C**

20 + 60 – 45 = 35 days

 **Test your understanding 10**

**Answer B**

50 day cash cycle = Inventory days + 30 receivable days – 40 payable days

Inventory days = 50 day cash cycle – 30 receivable days + 40 payable days = 60 days

 **Test your understanding 11**

Receivable days = 8/(60 × 0.8) × 365 = 61 days

Inventory days = 8.6/50 × 365 = 63 days

Payable days = 4/36 × 365 = 41 days

Operating cycle = 61 + 63 – 41 = 83 days

# Spreadsheets for management accounts

## Introduction

The TYU in this chapter are designed to test your knowledge on the techniques shown in this chapter. You will need to download the spreadsheets from MyKaplan. Suggested answers are available on MyKaplan, although it is better to refer to the notes and try to understand the methods than look straight at the answers.

### ASSESSMENT CRITERIA

Organise, record and format data (5.1)

Use tools to manipulate, analyse and verify data (5.2)

Use tools to prepare, protect and present accounting information (5.3)

## CONTENTS

# 1 Spreadsheet basics

## 1.1 Spreadsheet structure

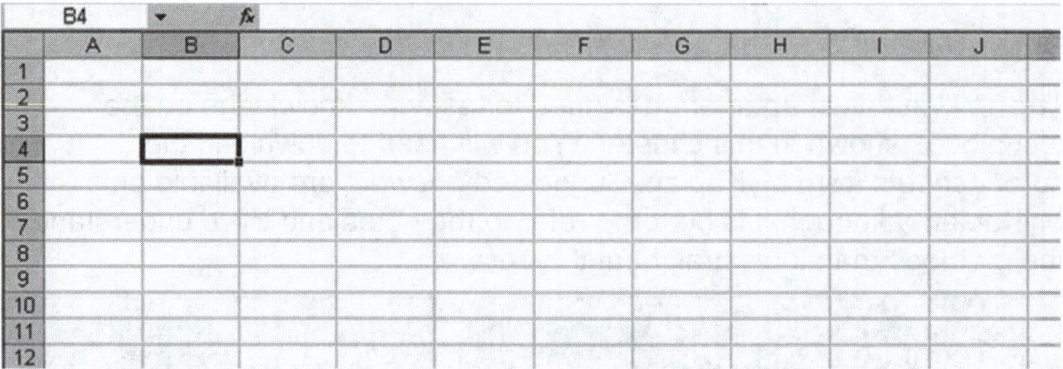

The spreadsheet (worksheet) shown above is made up of 'Rows', 'Columns' and 'Cells:

- The 'Rows' are numbered down the left hand-side from 1 onwards.

- The 'Columns' are lettered along the top from A onwards.

- The 'Cells' are the junction of columns and rows [example cell A1 is the junction of Column A and Row 1].

- The 'Active' cell is where you are be able to enter data and is highlighted with a bold border [See B4 above]. Both the column letter and the row number are also highlighted.

## 1.2 Selecting cells

To select a cell, left click on the cell you wish to select. This is now the Active Cell. The value or formula in the Active Cell will be shown in the Formula Bar, and the Cell Reference will be shown in the Name Box.

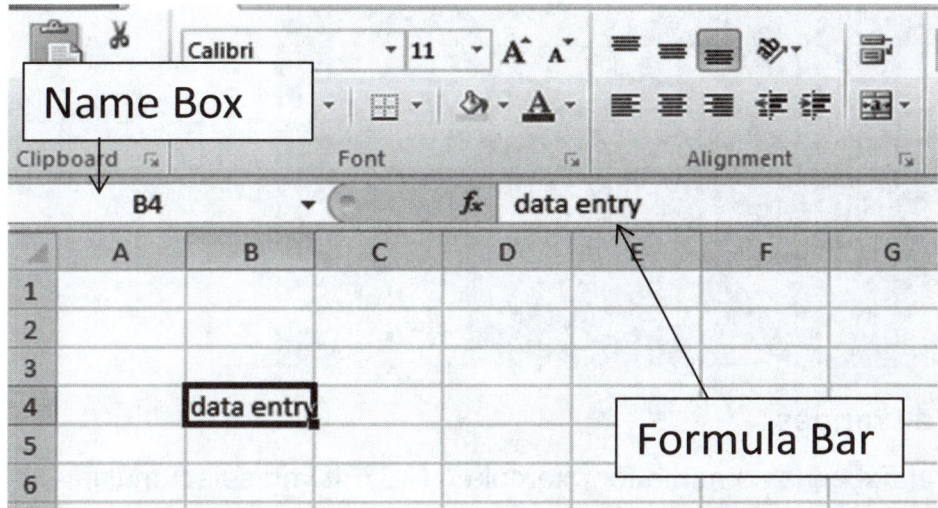

## 1.3 Selecting multiple cells

Selecting several cells at once is easiest using the mouse. Using the mouse, Left-Click on a cell to select it, but HOLD DOWN the mouse button then DRAG the mouse pointer to select neighbouring cells. While the mouse button is held down, the dimensions of the box chosen, rows (R) and columns (C) will be shown in the Name Box – this will disappear when the mouse button is released. If you wish to select cells that are not next to each other, press the Ctrl key while selecting individual cells.

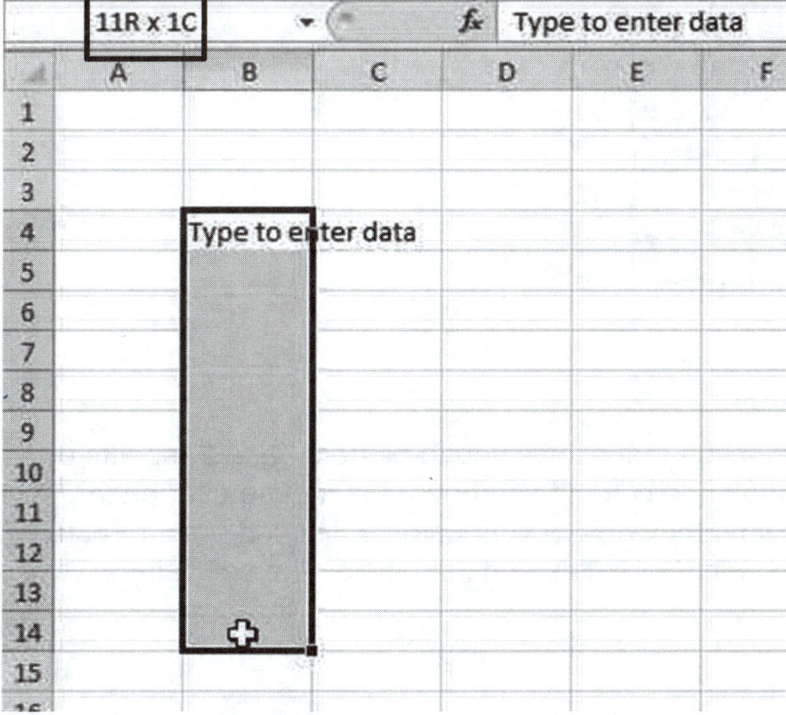

To select **ALL** cells in a worksheet, click on the box in the top-left of the sheet.

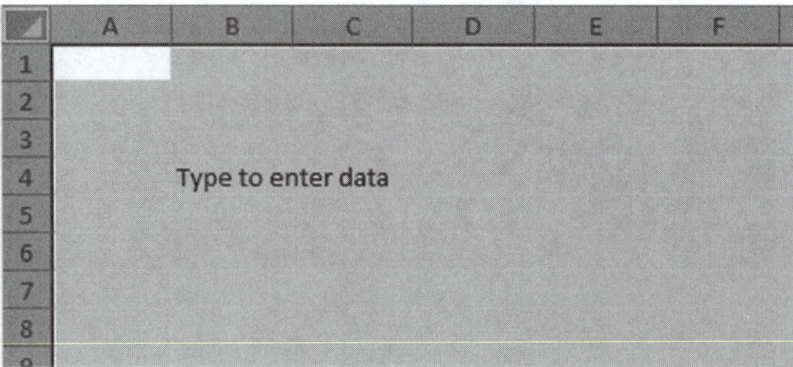

## 1.4 Cell ranges

Each cell in Excel has a name for example A1, B7. If you select multiple cells, this is a RANGE of cells. If you select 2 separate cells, for example C2 and E5, the cells would be separated by a comma, so this would be displayed as (C2, E5). If a BLOCK of cells is selected, these are displayed as:

(Top left cell:Bottom right cell)

For example, to refer to the cells selected, we would enter (A3:C8). This notation becomes important when we deal with functions later.

## 1.5 Paste Special

'Paste Special' is a function that allows you to paste different aspects of what could be contained in a cell. If you hover the mouse over each button, you can see what they do – a very commonly used one in Paste Values, which removes any formulas and just pastes the cell values.

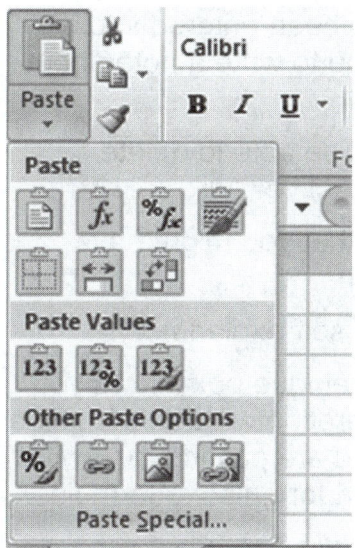

If you chose the Paste Special menu it gives all of the options available:

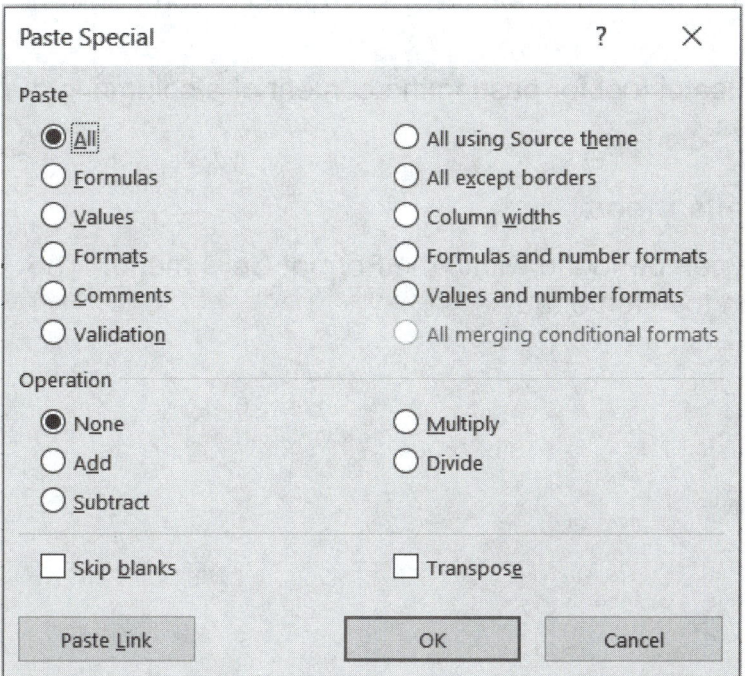

(i)     **'All'** pastes content, formula and formatting but it will not alter column width.

(ii)    **'Formulas'** pastes the formula from the cell(s) to the new location, without affecting the formatting of the destination cell.

(iii)   **'Values'** pastes the value of a cell and not the formula that may have created the value.

(iv)    **'Formats'** pastes any formatting that you might have carried out to the new cell(s). This includes cell shading, borders and number formats, but not column width.

(v)   **'Comments'** pastes any comments that have been entered into a cell to the new location. **'Comments'** allow you to write a note about a particular cell for you – and others – to see.

Once you have written your comment you will be able to delete and/or hide it by 'Right-Clicking' again in the 'Active Cell'.

(vi)  **'Validation'** pastes any data validation rules that you might have created. This will be covered in a later session.

(vii) The others are versions of the above and are self-explanatory.

You will also note that part of the 'Paste-Special' dialogue box allows you to carry out operations. For example, the **'add'** operation will add the value of the 'Active Cell' to the value of the cell(s) that you are pasting to. It will add formula outcomes to values, and it will also add formulas to formulas.

The last part of the 'Paste-Special' dialogue box allows two other actions.

(i)   **'Skip Blanks'** ignores the content – formatting etc – of a cell with no data in it. However, it does maintain the gaps between non-adjacent cells.

(ii)  **'Transpose'** is a useful tool for pasting the content of a column into a row, and vice-versa.

## 1.6   The format cells menu

Most formatting options can be found within the Format Cells menu.  The Format Cells menu is on the Home tab.

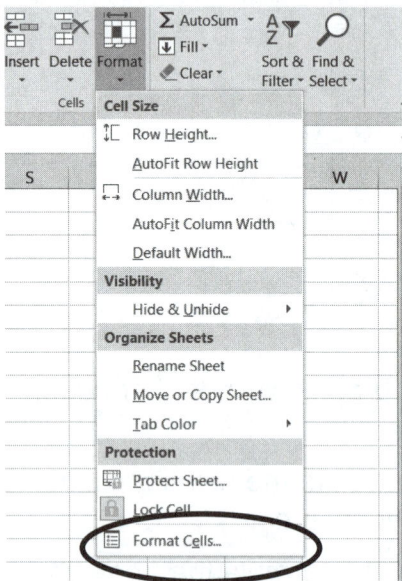

The **Format Cells** menu has several options, as summarised below:

## Number

Changes number formats, for example the number of decimal places, currency type or percentages. Percentages enables numbers to be displayed with a '%' symbol at the end and also multiplies the value in the cell by 100.

It is worth noting that changing the number format of a cell has no effect on the actual number within the cell. For example, if the cell contains the value 15.6, and you change the format to zero decimal places, the value of the cell used in calculations will still be 15.6, even though 16 will be displayed.

## Alignment

Allows adjustment of where data is shown within a cell for example left or right alignment and merging cells together.

## Font

Allows the appearance and size of text, along with special features like bold and underline to be changed.

## Border

Affects the cell itself, rather than the data within – place lines of varying size and colours around the cell.

## Fill

Colour the cell in various shades and patterns.

## Protection

Affects whether a cell can be edited.

To Exit the menu, click OK to accept any changes, or Cancel to reject them.

## 1.7    AutoFit all rows/columns

After your work is finished, it is sensible to AutoFit all rows/columns to ensure that everything is visible. This is quickly and easily achieved as follows:

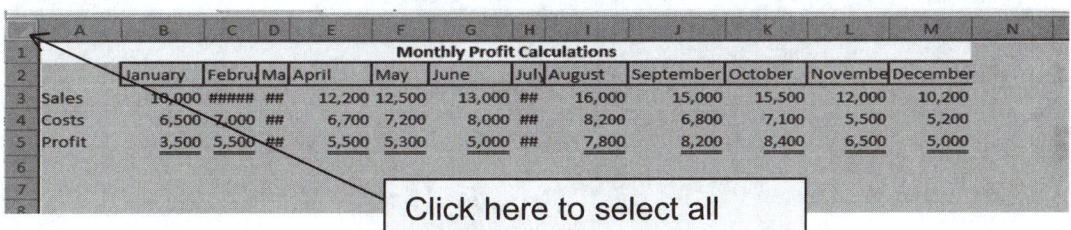

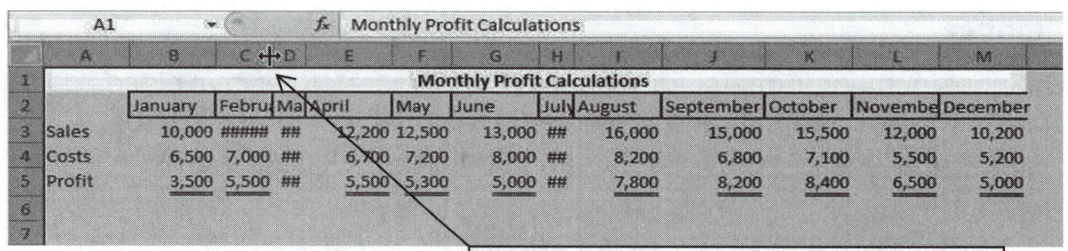

Double click between any two columns to Autofit all the columns

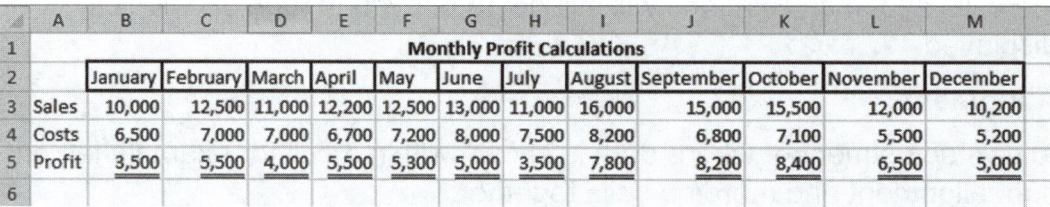

All columns are now wide enough to display their data.

---

### 📝 Test your understanding 1

This activity allows you to practice essential formatting techniques.

(a) Open the 'Unformatted Report' file.

(b) Merge and Center the title on the Summary report sheet across the data. Bold and Underline the title and change the font size to 16.

(c) Change the number format of the numbers to Number, with 0 decimal places and 1000 separator.

(d) Apply a double accounting underline to the profit figures.

(e) Fill the Half year information in cells H2:H4 using yellow. Place a single line border around the edge of cells H2:H4 and remove the double underline from cell H4.

(f) Insert a row between the title and Months.

(g) Autofit all column widths.

(h) Save the file.

---

## 1.8 Headers and Footers

Headers and Footers are used to provide information in a document such as document titles, data owner, version numbers, page numbers, dates etc.

To add them, use the **Insert** tab, then **Header & Footer**.

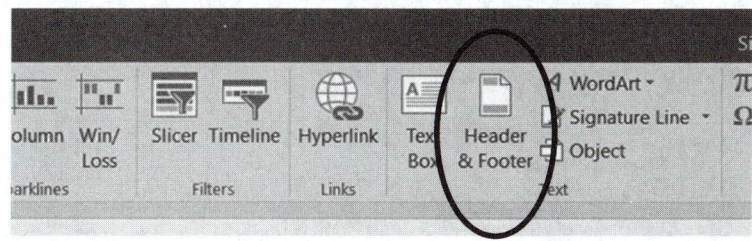

You will be taken to the Header – the page is split into three sections, where you can type in the header required.

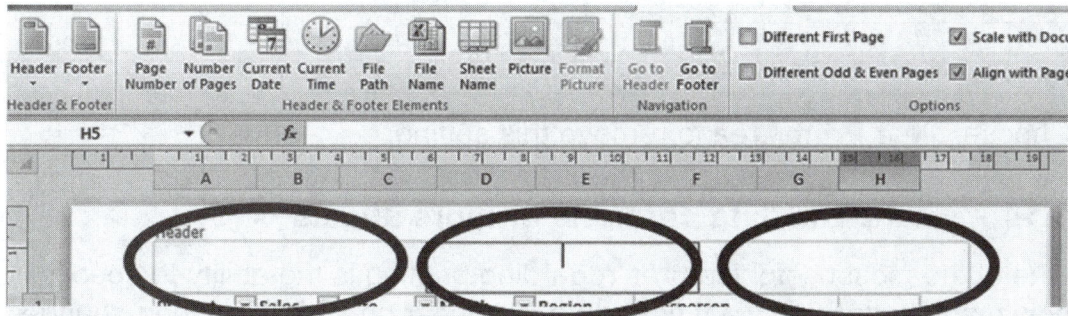

To edit the **Footer**, either navigate to the bottom of the page and click in the footer or click the **Go to Footer** button.

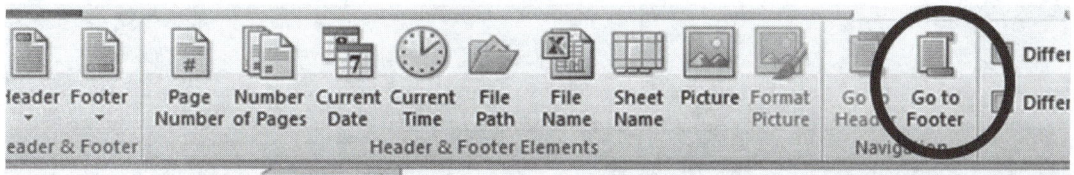

## 1.9 Print Area

Sometimes you may want to print only part of a document. This is quite easy to do. Simply highlight the cells you wish to print, and click the **Set Print Area** button on the **Page Layout** tab.

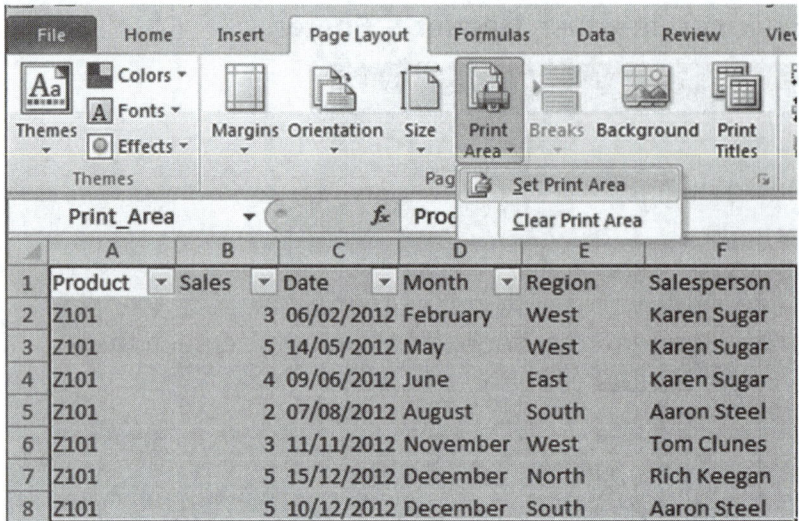

Choose **Clear Print Area** to remove this setting.

## 1.10 Fitting the data onto one or more sheets

One of the most useful features regarding printing is the ability to specify how many pages you want your data to appear on. Excel will then change the size of the font accordingly.

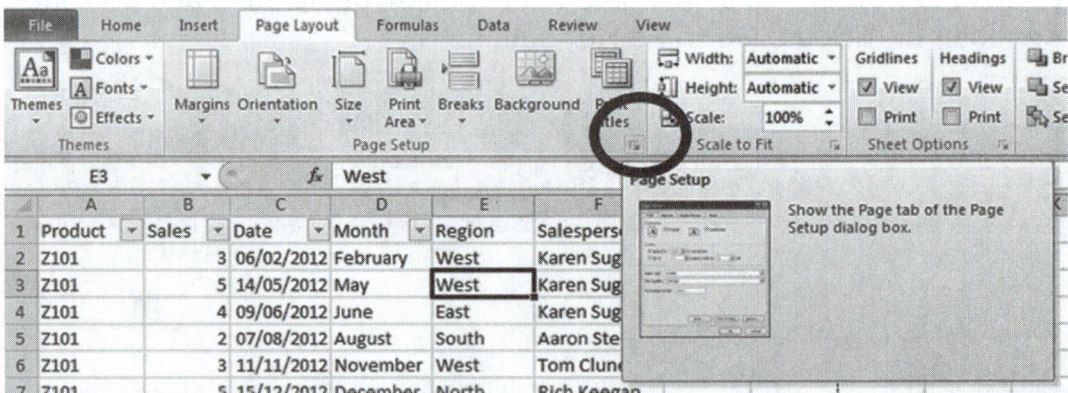

One way to do this is using the **Page Setup** menu. This is accessed by clicking on the arrow in the bottom corner of the Page Setup section of the **Page Layout** menu. Use the **Fit to** option to select the number of pages required.

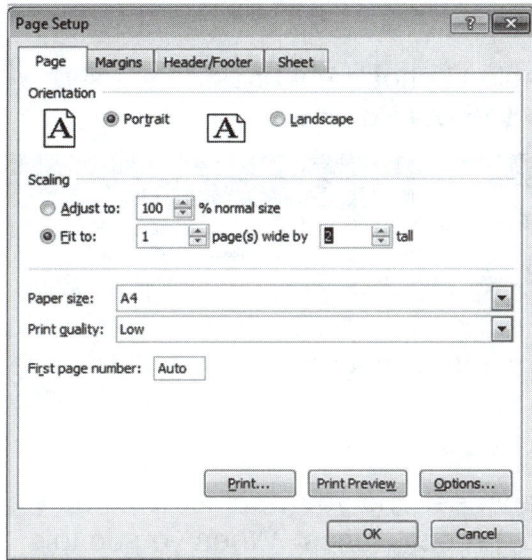

Use Print Preview to check that the final printout will look as desired.

## 1.11    Print preview and printing

Print Preview is found within the **File** tab, by clicking **Print**.

Having made all the adjustments to the data, format etc you will be in a position to print your document. Before you do this, you should review it using the 'Print Preview'.  When you are happy that your document is in the condition that you want it to be then you are in a position to 'Print'. Some changes, for example orientation and margins, can be completed on this screen

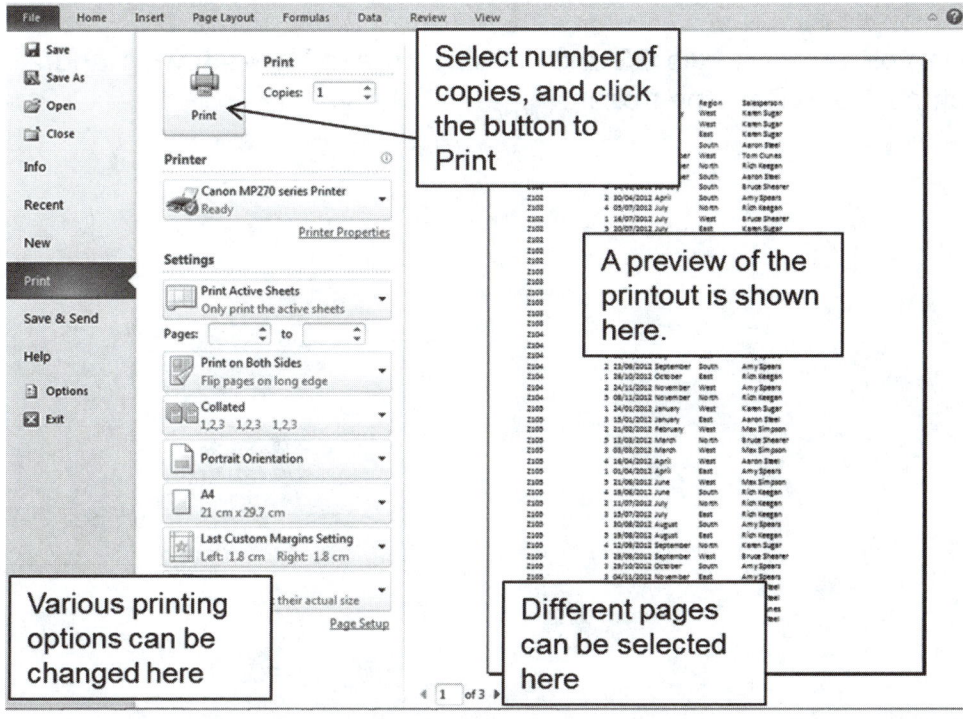

## 1.12    Viewing formulas

Viewing formulas is very useful to be able to check what has been used and where.  In the **Formulas** tab, select **Show Formulas**.

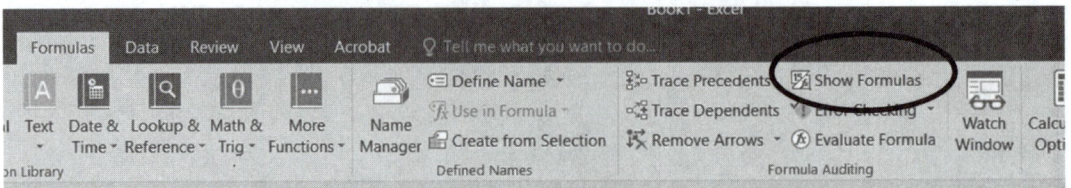

**Ctrl +  `** [control and grave] will do the same as above.

## 1.13    Freeze panes

When you have a lot of data in a spreadsheet and you want to scroll down or across, it is very handy to be able to 'Freeze Panes'. When you do this Excel will 'freeze' in position all rows above the 'Active Cell' and all columns to the left of the 'Active Cell'.

Click on the **Freeze Panes** button within the **View** tab to turn freeze on or off.

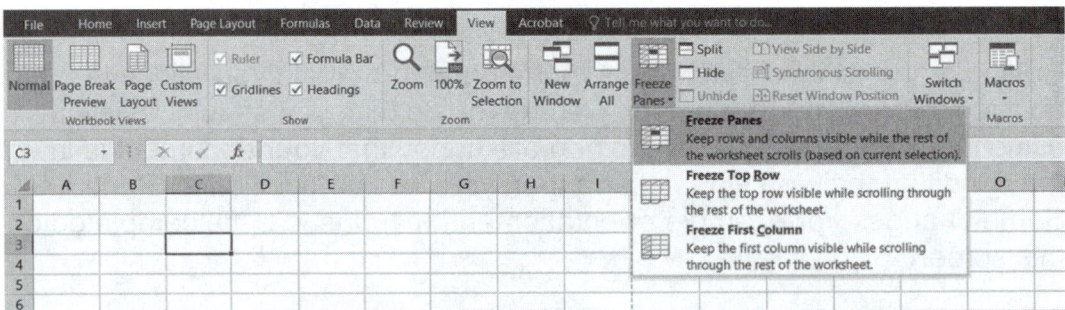

In this example by clicking in C3 and chosing Freeze Panes rows 1 and 2 and columns A and B will be frozen.

**Test your understanding 2**

This activity requires you to setup a document ready for printing.

(a)  Open the Report for Printing file.

(b)  Add a Footer to the document – with your name in the left section, and today's date in the right.

Note you can use the Design tab to insert the date, or just type it in.

(c)  Return to Normal view (use the View tab).

(d)  Change the Orientation to Landscape. Notice how the page breaks move.

(e)  Go to Print Preview. Notice that the report requires two pages.

(f)  Use Page Setup to fit the report to 1 page wide by 1 page tall.

(g)  Note that the Print Preview shows the whole report.

(h)  Save the file.

# 2 Sort and filter

## 2.1 Sorting data

Sometimes you will need to change the order of your data so that it is sorted according to your requirements. This can be performed quickly and easily, using the Sort function, located in both the **Home** tab and the **Data** tab.

| Home tab | Data tab |
|:---:|:---:|
| 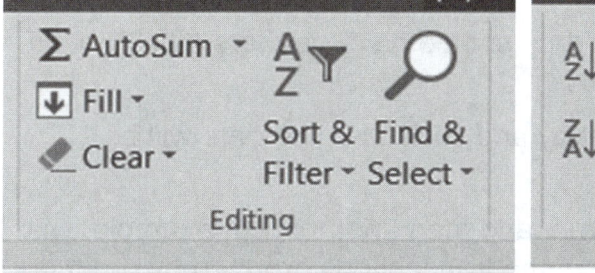 | 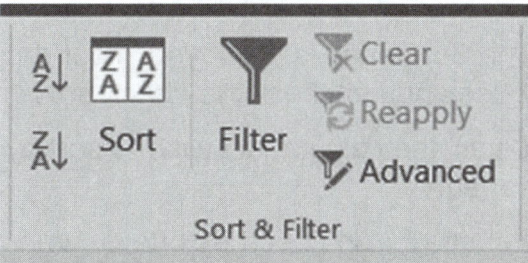 |

To sort, select the data you wish to sort, and click on the Sort button.

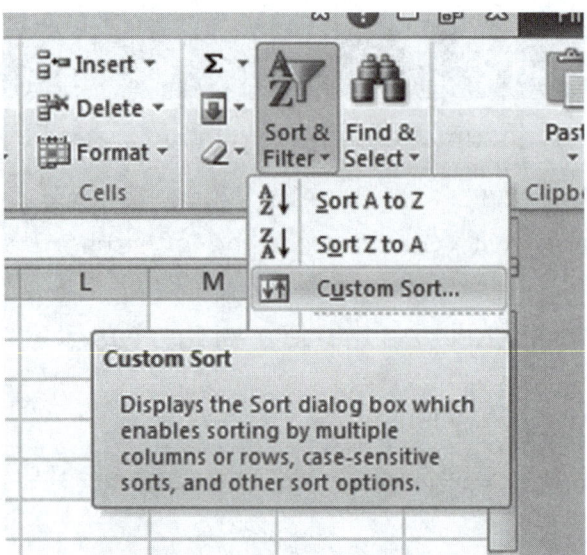

Sort A to Z and Z to A will sort data into either ascending order or descending order. This may not be what you need, so Custom Sort is usually what is required.

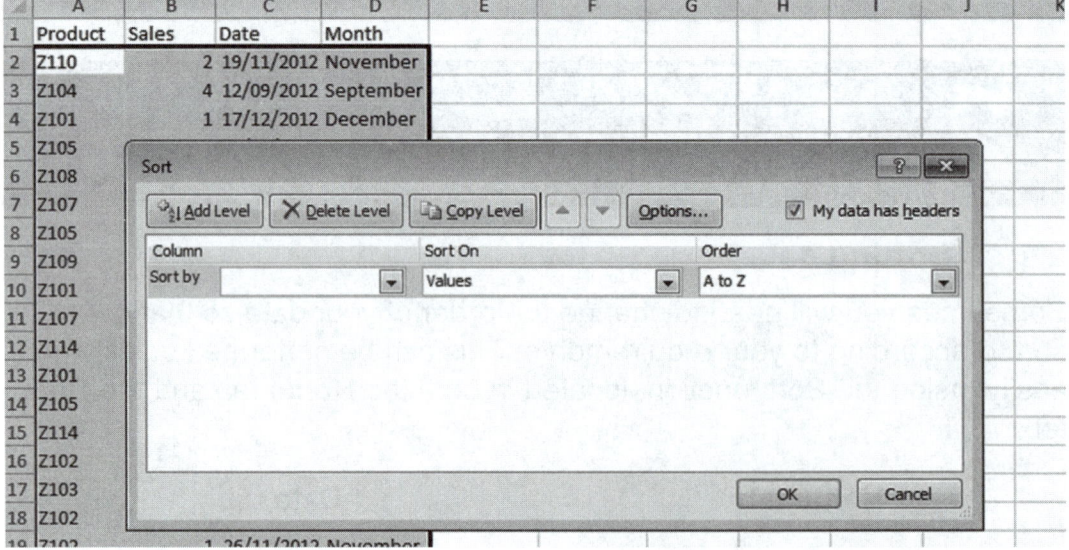

The Sort menu is displayed. Your data should have headers (titles), but if it does not, uncheck the check box.

Select the column you wish to sort by and click OK. The data will be sorted.

You may wish to sort by one column, and then another. For example, with this data set, we might want to have the transactions grouped by product, then by sales volume. This is also done with a custom sort:

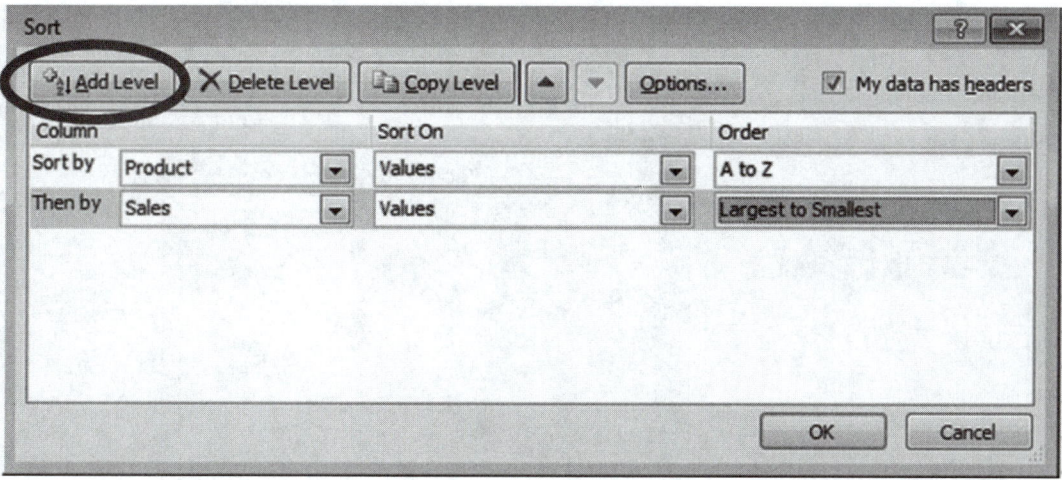

Clicking on **Add Level** will allow you to add more sort criteria. Delete Level will remove any unwanted levels.

### Sorting by date

It is very common to want to sort by day/date. If we sort on a column containing months, for example, these will be sorted in alphabetical order rather than chronological order. Choose custom list when sorting by month or days, and select the relevant list required. The data will then be sorted as required.

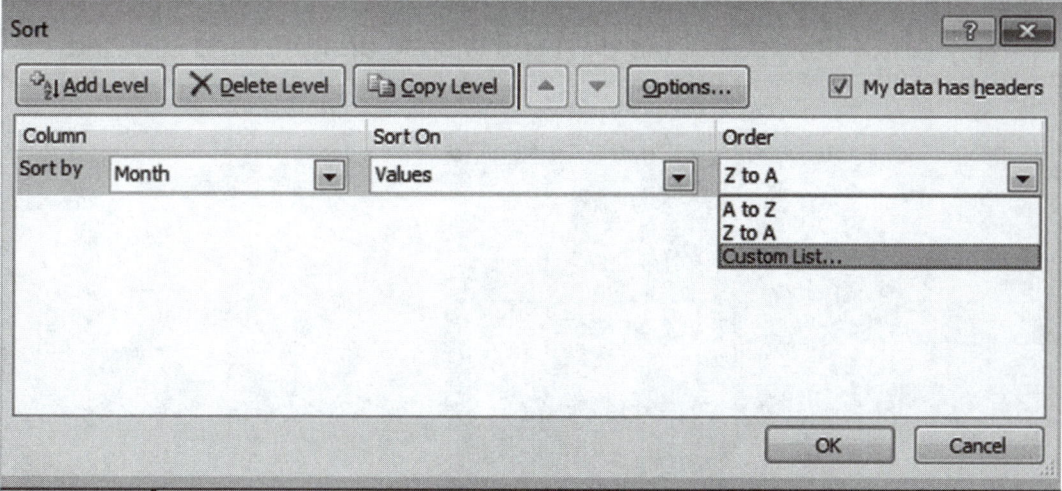

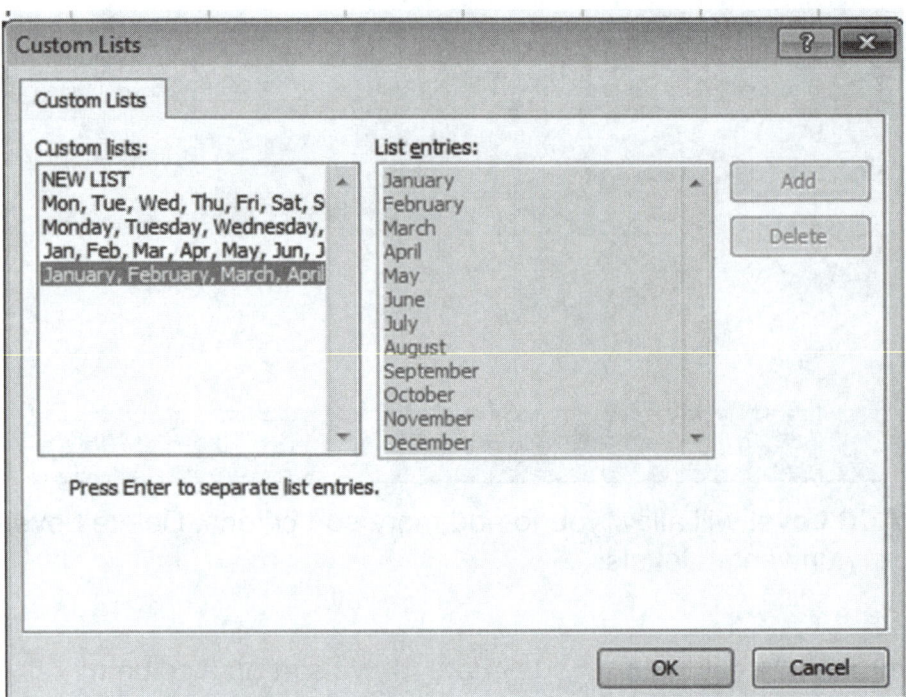

## 2.2 Filtering data

Filtering data is a powerful way of quickly analysing large data sets to find the information you need.

To apply **AutoFilter**, select the data you wish to analyse, and click the Filter button.

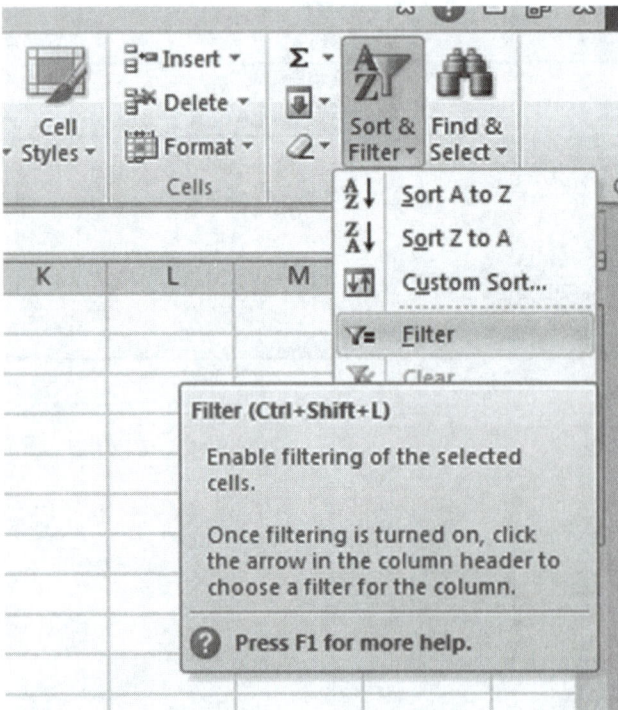

The arrows at the top of each column are the Filters – click on one to apply a Filter. Once the filter is in place, rows which do not meet the criteria applied will be hidden.

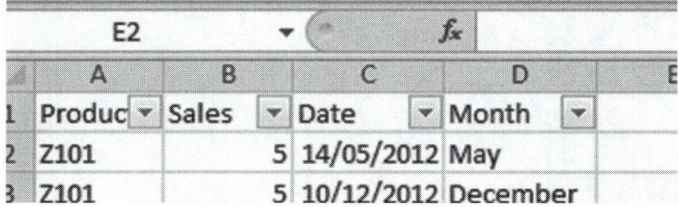

Clicking on the Filter at the top of a column also gives the option to Sort your data. You can simply check/uncheck the items you wish to see/not see. Clicking the (Select All) box will also deselect all items if they are all selected.

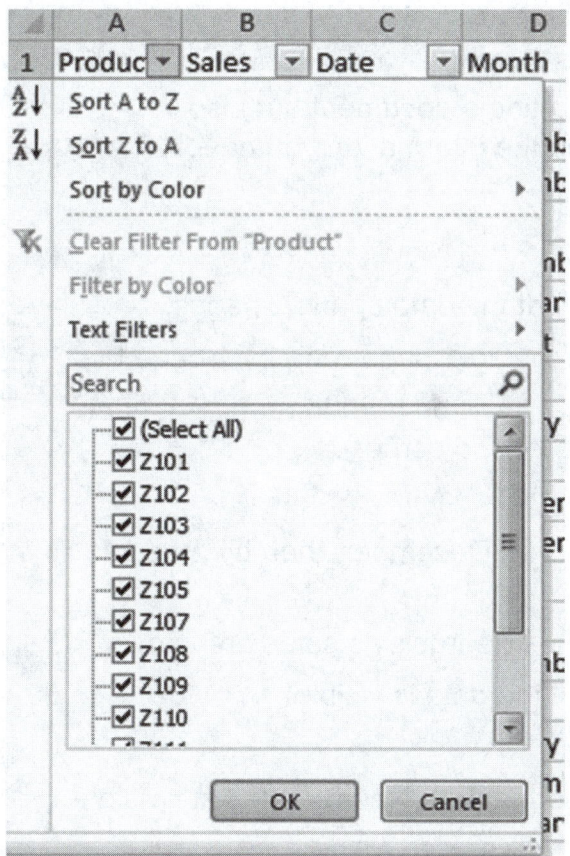

To remove a filter either click back in the filter and **Select All**, or within the **Sort & Filter** button, click the **Clear** option.

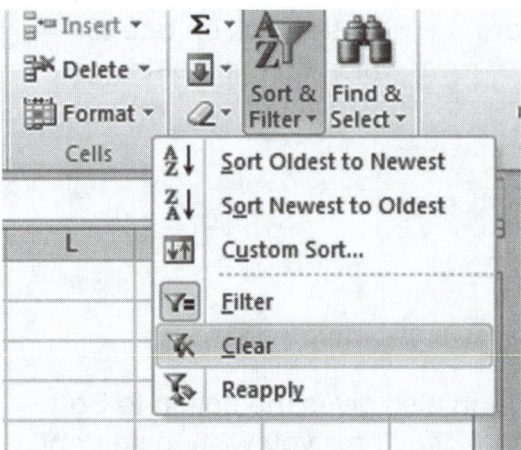

### Test your understanding 3

This activity is again centred on Printing a document but also highlighting the use of Filters to find the information you need.

(a)   Open the Eastern Region 2 file.

(b)   AutoFit Column widths.

(c)   Go to Print Preview – notice that the data spans 2 pages.

(d)   Use Page Setup to fit the printout to 1 page wide by 1 page tall.

(e)   Note that while this is possible, it will be hard to read. Exit print preview (click the arrow top left-hand corner).

(f)   Apply an Autofilter to the data.

(g)   Sort the data by month – January-December, then by product code, A-Z.

(h)   Apply a filter so that only James Beardsley's sales are shown.

(i)   Go to Print Preview – see that the data is visible!

(j)   Save the file (part 1).

(k)   Go back to the data – Filter so that Eva Nasri's sales are visible.

(l)   Save the file (part 2).

**Test your understanding 4**

This activity allows you to practice Sorting and Filtering Data. It is important that after each step you check that the data is in the correct order.

(a)   Open the Eastern Region file in the Activities folder.

(b)   Autofit the Column Widths so the data can be viewed.

(c)   Sort the data by Salesperson (A to Z) (remove sort).

(d)   Sort the data by Month – January-December (remove sort).

(e)   Sort the data by Month (January – December), then by Product code (add level).

(f)   Add an AutoFilter to the data.

(g)   Apply a filter to column A to only show sales from June and July.

(h)   Apply a filter to column F to only show James Beardsley's data.

(i)   Apply a filter to column C to only show amounts greater than or equal to 100.

(j)   Save the file.

# 3 Formulas and basic functions

## 3.1   Simple calculations

Excel's primary purpose is to manipulate raw data through calculations and formulas. One of the main things you will use Excel for is simple calculations. The most basic calculations are the mathematical functions addition +, subtraction -, multiplication * and divide /.

To use these, you need to tell Excel that you are using a **FUNCTION**. To do this, enter an equals sign, '**=**', before the calculation you require.

So, to find the answer to 3+5, type in any cell

**=3+5** and press **Enter**.

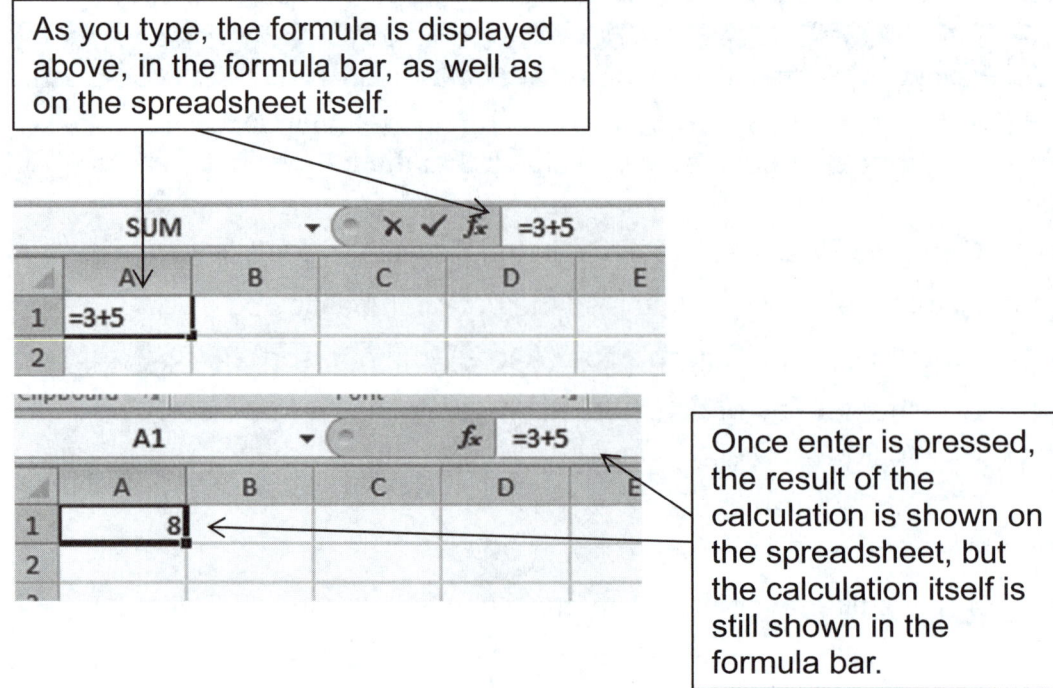

As you type, the formula is displayed above, in the formula bar, as well as on the spreadsheet itself.

Once enter is pressed, the result of the calculation is shown on the spreadsheet, but the calculation itself is still shown in the formula bar.

Excel can be used in this way as a simple calculator by entering the calculation required, using +, -, * or /.

### 3.2    Calculations using existing values

The real power of Excel comes to the fore when using the values in other cells as part of your calculations. Take the following example:

We need to find each person's pay (hourly rate × hours worked). You could simply type each one in but instead we can tell Excel to 'take the value in cell B2 and multiply by the value in cell C2'

| | A | B | C | D | E |
|---|---|---|---|---|---|
| 1 | Name | Hourly Rate | Hours Worked | Pay | |
| 2 | Srnicek | £8.60 | 30 | =b2*c2 | |
| 3 | Watson | £8.60 | 20 | | |
| 4 | Peacock | £9.00 | 20 | | |
| 5 | Albert | £11.50 | 25 | | |
| 6 | Beresford | £10.50 | 30 | | |
| 7 | Batty | £12.00 | 40 | | |
| 8 | Lee | £13.00 | 42 | | |
| 9 | Beardsley | £14.00 | 35 | | |
| 10 | Ginola | £16.00 | 15 | | |
| 11 | Shearer | £18.00 | 35 | | |
| 12 | Ferdinand | £16.00 | 32 | | |
| 13 | | | | | |

**Test your understanding 5**

This activity tests some simple calculations, including percentages, along with some basic data entry.

(a)   Open the Formatted Report file.

(b)   Select the Summary Report worksheet.

(c)   Look at the Half Year data in cells H4 and H5 – this is hard coded in. Enter a formula in cell H4 to add the numbers in cells B4 to G4.

(d)   Copy the formula into cell H5. You may notice that the border around H5 is changed. This can be avoided by using Paste Special and only pasting formulas.

(e)   In row 6, you need to calculate Profit Margin. This is the profit figure as a percentage of sales. The calculation for this is:

   Profit/Sales*100

   Enter 'Profit Margin' in A6, and add a formula to divide profit by sales in columns B-K.

| | A | B | C | D | E | F | G | H | I | J | K |
|---|---|---|---|---|---|---|---|---|---|---|---|
| 1 | | | **BallCo Management Accounts Data** | | | | | | | | |
| 2 | | | | | | | | | | | |
| 3 | | January | February | March | April | May | June | Half year | July | August | September |
| 4 | Sales | 8,648 | 6,850 | 8,264 | 6,823 | 7,176 | 7,083 | 44,844 | 6,019 | 7,223 | 7,579 |
| 5 | Profit | 4,701 | 3,496 | 5,202 | 3,641 | 3,967 | 2,732 | 23,739 | 2,081 | 4,219 | 3,444 |
| 6 | Profit | 0.54359 | 0.510365 | 0.629 | 0.53 | 0.55 | 0.39 | 0.529368 | 0.35 | 0.5841 | 0.45441351 |
| 7 | | | | | | | | | | | |

(f)   Now change the format of these numbers to percentage, 1 decimal place. When using the percentage format, the *100 is not required so you may need to amend your original formula.

(g)   The final quarter's results are:

   Oct – Sales 8243, Profit 4343

   Nov – Sales 8496, Profit 4611

   Dec – Sales 7199, Profit 3290

   Add this information to the report, along with the Profit Margin calculations.

(h)   Add a total in column O for the second half of the year. Copy and paste the half year formulas and formatting – they will add up the previous 6 months' data.

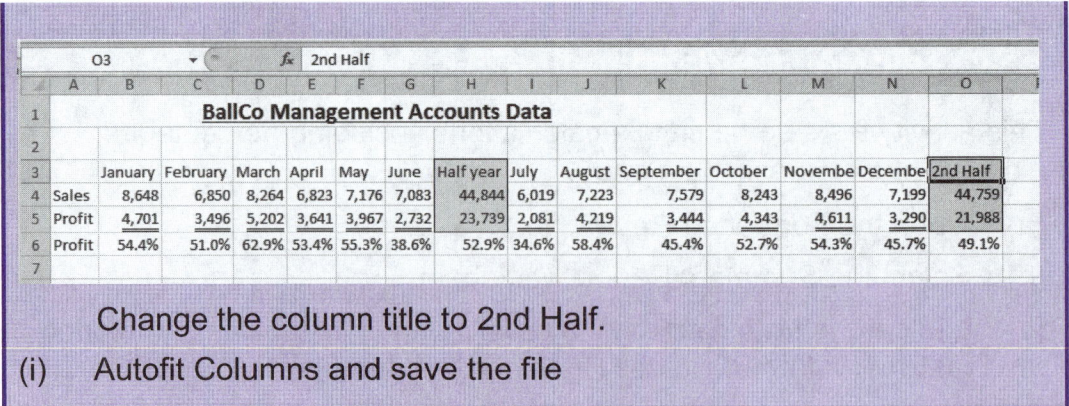

| | January | February | March | April | May | June | Half year | July | August | September | October | November | December | 2nd Half |
|---|---|---|---|---|---|---|---|---|---|---|---|---|---|---|
| Sales | 8,648 | 6,850 | 8,264 | 6,823 | 7,176 | 7,083 | 44,844 | 6,019 | 7,223 | 7,579 | 8,243 | 8,496 | 7,199 | 44,759 |
| Profit | 4,701 | 3,496 | 5,202 | 3,641 | 3,967 | 2,732 | 23,739 | 2,081 | 4,219 | 3,444 | 4,343 | 4,611 | 3,290 | 21,988 |
| Profit | 54.4% | 51.0% | 62.9% | 53.4% | 55.3% | 38.6% | 52.9% | 34.6% | 58.4% | 45.4% | 52.7% | 54.3% | 45.7% | 49.1% |

Change the column title to 2nd Half.

(i)    Autofit Columns and save the file

## 3.3 Functions

These are specific words which tell Excel to perform much more than just adding up a couple of cell values. They range from the relatively simple functions to more complicated tools.

## 3.4 Using a function

To enter a function into a cell, always start with an **EQUALS SIGN** first.

You then type the **NAME** of the function, followed by an **OPEN BRACKET** '('.

The **ARGUMENTS** of the function are then required. These tell Excel exactly what to do and depend on the function required. If more than one argument is needed, they must be separated by a **COMMA**.

The function is ended with a **CLOSE BRACKET** ')'.

This will become more important as we look at different functions.

## 3.5    The Insert Function button

A great way of getting used to functions within Excel is the **Insert Function** button $f_x$ located just above the column names.

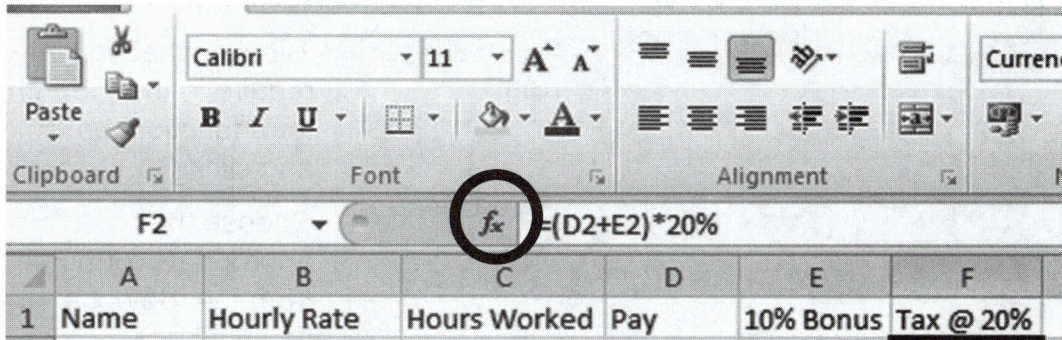

Clicking this button brings up the **Insert Function** menu, which can help work out which function is required.  This allows you to type in what you require, and several options will be provided based on your search.

Using **Insert Function** also provides a more user-friendly way of entering the calculation you require.

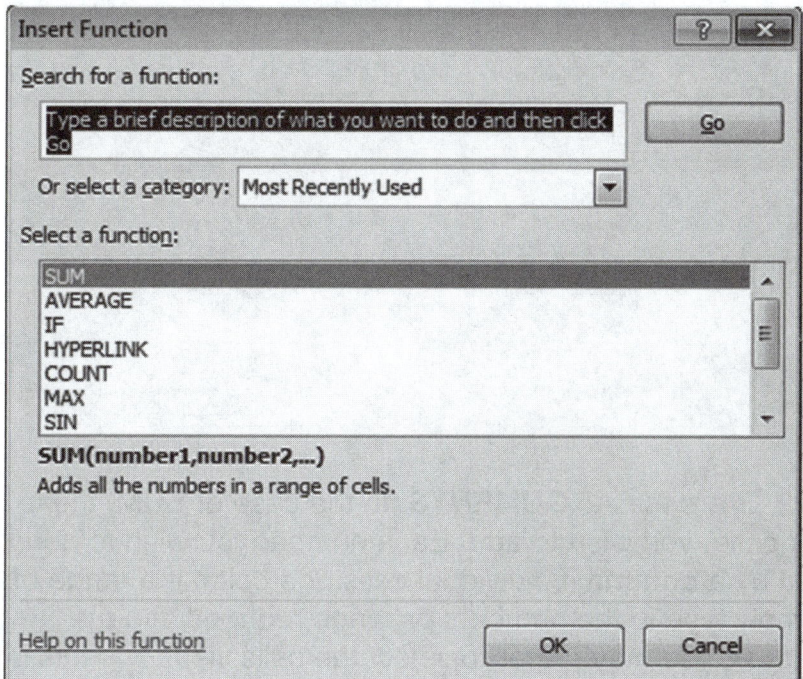

## 3.6   SUM

**SUM** is probably the most commonly used function in Excel. As the name suggests, it is used to add up a selection of numbers.

Using the sum function, we will demonstrate the **Insert Function** button.

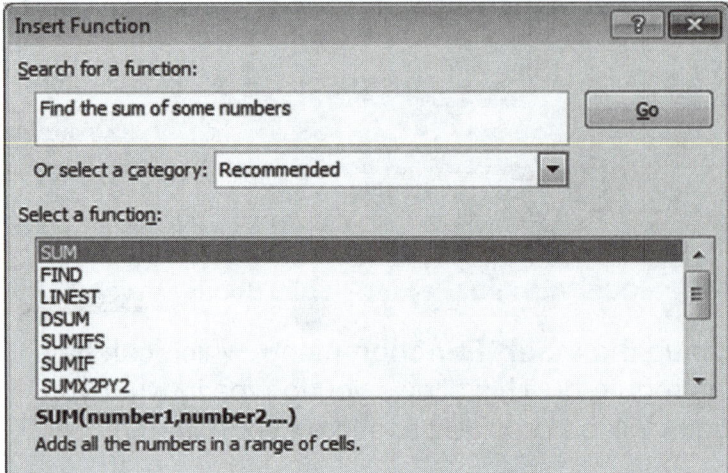

Type in what you require in the 'Search for a function' box and click **Go**.

Choose the appropriate formula from the 'Select a function' box.

Check the description to see if it going to perform the correct function.

Click **OK**.

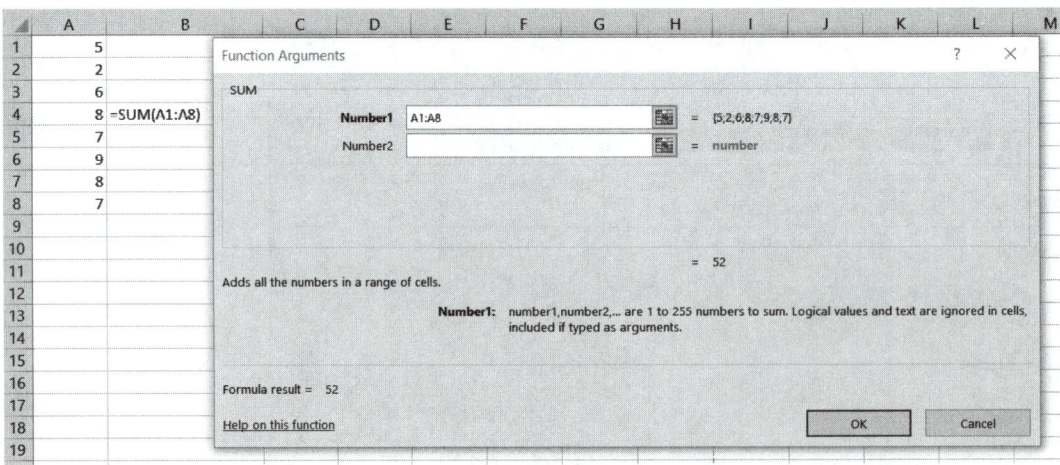

**Number1, number2,...** are the **ARGUMENTS**. In the case of SUM, these are the numbers (or cells) you wish to add. Each number you wish to add should be separated by a **comma** if individual cells or a colon if a range of cells.  You could simply type in the numbers or range required into the Number1 box. However, you may prefer to select the cells visually – this is also possible. The ![reference button] button at the end of the box is a **REFERENCE BUTTON**, which appears throughout Excel. If you click on this, you can then select the cells required.

Just like using **+**, you can also subtract cell values. In the example below, we want to find Net Pay as the sum of Pay and Bonus, less Tax; this can be done using SUM, note the minus sign before the F2 reference to indicate a subtraction.

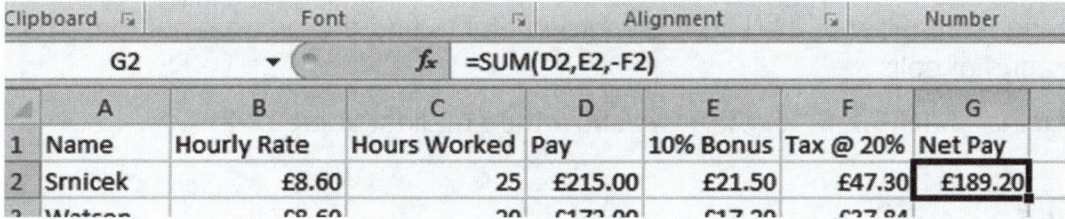

| | Clipboard | Font | | Alignment | | Number |
|---|---|---|---|---|---|---|
| G2 | | | $f_x$ | =SUM(D2,E2,-F2) | | |

| | A | B | C | D | E | F | G |
|---|---|---|---|---|---|---|---|
| 1 | Name | Hourly Rate | Hours Worked | Pay | 10% Bonus | Tax @ 20% | Net Pay |
| 2 | Srnicek | £8.60 | 25 | £215.00 | £21.50 | £47.30 | £189.20 |

## 3.7 Average

Another commonly used function is **AVERAGE**. This takes the average of a selection of numbers by adding them all up and dividing by how many numbers there are (arithmetic mean). It works in exactly the same way as SUM – the arguments are all the numbers or cells you wish to take the average of.

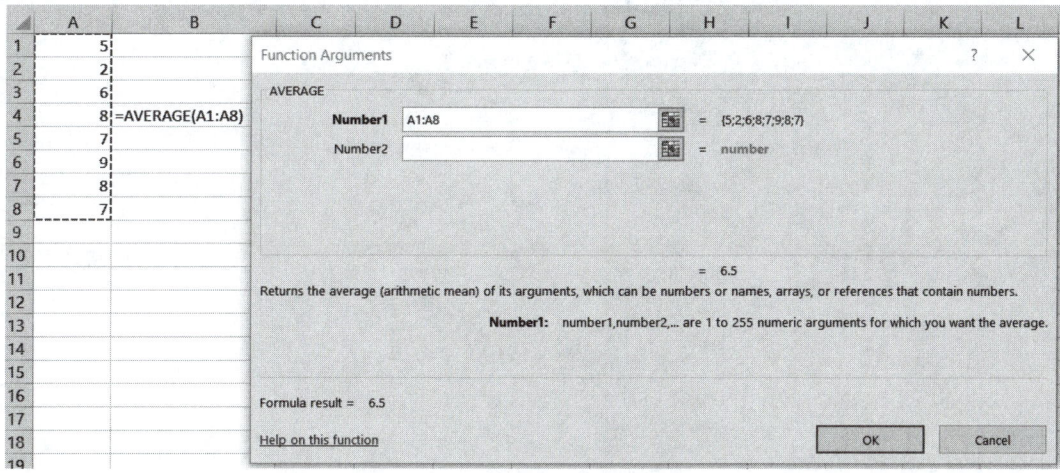

**Note** – the results can be checked – whenever cells are selected, the **Status Bar** at the bottom of the screen gives information, including the average, about those cells.

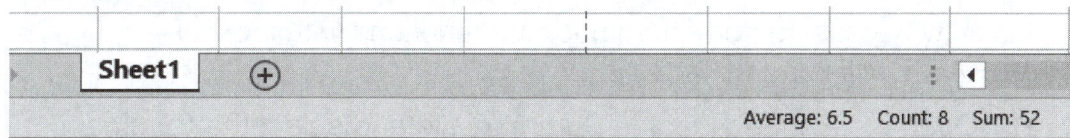

The average and sum are shown. Count is the number of cells with a value in.

### 3.8 MAX and MIN

You may be asked to find the biggest or smallest number in a list – use the **MAX** and **MIN** functions to do this. The format is again the same as **SUM**, for example **=MAX(3,2,6,15,12,9)** will return the value 15, as this is the biggest number in the list. It is more useful to find the biggest number in a range of cells:

Using **=MIN(3,2,6,15,12,9)** will show the smallest value of 2

### 3.9 AutoSum

**AutoSum** is a useful shortcut to perform any of the above functions (and a few others) quickly and easily. The **AutoSum** button can be found in the top right of the **Home** menu. These are the most commonly required functions, although selecting the 'More Functions' option actually allows you to select any function available within Excel.

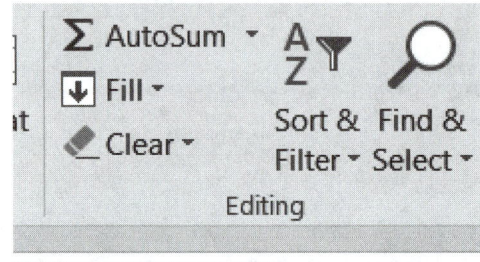

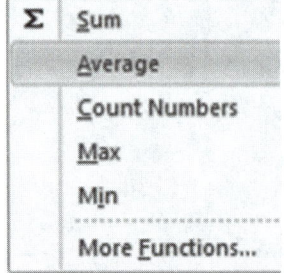

 **Test your understanding 6**

This activity uses some of the important functions within excel – AVERAGE, MIN and MAX.

(a)   Open the Report Needing Summary file and select the Summary Report worksheet.

(b)   We need to create a summary of the information underneath the report. This will show the monthly averages, as well as best and worst performance.

(c)   In cell A9, type 'Biggest sales' and use a function in cell B9 to return the largest monthly sales figure.

(d) In cell A10, type 'Lowest sales', and use a function in B10 to find the worst monthly sales.

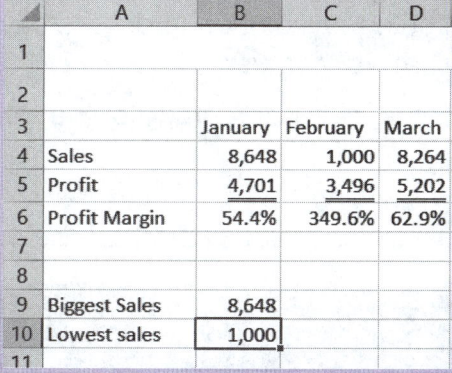

| | A | B | C | D |
|---|---|---|---|---|
| 1 | | | **BallCo Mana** | |
| 2 | | | | |
| 3 | | January | February | March |
| 4 | Sales | 8,648 | 6,850 | 8,264 |
| 5 | Profit | 4,701 | 3,496 | 5,202 |
| 6 | Profit Margin | 54.4% | 51.0% | 62.9% |
| 7 | | | | |
| 8 | | | | |
| 9 | Biggest Sales | 8,648 | | |
| 10 | Lowest sales | 6,019 | | |
| 11 | | | | |

(e) Change the value in C4 to 1000 – check that the value in B10 alters to reflect this.

| | A | B | C | D |
|---|---|---|---|---|
| 1 | | | | |
| 2 | | | | |
| 3 | | January | February | March |
| 4 | Sales | 8,648 | 1,000 | 8,264 |
| 5 | Profit | 4,701 | 3,496 | 5,202 |
| 6 | Profit Margin | 54.4% | 349.6% | 62.9% |
| 7 | | | | |
| 8 | | | | |
| 9 | Biggest Sales | 8,648 | | |
| 10 | Lowest sales | 1,000 | | |
| 11 | | | | |

(f) Undo the last command to restore February's sales.

(g) In A12, type 'Average Profit', and use a formula in B12 to calculate the average monthly profit figure.

(h) Merge and Center the title so that it is centered across all of the information.

(j) Autofit Column widths and save the file

**Test your understanding 7**

This activity is primarily included to allow more practice with percentage calculations, and use of brackets in a calculation. It also reinforces the functions already introduced.

(a)   Open the Southern Sales data workbook.  This contains sales by month for 5 salespeople. We need to populate the Annual Statistics 20X2 table.

(b)   The Sales row is already populated. Use a similar approach to find the Average, Maximum and Minimum for each salesperson, and the totals on the right-hand side.

(c)   We now need the percentage increase. This is the percentage increase in sales from January to December.

(d)   If you are struggling to get the percentages to work, remember that you need to put the increase in sales calculation in brackets so that is calculated before dividing by January sales.

(e)   Calculate each salesperson's sales as a percentage of the total (K21) to 1 decimal place.

(f)   Save the file.

# 4 Cell referencing

## 4.1   Introduction

In some calculations you may want to refer to one (or more) cells in repeated calculations.  This is particularly useful when you are using a particular number in a calculation that is used in different places and is also prone to change – such as a percentage increase for a budget.

There are three types of cell referencing:

1   Relative cell referencing

2   Absolute cell referencing

3   Mixed cell referencing.

**Note** – the type of cell referencing used only matters when you COPY the formulas to other cells within the spreadsheet.

You may also need to refer to cells on another workbook or worksheet. This is relatively straightforward but can create complicated looking formulas.

## 4.2 Relative cell referencing

If you copy a formula down, the row number is updated. Likewise, if you copy a formula across, the column is updated. This is relative referencing.

The formula in cell C4 is **=B2**. This means that when the value in cell B2 is changed, C4 will be updated to show this.

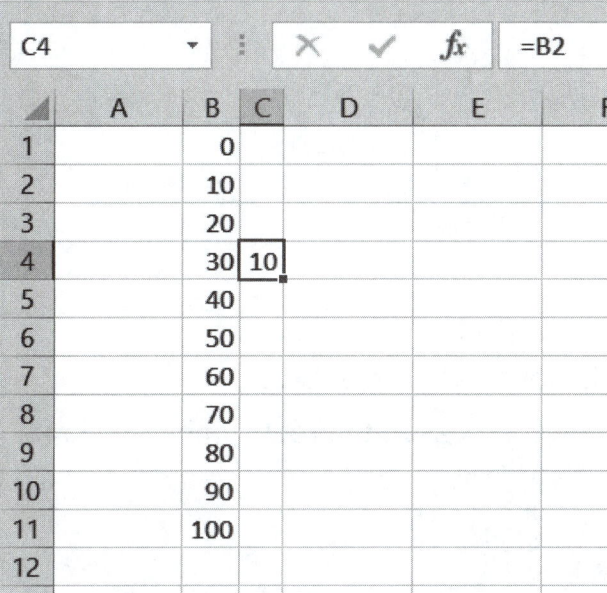

With relative referencing like this, if you **Copy** and **Paste** the formula in cell C4 into another cell, the reference to B2 will change.

The way it works is as follows:

- If you copy the formula **UP**, the row number decreases.

- If you copy the formula **DOWN**, the row number increases.

- If you copy the formula **RIGHT**, the column letter increases.

- If you copy the formula **LEFT**, the column letter decreases.

It is easiest to see this in action. If we copy the formula into cell C3:

Here you can see the formula has been copied **UP** a row, so the row number in the reference has reduced by one. The result is shown as 0 – the contents of Cell B1.

| C3 | | × | ✓ | *fx* | =B1 |
|---|---|---|---|---|---|

| | A | B | C | D | E |
|---|---|---|---|---|---|
| 1 | | 0 | | | |
| 2 | | 10 | | | |
| 3 | | 20 | 0 | | |
| 4 | | 30 | 10 | | |
| 5 | | 40 | | | |
| 6 | | 50 | | | |
| 7 | | 60 | | | |
| 8 | | 70 | | | |
| 9 | | 80 | | | |
| 10 | | 90 | | | |
| 11 | | 100 | | | |
| 12 | | | | | |

Similarly, we can copy the formula down, say three rows:

Copying the formula down three rows increases the row number by three.

| C7 | | × | ✓ | *fx* | =B5 |
|---|---|---|---|---|---|

| | A | B | C | D | E |
|---|---|---|---|---|---|
| 1 | | 0 | | | |
| 2 | | 10 | | | |
| 3 | | 20 | 0 | | |
| 4 | | 30 | 10 | | |
| 5 | | 40 | | | |
| 6 | | 50 | | | |
| 7 | | 60 | 40 | | |
| 8 | | 70 | | | |
| 9 | | 80 | | | |
| 10 | | 90 | | | |
| 11 | | 100 | | | |
| 12 | | | | | |

Copying the formula across works in the same way. Copying across two columns would update the "B" column reference to a "D" column reference in the formula, as D is two letters after B in the alphabet.

## 4.3　Absolute cell referencing

This is used to ensure that a formula always looks at the content of a particular cell.

To create an **Absolute** reference we use a **$** sign before the letter and the number in the cell reference.

| C4 | | ⋮ | ✕ | ✓ | fx | =$B$2 |

| ◢ | A | B | C | D | E |
|---|---|---|---|---|---|
| 1 | | 0 | | | |
| 2 | | 10 | | | |
| 3 | | 20 | | | |
| 4 | | 30 | 10 | | |
| 5 | | 40 | | | |
| 6 | | 50 | | | |
| 7 | | 60 | | | |
| 8 | | 70 | | | |
| 9 | | 80 | | | |
| 10 | | 90 | | | |
| 11 | | 100 | | | |
| 12 | | | | | |

Although the result is the same at first, if you copy this formula, it will **ALWAYS** refer to cell B2.

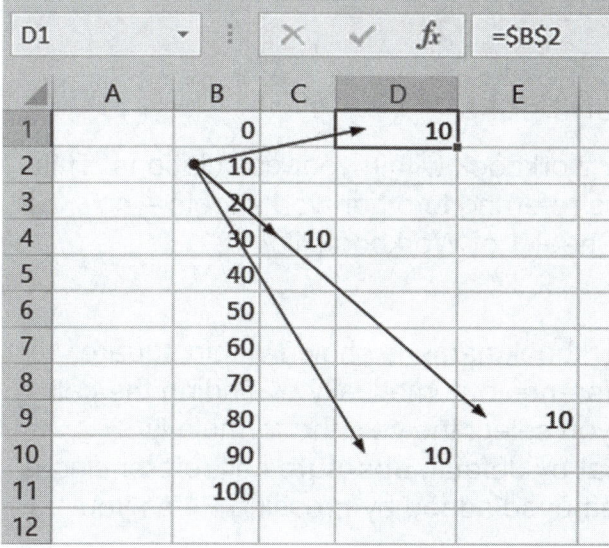

| D1 | | ⋮ | ✕ | ✓ | fx | =$B$2 |

| ◢ | A | B | C | D | E |
|---|---|---|---|---|---|
| 1 | | 0 | | 10 | |
| 2 | | 10 | | | |
| 3 | | 20 | | | |
| 4 | | 30 | 10 | | |
| 5 | | 40 | | | |
| 6 | | 50 | | | |
| 7 | | 60 | | | |
| 8 | | 70 | | | |
| 9 | | 80 | | | 10 |
| 10 | | 90 | | 10 | |
| 11 | | 100 | | | |
| 12 | | | | | |

**Absolute** cell referencing can save lots of time when using formulas.

## 4.4    Mixed cell referencing

This is a combination of both **Absolute** and **Relative** referencing. Remember, the type of referencing is only relevant when you copy a formula. You might want the row number to be relative (i.e. change when you copy), but the column to remain fixed.

The **$** sign used in absolute referencing above is key here. When we used the absolute reference **$B$1**, what we really said was "keep the column and the row fixed." It can be broken up as **$B** – keep the column fixed, and **$1**, keep the row fixed.

When entering a cell reference in a formula, pressing **F4** repeatedly will cycle through the different types of referencing by adding/removing $ signs as required

## 4.5    Referencing other worksheets

It is very common that a calculation will need to refer to a cell on another worksheet within the same workbook. This works in the same way, but now instead of saying "Use the value in cell A1", we need to say "Use the value on Sheet 2 in Cell A1" (for example). The format for this would be:

**=Sheet2!A1**

Remember that when entering a formula, you can click on the cell you wish to use rather than typing its reference. This is true whether the cell is on the current worksheet or not.

## 4.6    Referencing other workbooks

You may wish to refer to another workbook within your calculations. This works in exactly the same way as referring to other worksheets – now our reference would be 'Cell A1 on Sheet 1 of Workbook 1'.

**=[Book 1.xlsx]Sheet 1!$A$1**

The only difference being the workbook name is shown within square brackets. You can create this reference automatically by finding the cell you need and clicking on it.  As you select the cell, the formula is populated automatically. Note that by default, **absolute** cell referencing is used – the dollar signs can be removed/added by pressing **F4** as you enter the formula, or manually.

## 4.7    Links

Once a formula is set up referencing another workbook, a **link** has been created.  These can be managed using the **Edit links** option in the **Data** tab.

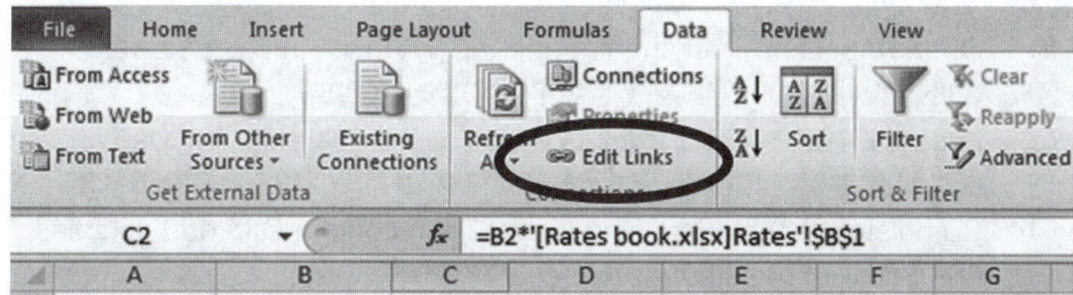

Here, links can be managed if necessary. Break link removes the link from the formula – the current value of the formula will be retained.

## 4.8    Naming cells

Naming cells and ranges of cells can make formulas easier to understand. As we have already seen, each cell has a **reference** made up of its column and row position. Instead of this, it can be given a name. The simplest way to do this is by using the **Name Box**.

To give the cell a **name**, simply type the name in the **Name Box**.

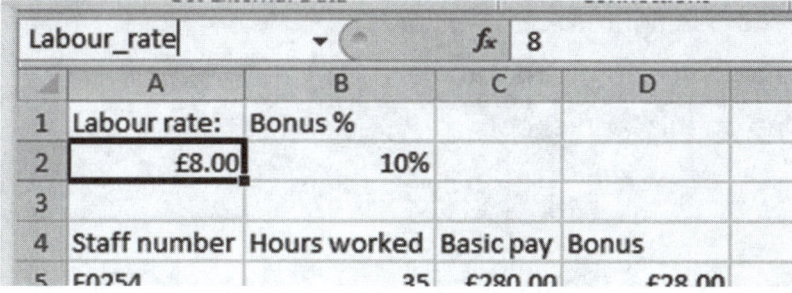

There are a few rules for cell names:

- No spaces (underscore is often used instead).

- Your name cannot be a valid cell reference (e.g. AB123).

- The name must be less than 256 characters.

- The name must start with a letter, an underscore or a backslash (\\).

- Other valid characters after the first letter are letters, numbers, backslash, full stop and underscore, £ signs should NOT be used.

- Names are not case sensitive.

This has the advantage of automatically making the cell reference **absolute**, when it is copied down.

**Test your understanding 8**

This activity tests your use of absolute references.

(a)   Open the Referencing 1 workbook.

(b)   On the Absolute worksheet, enter the VAT rate in cell B1 as 20% (this should automatically format as percentage).

(c)   In cells B4-B8 enter a formula which calculates the VAT. Use an Absolute Reference in cell B4 and copy it down to the other cells.

(d)   Complete the table by using a formula in column C to add up sales and VAT (there is more than one correct formula).

(e)   Save the file.

 **Test your understanding 9**

This activity tests your use of relative references.

(a)   Open the Referencing 2 workbook.

(b)   On the Relative worksheet. Notice that there are 3 sets of data here – the calculations for the first set are complete. Copy the formulas from C4:E8 into Cells I4:K8 – the references will update to use the correct sales figures.

(c)   Repeat this to copy the formulas into cells O4:Q4.

(d)   Show Formulas on this worksheet.

(e)   Save the file.

**Test your understanding 10**

This activity tests your use of mixed referencing.

(a)   Open the Referencing 3 workbook.

(b)   Select the Mixed Referencing worksheet. The table will show how our sales will change with varying volume, and with different percentage increases added. Firstly, calculate forecast sales in column B. An absolute reference should be used on B1.

| B14 | | $f_x$ =A14*$B$1 | | | | | | |
|---|---|---|---|---|---|---|---|---|
| | A | B | C | D | E | F | G | H |
| 1 | Forecast Selling Price | £100 | Forecast Sales + | Forecast Sales + | Forecast Sales + | Forecast Sales + | Forecast Sales + | Forecast Sales + |
| 2 | Forecast Sales Volume (Units) | Forecast Sales | 5% | 6% | 7% | 8% | 9% | 10% |
| 3 | 1000 | £100,000 | | | | | | |
| 4 | 1500 | £150,000 | | | | | | |
| 5 | 2000 | £200,000 | | | | | | |
| 6 | 2500 | £250,000 | | | | | | |
| 7 | 3000 | £300,000 | | | | | | |
| 8 | 3500 | £350,000 | | | | | | |
| 9 | 4000 | £400,000 | | | | | | |
| 10 | 4500 | £450,000 | | | | | | |
| 11 | 5000 | £500,000 | | | | | | |
| 12 | 5500 | £550,000 | | | | | | |
| 13 | 6000 | £600,000 | | | | | | |
| 14 | 6500 | £650,000 | | | | | | |
| 15 | | | | | | | | |

(c)   We now need to calculate the forecast sales plus the percentage increase. This calculation could be:

Forecast sales*(1+percentage increase)

We need to be careful with the referencing. If we start in cell C3, the calculation is =B3*(1+C2). This will give the correct answer of £105,000.

However, when we copy the formula across to the other columns, it will not work. If we copy across into column D, the formula will become =C3*(1+D2). This is not correct, as we need to always refer to column B for the Forecast sales.

So, the formula becomes =$B3*(1+C2). If this is copied across, the top row will be correct.

We also have to consider the reference to C2. If we copy this down a row, the formula will become =$B4*(1+C3) which is no longer multiplying by the correct percentage. We need to always refer to the row in this part of the formula, which becomes =$B4*(1+C$2)

Note: There are different formulas that can be used to calculate the forecast sale plus the percentage increase.  The formula could also be =$B3+$B3*C$2

The final result looks like this:

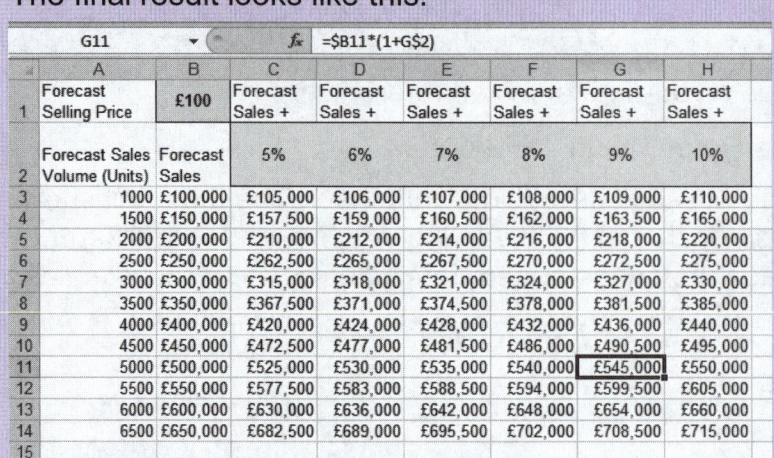

| | G11 | | | $f_x$ | =$B11*(1+G$2) | | | |
|---|---|---|---|---|---|---|---|---|
| | A | B | C | D | E | F | G | H |
| 1 | Forecast Selling Price | £100 | Forecast Sales + | Forecast Sales + | Forecast Sales + | Forecast Sales + | Forecast Sales + | Forecast Sales + |
| 2 | Forecast Sales Volume (Units) | Forecast Sales | 5% | 6% | 7% | 8% | 9% | 10% |
| 3 | 1000 | £100,000 | £105,000 | £106,000 | £107,000 | £108,000 | £109,000 | £110,000 |
| 4 | 1500 | £150,000 | £157,500 | £159,000 | £160,500 | £162,000 | £163,500 | £165,000 |
| 5 | 2000 | £200,000 | £210,000 | £212,000 | £214,000 | £216,000 | £218,000 | £220,000 |
| 6 | 2500 | £250,000 | £262,500 | £265,000 | £267,500 | £270,000 | £272,500 | £275,000 |
| 7 | 3000 | £300,000 | £315,000 | £318,000 | £321,000 | £324,000 | £327,000 | £330,000 |
| 8 | 3500 | £350,000 | £367,500 | £371,000 | £374,500 | £378,000 | £381,500 | £385,000 |
| 9 | 4000 | £400,000 | £420,000 | £424,000 | £428,000 | £432,000 | £436,000 | £440,000 |
| 10 | 4500 | £450,000 | £472,500 | £477,000 | £481,500 | £486,000 | £490,500 | £495,000 |
| 11 | 5000 | £500,000 | £525,000 | £530,000 | £535,000 | £540,000 | £545,000 | £550,000 |
| 12 | 5500 | £550,000 | £577,500 | £583,000 | £588,500 | £594,000 | £599,500 | £605,000 |
| 13 | 6000 | £600,000 | £630,000 | £636,000 | £642,000 | £648,000 | £654,000 | £660,000 |
| 14 | 6500 | £650,000 | £682,500 | £689,000 | £695,500 | £702,000 | £708,500 | £715,000 |
| 15 | | | | | | | | |

(d)    Save the file.

---

 **Test your understanding 11**

This activity uses a named range to calculate values.

(a)    Open the Referencing 4 workbook.

(b)    On the Absolute worksheet enter the VAT rate in cell B1 as 20%.

(c)    Name cell B1 vat_rate.

(d)    Calculate the VAT in cells B4:B8 using the name vat_rate.

(e)    Complete the Total column.

(f)    Show Formulas.

(g)    Save the file.

---

 **Test your understanding 12**

This activity tests your use of formulas referencing different worksheets.

(a)    Open the Regional Combined workbook.

(b)    The Regional Combined Sales worksheet needs populating with the sum of the values on District 1 and District 2 worksheets.

(c)    Enter a formula in cell B2 on the totals worksheet which adds cell B2 from District 1 to B2 from District 2.

(d)    Copy the formula down and across into the other cells.

(e)    Format the numbers in Number format, to zero decimal places with a 1000 separator comma.

(f)    Save the file.

# 5 Conditional formatting

## 5.1 Conditional formatting

**Conditional Formatting** is where you can change the format of a cell based on certain conditions.

To see any conditional formatting already in place, or to create a conditional format, select the cell(s) you wish to format, and in the **Home Menu**, select **Conditional Formatting**. Several options appear.

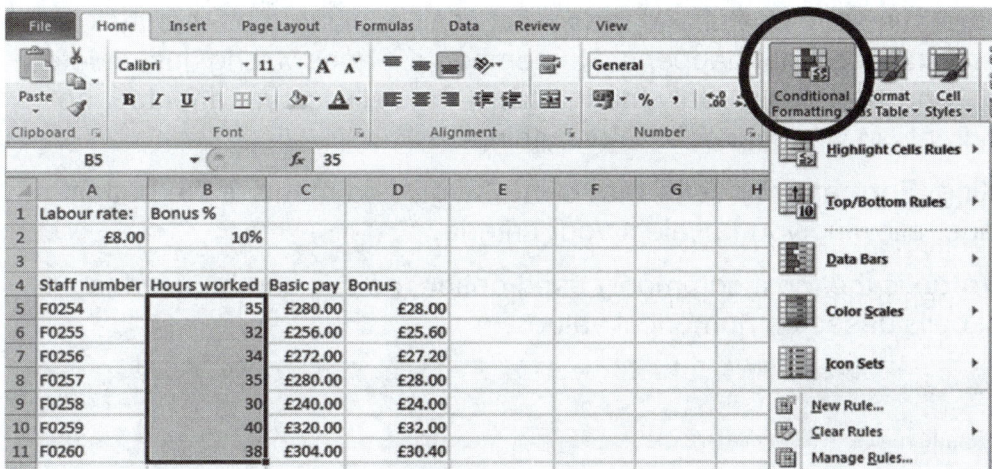

Select **Manage Rules** to bring up the Conditional Formatting Rules Manager .

From here you can create a new rule, edit a rule, delete a rule or change the order in which the rules apply.

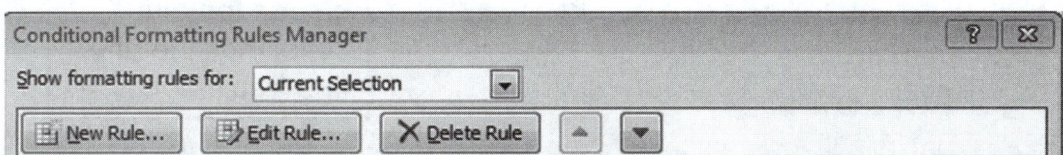

## 5.2 Creating a new rule

Clicking **New Rule** from the **Rules Manager** menu brings up the following options:

The most frequently used rule is 'Format only cells that contain'.

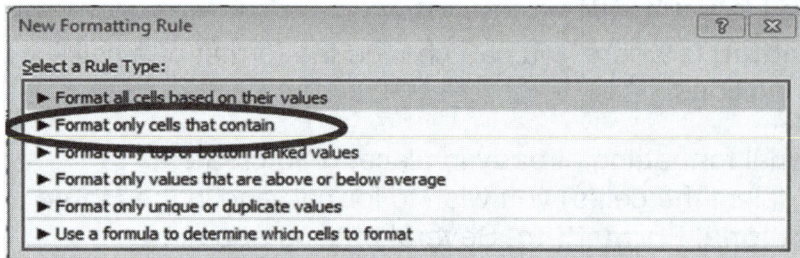

The other rules are useful and reasonably self-explanatory – the trick is to try them and see what happens. Remember, if it goes wrong, just delete the rule and start again. Only the format of the cells is ever affected, not the content, so you cannot break anything

Selecting '**Format only cells that contain**' gives a menu at the bottom of the page, allowing you to select your criteria.

**Cell Value** is the most commonly used option, as this can be used to format cells based on numerical values.

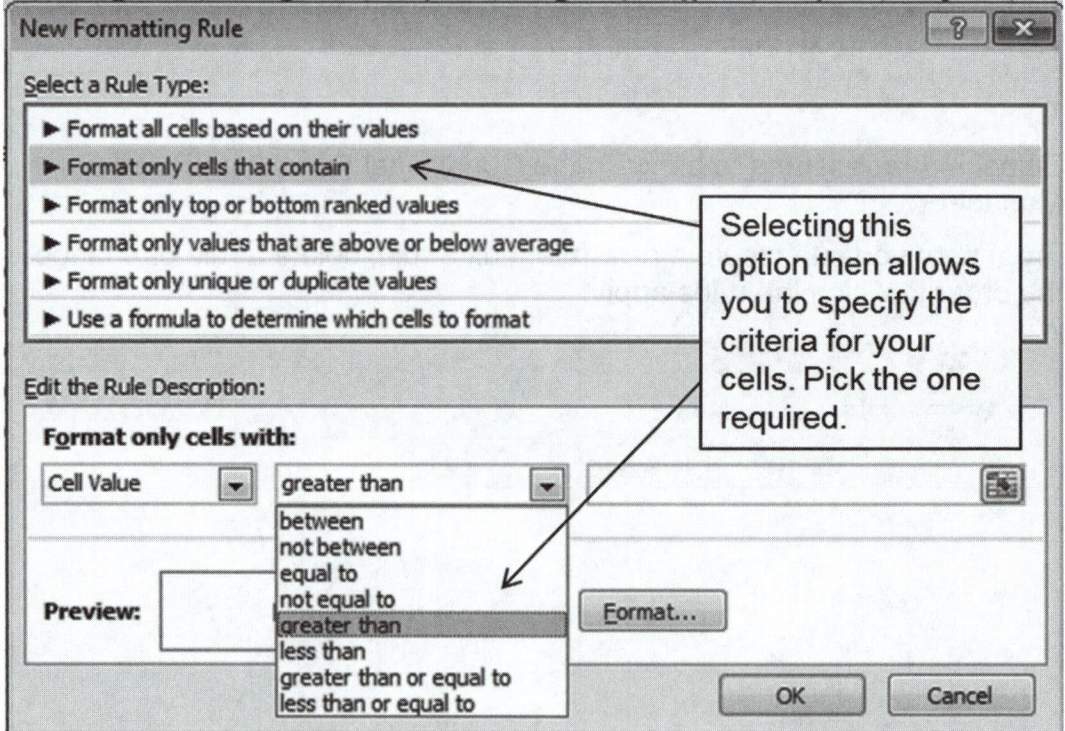

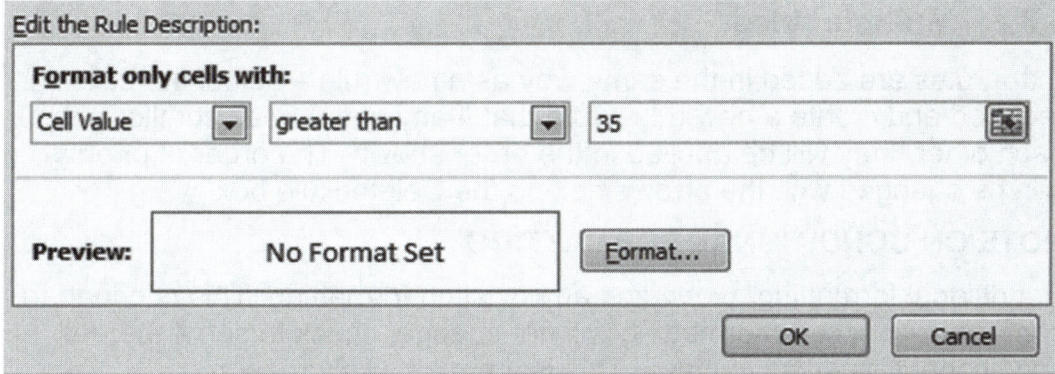

The rule is set up – the formatting will change for any cell (out of the ones selected) whose value is greater than 35. However, no special format has been set. To do this, click the **Format** button.

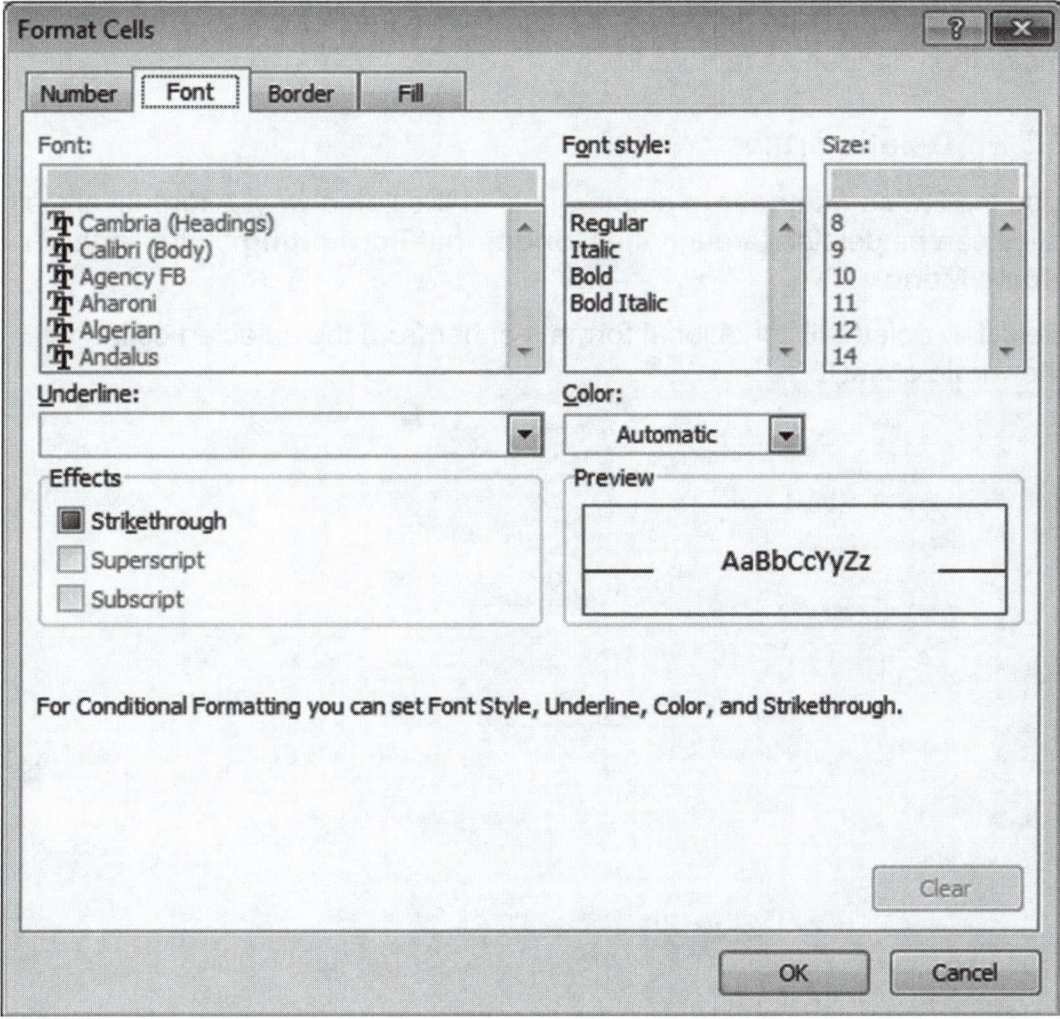

## 5.3 Multiple rules

Extra rules are added in the same way as a new rule – select the cells required and create a new rule. Note that if any of the rules conflict with each other, they will be applied in the order shown. The order of priority can be changed with the arrows next to the Delete Rule box.

**NOTE ON CONDITIONAL FORMATTING**

Conditional formatting overwrites any existing formatting. This can lead to confusion – if a cell's formatting will not change, check to see if there is conditional formatting in place. This is the most likely reason.

## 5.4 Editing rules

**Edit** rules from within the **Rules Manager** box.

Clicking on **Edit Rule** brings up the same menu as for a New Rule, so make the changes as required.

## 5.5 Deleting rules

Use the **Rules Manager** to delete a rule in the same way. Alternatively, all rules can be deleted through the **Conditional Formatting** button in the **Home Menu**.

Select to delete all conditional formats either from the selected cell(s) or the whole sheet.

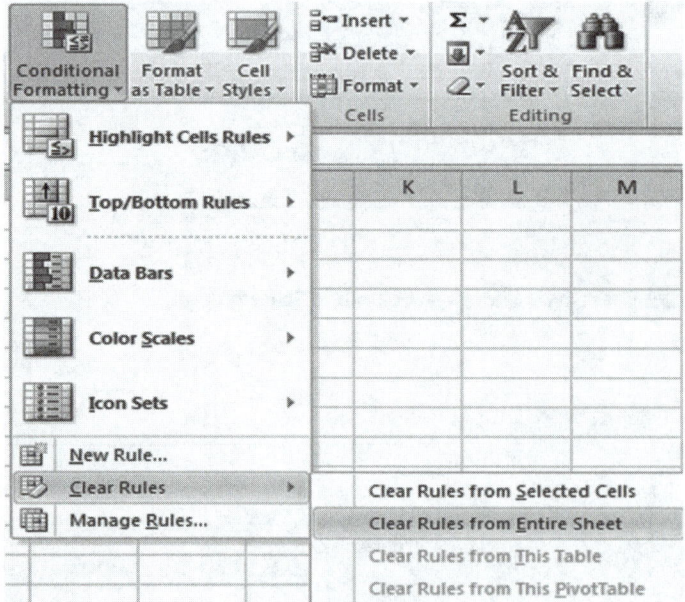

**KAPLAN** PUBLISHING

## Test your understanding 13

This activity tests several aspects of conditional formatting and referencing, along with some management accounting calculations.

(a)   Open the Conditional workbook.

(b)   The values in cells B6:G13 need to be populated.

Column B is revenue.  The sales volume needs to be used in each row, so the row number in cell G1 must be fixed – you can either use an absolute reference, $G$1, or mixed, G$1, it doesn't matter as long as the '1' is held.

Column C is the total variable costs.  Again, this will be the same in rows 6-13, so make sure the row numbers in the calculation are fixed.

Column D is the total contribution.

Column E is the Fixed costs (use an absolute reference)

Column F is the total costs

Column G is the profit (which could be calculated in a number of ways from this set of data)

(h)   Now the figures are populated, we can add some conditional formats.

Select cell G6, and using the Manage Rules menu, apply the following conditional formats:

Cell value<0 – Fill Red

Cell value=0 – Fill Yellow

Cell value>0 – Fill Green

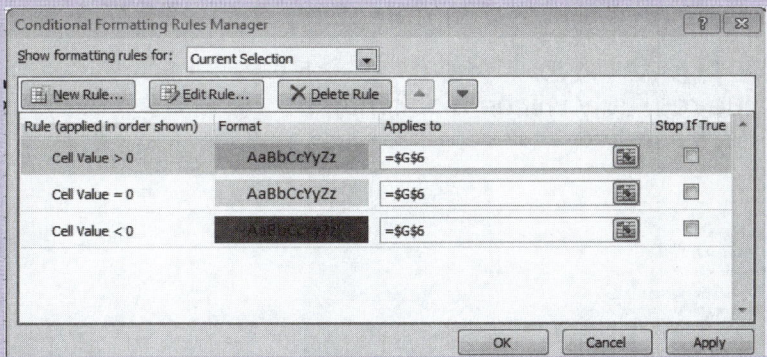

The cell should turn yellow, as profit is zero.

(i)   Copy the format down onto cells G7:G13.  The remaining cells should turn green, as their values are all greater than zero.

(j)  Change the sales volume in cell G1 to 20,000. Note the change in colour of the formatted cells.

(k)  Save the file.

---

  **Test your understanding 14**

This activity uses slightly more difficult conditional formatting, based on the value in another cell.

(a)  Open the CF Report file.

(b)  We want to highlight the largest sales figure in the data – use conditional formatting to fill this cell as green. Select cells B4:M4 and set up a new conditional formatting rule. The largest sales figure in cell B9 so we want to format the cell which is equal to this. This screen shot shows one way of doing this:

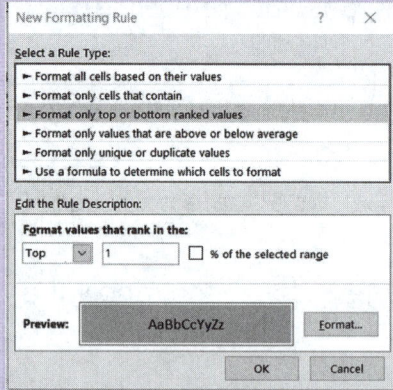

(c)  Change the value in cell J4 to 10,000. The value in B9 will change, and cell J4 will be coloured green.

(d)  Undo the last command to return September sales to 7,579.

(e)  Apply a similar conditional format to the sales figures to colour the lowest value red. July will be highlighted.

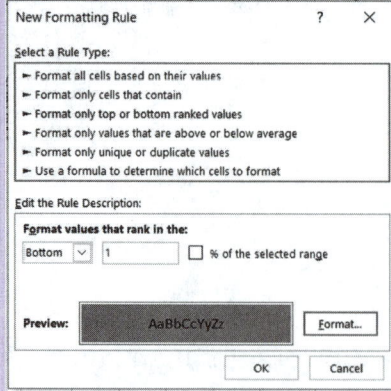

(f)     Apply conditional formatting to cells B5:M5 to bold any profits lower than average and fill the cell blue.

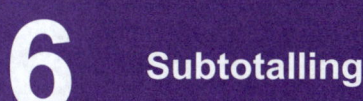

New Formatting Rule

Select a Rule Type:
- ► Format all cells based on their values
- ► Format only cells that contain
- ► Format only top or bottom ranked values
- ► Format only values that are above or below average
- ► Format only unique or duplicate values
- ► Use a formula to determine which cells to format

Edit the Rule Description:

**Format only cells with:**

| Cell Value | less than | =$B$12 |

Preview:     AaBbCcYyZz     Format...

OK     Cancel

(g)     Save the file.

# 6 Subtotalling

## 6.1 Introduction

Excel has a tool that allows you to insert subtotals. The Subtotal function is found in the Data tab, in the Outline menu.

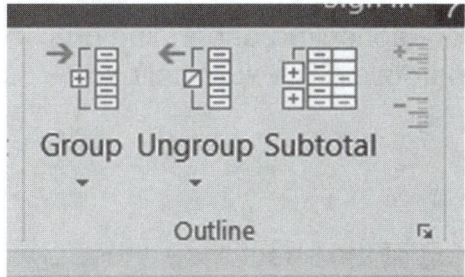

## 6.2 Creating subtotals

**Important note** – in order for a subtotal to work, the data MUST be sorted first, in the same order as the column(s) you wish to subtotal by. We may wish to add a subtotal to a worksheet show the total sales by each product. To do this, we must sort by product first.

Once the data is sorted, select it, and click the subtotal button.

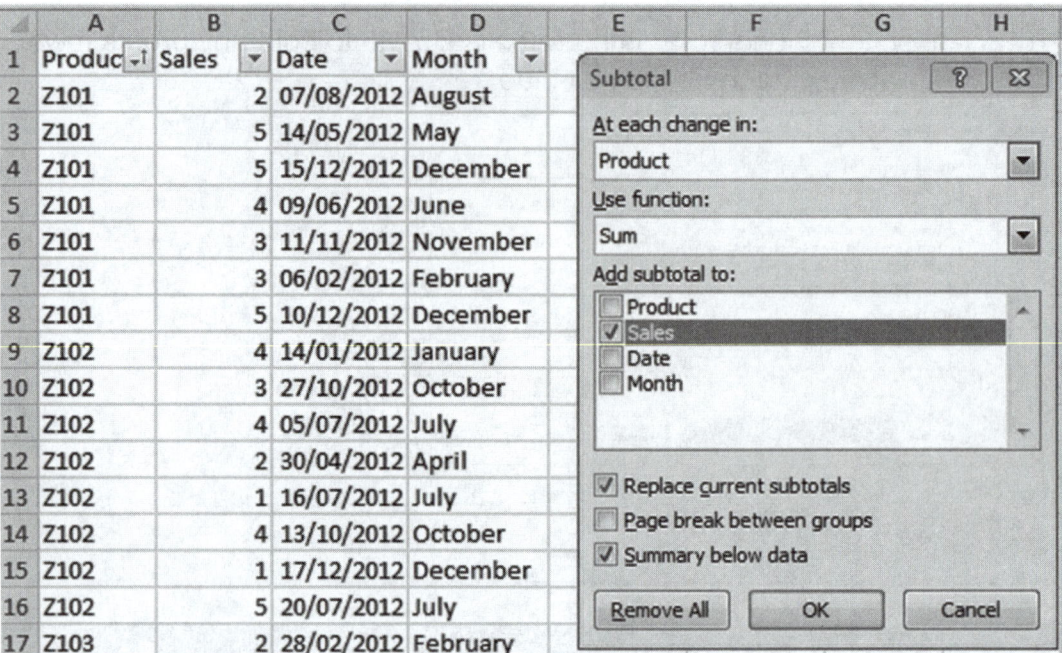

The Subtotal dialogue box will appear:

'**At each change in:**' – we wish to add a subtotal at each change in product.

'**Use function:**' – we want a total of the sales, so use SUM.

'**Add subtotal to:**' – as we want to find the total sales, this is the column we need a subtotal for – note that more than one column can be chosen.

The options at the bottom can be checked or unchecked depending on what you need. Click OK to complete the subtotals.  The subtotals are added below each set of data, as required.

### 6.3    Grouping

Some extra buttons have appeared on the left of the sheet too – these allow you to quickly hide and show data. Clicking on the [–] boxes will hide the data and they become [+].  Clicking the [+] will unhide the data.

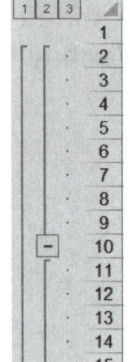

This enables you to specify what level of data is shown with the 1, 2, 3 buttons in the top left of the screen. The higher the number the more data is shown – clicking **3** will show all data. **2** will hide the lowest level of data.  This is useful to show a summary by product.

## 6.4 Removing subtotals

Removing subtotals is done in a similar way to adding subtotals – select the data with the subtotals on and click the **Subtotal** button.

Click the **Remove All** button the remove the subtotals.

## 6.5 Multiple subtotals

It is possible to have more than one subtotal on a data set. For example, we may wish to show sales by product but then summarised by month within each product.

As with normal subtotalling, the data must be sorted accordingly – if we need to subtotal on two bases, we must sort by the column we are subtotalling on first, then by the second subtotal column.

Add the first subtotal in the normal way:

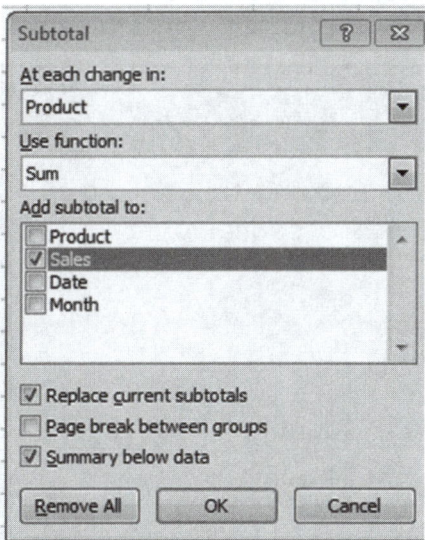

If you already have a subtotal in place, it will be overwritten as **Replace current subtotals** is selected.

To add the second subtotal, simply select the data again and click subtotal again.

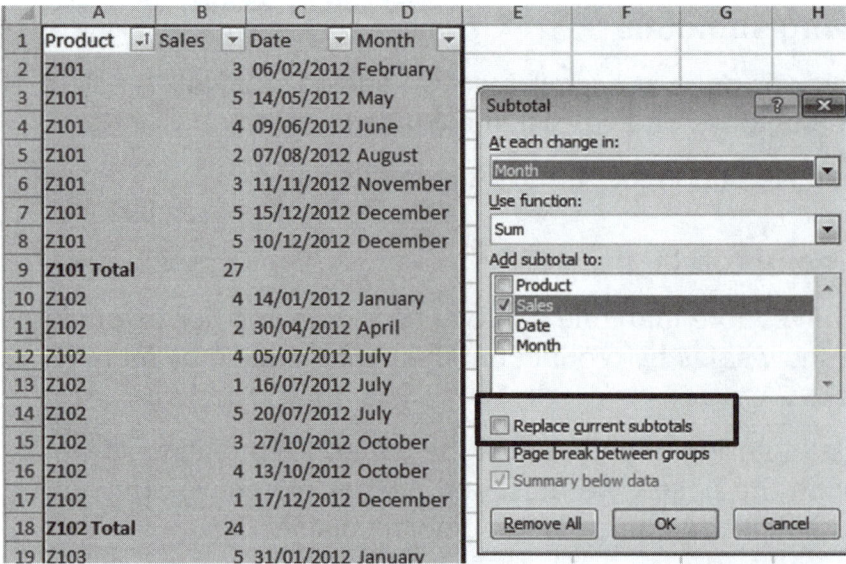

It is essential here that **Replace current subtotals** is unchecked, otherwise the first subtotal will be overwritten.

 **Test your understanding 15**

This activity allows you to practice adding and removing subtotals. It also acts as a reminder on Sorting data, as this is essential for subtotalling.

(a)  Open the Subtotal file.

(b)  Remove the subtotals.

(c)  Add subtotals for Quantity and Revenue by Month.

(d)  Select grouping level 2 – to show the monthly totals.

(e)  Save the file.

 **Test your understanding 16**

This activity allows you to practice adding and removing subtotals. It also acts as a reminder on Sorting data, as this is essential for subtotalling.

(a)  Open the Subtotal 1 file.

(b)  Remove the subtotals.

(c)  Sort the data by Month and by Product Code.

(d)  Add a subtotal of Sales Quantity and Revenue **by** Month.

(d)  Add another subtotal **by** Product Code (remember to uncheck 'Replace current subtotals').

(e)   Select grouping level 3 – to show the monthly and product subtotals.

(f)   Save the file.

# 7    Useful and logical functions

## 7.1   ROUND

Instead of changing the format, you may wish to instruct Excel to round the numbers to a certain number of decimal places – this is often useful when dealing with currency – round to 2 decimal places. To do this, use the **ROUND** function. Like all functions in Excel, it has a set format:

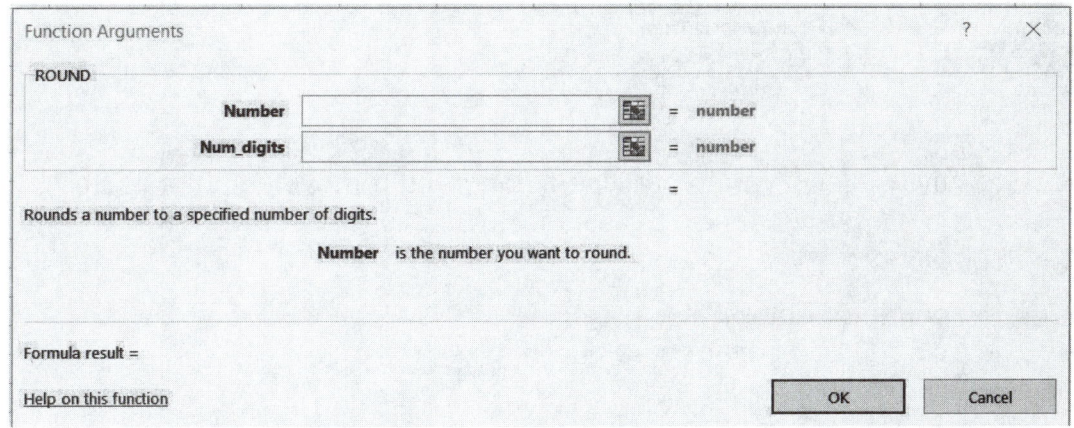

**=ROUND(number,num_digits)**

- 'number' and 'num_digits' are the ARGUMENTS

- **number** is the number or cell reference which needs rounding

- **num_digits** is the number of decimal places you wish to round to.

For example, if you type =ROUND(4.5682,3), the value shown will be 4.568 – rounded to 3 decimal places:

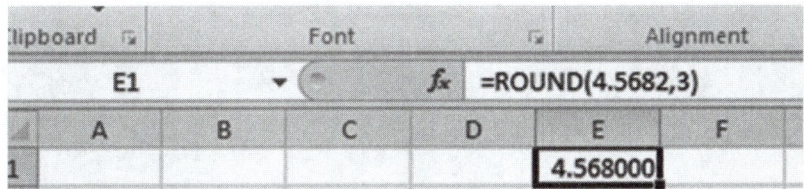

The formatting is shown to 6 decimal places, but the number has been rounded to 3.  To round to the nearest number, use 0 for **num_digits**. The Round function follows normal mathematical rounding rules – 0-4 are rounded down and 5-9 are rounded up.

You can also use =Round to round calculations:

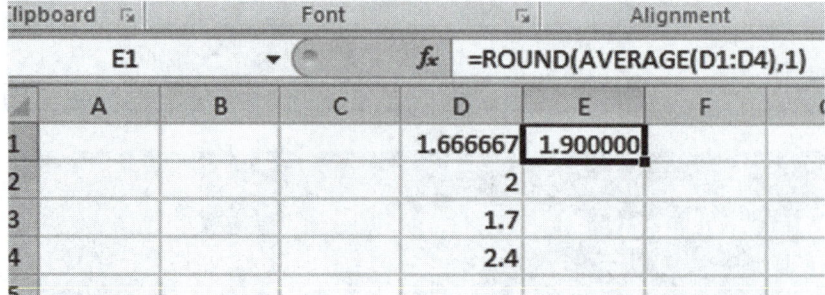

## 7.2    ROUNDUP and ROUNDDOWN

Sometimes you will want to force a number to be rounded up or down, and ROUNDUP or ROUNDDOWN will do this.

Roundup and Rounddown have exactly the same arguments as ROUND:

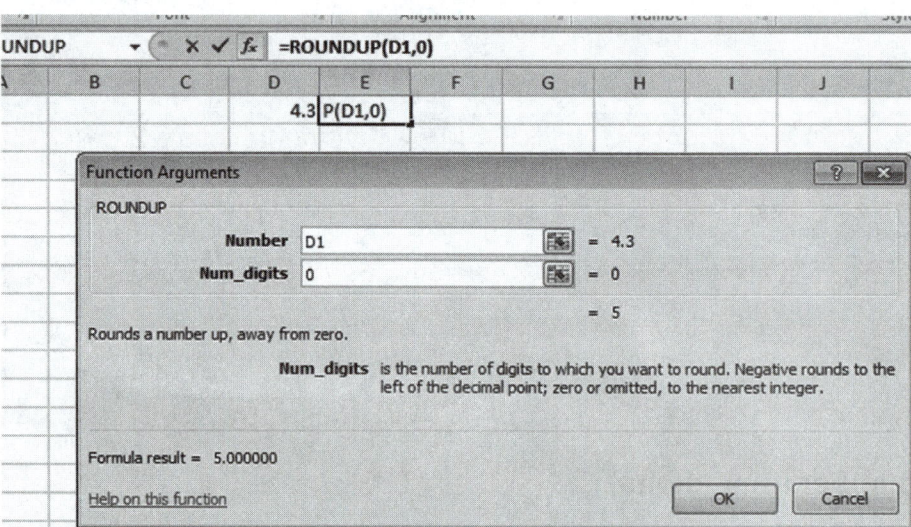

Rounddown works in exactly the same way:

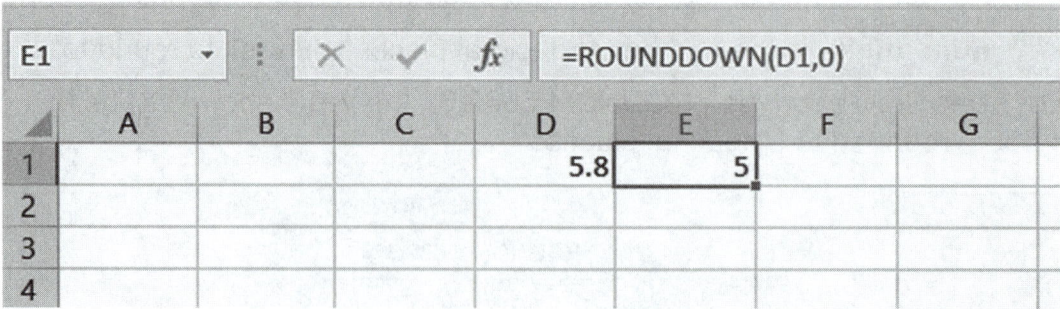

## Test your understanding 17

This activity mainly tests use of the ROUND function, along with some conditional formatting and simple functions.

(a)   Open the Inventory list file.

(b)   Note the information – we have a list of products, the quantity of the product and the total value of the products in inventory. In column E, we need to calculate the cost per unit of product.

(c)   In column E, calculate the cost per unit, rounded to 2 decimal places.

(d)   Format the figures in column E showing the figures to 3 decimal places, with a £ sign in front of the numbers (currency format).

(e)   In cells E16, E17 and E18, enter formulas to show the average, smallest and largest cost per unit respectively.

(f)   Label these as Average, Lowest and Highest in cells D16-D18.

(g)   Use conditional formatting to fill the largest value in cells E2:E15 in yellow.

(h)   Change the value in cell C3 to 5 – Note that this should change the value in E18 to £45.60 and the E3 should fill yellow.

(i)   Save the file.

## 7.3   LOOKUP Function

The LOOKUP function can be used to find a value either from a one-row or one-column range or from a set of data.  Data can be a column or a row.  It can look forwards or backwards in a set of data.  A Lookup will return the value that is closest match to what it is asked to find so sometime is not as accurate.

For example, excel is looking for the contents of cell C2 (Lookup_value) in column A2:A6 (Lookup_vector) and looking in the same row in column B2:B6 (Result_vector) to return the size that relates to the product code.

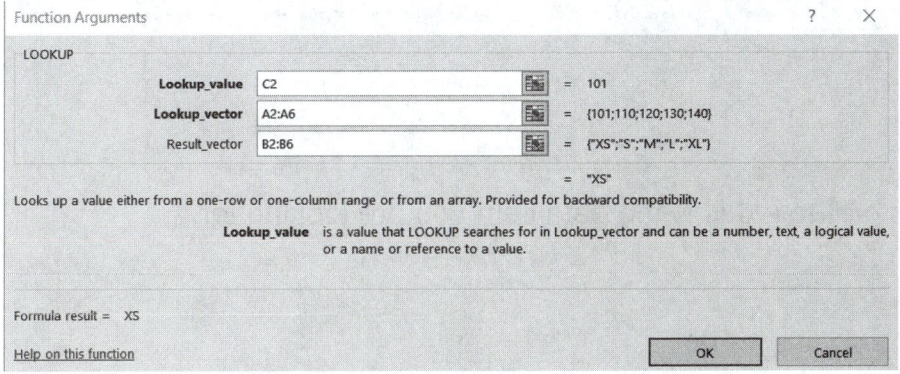

The result is fine – Product code 101 is XS.

| | A | B | C | D |
|---|---|---|---|---|
| 1 | Product code | Size | | |
| 2 | 101 | XS | 101 | XS |
| 3 | 110 | S | | |
| 4 | 120 | M | | |
| 5 | 130 | L | | |
| 6 | 140 | XL | | |

But if the product code is change to 104 excel still returns XS, even though code 104 does not exist, as it is looking for the best match possible:

| | A | B | C | D |
|---|---|---|---|---|
| 1 | Product code | Size | | |
| 2 | 101 | XS | 104 | XS |
| 3 | 110 | S | | |
| 4 | 120 | M | | |
| 5 | 130 | L | | |
| 6 | 140 | XL | | |
| 7 | | | | |

**The VLOOKUP Function**

VLOOKUPs are used is the same way as a Lookup but there are slightly different features.

The Vlookup will look in the leftmost column in a set of data and then return a value in the same row from a specified column. It is also possible to specify that exact matches are required.

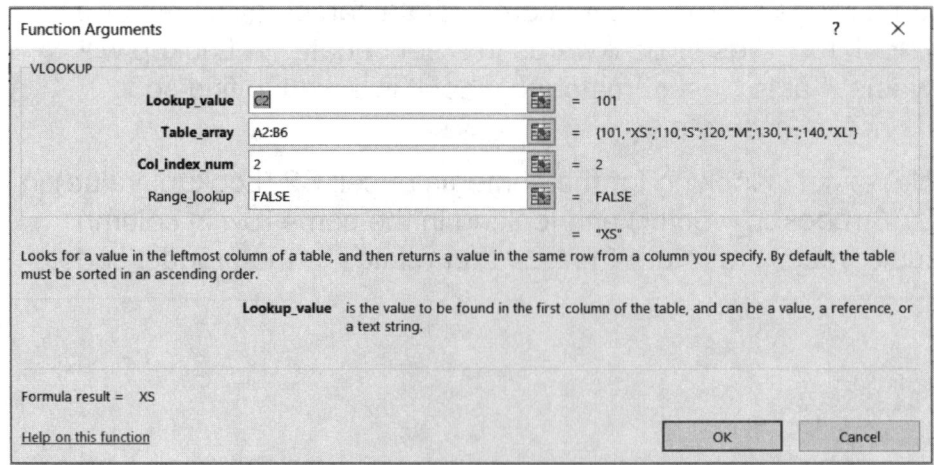

* **lookup_value** – this is the data item you are looking for.

- **table_array** – this is the range the data is in – i.e. where you are looking. The first column should contain the item being looked up; this is not necessarily the first column in the worksheet. If the vlookup is being used in more than one cell absolute referencing needs to be added to ensure that Excel continues to look at the correct data.

- **col_index_number** – this is the column number we want to use from the table_array.

- **range lookup** – this should either be TRUE or FALSE. If you leave it out then Excel will assume its value is TRUE.

  FALSE means that an exact match to the lookup_value must be found – useful for looking up specific items in a list.

  TRUE means the nearest value to the lookup_value will be found – useful if there is a range of values that the lookup_value lies between.

For example, if we want excel to look in some data, find a product code and return a quantity we would do the following:

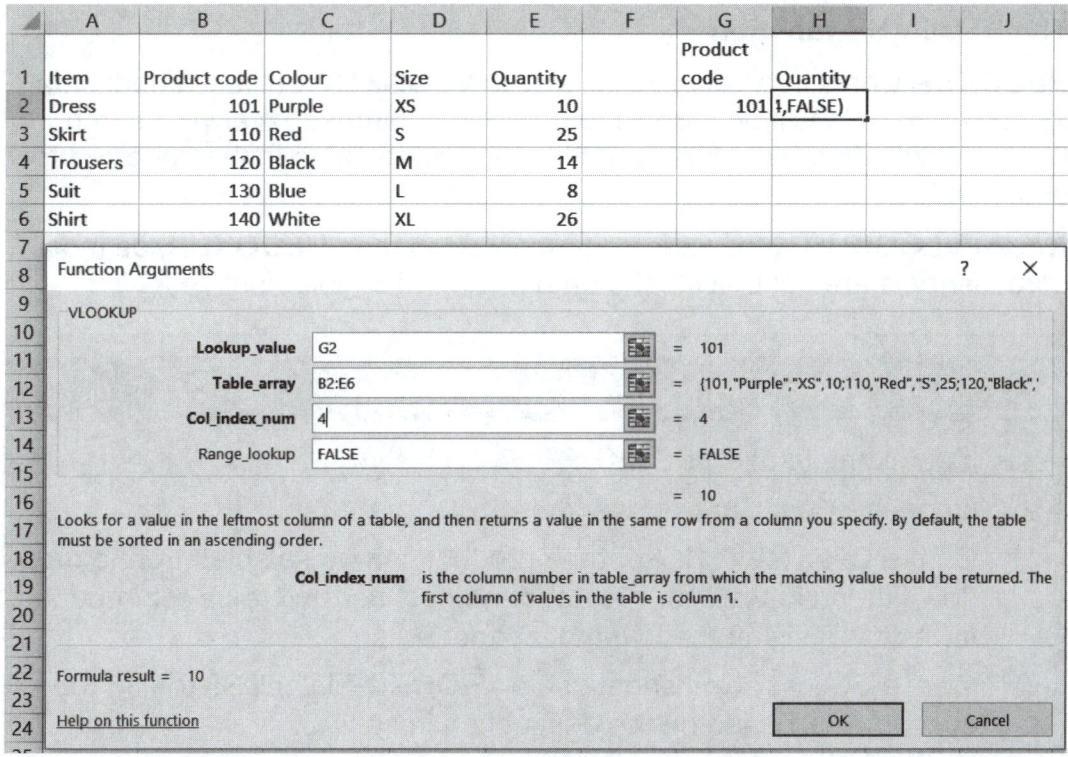

Note that the Table_array starts with column B as this is where the value to find is located and then returns the value from column E (4th column in the table). False is also chosen so an exact match to the product code is found.

You can copy this formula and use it in other cells but an absolute reference would need to be applied to the table_array so excel would continue looking at the same data.

**How does it work?**

It is easier to use VLOOKUP if you understand what it is doing. If we use the above example, we are looking for the quantity of the product in cell G2, in the cells from B2 to E6, and want the value in the 4th column.

Excel 'looks' down the 1st column until it finds a match, then returns the value in the 4th column of the table. The value 10 will be returned.

**Limitations of VLOOKUP**

**Duplicates** – Excel looks down each row of the first column until it finds a match – any matches below this will be ignored.

**First column only** – only the first column of the table is 'searched' for the **lookup_value**.

**Cannot Look 'Backwards'** – VLOOKUP 'finds' a value in the first column of a table, then returns the value from the appropriate column to the right. One way round this problem is to swap the columns over in the original data, as shown below.

**The HLOOKUP function**

**HLOOKUP** works in a very similar way to **VLOOKUP** but it is a horizontal lookup – the data will be in rows rather than columns. Excel will search along a row to find the value, and then return the value in the specified row of the table:

**Note** – **VLOOKUP** is far more commonly used than **HLOOKUP**, as most spreadsheets are set up with the data arranged in columns.

---

 **Test your understanding 18**

This is an example of a VLOOKUP.

(a)    Open the Cost Checker workbook.

(b)    On the Checker worksheet the product can be selected from a drop down menu in Cell A3. We need the cost per unit to be returned from column E on the Inventory sheet.

(c)    On the Checker worksheet use a VLOOKUP in cell B3 to find the cost per unit based on the description in cell A3.

(d)    Change the product in A3 to 'Doodad 2'. Click in A3 and select the drop down menu to change the product.

(e)    The value in B3 should change to 12.01.

(f)    Save the file.

---

## 7.4 Logical functions

Logical functions give an answer of either **TRUE** or **FALSE**. A very simple logical function would be:

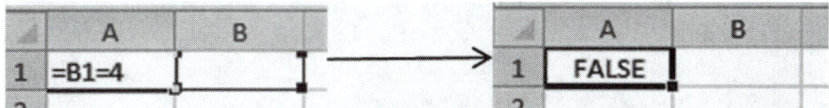

The first '=' is just there to tell Excel that this is a formula. The logical test is B1=4. This can either be TRUE – if B1 does equal 4, or FALSE, if it does not. As there is no value in cell B1, the answer is FALSE.

If you enter 4 into B1, the answer changes to TRUE.

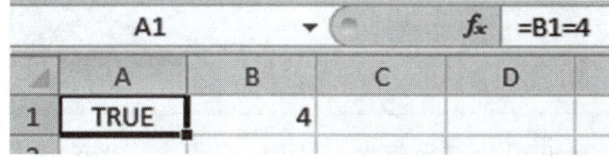

This is very useful for checking if two cells which should have the same value do have the same value!

The full list of logical checks is as follows:

| Check | Symbol |
|---|---|
| Equal to | = |
| Less than | < |
| Less than or equal to | <= |
| Greater than | > |
| Greater than or equal to | >= |
| Not equal to | <> |

Note the 'Not equal to' and 'Less/greater than or equal to' – the order of the symbols is important.

We are going to look at the following logical functions – IF, AND, OR

### IF

Logical checks are very useful, but it may be more appropriate to have something other than TRUE or FALSE as a response, an IF function can do this.

The **IF** function has 3 arguments, as follows:

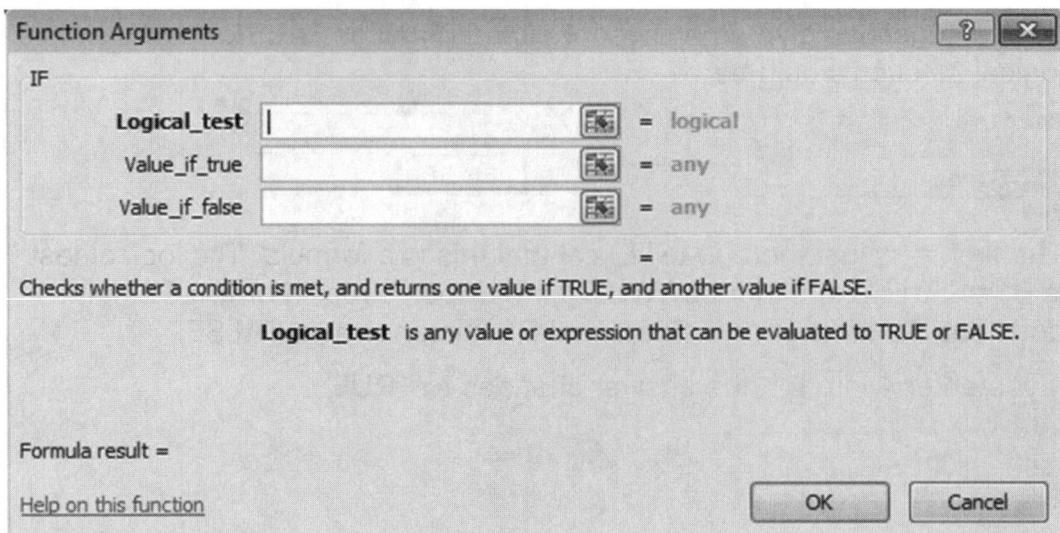

- **Logical_test** – as above, a logical test is a test that will have the value TRUE or FALSE. **What are we testing?**

- **Value_if_true** – enter here what you would like to do if the test is true – this could be a calculation, some text or even another Excel function. **What to do if the test is true.**

- **Value_if_false** – enter here what to do if the test is false, in the same way. **What to do if the test is false**.

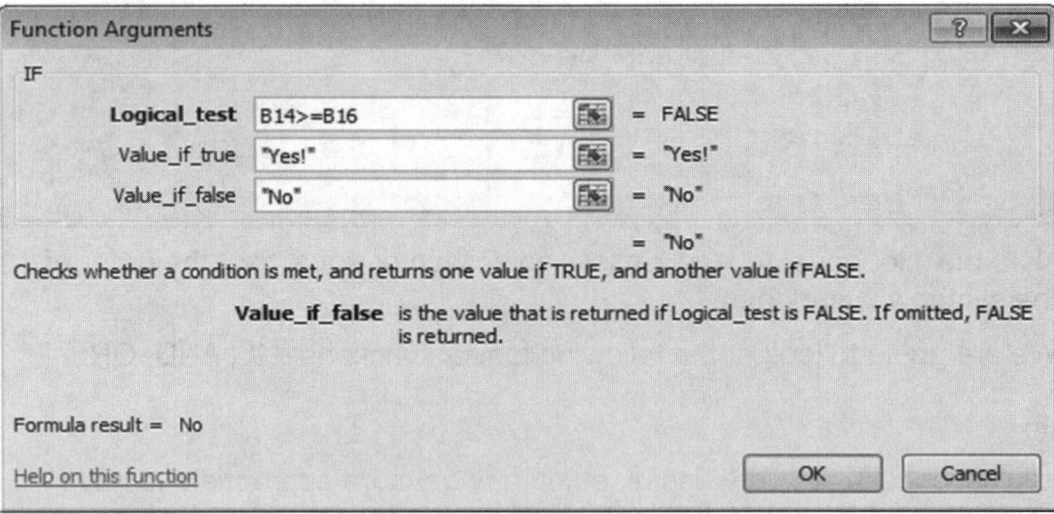

The logical test is asking if the content in cell B14 is greater than or equal to the content in cell B16. If it is, we want text saying "Yes!", otherwise "No". Note that the quote marks ("") are required to tell Excel to show text.

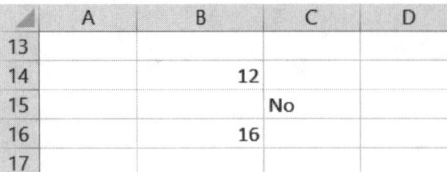

|  | A | B | C | D |
|---|---|---|---|---|
| 13 |  |  |  |  |
| 14 |  | 12 |  |  |
| 15 |  |  | No |  |
| 16 |  | 16 |  |  |
| 17 |  |  |  |  |

Going back to the Vlookup example, we might want to check that we have enough of a product in inventory to meet an order.

An IF function can be built around a Vlookup – the Vlookup becomes part of the logical test.

Start by creating the Vlookup to look up the product code and return the quantity in inventory:

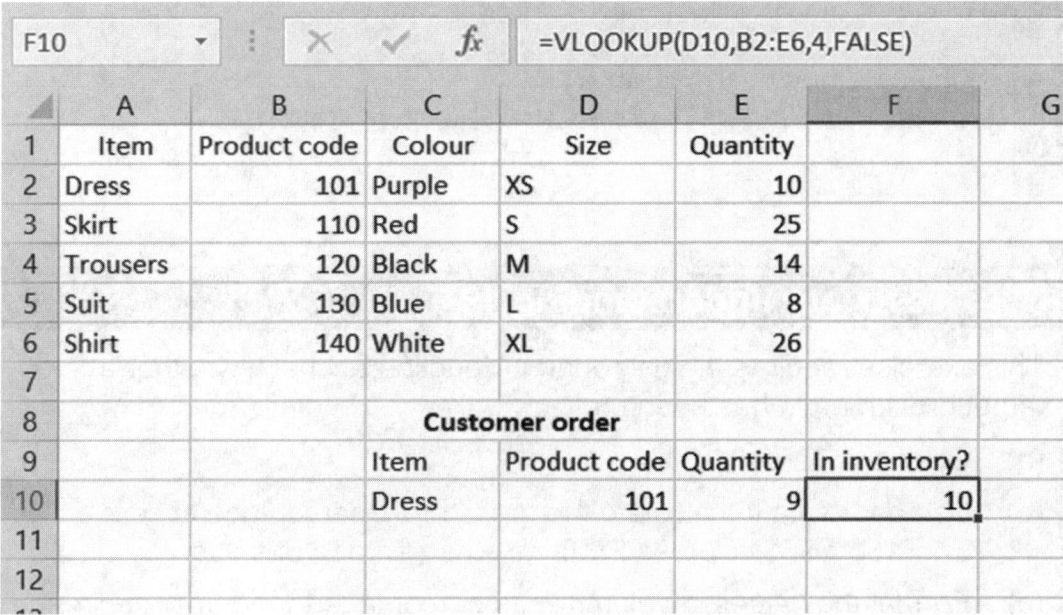

We now want to see **IF** the order size is less than or equal to the number in inventory.

The IF function can be built around it. Type **IF(** between the = and Vlookup click on the word IF in the formula bar and then the **Insert Function** button to bring up the appropriate menu, complete the logical test, add the values if true or false, click ok.

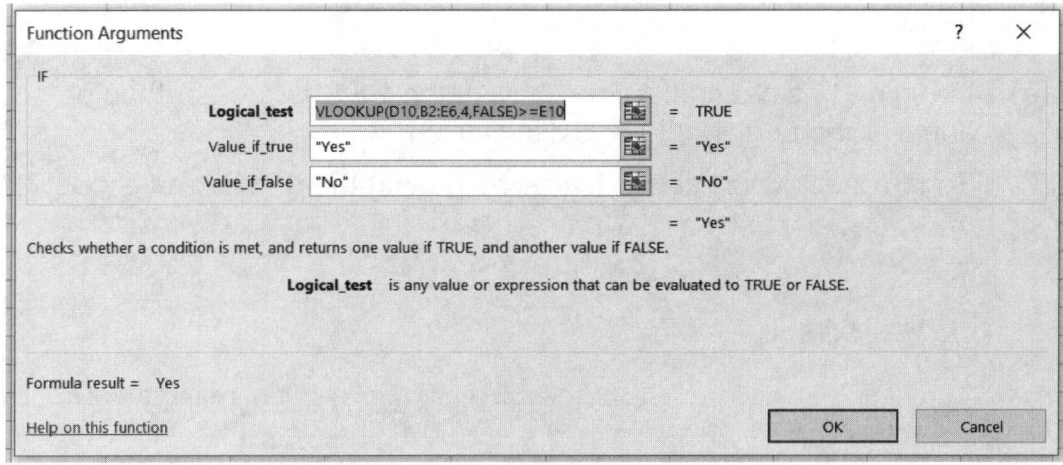

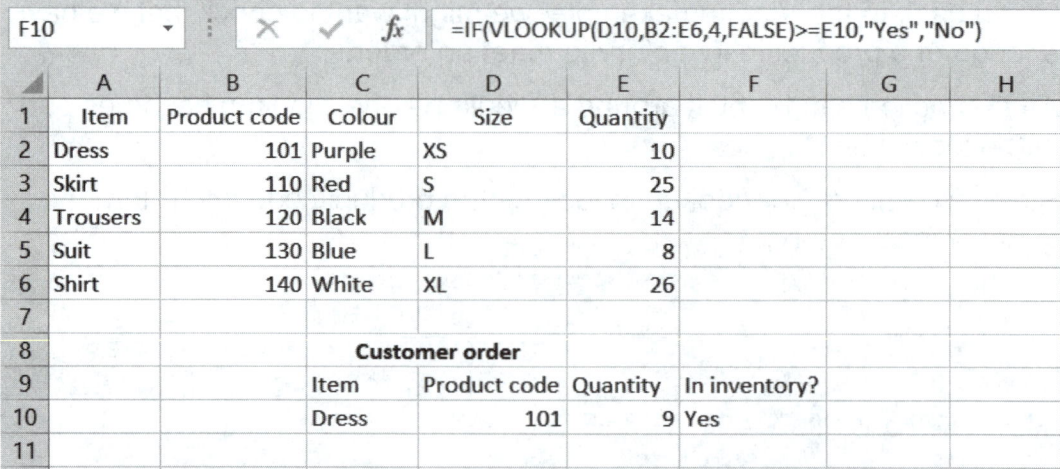

| F10 | | | $f_x$ | =IF(VLOOKUP(D10,B2:E6,4,FALSE)>=E10,"Yes","No") | | | |
|---|---|---|---|---|---|---|---|
| | A | B | C | D | E | F | G | H |
| 1 | Item | Product code | Colour | Size | Quantity | | | |
| 2 | Dress | 101 | Purple | XS | 10 | | | |
| 3 | Skirt | 110 | Red | S | 25 | | | |
| 4 | Trousers | 120 | Black | M | 14 | | | |
| 5 | Suit | 130 | Blue | L | 8 | | | |
| 6 | Shirt | 140 | White | XL | 26 | | | |
| 7 | | | | | | | | |
| 8 | | | **Customer order** | | | | | |
| 9 | | | Item | Product code | Quantity | In inventory? | | |
| 10 | | | Dress | 101 | 9 | Yes | | |
| 11 | | | | | | | | |

 **Test your understanding 19**

This exercise requires the use of an IF function to check whether a target profit margin has been met.

(a) Open the Target GP file.

(b) Use a formula to calculate the gross profit percentage in cells E4:E15. GP% is Gross Profit as a percentage of sales.

(c) Format the values in column E as percentage format to 1 decimal place.

(d) Your spreadsheet should look like this

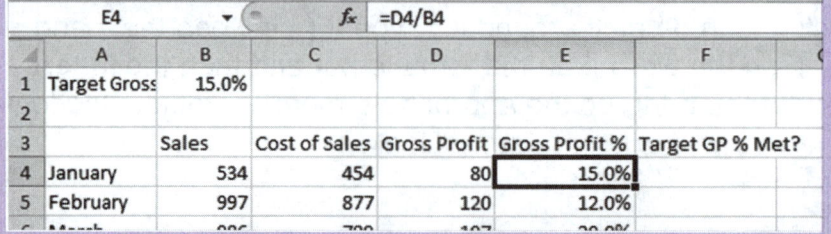

| E4 | | | $f_x$ | =D4/B4 | | |
|---|---|---|---|---|---|---|
| | A | B | C | D | E | F |
| 1 | Target Gross | 15.0% | | | | |
| 2 | | | | | | |
| 3 | | Sales | Cost of Sales | Gross Profit | Gross Profit % | Target GP % Met? |
| 4 | January | 534 | 454 | 80 | 15.0% | |
| 5 | February | 997 | 877 | 120 | 12.0% | |

(e) Using an IF statement, return 'Yes' if the GP% is greater than or equal to the target in B1 and 'No' if it is not.

(f) Sense check your results – are you getting the results you expect?

(g)

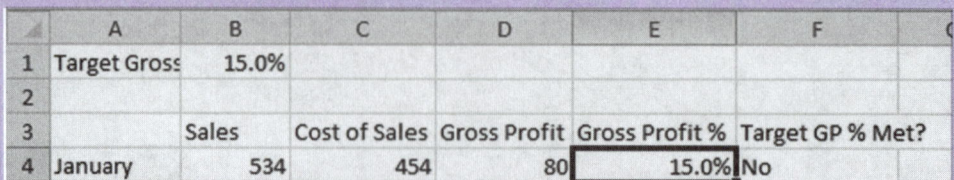

| | A | B | C | D | E | F |
|---|---|---|---|---|---|---|
| 1 | Target Gross | 15.0% | | | | |
| 2 | | | | | | |
| 3 | | Sales | Cost of Sales | Gross Profit | Gross Profit % | Target GP % Met? |
| 4 | January | 534 | 454 | 80 | 15.0% | No |

You may find you get the above – this should be Yes – the target has been met! Let us see why it is not working.

(h) Change the format in column E to 2 decimal places.

(i) As this calculation is unrounded, the target has not been met.

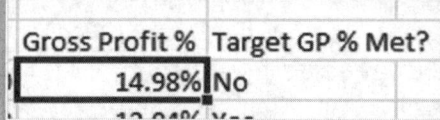

| Gross Profit % | Target GP % Met? |
|---|---|
| 14.98% | No |
| 12.04% | Yes |

(j) Use the ROUND function in column E to round the calculation to 3 decimal places. Note that for percentages, 14.98% is equivalent to 0.1498, so we need to round to 3 decimal places.

(k) Your Formulas should now work. If you are not getting the results you expect, check the formula that is not working – see which cells are being used. It is usually a problem with absolute/relative references.

(l) Change the value in B1 to 20% – see how column F changes.

(m) AutoFit the column widths and save.

### Test your understanding 20

This example uses calculations across worksheets, as well as requiring an IF formula.

(a) Open the Boat sales file.

(b) This workbook contains four worksheets:

Sales Volume – shows the sales to four customers of two different products.

Pricing – shows the price of the two products.

Discounting – shows the discount offered to each customer if target sales are met.

Monthly sales – calculates revenue, and any discount offered.

The calculations are required on the Monthly Sales worksheet.

(c) On the Monthly Sales sheet, in cells C4:D7, calculate the sales revenue from each product by customer. Note that a combination of relative and mixed referencing is required.

(d) Calculate the totals by product and customer in cells E4:E7 and C9:E9.

(e)     In cells F4:F7 we need to calculate the value of the discount. A discount is given IF the actual sales (from the Sales Volume sheet) are greater than or equal to the volume target for each customer – in cells B4:B7.

The discount offered will be the total sales figure multiplied by the discount on the Discounting sheet.

(f)     Calculate the discounted sales in column G and copy the totals across in row 9.

(g)     In H4:H7 you need a formula to say 'Yes' if a discount has been given and 'No' if it has not. There are several ways to achieve this.

(h)     Save the file.

**AND**

**AND** is used when you want to check more than one thing is true. As it is a logical function, the result of an **AND** function will be TRUE or FALSE. The basic idea is to say:

Is this true **and** is this true **and** is this true **and**…

The **AND** function will return a value of TRUE if **ALL** of the checks are TRUE. If any are FALSE, then the answer will be FALSE. You can test up to 255 logical checks.

Using the Insert Function button breaks this down nicely, in this example, three things are being checked – is 3 greater than 1, is 2 equal to 2 and is 7 not equal to 10:

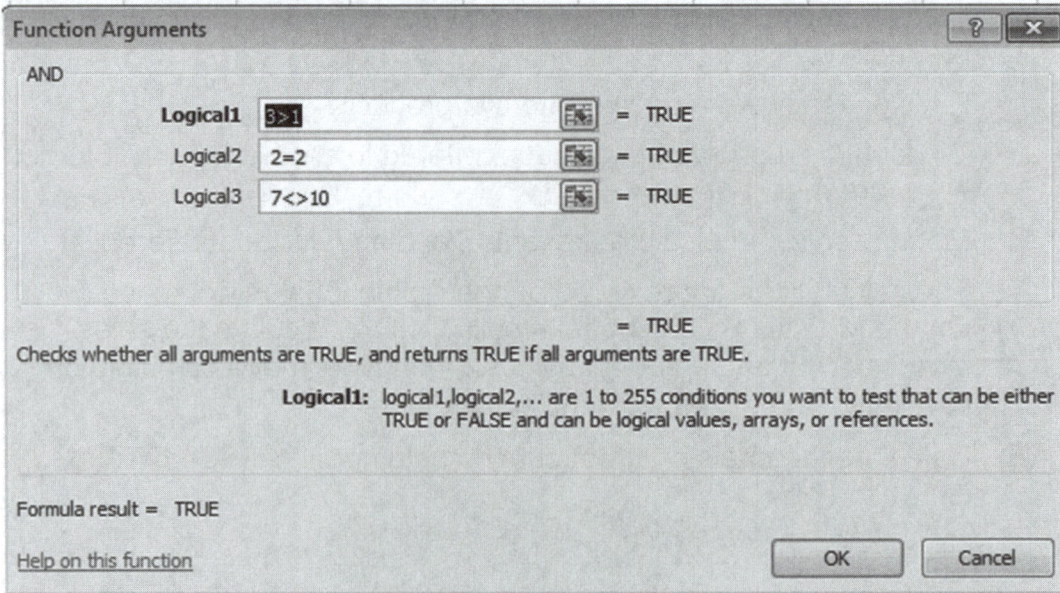

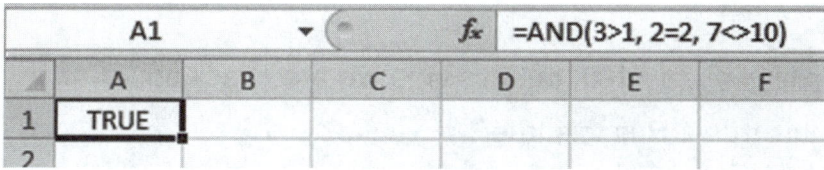

If we change the arguments so that only one is false, this will affect the outcome:

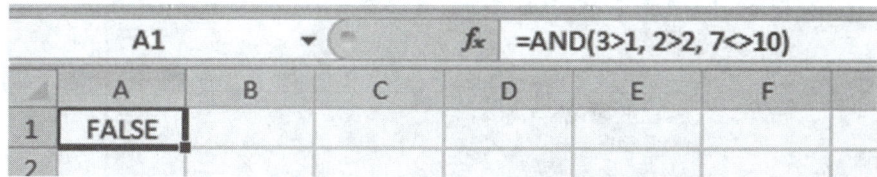

2 is not greater than 2, so the value is FALSE!

 **Test your understanding 21**

This example requires the use of an IF with an AND formula.

(a)   Open the Boat Sales Two file.

(b)   This workbook contains four worksheets:

Sales Volume – shows the sales to four customers of two different products.

Pricing – shows the price of the two products.

Discounting – shows the discount offered to each customer if target sales are met.

Monthly sales – calculates revenue, and any discount offered.

The calculations are required on the Monthly Sales worksheet.

(c)   In cells F4:F7 we need to calculate the value of the discount. A discount is now given **IF** the actual sales (from the Sales Volume sheet) **FOR BOTH PRODUCTS** are greater than or equal to the volume target for each customer – in cells B4:B7. The sales for SuperCruise **AND** the sales for WindSail must be bigger than target – this will form your logical test.

The discount offered will be the total sales figure multiplied by the discount on the Discounting sheet.

(d)   Calculate the discounted sales in column G and copy the totals across in row 9.

(e)   In H4:H7 you need a formula to say 'Yes' if a discount has been given and 'No' if it has not. There are several ways to achieve this.

(f)   Save the file.

## OR

**OR** works in a similar way to **AND**, but this time we are checking:

Is this true **OR** is this true **OR** is this true….

As a result, only ONE of the logical checks needs to be true for the value to be TRUE.

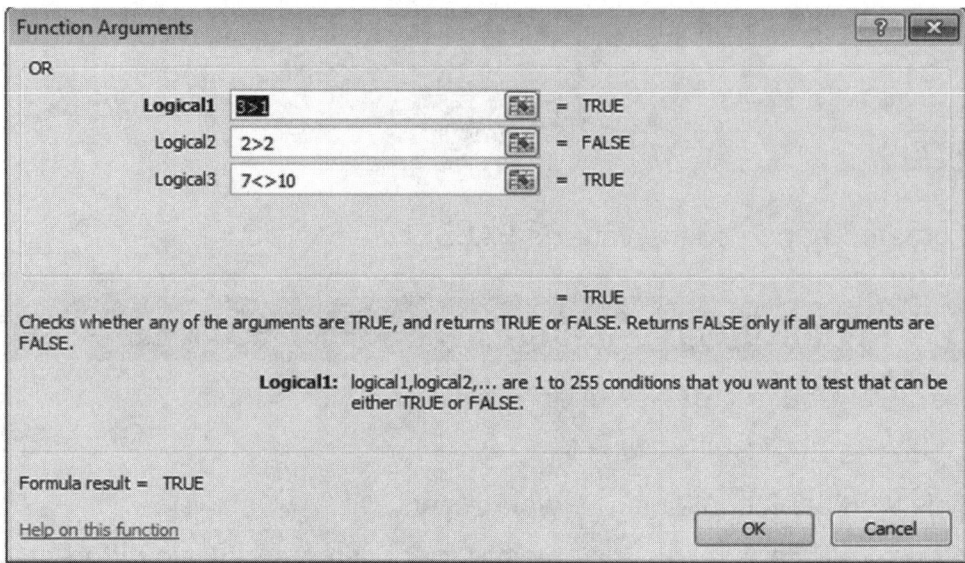

Taking the same checks as the previous example, as at least one is TRUE, the value returned is TRUE.

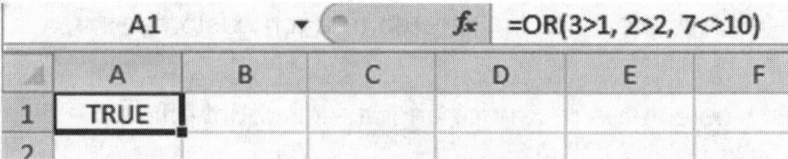

As explained in the function box OR will only give a FALSE answer if ALL of the checks are FALSE.

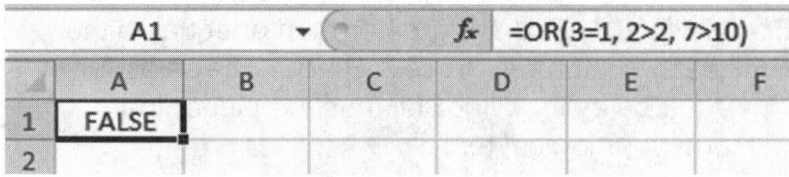

All three checks are FALSE.

### Using AND OR

The main use of these will be within an **IF** statement. If, for example, you wish to check two things, the logical test part of the **IF** formula would be an **AND** function. Remember, the first argument in an **IF** statement is a logical test with the answer TRUE or FALSE – an **AND** function will give this.

We might want to check that the weather is going to be sunny or cloudy for a picnic.

| | A | B | C | D |
|---|---|---|---|---|
| 1 | Day | Weather | Picnic? | |
| 2 | Monday | Rainy | | |
| 3 | Tuesday | Cloudy | | |
| 4 | Wednesday | Sunny | | |
| 5 | Thursday | Sunny | | |
| 6 | Friday | Rainy | | |
| 7 | Saturday | Sunny | | |
| 8 | Sunday | Cloudy | | |
| 9 | | | | |

Set up the logical check first (is the value in B2 'Cloudy' or 'Sunny'?).

| C2 | | | $f_x$ | =OR(B2="Cloudy",B2="Sunny") | | |
|---|---|---|---|---|---|---|
| | A | B | C | D | E | F |
| 1 | Day | Weather | Picnic? | | | |
| 2 | Monday | Rainy | FALSE | | | |
| 3 | Tuesday | Cloudy | TRUE | | | |
| 4 | Wednesday | Sunny | TRUE | | | |
| 5 | Thursday | Sunny | TRUE | | | |
| 6 | Friday | Rainy | FALSE | | | |
| 7 | Saturday | Sunny | TRUE | | | |
| 8 | Sunday | Cloudy | TRUE | | | |

This OR function can be used as the logical check in an IF statement:

Start entering the IF statement, with the open bracket.

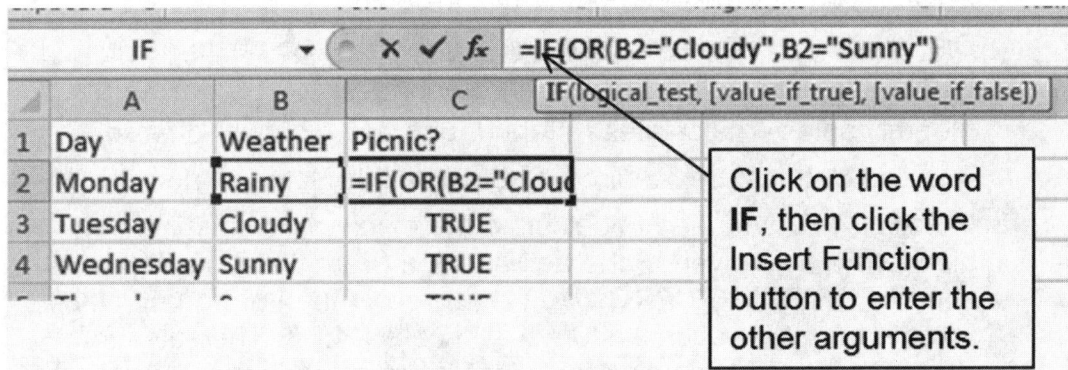

| IF | | | X ✔ $f_x$ | =IF(OR(B2="Cloudy",B2="Sunny") |
|---|---|---|---|---|

IF(logical_test, [value_if_true], [value_if_false])

| | A | B | C |
|---|---|---|---|
| 1 | Day | Weather | Picnic? |
| 2 | Monday | Rainy | =IF(OR(B2="Clou |
| 3 | Tuesday | Cloudy | TRUE |
| 4 | Wednesday | Sunny | TRUE |

Click on the word **IF**, then click the Insert Function button to enter the other arguments.

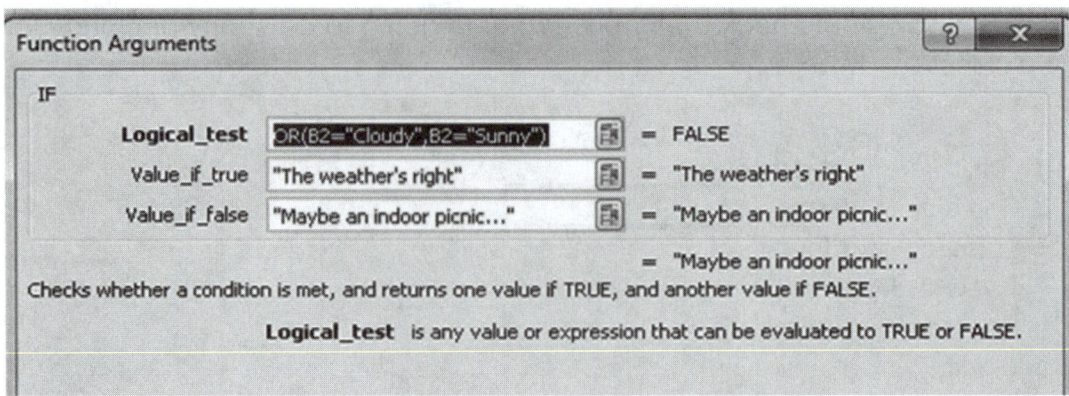

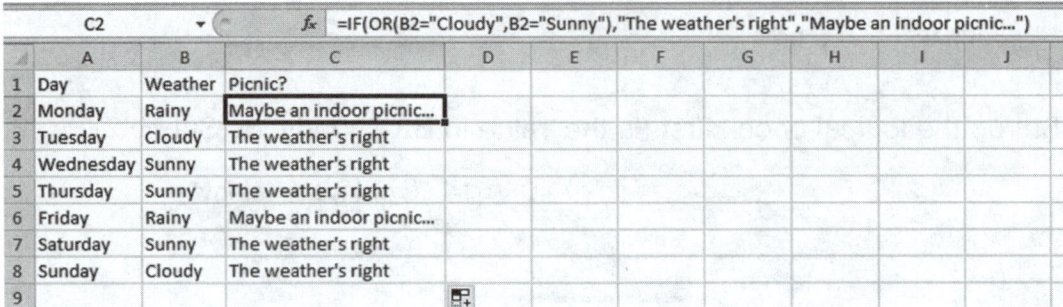

 **Test your understanding 22**

This example requires the use of an IF with an OR formula.

(a) Open the Boat Sales Three file.

(b) This workbook contains four worksheets:

Sales Volume – shows the sales to four customers of two different products.

Pricing – shows the price of the two products.

Discounting – shows the discount offered to each customer if target sales are met.

Monthly sales – calculates revenue, and any discount offered.

The calculations are required on the Monthly Sales worksheet.

(e) In cells F4:F7 we need to calculate the discounted sales. A discount is now given IF the actual sales (from the Sales Volume sheet) **FOR EITHER PRODUCT** are greater than or equal to the volume target for each customer – in cells B4:B7. The sales for SuperCruise **OR** the sales for WindSail must be bigger than target – this will form your logical test.

(f) Copy the totals across in row 9.

(g) In G4:G7 you need a formula to say 'Yes' if a discount has been given and 'No' if it has not. There are several ways to achieve this.

(h) Save the file.

## 7.5    SUMIF function

SUMIF can be used to add cells specified by a given condition or criteria. For example, suppose that in a set of data that consists of numbers, you want to sum only the negative values, (if the value is <0).

|  | A | B | C | D | E | F |
|---|---|---|---|---|---|---|
| 1 |  |  |  | Percentage change fron | 80.00% |  |
| 2 |  |  |  |  |  |  |
| 3 |  | Budget | Flexed budget | Actual | Variance |  |
| 4 |  | £ | £ | £ | £ |  |
| 5 | Volume sold and produced | 1,000 | 1,800 | 1,800 |  |  |
| 6 | Sales revenue | 40,000 | 72,000 | 60,000 | - 12,000 |  |
| 7 | Direct materials | 4,000 | 7,200 | 6,000 | 1,200 |  |
| 8 | Direct labour | 3,800 | 6,840 | 5,300 | 1,540 |  |
| 9 | Fixed overheads | 10,700 | 10,700 | 13,600 | - 2,900 |  |
| 10 | Operating profit | 21,500 | 47,260 | 35,100 | - 12,160 |  |
| 11 |  |  |  |  |  |  |

You can use the following formula:

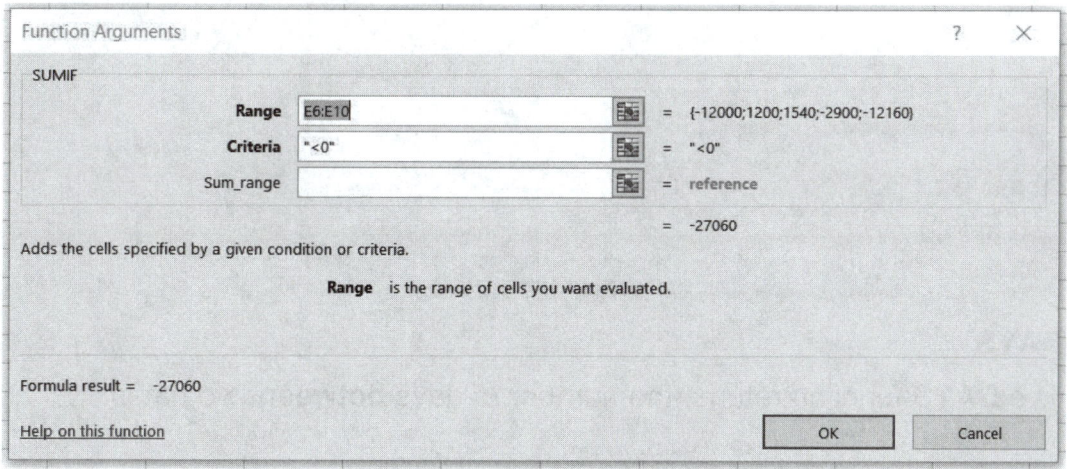

## 7.6    DATE function

The DATE function can be used to insert dates into worksheets so that they are always current, or they can be used in formulas to help calculations.

To deal with dates, Excel treats every date as a number – how it is displayed is based on the format you choose in the Format Cells menu.

Dates 'start' from 1 January 1900, i.e. this day is represented by the number 1. Every day beyond this the number increases by 1. For example:

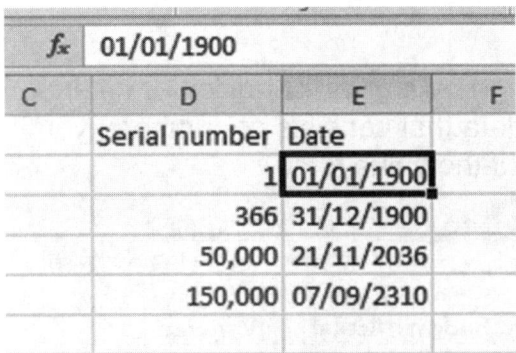

These two columns are identical. However, the FORMAT of the 2nd column has been changed to be dates.

This can also be achieved by using the function **=DATE**. The date of 16th July 2021 is represented by the number 44393.

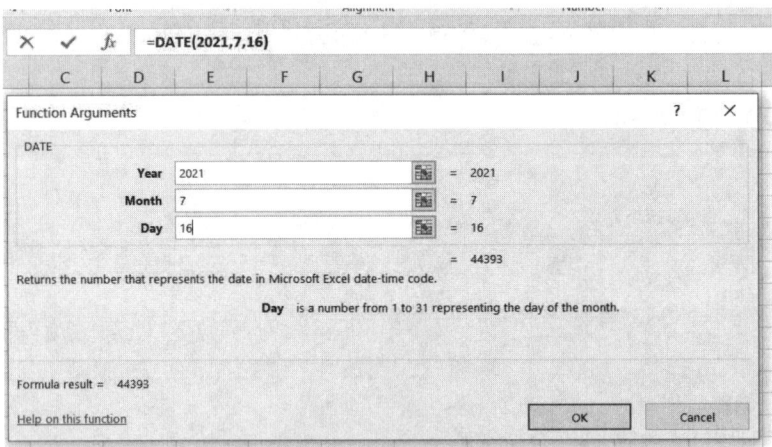

## DAYS

The **DAYS** function returns the number of days **between** two dates.

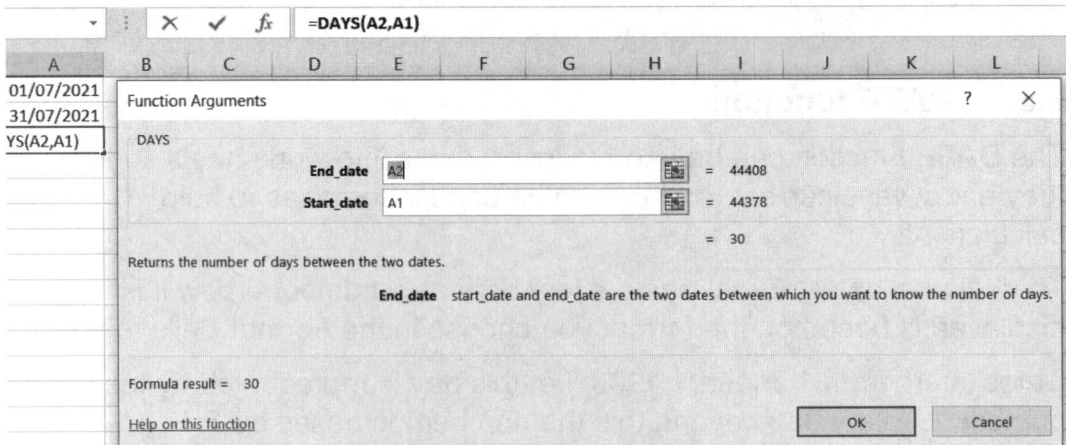

The number of days **between** the 1st July 2021 and 31st July 2021 is given as 30.

**KAPLAN** PUBLISHING

Be careful, if you are asked how many days there are in total you would need to add one each time.

## 7.7    FORECAST function

Excel contains a number of functions that allow you to forecast future figures based on current and historic data. One that you need to be familiar with is the FORECAST function.

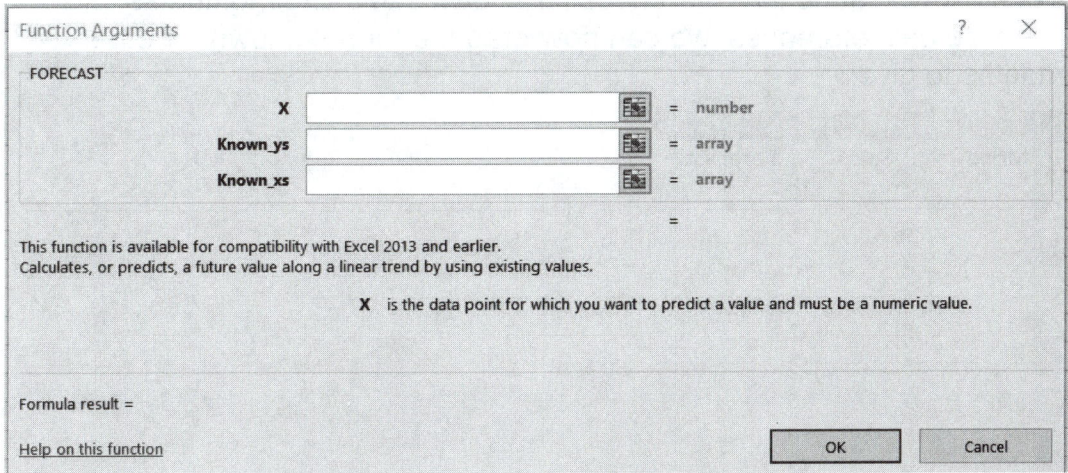

- "x" is the independent variable for the forecast – e.g. the future month you want

- "known_y's" are the known dependent variables – e.g. sales figures we already have

- "known_x's" are the known independent variables – e.g. the months for which we already have sales figures

It is best to use absolute referencing for known_y's and known_x's in order to move the formula around.

Suppose you are given sales for the first 9 months of the year and want to forecast sales for the last quarter of the year.  Using 'insert function' we can calculate the required values:

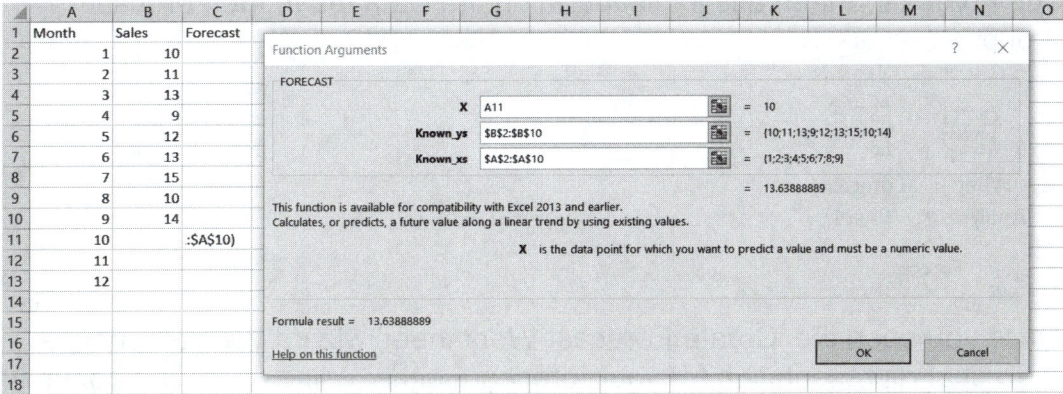

- The first element, **A11**, gives the "x" value of the month for which we need a forecast (month 10)

- The second, **$B$2:$B$10**, gives the range of sales figures ("y" values) we know

- Finally, **$A$2:$A$10** gives the range of months ("x" values) for which we know sales figures

Because we set up the references for known sales and months as absolute cell references, we can now drag the formula down for other months to give:

| | A | B | C |
|---|---|---|---|
| 1 | Month | Sales | Forecast |
| 2 | 1 | 10 | |
| 3 | 2 | 11 | |
| 4 | 3 | 13 | |
| 5 | 4 | 9 | |
| 6 | 5 | 12 | |
| 7 | 6 | 13 | |
| 8 | 7 | 15 | |
| 9 | 8 | 10 | |
| 10 | 9 | 14 | |
| 11 | 10 | | 13.63889 |
| 12 | 11 | | 13.98889 |
| 13 | 12 | | 14.33889 |

We can then reformat column C and use the forecast in any other way we need – we could add =ROUND or use the formatting features to change the decimal places.

## 7.8 FORECAST SHEETS

Creating a forecast sheet in Excel is a useful way to predict future trends based on historical data.

**Creating a forecast sheet in Excel**

The Forecast Sheet function is found on the Data tab in the Forecast group.

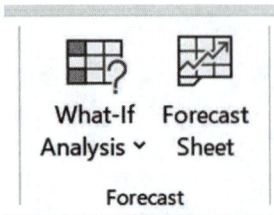

Once you open the 'Create Forecast Worksheet' wizard you can choose the visual representation for your forecast - either a line chart or a column chart. You will see the options in the top right-hand corner of the window.

On the same pop out window you can set the end date for your forecast period in the 'Forecast End' box in the bottom left-hand corner of the window (above Options). This could be a number of time periods or a date.

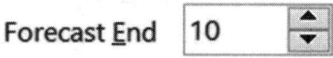

Then click the 'Create' button in the bottom right-hand corner of the window.

## More advanced options

There are some more advanced options available within the 'Create Forecast worksheet' window in Excel. To access these, you need to click on 'Options' in the bottom left of the window. These options enable you to customise settings such as confidence intervals, seasonality, and more.

### Confidence interval

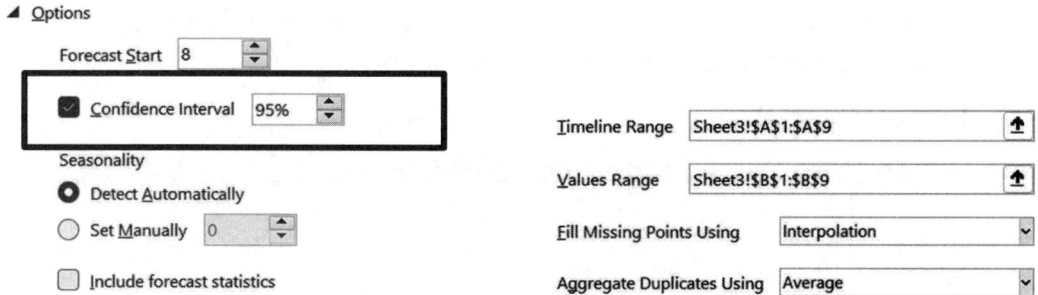

A confidence interval provides an estimated range of possible forecast values based on a specified level of confidence. It shows that your forecast might not be perfect, and it gives you an idea of how much it could vary.

The confidence interval gives you an upper and lower band around your forecasted value. This range helps account for the uncertainty and variability in any forecast.

## Confidence level (the % chosen)

The confidence level indicates how sure you want to be that the actual future values will fall within the confidence interval.

- The range or width of the confidence interval is directly related to the confidence level because it reflects how certain you want to be about your prediction.

- Higher confidence levels will have wider intervals, a larger range.

  When you choose a higher confidence level, like 95%, you want to be more certain that the true value will fall within the interval. To achieve this high certainty, you need to allow for a larger range of possible values. This means the interval will be wider, covering more ground to make sure the actual value is included.

- Lower confidence levels will have narrower intervals, a smaller range.

  When you choose a lower confidence level, like 50%, you are okay with being less certain about the prediction.  The range will be narrower, but there is only a 50% chance of the outcome falling within this range, so a higher risk of the actual outcome being outside of it.

It's a trade-off between certainty and precision. Higher confidence levels give you more certainty but less precision (wider range), while lower confidence levels give you more precision but less certainty (narrower range).

To set the confidence interval in Excel forecast sheets choose the confidence interval using the up and down arrows.

## Handling missing data

Any missing data can be filled by interpolating values:

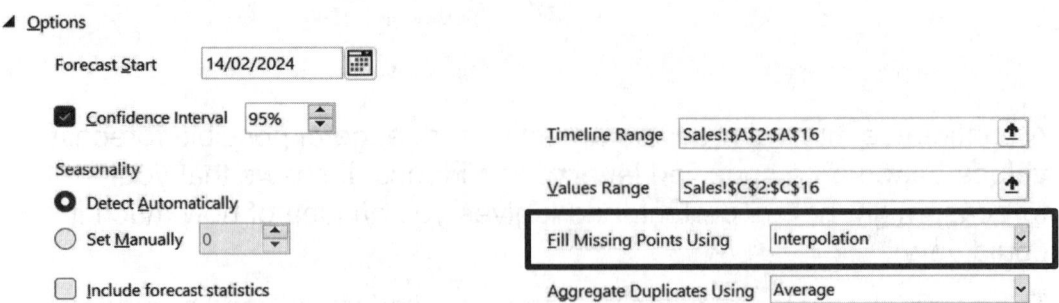

**KAPLAN** PUBLISHING

Or excel will fill the blanks by adding zeros:

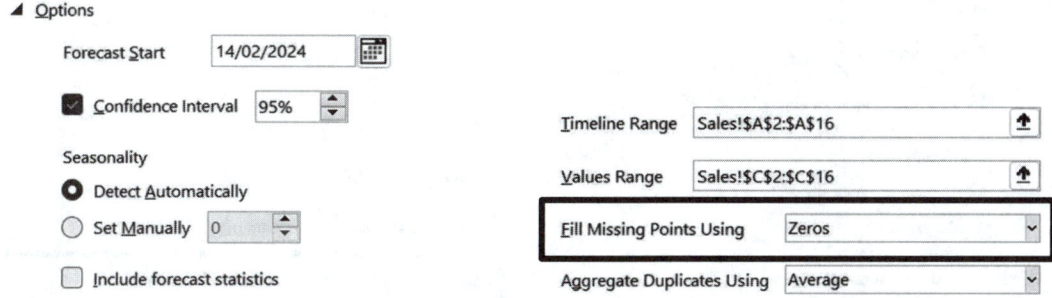

## Seasonality

Seasonality refers to periodic fluctuations or patterns in data that occur at regular intervals. These patterns can be influenced by various factors such as time of year, day of the week, or specific events. In the context of creating forecast sheets in Excel, accounting for seasonality is crucial to produce more accurate forecasts.

Seasonality occurs at regular, predictable intervals. For example, ice cream sales may increase during the summer every year, or electricity usage may peak during the winter months.

The patterns repeat over a consistent period, such as weekly, monthly, quarterly, or annually.

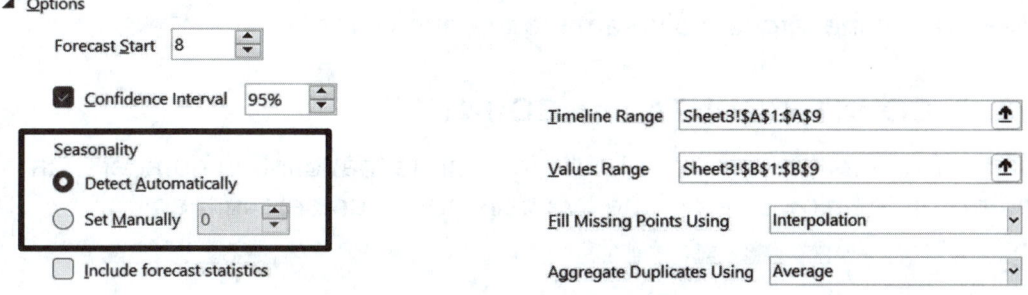

Excel's forecast sheet tool can automatically detect and incorporate seasonality, but you can also set it manually if needed:

**Automatic Detection:** By default, Excel attempts to automatically detect seasonality in your data. This is useful if you are unsure about the specific seasonal pattern.

**Manual Configuration:** If you have a good understanding of the seasonal pattern (e.g. weekly, monthly, quarterly), you can specify the seasonality manually.

**What does 'Aggregate Duplicates Using' do?**

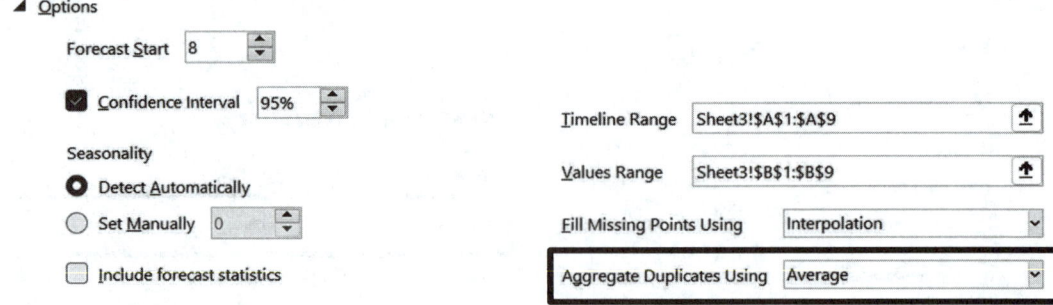

When creating a forecast sheet in Excel, the 'Aggregate duplicates using' option is used to handle duplicate time points within your historical data. Duplicate time points occur when you have multiple entries for the same date or time period. Aggregating these duplicates ensures that your forecast is based on summarised data rather than multiple individual entries for the same period, which could skew the results.

You can choose different methods to aggregate the duplicates, such as:

**Average:** Calculates the mean of the duplicate values.

**Sum:** Adds up all the duplicate values.

**Count:** Counts the number of duplicate entries.

**Min:** Takes the smallest value among the duplicates.

**Max:** Takes the largest value among the duplicates.

### 7.9    COUNT, COUNTA and COUNTIF

**COUNT** counts the number of cells in a range that contain numbers.  In the example below three of the five cells have numbers in them.

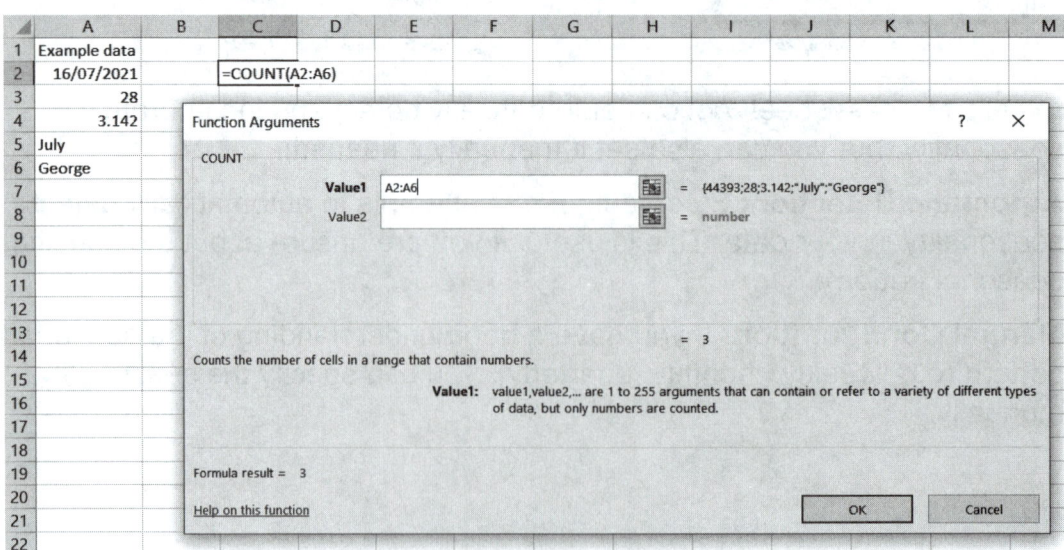

**COUNTA** counts the number of cells in a range that are not empty, which is useful if you have text rather than number in the worksheet. In the example below five of the eight cells selected are not empty i.e. have numbers or text in them.

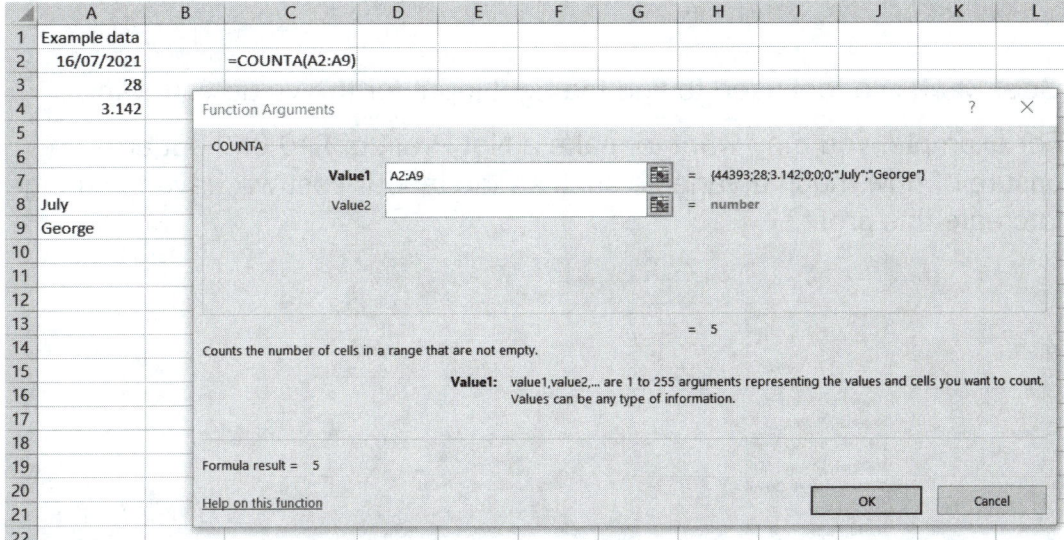

**COUNTIF** will count the number of cells within a range that meet a given condition. In the example below the criteria is that the cell value must equal 28. Result shows one cell meets that criterion.

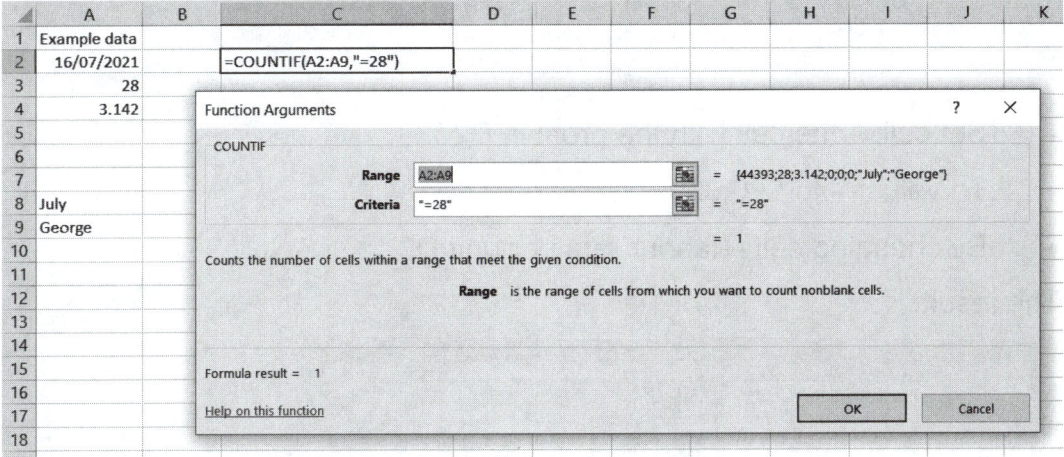

## 7.10 Goal seek

Goal Seek can be found in the **Data** tab, in the **Forecast** section within the What-if Analysis menu.

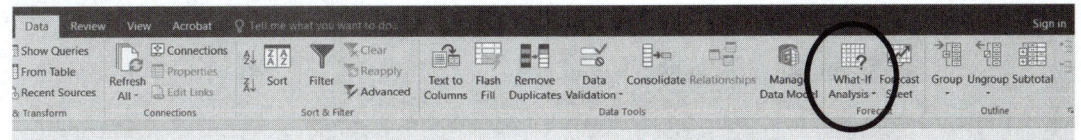

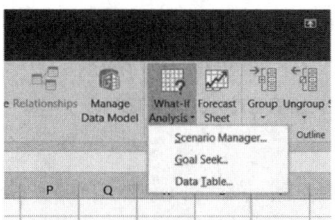

**Goal Seek** is a tool used to find the right input for the value you want.

For example, you may want to make a Net Profit of £10,000 but are unsure of how much a variable such as the labour cost will have to change to create this profit.

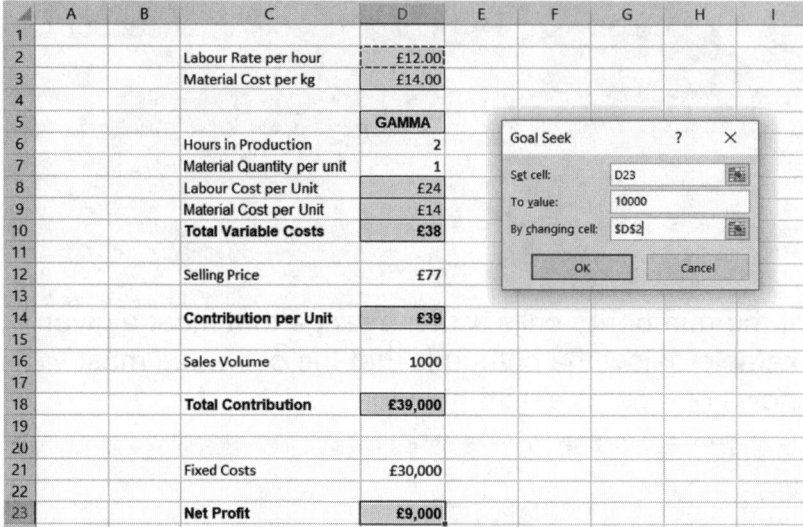

- Set cell: – the cell with the profit in D23

- To value: – to £10,000

- By changing cell – labour rate per unit D2.

The result:

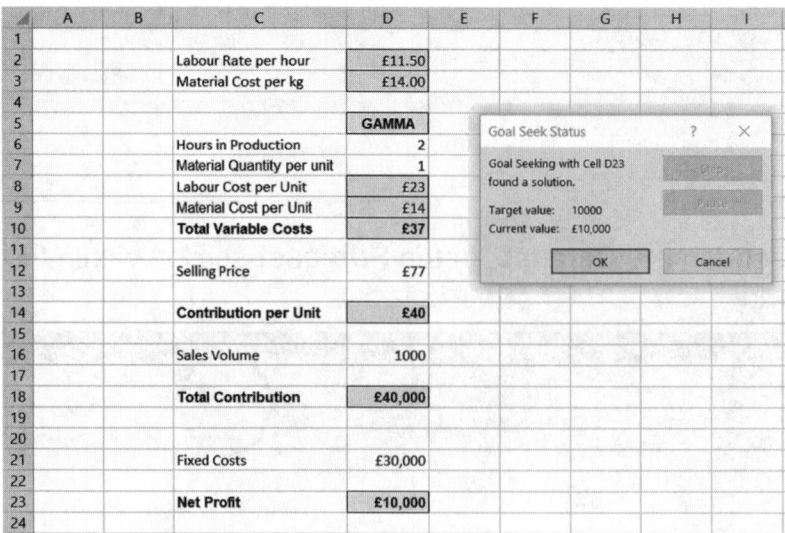

Sometimes a solution cannot be found. If this is the case, you will need to adjust the values you are asking **Goal Seek** to find till you get a correct answer. Don't forget to check that the variable is actually involved in the calculation.

 **Test your understanding 23**

This activity shows the use of Goal Seek in What-If Analysis.

(a)   Open the Goal Seek file.

(b)   We can use Goal Seek to find, for example, what material cost per kg would be required to give us a profit of £10,000 for a product.

(c)   Select the Alpha Net Profit cell, D27, and launch Goal Seek.

(d)   We wish to set cell D27 to a value of 10000 by changing D3.

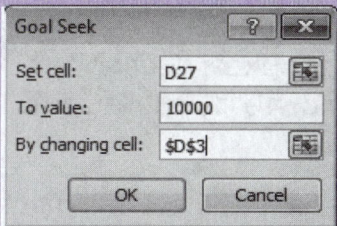

(e)   A success message should be shown:

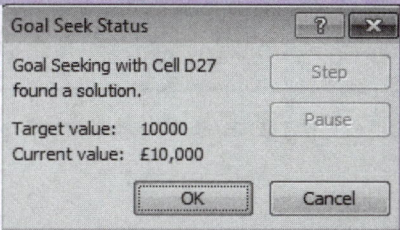

(f)   Note that the material cost has been changed to give the required profit. Try other combinations. Remember, you can 'undo' (Ctrl-Z) a Goal Seek, if you don't like the results.

(g)   Save the file.

# 8 Formula Auditing

## 8.1 Errors

You need to be aware of a number of different types of error. The errors below will be displayed in the cell where the problem is.

| Error | Description |
|---|---|
| #DIV/0! | This occurs if we have tried to divide by zero or a blank cell. |
| #N/A | This occurs if data is not available. It is common in LOOKUP functions. |
| #NAME? | This occurs if we use a name that Excel doesn't recognise. This is common in incorrectly spelled function names. |
| #NUM! | This occurs if you place an invalid argument in a function. |
| #REF! | This occurs if a formula uses an invalid cell reference. |
| #VALUE! | This occurs if we attempt to use an incorrect data type. |

When you enter a formula Excel will place a flag in a cell if it thinks you are making an error.

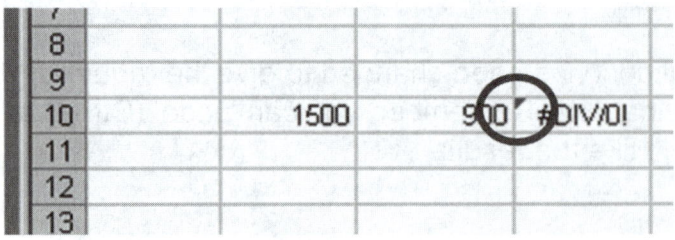

If you click into the error cell you will be given the option to review and deal with the error.

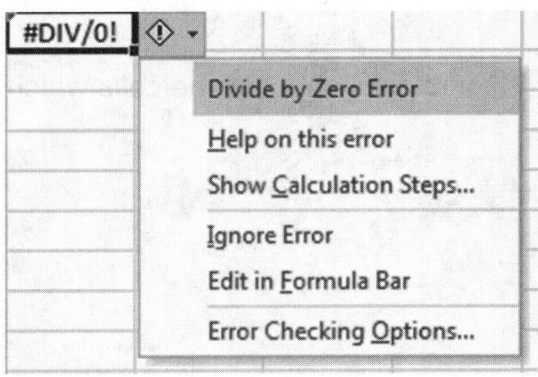

## 8.2 Formula Auditing Toolbar

The **Formula Auditing Toolbar** is a very useful tool for finding and controlling errors in spreadsheets – especially complex ones. It is found in the **Formulas** tab.

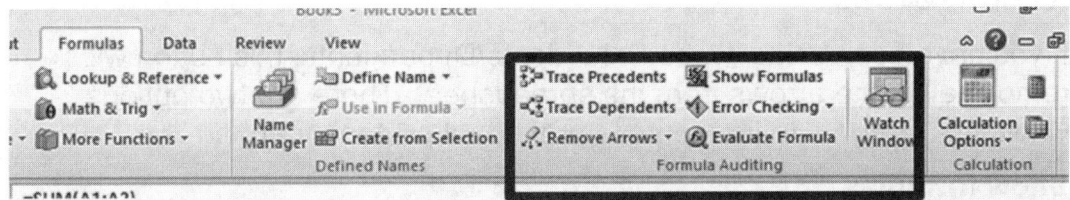

### Trace precedents

This useful tool allows you to see which cells are used in the calculation of your selected cell. This is helpful if you are trying to work out why a formula is giving an unexpected value or error.  Clicking the 'Trace Precedents' button with C7 selected will show which cells are being used.

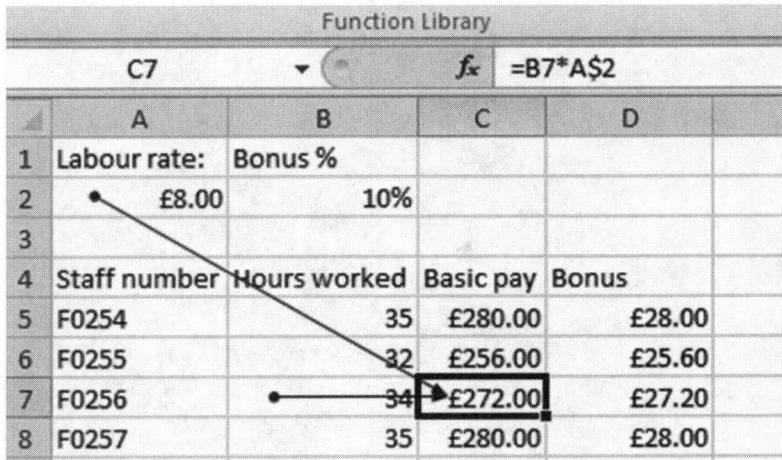

### Trace dependents

Similar to trace precedents, clicking this button will show all the cells which are referring to this cell in a formula.

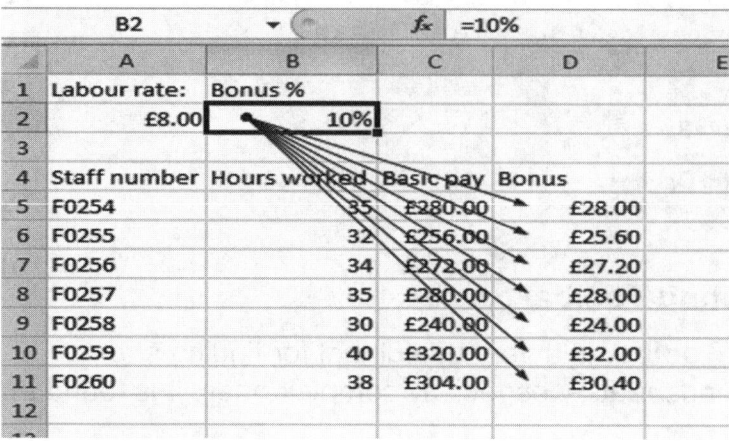

### Remove arrows

If you have been using Trace Precedents/Dependents, this button will remove all of the arrows from the spreadsheet. There are two options within this button – to just remove precedent or dependent arrows.

### Show formulas

This button toggles between showing the results of the formula in a cell and showing the formula itself.

# 9 Graphs and Charts

## 9.1 Chart and graph terminology

Listed below are the more common charting terms:

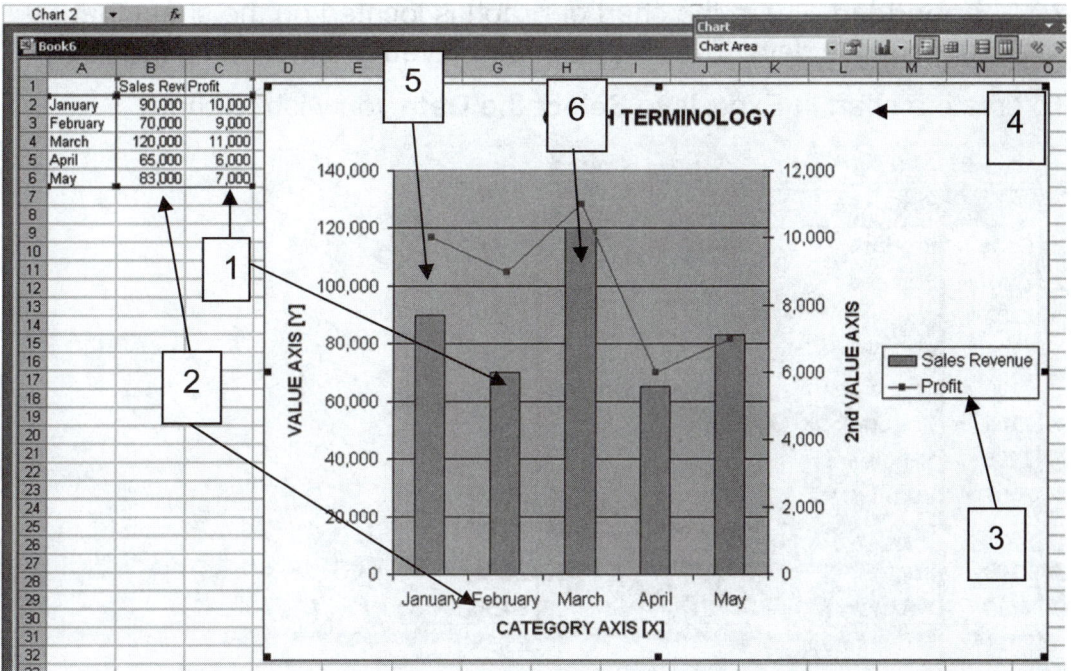

1   **Data Series** – these are the numbers **[values]** from which Excel is creating the graph. These are plotted on the **Value or 'Y' axis**.

2   **Category** – the information that identifies the data series. This is plotted along the **Category or 'X' axis**.

3   **Legend** – this identifies the different data series.

4   **Title** – gives meaning to the graph.

5   **Scale** – both the 'X' and the 'Y' axis (if numerical) can have a scale. These identify the range of values in the data series.

6   **Data Point** – this denotes the value of a particular data series. **Data Labels** can be placed next to data points to give greater meaning. Data Points have Data Markers. **Data Markers** are different shapes and colours for each data series.

## 9.2    Creating charts and graphs

Within Excel there are two basic ways to display charts and graphs. There is no right or wrong way; it is down to user preference. It is also a simple matter to switch between the two types.

1    **Chart Sheet** – here the chart or graph becomes the entire worksheet.

2    **Embedded** – here the chart or graph is located on the sheet that contains the data. The chart can be moved around to suit the user.

To create a chart in Excel is to **Select** the **Data** you wish to chart,

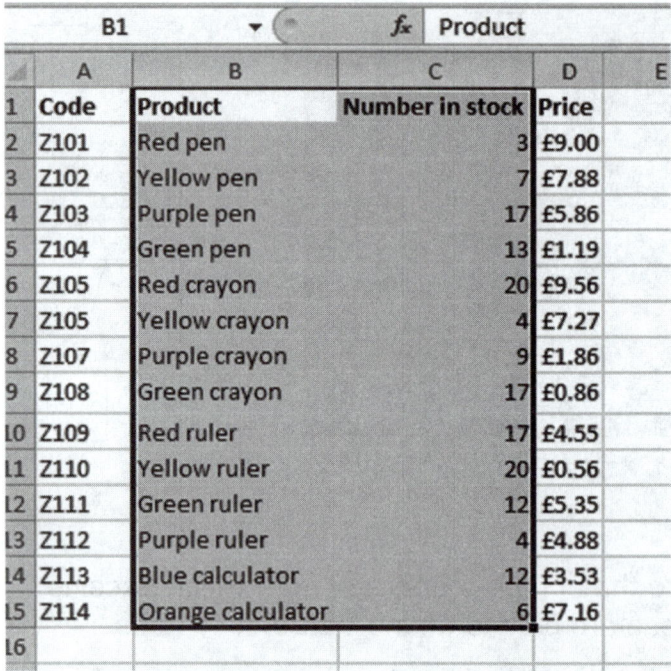

and on the **Insert** tab, select the chart type you want. If you cannot see the chart you need, click the little arrow in the corner of the **Charts** menu, and all available charts will be shown.

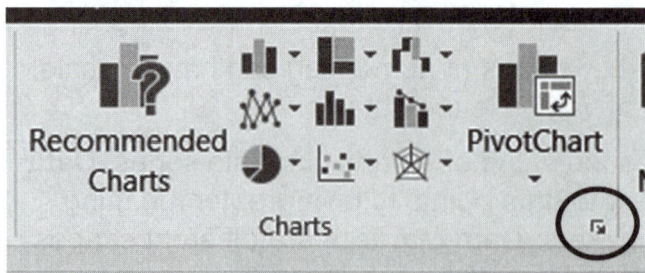

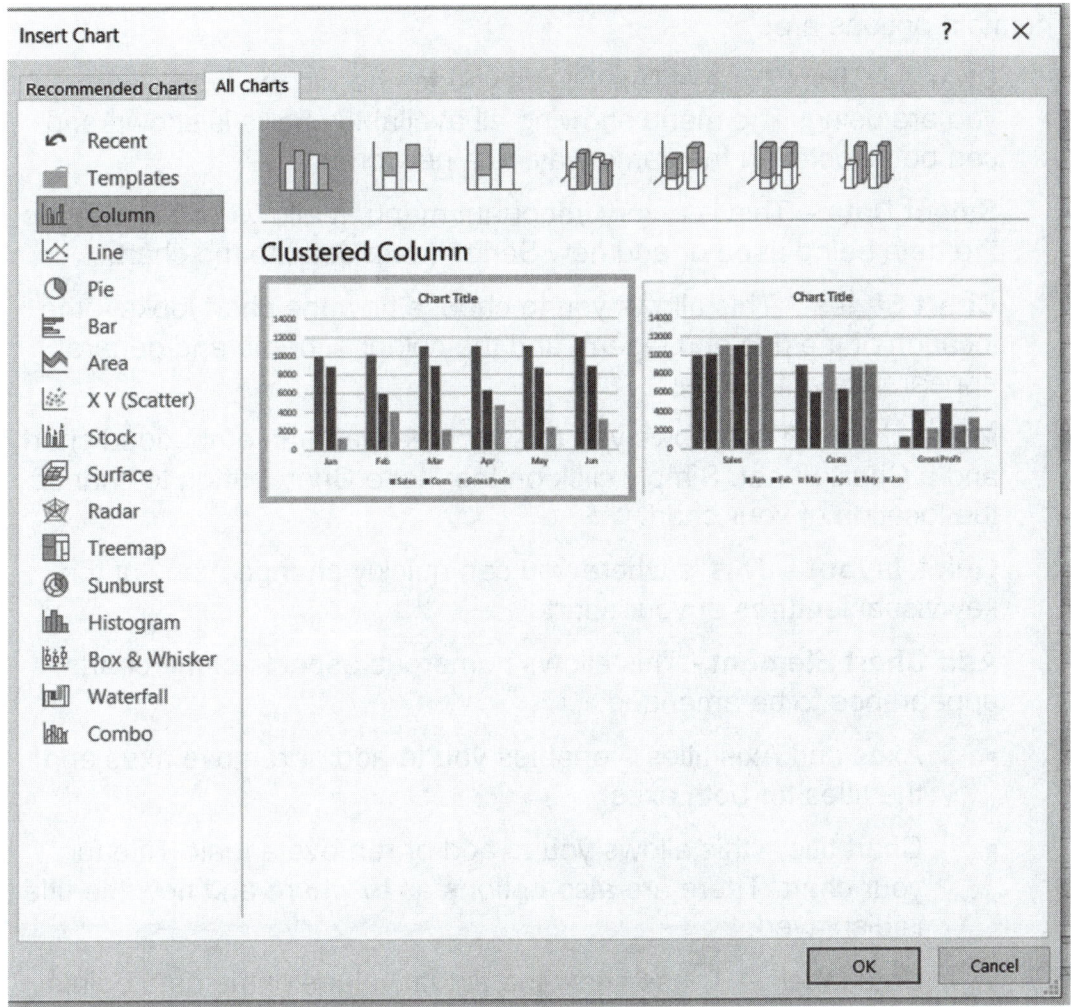

If you are asked for a **Clustered Column chart**, and do not know what it is – go into this menu and hover over the options to find what you need. Click **OK** once you have found what you need, and the chart will be shown.

## 9.3 The chart tools tabs

When you create a chart, or have one selected, the chart tools tabs will become available on the Ribbon. These will allow you to change the features of your chart.

There are two tabs within the Chart Tools menu – the Design tab and Format tab.

**Design Tab**

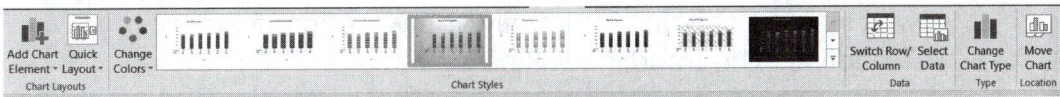

This is to do with the fundamental features of your chart – what sort of chart it is, the data used and where it is shown on your spreadsheet.

The main options are:

- **Change Chart Type** – This allows you to change the type of chart you are using. The menu showing all available charts is shown and can be selected in the same way as a new chart.

- **Select Data** – This is a very important menu. It allows you to change the data being used or add new Series (data sets) to the chart.

- **Chart Styles** – This allows you to choose how the chart looks – the location of the title and legend and the colour scheme and general appearance of the chart.

- **Move chart** – This allows you to switch between an embedded chart and a Chart Sheet. Simply click on the Move Chart button to change the location of your chart.

- **Quick layout** – This is where you can quickly change many of the key visual features of your chart

- **Add Chart Element** - This allows numerous aspects of the charts appearance to be amended:

  - Axes and Axis titles – enables you to add or remove axes and the titles for both axes.

  - Chart title – this allows you to add or remove a main Title for your chart. There are also options as to where and how the title is displayed.

  - Data labels – These show the actual values of the data points on the graph. You can turn them on or off, as well as where they appear on the chart.

  - Data table – A data table shows the actual data points being used to make the chart – like data labels but shown beneath the chart. Use this option to add/remove a data table, with or without a legend (key). The example below shows a data table with a legend key.

  - Legend – the Legend is the 'key' which explains what the different colours or bars on the graph correspond to. Use this button to add or remove a Legend, as well as change the location of the Legend.

  - Trend line shows the general pattern of movement in your data set. Use the Trend Line button to do this. You will be presented with several options – normally you will choose Linear Trendline. The trendline will be added.

**Format Tab**

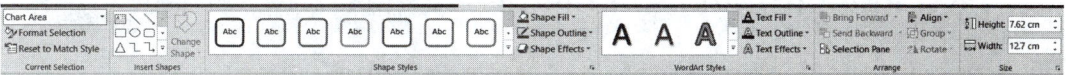

This tab allows you to change the format of any aspect of your graph – colours, thickness of lines and several other formatting options. Select, left-click, on the area of the graph you need to format and then select the option you need.

## 9.4 Adding another data set

More data series can be added if you want to show more information on your graph. This is done within the **Select Data** option in the Design tab. Click **Add** to add more data.

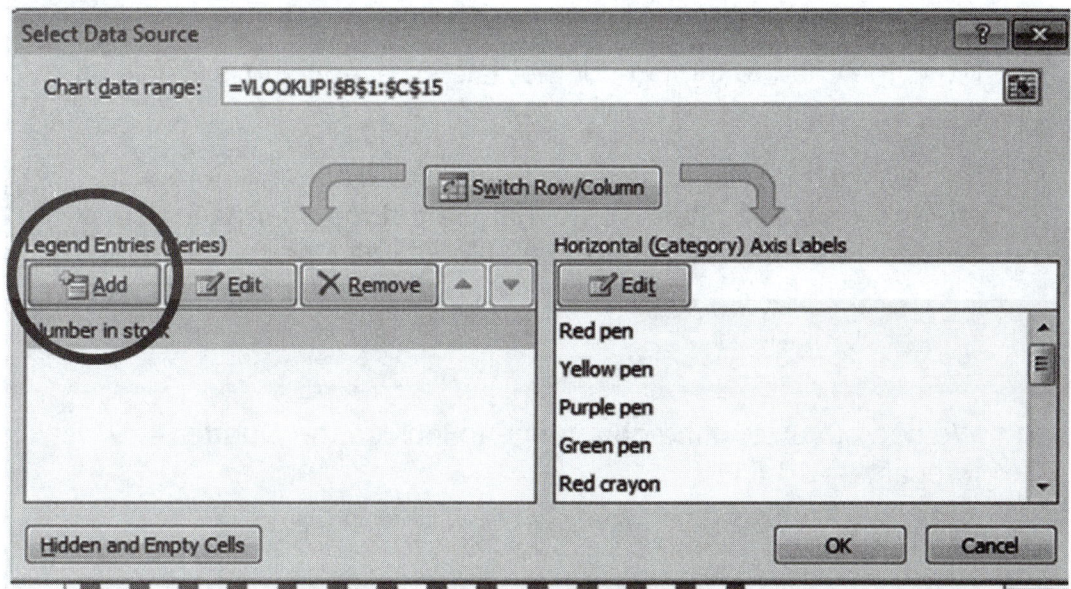

The **Series name** box allows you to select the name for your new data set – this can either be a cell reference or typed value.

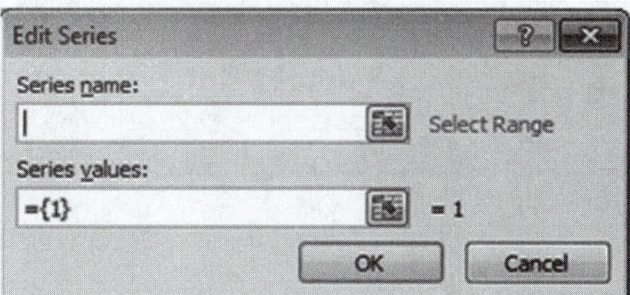

**Test your understanding 24**

This activity allows you to practice creating a simple chart.

(a)    Open the **Graph Sales Data**.

(b)    On monthly data worksheet you need to draw a **Clustered Column** chart showing the first 3 Quarters' results for each area. To do this, select all of the data – cells B13:E16, and insert the chart.

(c)    Add a title to the chart – **Quarterly Sales 20X0**.

Add a title to the y-axis – **£000**.

Delete the Legend.

Add a data table to the graph – with a legend.

(d)    Move the chart to the right of the data so everything is visible.

(e)    Save the file

(f)    The aim of this next exercise is to add the Quarter 4 Forecast information to the chart. To do this, **Select** the chart, and use **Select Data** from the **Design** tab. Notice the Chart data range:

(g)    We need to extend the data range to include the Quarter 4 forecast – F13:F16.

(h)    Change the **Forecast Increase** figure in cell A2 to 100%. The Quarter 4 forecast is based on this – the figures, and the chart, will update. Change it back to 10%.

(i)    **Move** the chart to a chart sheet.

(j)    Save the workbook.

**Test your understanding 25**

This activity allows you to change the chart type being used, add a trendline, and deal with formatting of chart items.

(a) Open the **Graph Sales Data 2** workbook and select **Comparison** worksheet.

(b) This is a stacked column chart, showing sales, costs and gross profit. It is not a meaningful representation of the data. For example, the first bar, for January, shows a total of £20,000. This is the sum of sales, costs and profit. The individual coloured sections do indicate the size of each item, but it is hard to interpret.

(c) The first thing to do is change the gross profit series to show as a line. **Select** the gross profit data series (click on any part of the chart coloured in cream).

(d) In the **Design** tab, select **Change Chart Type**, and select **Line**.

(e) **Delete** the costs data series and change the title to **Sales and Profit comparison**.

(f) Add a secondary axis for the gross profit data series by using the **Change Chart type** menu.

(g) Add a **linear trendline** to the gross profit data series.

(h) **Select** the trendline. Change the format so that it is a thick line (3pt), coloured bright green.

(i) Save the file.

# 10 Data validation

## 10.1 Data validation

Data validation allows a user to restrict what values can be entered into a cell. This can prevent incorrect data entry or allow another user to select from a Dropdown list, making data entry easier.

To add data validation, select the cell(s) required, then in the **Data** tab, select **Data Validation**.

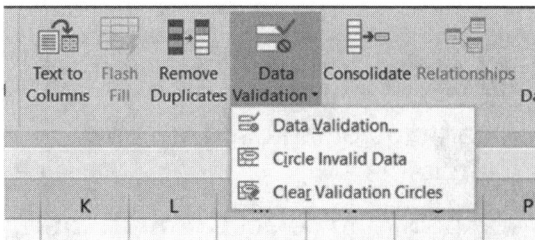

The Data Validation menu has three tabs – Settings, Input Message and Error Alert.

### Settings

This is where you define exactly how you would like to restrict your cell entry. The default is as shown above – **Allow: any value**. Selecting this dropdown box shows the options available.

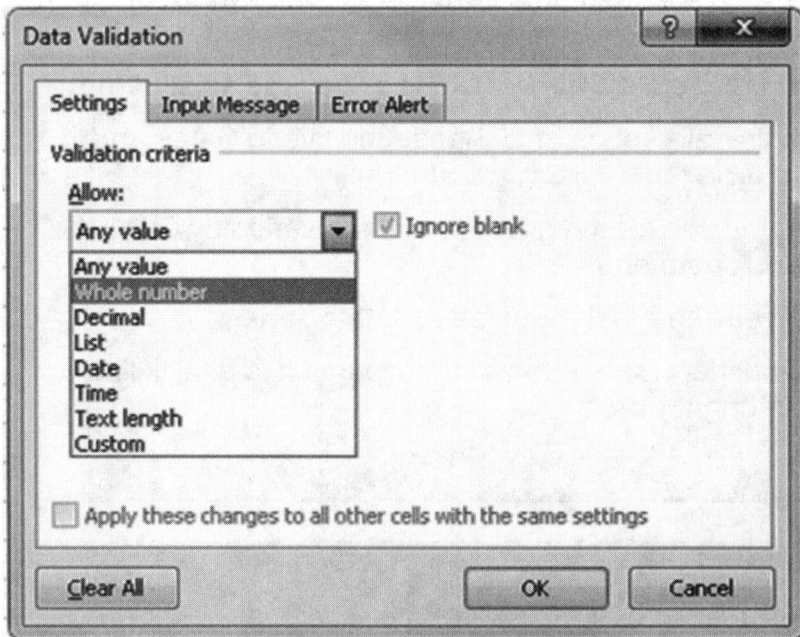

When an option is selected, more options become available. For example, whole number only allows whole numbers, but you can further restrict the range. As on many other options, you can restrict to certain ranges, or above or below other numbers (which can be based on cell values).

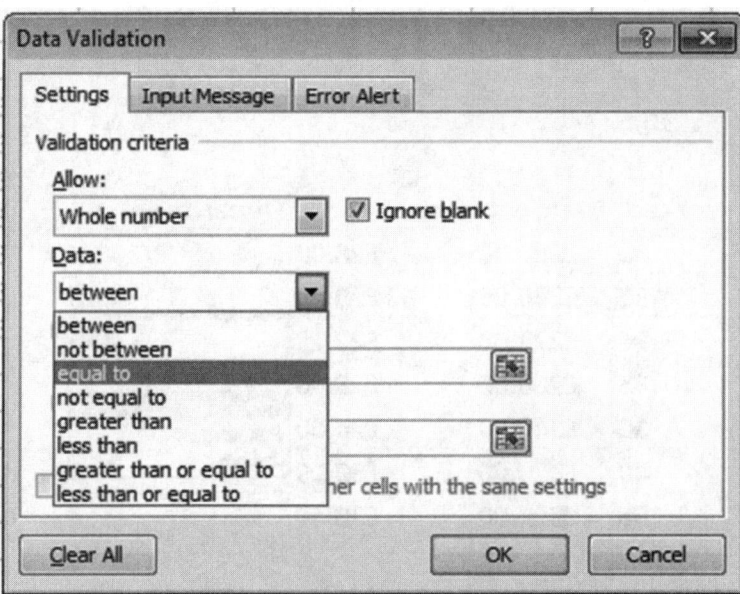

You can also restrict to a list of options. This is very useful when a cell should only contain certain entries.

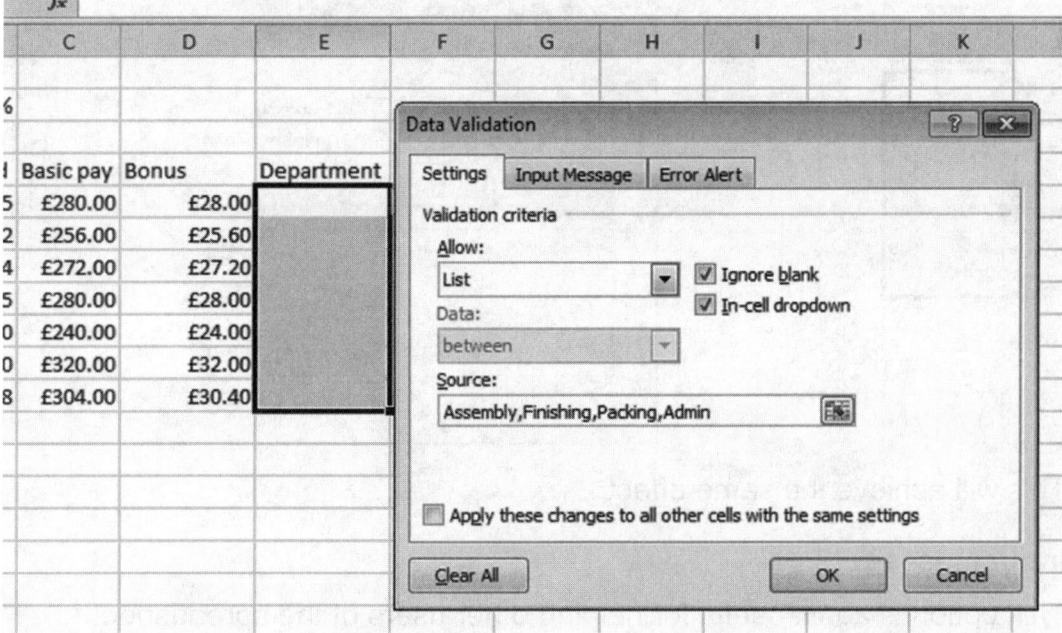

In the Data Validation menu, select Allow **List**, and type the possible options in the box, separated by a comma. Notice the **In-cell dropdown** option is checked. Click **OK**.

Now, when the cell is clicked on, the four options are shown. You can still type in the cell, as well as using the dropdown. If you type something that is not in the list an error message will show.

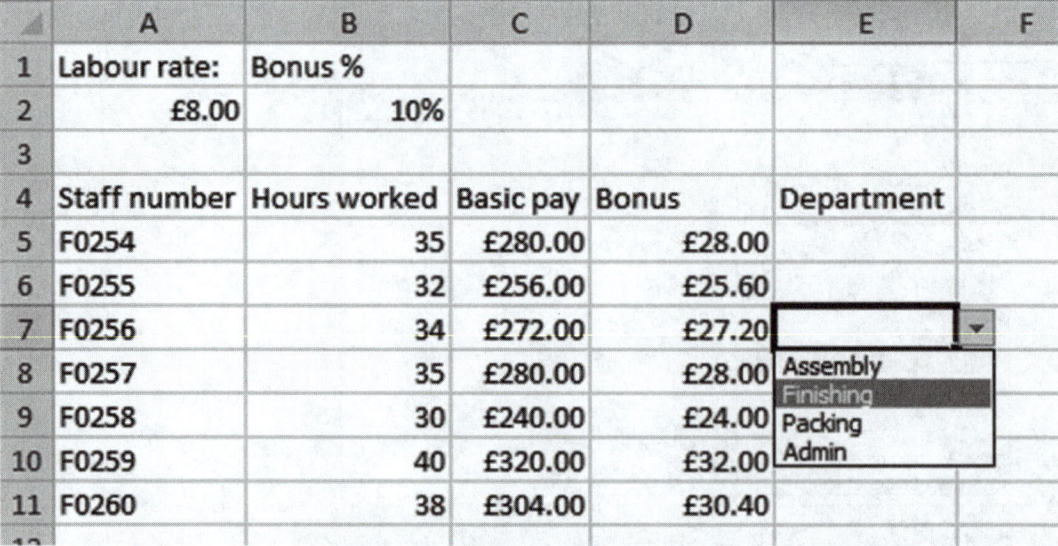

Rather than typing the values in, you can also refer to a range of cells.

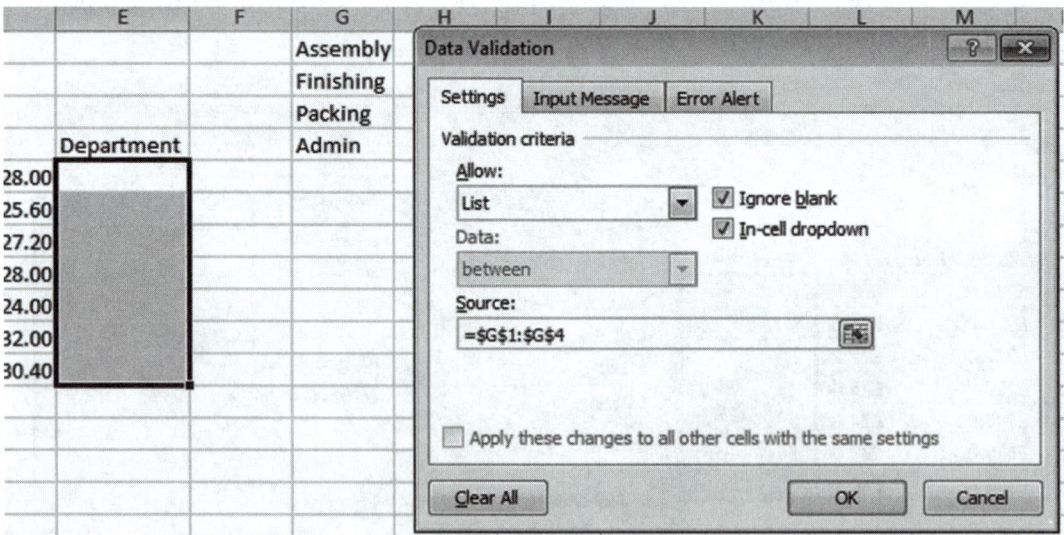

This will achieve the same effect.

**Input message**

This option is again useful for helping other users of the spreadsheet to enter the correct data. If activated, when the cell is selected a message will be displayed giving help on what can be entered. The message shown should provide useful information for the spreadsheet user.

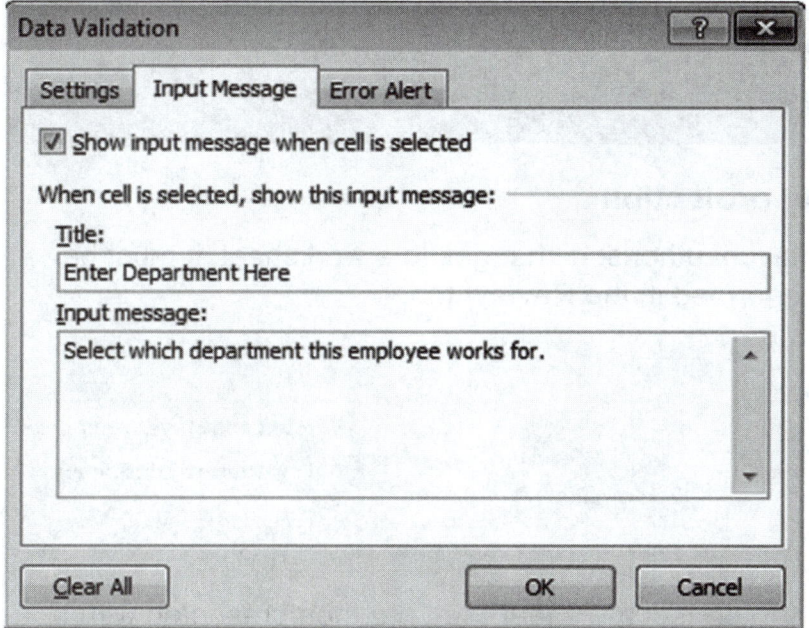

## Error alert

This tab allows you to select the error message that is shown if incorrect data is entered. By default, if the data validation restrictions are not met, the following error is shown:

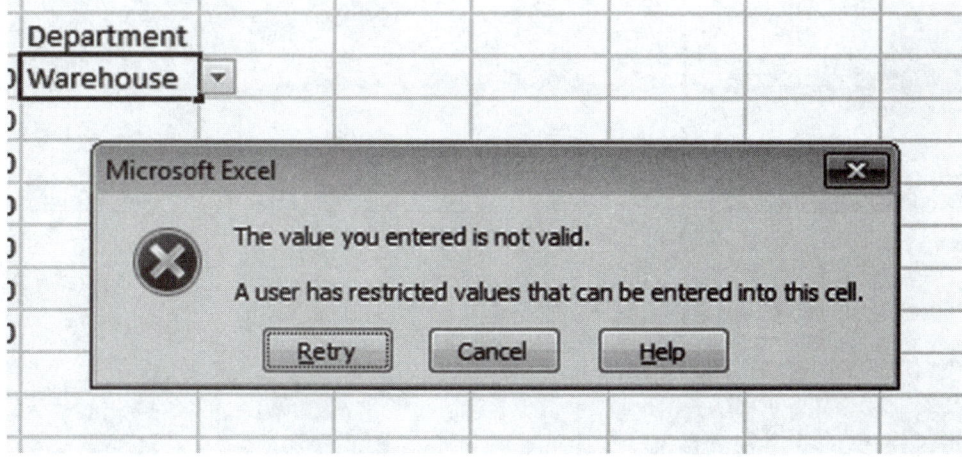

# 11 Protecting your data

## 11.1 Worksheet protection

To prevent accidental/unauthorised changes to a worksheet, it must be protected. This is performed in the **Review** tab.

Click **Protect Sheet** to protect the sheet. You are then presented with a series of options giving you the power to restrict various activities. Check/uncheck the boxes as required, depending on what access you wish to give/remove. You can also set a password if required. If you enter a password, you will be required to confirm it. This password will then be required to unprotect the sheet.

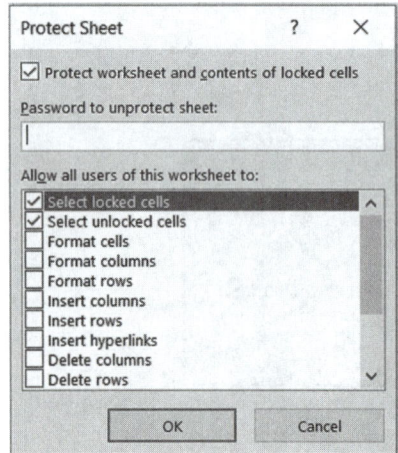

Note the warning. If you forget the password to unprotect a worksheet, then it cannot be recovered.

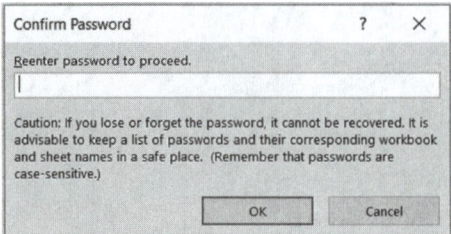

When you protect a spreadsheet, only LOCKED cells will be affected. All cells in a workbook are locked by default.

If a sheet is protected, then use the **Unprotect Sheet** option to remove protection.

## 11.2 Cell protection

If you wish to protect one cell or a range of cells in a worksheet you can use **Allow Users to Edit Ranges** on the Review tab.

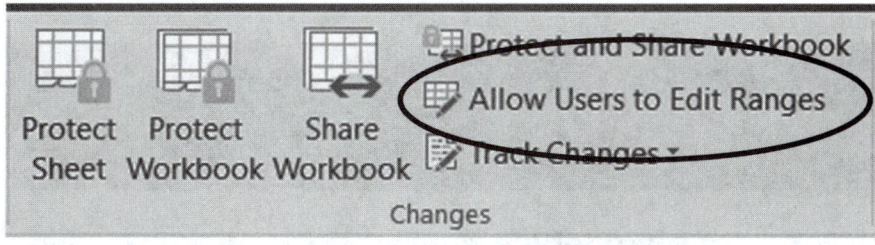

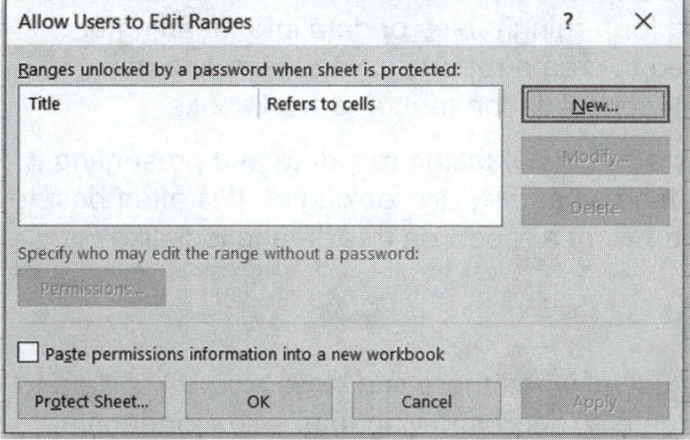

Click on 'New', give the range of cells a title (not essential), select the cells the protection refers to, add a password (if required) and click OK.

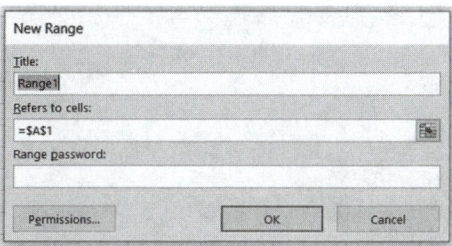

Click Apply and then protect the worksheetsheet. With the range selected below it would mean that the whole worksheet except cell A1 will be protected.

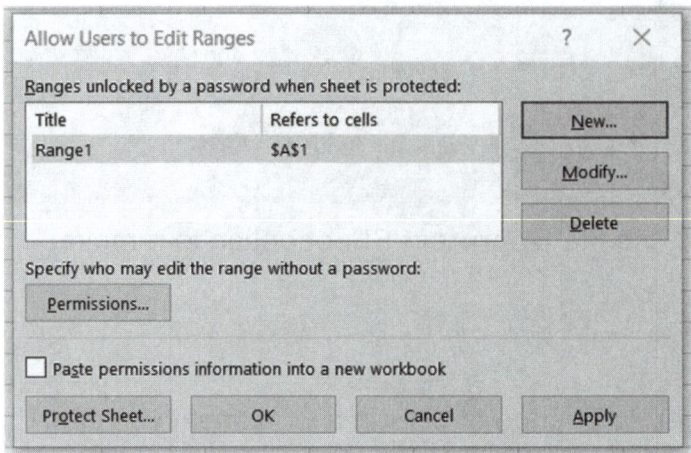

# 12 Pivot tables

## 12.1 Construction of pivot tables

A **Pivot Table** is a tool used for turning tables of data into meaningful reports. The tool can be used to create reports from external sources, multiple-workbooks (another consolidation tool) and workbooks.

In essence a **Pivot Table** is a means of taking raw data and presenting it so that the user can understand what they are looking at. It is often best to think in terms of 'what would I want a report on this data to look like?'

## 12.2 Creating a report

Pivot tables are particularly useful when there is a large amount of data to analyse. If we wanted to create a report showing total sales for each month, split by region. We can use the Pivot Table to show this very easily.

To create a pivot table, select the data (**including headers**) you wish to use, then on the **Insert** tab, select **Pivot Table**.

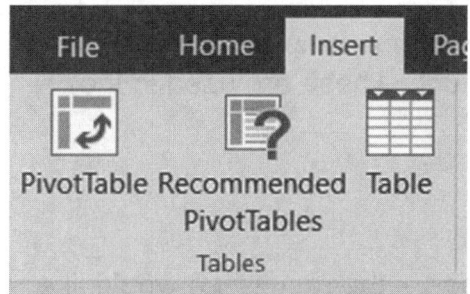

This opens the **PivotTable Wizard**.

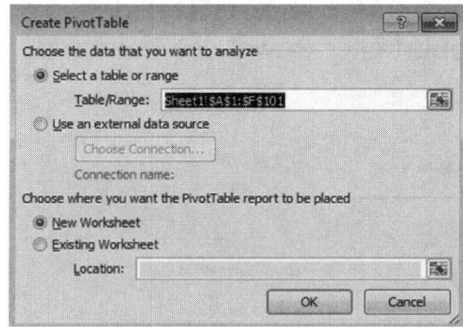

You can choose whether to create the table in a new worksheet or place it somewhere on your existing sheet. Click OK.

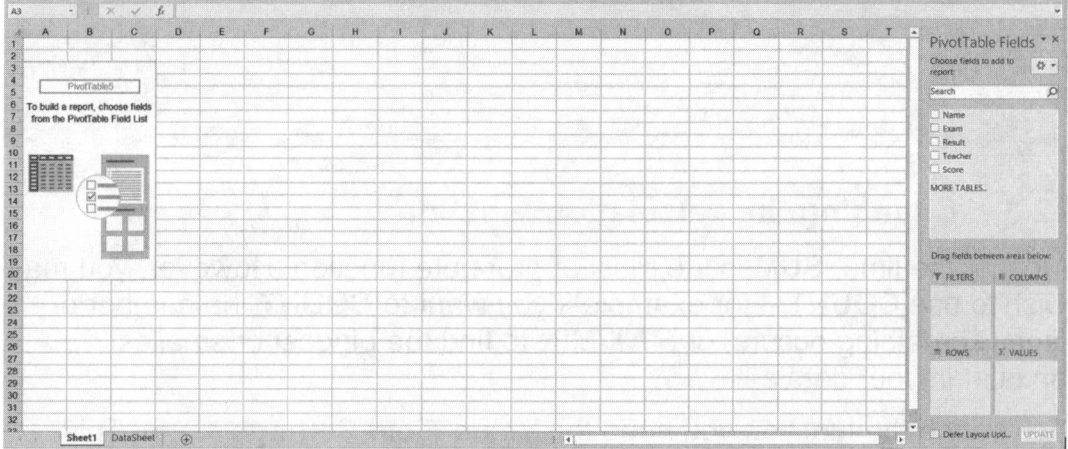

This view allows you to build your report. The following terms are used:

- **Pivot Table Fields** – are the data headings used to make the report.

- **Filter** – this is the 'pages' of the report. For example, we might have a page for every month, or every product. These are used in the same way as AutoFilters.

- **Rows** – the rows of our report.

- **Columns** – the columns in our report.

- $\sum$ **Values** – this is the 'data' in our report – the results we would like to show.

The box on the left of the sheet is where the report is shown. The idea is to 'drag' the fields into the required field – report filter, rows, columns and values.

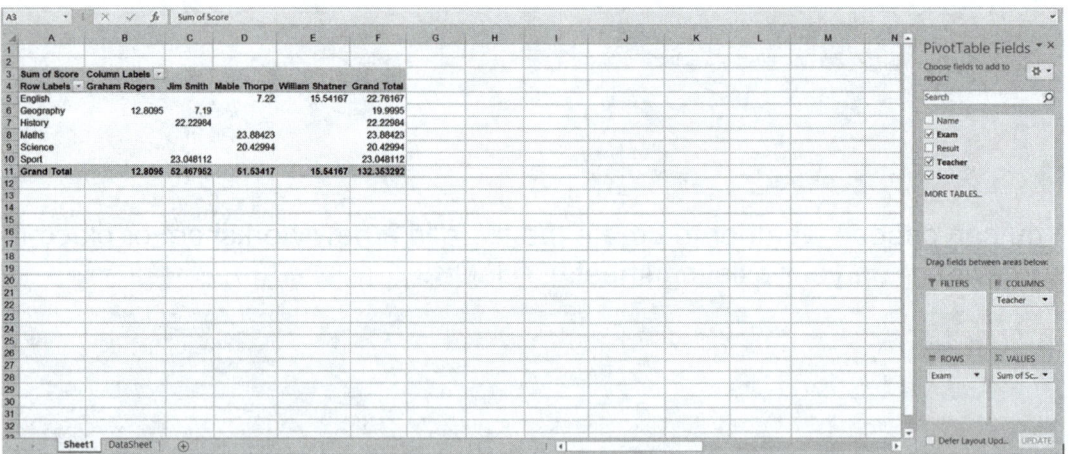

## 12.3    Changing the calculation function

Most of the time, **SUM** is the most appropriate function. However, you may wish to use **COUNT** – for example if you want to **COUNT** the number of times something occurs, or **MAX/MIN** to find the biggest or smallest amount in your data set.

To change the function you need the **Value Field Settings** menu. This can be found by either **Right-Clicking** in the pivot table, or by going to the **PivotTable Tools/Options** tab.

Select the function you want here.

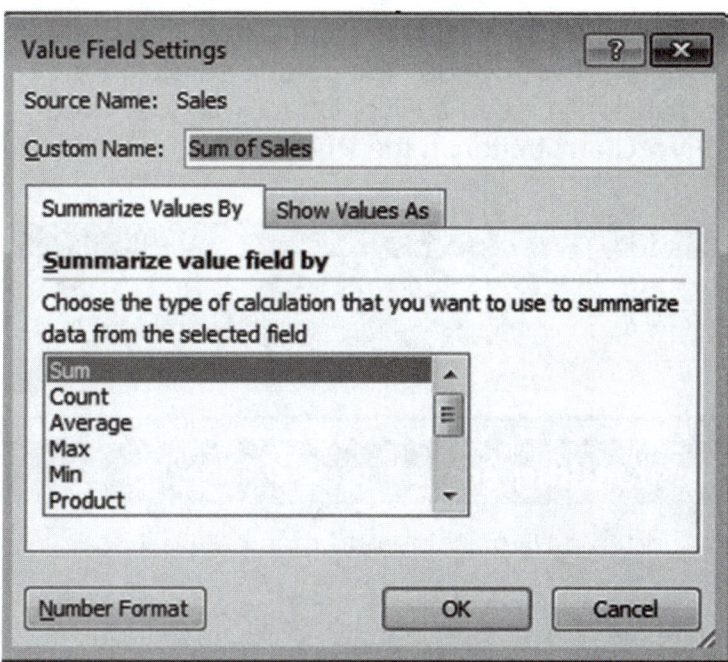

## 12.4 Refreshing data

If there are any updates to the original data, the **Pivot Table** will need to be updated to reflect this change. Note that this **does not** happen automatically. It is a simple process – either **right-click** on the table and choose refresh.

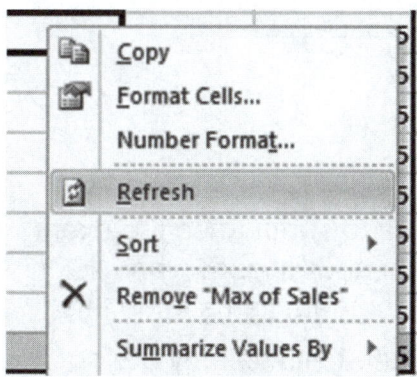

Or use the **Refresh** button in the **PivotTable Tools/Analyze** tab.

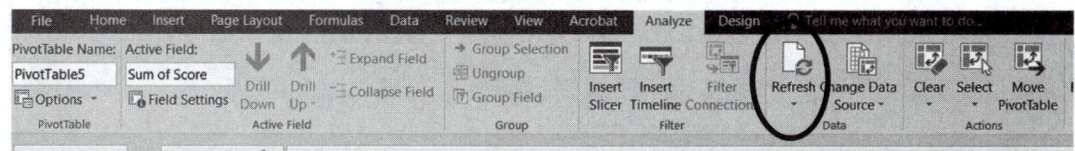

## 12.5    Pivot charts

A Pivot Chart is just a chart based on a pivot table. They work in exactly the same way as a normal chart. Pivot Charts change according to the filters applied to your PivotTable.  To insert a Pivot Chart, with the Pivot Table selected, click the **PivotChart** button in the **PivotTable Tools/Analyze** tab.

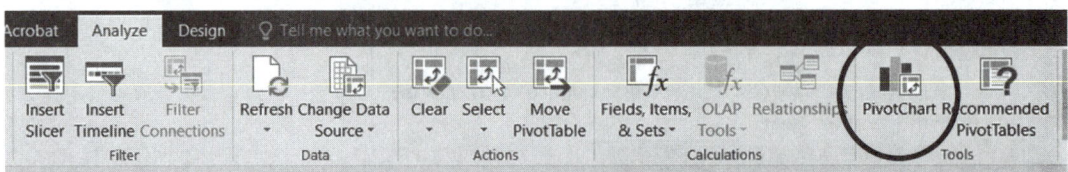

 **Test your understanding 26**

This activity allows you to create a Pivot Table and manipulate it as necessary.

(a)    Open the ResultsPivotData.  This only contains one sheet, which contains a data set of exam results.

(b)    Create a Pivot Table on a new worksheet that enables us to know (count) how many students ($\sum$values) were taught by each teacher (column) and sat each exam (row).  We will want to filter our report to show the results (pass or fail)

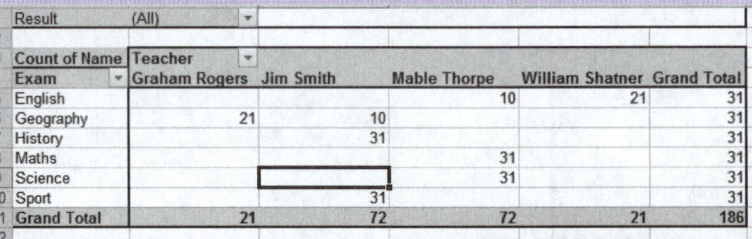

| Result | (All) | | | | |
|---|---|---|---|---|---|
| Count of Name | Teacher | | | | |
| Exam | Graham Rogers | Jim Smith | Mable Thorpe | William Shatner | Grand Total |
| English | | | 10 | 21 | 31 |
| Geography | 21 | 10 | | | 31 |
| History | | 31 | | | 31 |
| Maths | | | 31 | | 31 |
| Science | | | 31 | | 31 |
| Sport | | 31 | | | 31 |
| Grand Total | 21 | 72 | 72 | 21 | 186 |

(c)    We now want to use the same Pivot Table to summarise the exam subjects as Core subjects (English, Maths and Science), and Sundry (everything else). We can group the data items to do this.

You will need to hold down Ctrl to select the cells as they are not adjacent.

Group these items using Group Selection on the Group section of the Analyze tab. Rename the groups – Core and Sundry by typing in the cell.

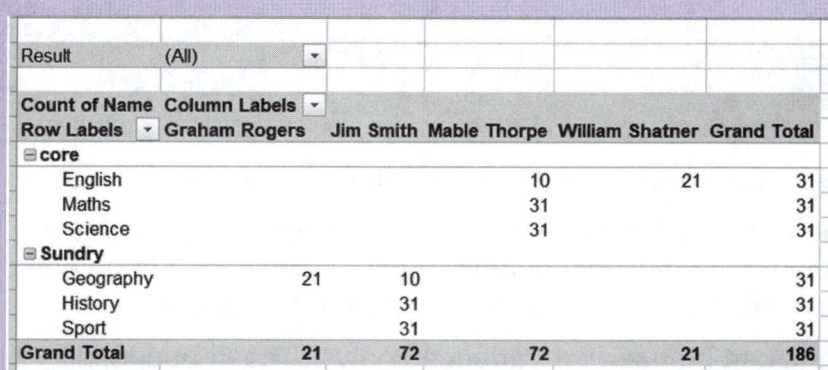

| Result | (All) | | | | | |
|---|---|---|---|---|---|---|
| **Count of Name** | **Column Labels** | | | | | |
| **Row Labels** | **Graham Rogers** | **Jim Smith** | **Mable Thorpe** | **William Shatner** | **Grand Total** | |
| **core** | | | | | | |
| English | | | 10 | 21 | 31 | |
| Maths | | | 31 | | 31 | |
| Science | | | 31 | | 31 | |
| **Sundry** | | | | | | |
| Geography | 21 | 10 | | | 31 | |
| History | | 31 | | | 31 | |
| Sport | | 31 | | | 31 | |
| **Grand Total** | **21** | **72** | **72** | **21** | **186** | |

(d)   Move the Exam 2 field into the Report Filter area. Move Result into the Row Labels (it should be below Exam in the row box). You can now select to just see core subjects, sundry subjects, or both. Select Core.

(e)   Save the file.

 **Test your understanding 27**

This activity takes you through the steps of creating a PivotChart.

(a)   Open the ResultsPivotData2 workbook.

(b)   Create a PivotTable from the data. Use the following settings:

Report Filter = Name

Row Field = Result

Column Field = Exam

Value Field = Score.  We want to show the highest percentage (MAX) formatted to zero decimal places.

(c)   Remove the Grand Totals (Design tab, Layout, Grand Totals).

(d)   Now, create a PivotChart (Analyze tab, tools, PivotChart). Make a clustered bar chart. The graph will display the data shown in the table.

(e)   Add a title to the chart – Exam Results 2012.

(f)   Change the Name to select Gareth Jones and see how the chart changes to show their results.

(g)   Save the workbook.

# 13 Summary

Spreadsheets are a very useful tool for a management accountant.

It is possible to set up templates in a spreadsheet workbook that will, by using formulae and functions, enable regular calculations to be completed quickly and easily by only changing a couple of cell values.

Spreadsheets can be used for variance analysis, cash budgeting, forecasting, performance reports and to graphically display data.

Spreadsheets can be used to manipulate a large volume of data and information and allow processing of data to happen more quickly.

## Test your understanding answers

Suggested answers are available on MyKaplan.

**KAPLAN** PUBLISHING

# MOCK ASSESSMENT

# 1 Mock Assessment Questions

## Task 1 (24 marks)

This task is about costing techniques

**(a)** **Which TWO of the following statements relating to management information are TRUE?** **(2 marks)**

| | Tick |
|---|---|
| No strict rules govern the way in which the information is presented | ✓ |
| There is usually a legal requirement for the information to be produced | |
| It is produced for parties external to the organisation | |
| It may be presented in monetary or non-monetary terms | ✓ |

*financial accounting* ✓

**(b)** **Which of the following statements is NOT correct?** **(2 marks)**

(A) cost accounting can be used for inventory valuation to meet the requirements of internal reporting only.

B management accounting provides appropriate information for decision making, planning, control and performance evaluation.

C routine information can be used for both short-term and long-run decisions.

D financial accounting information can be used for internal reporting purposes.

The following information is available for product ZYQ:

Annual demand – 1,250,000 kilograms

Annual holding cost per kilogram – £5

Fixed ordering cost – £2

**(c)** **Calculate the Economic Order Quantity (EOQ) for ZYQ.**

**(3 marks)**

$$\sqrt{\frac{2 \times 2 \times 1,250,000}{5}} = 1,000$$

(d) Which of the following costs would never be included in the valuation of inventory? **(1 mark)**

A    marginal costs

B    prime costs

C    product costs

D    period costs

Below are extracts from Bounce Ltd's payroll for last week.

| Date | Labour cost |
|---|---|
| 6 July | Stores department<br>Employees pay £3,000 + 8% bonus |
| 13 July | Manufacturing<br>Production employees pay 400 hours at £8.00 per hour |

The cost codes for the different accounts are:

| | |
|---|---|
| Non-operating overheads | 7000 |
| Operating overheads | 8000 |
| Wages control account | 2000 |
| Manufacturing direct costs | 1020 |
| Assembly direct costs | 1025 |

(e) Complete the cost journal entries to record the four payroll payments made in July. **(4 marks)**

| Date | Code | Dr £ | Cr £ |
|---|---|---|---|
| 6 July | 8000 | 3,240 | |
| 6 July | 2000 | | 3,240 |
| 11 July | | | |
| 11 July | | | |
| 13 July | 1020 | 3,200 | |
| 13 July | 2000 | | 3,200 |
| 15 July | | | |
| 15 July | | | |

**KAPLAN** PUBLISHING

Information is available relating to the production of the 100,000 tins of cat food for the month of September:

| | |
|---|---|
| Total number of labour hours worked | 21,600 |
| Overtime hours worked | 4,900 |
| Standard hours for production in September | 22,400 |
| Basic rate per hour | £8 |
| Overtime payment per hour | £14.50 |

*800*

The company operates a group incentive scheme, whereby a bonus of 25% of the basic hourly rate is paid for hours saved.

**(f)   Calculate the total cost of direct labour for September, assuming that overtime and the bonus are due to a specific customer request.**                                                    **(5 marks)**

| | |
|---|---|
| Total basic pay (£) | 172,800 |
| Total overtime premium (£) | 31,850 |
| Hours saved (hours) | 800 |
| Bonus (£) | 1,600 |
| Total direct labour cost (£) | 206,250 |

**(g)   Calculate the total labour cost per tin of cat food in the month of September (to the nearest penny).**                    **(2 marks)**

The total labour cost of each tin in the month of September is:

£ 2.06

In October the bonus was based on equivalent units. Employees will receive 20% of the basic hourly rate for every equivalent unit in excess of target. Rates of pay are not due to change in October. The target production is 90,000 units.

At the end of October 60,000 units were completed and there were 50,000 units of closing work in progress that was 100% complete for material and 70% complete for labour.

**(h)   Calculate the number of equivalent units with regards to labour and the bonus payable.**            *1.6*                **(4 marks)**

| | |
|---|---|
| Equivalent units | 95,000 |
| Excess units | 5,000 |
| Bonus (£) | 8,000 |

**(i)** **Calculate the bonus per tin of cat food in the month of October to the nearest penny.** **(1 mark)**

The bonus per equivalent unit in the month of October is:

£  0.08

## Task 2 (24 marks)

This task is about attributing costs.

Icon Ltd has two production departments (Assembly and Finishing) and three service departments (Maintenance, Stores and Administration)

The following information is also available:

| Department | Carrying amount of machinery | Machinery power usage (KwH) | Floor space (square metres) | Number of employees |
|---|---|---|---|---|
| Assembly | 4,200,000 | 298,800 | | 15 |
| Finishing | 1,800,000 | 199,200 | | 10 |
| Maintenance | | | 18,000 | 4 |
| Stores | | | 10,800 | 3 |
| Administration | | | 7,200 | 8 |
| Total | 6,000,000 | 498,000 | 36,000 | 40 |

Overheads have been allocated or apportioned on the most appropriate basis across all five departments. The total overheads of the service departments are then reapportioned to the two production departments on the following bases:

- Maintenance overheads are reapportioned on the basis of the carry amount of the machinery.

- The stores cost centre makes 70% of its issues to the Assembly, and 30% to the Finishing.

- Administration supports the other departments on the basis of the number of employees.

(a) Complete the reapportionment table on the basis of the information given. Enter your answers to the nearest whole pound (£). Use minus signs or brackets to indicate any negative figures.
**(12 marks)**

| | Total £ | Assembly £ | Finishing £ | Maint. £ | Stores £ | Admin. £ |
|---|---|---|---|---|---|---|
| Totals | 2,020,750 | 1,006,995 | 508,855 | 164,950 | 74,330 | 265,620 |
| Administration | | 124509 | 83,006 | 33203 | 24902 | -265660 |
| Maintenance | | 138707 | 59446 | -198153 | | |
| Stores | | 69462 | 29770 | | -99232 | |
| Total | 2,020,750 | 1,339673 | 681,007 | | | |

Icon Ltd is considering changing from traditional absorption costing to activity based costing. They have calculated the costs to be assigned to two cost pools:

| | Machine set ups | Special parts handling |
|---|---|---|
| Budgeted overheads (£) | 1,350,000 | 700,000 |

They make two products that have the following details:

| | Idol | Image |
|---|---|---|
| Number of machine set ups per batch | 50 | 200 |
| Number of special parts per batch | 250 | 150 |
| Budgeted number of batches | 1,000 | 2,000 |

(b) What would be the cost driver rate per machine set up to two decimal places? (2 marks)

£ 3.00

1,000 × 50 = 50000
2,800 × 200 = 400,000
= 450,000
1,350,000 / 450,000 = £3.00

(c) What would be the cost driver rate per special part to two decimal places? (2 marks)

£ 1.27

1,000 × 250 = 250,000
2,000 × 150 = 300,000
550,000

**Additional data**

At the end of the quarter actual overheads incurred were found to be:

|  | Machine set ups | Special parts handling |
|---|---|---|
| Actual overheads (£) | 1,240,000 | 650,100 |

(d) **Calculate the overhead that was absorbed in each cost pool and state the under or over absorption that has occurred (answers to the nearest £)** (6 marks)

|  | Actual cost driver value | Absorbed amount £ | Under/over | Value £ |
|---|---|---|---|---|
| Machine set ups | 400,000 | 1,200,000 under | | 40,000 |
| Special parts handling | 600,000 | 762,000 over | | 111900 |

(e) **The management accountant's report shows that fixed production overheads were over-absorbed in the last accounting period. The combination that is certain to lead to this situation is:** (2 marks)

A  production volume is lower than budget and actual expenditure is higher than budget

B  production volume is higher than budget and actual expenditure is lower than budget

C  production volume is higher than budget and actual expenditure is higher than budget

D  production volume and actual cost are as budgeted

## Task 3 (24 marks)

This task is about short-term decision making.

Product ZYQ has a selling price of £52 per unit with a total variable cost of £38 per unit. Icon Ltd estimates that the fixed costs per quarter associated with this product are £84,000.

(a) Calculate the contribution per unit of Product ZYQ (two decimal places) **(2 marks)**

| £ 14 |
|---|

(b) Calculate the budgeted breakeven, in units, for product ZYQ. **(2 marks)**

| 6,000 | units |
|---|---|

(c) Calculate the budgeted breakeven, in £, for product ZYQ. **(2 marks)**

| £ 312,000 |
|---|

(d) Complete the table below to show the budgeted margin of safety in units, and the margin of safety percentage if Icon Ltd sells 8,000 units or 9,000 units of product ZYQ. **(4 marks)**

| Units of ZYQ sold | 8,000 units | 9,000 units |
|---|---|---|
| Margin of safety (units) | 2,000 | 3,000 |
| Margin of safety percentage (to the nearest percent) | 25% | 33% |

(e) If Icon Ltd wishes to make a profit of £21,000, how many units of ZYQ must it sell? **(2 marks)**

| 7,500 | units |
|---|---|

(f) If Icon Ltd increases the selling price of ZYQ by £1, what will be the impact on the breakeven point and the margin of safety, assuming no change in the number of units sold? **(2 marks)**

A the breakeven point will decrease and the margin of safety will increase.

B the breakeven point will stay the same but the margin of safety will decrease.

C the breakeven point will decrease and the margin of safety will stay the same.

D the breakeven point will increase and the margin of safety will decrease.

Icon Ltd has prepared a forecast for the next quarter for one of its small wooden parts, ZYG. This component is produced in batches and the forecast is based on selling and producing 1,500 batches.

One of the customers of Icon Ltd has indicated that it may be increasing its order level for component ZYG for the next quarter and it appears that activity levels of 1,800 batches are feasible.

The semi-variable costs should be calculated using the high-low method. If 3,000 batches are sold the total semi-variable cost will be £14,000, and there is a constant unit variable cost up to this volume.

**(g)** **Complete the table below and calculate the estimated profit per unit of ZYG at the different activity levels.** **(9 marks)**

| Units produced and sold | 1,500 | 1,800 |
|---|---|---|
| | £ | £ |
| Sales revenue | 45,000 | 54,000 |
| Variable costs: | | |
| Direct materials | 7,500 | 9,000 |
| Direct labour | 9,000 | 10,800 |
| Overheads | 6,000 | 7,200 |
| Semi-variable costs: | 11,000 | |
| Variable element | | 3,600 |
| Fixed element | | 8,000 |
| Total cost | 33,500 | 38,600 |
| Profit for the period | 11,500 | 15,400 |
| Profit per unit (to 2 decimal places) | 7.67 | 8.56 |

**(h)** The profit per unit has **increased/decreased** because the cost per unit has **increased/decreased.** **(1 mark)**

1,500   £3,000
          2

## Task 4                                     (16 marks)

This task is about understanding principles of budgeting and of cash management.

**(a)** **What are the main purposes of budgeting (tick all that apply)?**

**(2 marks)**

|  | Tick |
|---|---|
| To give authority to spend | ✓ |
| To control expenditure | ✓ |
| To aid decision making |  |

**(b)** **Which of the following would NOT be included in a cash budget (tick all that apply)?**         **(2 marks)**

|  | Tick |
|---|---|
| Depreciation | ✓ |
| Provisions for doubtful debts | ✓ |
| Wages and salaries |  |

**(c)** **Which of the following statements are correct (tick all that apply)?**         **(2 marks)**

|  | Tick |
|---|---|
| A fixed budget is a budget that considers all of an organisation's costs and revenues for a single level of activity. | ✓ |
| A flexible budget is a budget that is produced during the budget period to recognise the effects of any changes in prices and methods of operation that have occurred. |  |
| Organisations can use budgets to communicate objectives to their managers. | ✓ |

**(d)** A company has annual sales of £40 million, annual cost of sales of £30 million and makes annual purchases of £15 million. Its Statement of financial position includes among assets and liabilities the following:

Trade receivables    36.5                    £4 million

Trade payables       73                      £3 million

Inventory                                    £8 million

(i)    **Calculate the trade receivables collection period in days (to 1 decimal place).** 36.5    **(2 marks)**

(ii)   **Calculate the trade payables payment period in days (to 1 decimal place).** 73.0    **(2 marks)**

(iii)  **Calculate the inventory holding period in days (to 1 decimal place).** 97.3    **(2 marks)**

(iv)   **What is the working capital cycle?**    **(2 marks)**

    A    206.5 days

    B    60.8 days

    C    36.5 days

    D    97.3 days

**(e)** **Which one of the following is the main function of liquidity management?**    **(2 marks)**

    A    keeping cash in the bank

    B    making a profit

    C    meeting any liabilities that are due

    D    investing in capital expenditure

## Task 5                                                                (16 marks)

This task is about the preparation of budgets.

Open the Walter file from MyKaplan

Walter is pet food manufacturer and produces two type of dog treats. They are developing their budget for 20X2. You have been provided with the 20X1 information on the 'Data' worksheet in the Walter workbook.

The plan is to increase sales in January by 10% on 20X1 figures.

On the 'budget' worksheet:

**(a)  using the data from the 'data' worksheet, in cells B4 and C4 use a formula to calculate the planned level of sales for Jan 20X2.**

**(1 mark)**

Walter would like to increase the selling price by 1%.

**(b)  using the data from the 'data worksheet' in cells B5 and C5 use a formula to calculate the total revenue Walter should hope to receive. Use a formula to round your answer to the nearest whole £**                                                                **(2 marks)**

Quantities of the two materials per unit is not due to change but the cost of the material will decrease by 2%.

**(c)  using the data from the 'data worksheet', in cells B8:C9, use a Vlookup to calculate the total quantity required for each product for each type of material.**                                                **(2 marks)**

**(d)  use formulae to complete cells D8:E9 to calculate the total cost of each material.**                                                                **(2 marks)**

**(e)  using the data from the 'data worksheet', use formulae to calculate the labour costs for each product in cells B12:B13**

**(1 mark)**

Walter's sales are split into 60% cash sales, 20% 1 month after sale and the remainder 2 months after sale.

Walter pays the material suppliers 40% one month after receiving the goods and the rest two months after. The wages are paid in the month of production.

On the 'Cash' worksheet:

Show how January's production and sales will impact the opening cash balance of £6,850.

**(f)  link the figures from the budget worksheet and using formulas and the information on the budget worksheet complete cells B3:D3 and B6:D8**                                                                **(5 marks)**

**(g)  use formulas to complete cells B10:D12 and use conditional formatting to highlight any negative figures in red text    (3 mark)**

## Task 6 (16 marks)

This task is about budgets and deviations.

Meryl Ltd has many different departments and you have been tasked with comparing the original budget and actual performance for the business as a whole for the year ending 31 April.

On the 'Data' worksheet

**(a)** **copy and paste the data to a new worksheet and call it Data 2**

(1 mark)

On the 'Data' worksheet

**(b)** **add subtotals as follows (both subtotals should be visible):**

    (i)    for each change in department sum the cost (£000)

    (ii)   for each change in cost element sum the cost (£000)

(2 marks)

On the 'Data 2' worksheet

**(c)** **produce a pivot table in cell G1 to show the total of each cost element for each department** (2 marks)

On the 'Variance' worksheet

**(d)** **use a Vlookup on the pivot table to input the Grand totals for each cost element into the relevant cells in the 'Variance' worksheet** (2 marks)

**(e)** **in cell C1 enter a formula to use to flex the original budget**

(1 mark)

**(f)** **in cells E8:E13 use formulas to calculate the variances, adverse variances should be shown with a minus sign** (2 marks)

**(g)** **in cell E15 produce an IF statement that says OK if the operating profit variance is favourable and INVESTIGATE if the operating profit is adverse** (2 marks)

**(h)** **in cells F8:F13 calculate the variance as a percentage of the flexed budget. Use a function to round up to nearest whole percent** (2 marks)

**(i)** **produce a column chart that shows the variance percentages. Add data labels to the chart to show what the revenue or cost type the columns refer to. Turn the adverse variance columns red and the favourable variance columns green** (2 marks)

     **KAPLAN** PUBLISHING

# 2 Mock Assessment Answers

## Task 1

(a) Which TWO of the following statements relating to management information are TRUE? (2 marks)

| | Tick |
|---|---|
| No strict rules govern the way in which the information is presented | ✓ |
| There is usually a legal requirement for the information to be produced | |
| It is produced for parties external to the organisation | |
| It may be presented in monetary or non-monetary terms | ✓ |

(b) Which of the following statements is NOT correct? (2 marks)

A     cost accounting can be used for inventory valuation to meet the requirements of internal reporting only.

(c) The EOQ is $\sqrt{\dfrac{2 \times 2 \times 1{,}250{,}000}{5}}$ = 1,000 kg (3 marks)

(d) **D** (1 mark)

Period costs

(e) (4 marks)

| Date | Code | Dr £ | Cr £ |
|---|---|---|---|
| 6 July | 8000 | £3,000 × 1.08 = 3,240 | |
| 6 July | 2000 | | 3,240 |
| 13 July | 1020 | 400 × £8 = 3,200 | |
| 13 July | 2000 | | 3,200 |

**(f)** **(5 marks)**

| Total basic pay (£) | 21,600 × £8 = **£172,800** |
|---|---|
| Total overtime premium (£) | 4,900 × (£14.50 – £8) = **£31,850** |
| Hours saved (hours) | 22,400 – 21,600 = **800** |
| Bonus (£) | 800 × £8 × 25% = **£1,600** |
| Total direct labour cost (£) | **£206,250** |

**(g)** £206,250 ÷ 100,000 = **£2.06** **(2 marks)**

**(h)** **(4 marks)**

| | |
|---|---|
| Equivalent units | Completed = 60,000 × 100% = 60,000 |
| | CWIP = 50,000 × 70% = 35,000 |
| | Total = 60,000 + 35,000 = **95,000 EU** |
| Excess units | 95,000 – 90,000 = **5,000 EU** |
| Bonus (£) | 5,000 × £8 × 20% = **£8,000** |

**(i)** £8,000 ÷ 95,000 = **£0.08** **(1 mark)**

## Task 2

**(a)** **(12 marks)**

| | Total £ | Assembly £ | Finishing £ | Maint. £ | Stores £ | Admin. £ |
|---|---|---|---|---|---|---|
| Totals | 2,020,750 | 1,006,995 | 508,855 | 164,950 | 74,330 | 265,620 |
| Administration | | 124,509 | 83,006 | 33,203 | 24,902 | (265,620) |
| Maintenance | | 138,707 | 59,446 | (198,153) | | |
| Stores | | 69,462 | 29,770 | | (99,232) | |
| Total | 2,020,750 | 1,339,673 | 681,077 | | | |

**(b)** £1,350,000/(50 × 1,000 + 200 × 2,000) = **£3.00** **(2 marks)**

**(c)** £700,000/(250 × 1,000 + 150 × 2,000) = **£1.27** **(2 marks)**

**(d)** (6 marks)

|  | Actual cost driver value | Absorbed amount £ | Under/over | Value £ |
|---|---|---|---|---|
| Machine set ups | 400,000 | 1,200,000 | Under | 40,000 |
| Special parts handling | 600,000 | 762,000 | Over | 111,900 |

**(e)** **B** (2 marks)

Fixed production overheads are over-absorbed when actual expenditure is less than budget and/or actual production volume is higher than budget.

## Task 3

**(a)** £52 – £38 = **£14.00** (2 marks)

**(b)** £84,000/(£14) = **6,000 units** (2 marks)

**(c)** 6,000 × £52 = **£312,000** (2 marks)

**(d)** (4 marks)

| Units of ZYQ sold | 8,000 units | 9,000 units |
|---|---|---|
| Margin of safety (units) | 8,000 – 6,000 = **2,000** | 9,000 – 6,000 = **3,000** |
| Margin of safety percentage (to the nearest percent) | 2,000/8,000 × 100 = **25%** | 3,000/9,000 × 100 = **33%** |

**(e)** (£84,000 + £21,000)/(£14) = **7,500 units** (2 marks)

**(f)** **A** (2 marks)

An increase in the selling price per unit will increase the contribution per unit. An increase in contribution per unit will reduce the number of units needed to breakeven. This in turn will increase the margin of safety.

**(g)**                                                                      **(9 marks)**

| Units produced and sold | 1,500 | 1,800 |
|---|---|---|
|  | £ | £ |
| Sales revenue | 45,000 | 54,000 |
| Variable costs: |  |  |
| Direct materials | 7,500 | 9,000 |
| Direct labour | 9,000 | 10,800 |
| Overheads | 6,000 | 7,200 |
| Semi-variable costs: | 11,000 |  |
| Variable element |  | 3,600 |
| Fixed element |  | 8,000 |
| Total cost | 33,500 | 38,600 |
| Profit for the period | 11,500 | 15,400 |
| Profit per unit (to 2 decimal places) | 7.67 | 8.56 |

**(h)** The profit per unit has **increased** because the cost per unit has **decreased**.                                                                **(1 mark)**

## Task 4

**(a)** **What are the main purposes of budgeting (tick all that apply)?**
                                                                      **(2 marks)**

|  | Tick |
|---|---|
| To give authority to spend | ✓ |
| To control expenditure | ✓ |
| To aid decision making |  |

The main purposes of budgeting are to plan and control. Budgets also usually give authority to spend up to the budget limit. Budgets are not primarily used for decision making.

(b) **Which of the following would NOT be included in a cash budget (tick all that apply)?** **(2 marks)**

|  | Tick |
|---|---|
| Depreciation | ✓ |
| Provisions for doubtful debts | ✓ |
| Wages and salaries |  |

Depreciation and the provision for doubtful debts are not cash flow items and so would not be included in a cash budget.

(c) **Which of the following statements are correct?** **(2 marks)**

|  | Tick |
|---|---|
| A fixed budget is a budget that considers all of an organisation's costs and revenues for a single level of activity. | ✓ |
| A flexible budget is a budget that is produced during the budget period to recognise the effects of any changes in prices and methods of operation that have occurred. |  |
| Organisations can use budgets to communicate objectives to their managers. | ✓ |

Statement (i) is correct. A fixed budget is prepared for a single level of activity.

Statement (ii) is incorrect. A flexible budget is prepared during the budget period but it recognises only the effects of changes in the volume of activity.

Statement (iii) is correct. A major purpose of the budgetary planning exercise is to communicate an organisation's objectives to its managers.

(d) A company has annual sales of £40 million, annual cost of sales of £30 million and makes annual credit purchases of £15 million. Its Statement of financial position includes among assets and liabilities the following:

Trade receivables    £4 million

Trade payables    £3 million

Inventory    £8 million

(i) **Calculate the trade receivables collection period in days (1 dp).**

4/40 × 365 = **36.5** (2 marks)

(ii) **Calculate the trade payables payment period in days. (1 dp)**

3/15 × 365 = **73.0** (2 marks)

(iii) **Calculate the inventory holding period in days.**

8/30 × 365 = **97.3** (2 marks)

(iv) **What is the working capital cycle?** (2 marks)

**B    60.8 days**

36.5 – 73.0 + 97.3 = 60.8

(e) **Which one of the following is the main function of liquidity management?** (2 marks)

C    meeting any liabilities due

## Task 5

Please see MyKaplan for the answers.

## Task 6

Please see MyKaplan for the answers.

# #

**KAPLAN** PUBLISHING